Handbook for Competitive Volleyball

ρόδος
2400 χρόνια

Dedicated to the city
of Rhodos, on the occasion
of its 2400-year jubilee,
and also to the island
on which this manual
was realised.

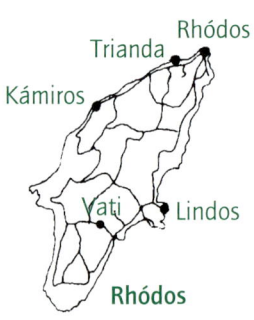

Rhódos
Trianda
Kámiros
Vati   Lindos
Rhódos

We would like to thank the
Institute for Sports Games at the German Sport University, Cologne,
for the friendly support.

Athanasios Papageorgiou
Willy Spitzley

Handbook for Competitive Volleyball

Meyer & Meyer Sport

Original title: Handbuch für Leistungsvolleyball
Aachen: Meyer und Meyer Verlag, 2000

Translated by Achim Ziegele
Edited by Tom Liagridonis

British Library Cataloguing in Publication Data
A catalogue for this book is available from the British Library

Papageorgiou / Spitzley:
Handbook for Competitive Volleyball
Athanasios Papageorgiou ; Willy Spitzley
Oxford: Meyer und Meyer, 2003
ISBN 1-84126-074-6

All rights reserved, especially the right to copy and distribute, including the translation rights.
No part of this work may be reproduced – including by photocopy, microfilm or any other means –
processed, stored electronically, copied or distributed in any form whatsoever without the written
permission of the publisher.

© 2003 by Meyer & Meyer Sport (UK) Ltd.
Aachen, Adelaide, Auckland, Budapest, Graz, Johannesburg,
Miami, Olten (CH), Oxford, Singapore, Toronto
Member of the World
Sports Publishers' Association
www.w-s-p-a.org
Printed and bound by Vimperk, AG
ISBN 1-84126-074-6
www.m-m-sports.com

Contents

1 The Goals and Teaching Concept of this Book 9
   1.1 The New Rules and their Effect on Practice and Matches 16
      1.1.1 The All Rally-Point Scoring System 16
      1.1.2 The Libero-Player Rule 23
      1.1.3 Rule Changes for the Service 24
      1.1.4 The New Rules and their Impact on Coaching 25

2 Organisation and Symbols....................................27

3 Learning Part 1:
Service Reception Formations and Individual Tactics
of the Server and the Service Reception Players 30
   3.1 Service Reception Formations 30
      3.1.1 Five-person Service Reception Formation 32
      3.1.2 Four-person Service Reception Formation 36
      3.1.3 Three-person Service Reception Formation 45
      3.1.4 Two-person Service Reception Formation 52
      3.1.5 Fake/Trick Formations 58
   3.2 Individual Tactics of the Service Reception Players 66
      3.2.1 The Libero as a Service Reception Player 77
   3.3 Individual Tactics of the Server 79
   3.4 Selected Drills to Train the Individual Tactics of the Server
      and the Service Reception Players, and the Training of
      the Service Reception Formation 88

4 Learning Part 2:
Offence: Setting, Offensive Combinations, Offensive Coverage,
and the Individual Tactics of the Setter and the Hitters 103
   4.1 Analysis of the Facts 103
   4.2 Offensive Combinations 106
   4.3 Covering Offensive Combinations 117
   4.4 Individual Tactics of the Setter 122
   4.5 Individual Tactics of the Hitter 127
      4.5.1 The Quick Hitter 129
      4.5.2 The Offside/Main Hitter 135
      4.5.3 The Back-court Hitter 136
      4.5.4 The Service Reception Outside Hitter 138
      4.5.5 The Second/Combination Hitter 139
      4.5.6 Individual Tactical Factors/Strategies 140

4.6 Selected Training Drills for the Individual Tactics of the Setter, the Outside Hitter, the Diagonal Hitter, the Back-court Hitter, and the Quick Hitter 143
    4.6.1 Preliminary Thoughts 143
    4.6.2 Sequence of Training to Improve upon Individual and Group/Team Tactics 147
    4.6.3 Drills for Training Offensive Tactics 160
    4.6.4 Special Training Drills for the Setter and the Attacker 162

5 Learning Part 3: Blocking and Defensive Formations and the Individual Tactics of the Blocking and Defensive Athlete! 167
5.1 Analysis of the Facts 167
5.2 Blocking and Defensive Formations 169
    5.2.1 Course of Action of a Defence with Position VI Playing Back ..170
5.3 Offence out of the Defence 190
5.4 Individual Tactics of the Blocker 195
    5.4.1 Individual Tactics of the Middle Blocker 197
    5.4.2 Individual Tactics of the Outside Blocker 202
    5.4.3 Individual Tactics of the Blocking Athletes at the Middle and Low Levels of Volleyball 205
5.5 Individual Tactics of the Defender 206
    5.5.1 The Libero as a Defensive Specialist 211
5.6 Selected Training Drills 213
    5.6.1 Individual Tactics of a Single Block and the Defenders 213
    5.6.2 Selected Training Drills for Block and Defence with a Special Focus on the Individual and Group Tactics of the Blocking and Defensive Athletes 218
    5.6.3 Selected Games for the Training of Blocking and Defensive Athletes 226
    5.6.4 Special Training Drills to Work on the Coordinative Skills and Abilities of the Defenders 233

6 Match Systems 236
6.1 Basic Starting Line-up 240
6.2 Match Systems with Two Setters 242
    6.2.1 The 4-2/4-2+L Match System with Four All-around/Universal Athletes 244
    6.2.2 The 2-1-3/2-1-3+L Match System with Three All-around/Universal Athletes 244
    6.2.3 The 2-2-2/2-1-3+L Match System with Two All-around/Universal Athletes 245
    6.2.4 The 2-3-1/2-3-1+L Match System with One All- .... around/Universal Athlete 246

6.3 Match Systems with One Setter 247
   6.3.1 Thoughts and Helpful Hints for the Development
       of a Basic Starting Line-up 247
   6.3.2 Setter with Five All-around/Universal Athletes 250
   6.3.3 Setter with Four Service Reception Athletes in a
       Three-person or Four-person Service Reception Formation
       and One Back-court Hitter (1-1-4/1-1-4+L Match Systems) 251
   6.3.4 Setter with Three Service Reception Athletes in a
       Two-person or a Three-person Service Reception Formation
       and Two Quick Hitters/Middle Blockers
       (1-2-3/1-2-3+L Match Systems) 253
   6.3.5 Setter with Two Main Service Reception Athletes in a
       Two-person Service Reception Formation and Three Middle
       Blockers/Quick Hitters (1-3-2 Match System) 257
   6.3.6 Setter with Two Main Service Reception Athletes in
       a Two-person Service Reception Formation, Three Middle
       Blockers/Quick Hitters, and a Libero
       (1-3-2+L Match System) 263
   6.3.7 Setter with One Main Service Reception Athlete in a
       Two-person Service Reception Formation, Four Middle
       Blockers/Quick Hitters, and a Libero
       (1-4-1+L Match System) 265
   6.3.8 Setter with Five Middle Blockers/Quick Hitters and a ....
       Libero (5-1+L Match System) 267
6.4 Switching/Changing Positions by the Athletes 267

7 Defensive and Offensive Strategies **274**
7.1 Strategies for the Starting Line-up 278
7.2 Serving Strategies 280
   7.2.1 Serving Strategies vs. a Two-person Service Reception
       Formation, which Utilises Two Service Reception Specialists
       but without a Libero 283
   7.2.2 Serving Strategies vs. a Two-person Service Reception
       Formation, which Utilises only One Service Reception
       Specialist or Libero 286
   7.2.3 Serving Strategies vs. a Three/Four-person Service
       Reception Formation, which Utilises Three/Four Service
       Reception Athletes 287
   7.2.4 Serving Strategies During a Tiebreak 288
   7.2.5 General Principles for a Serving Strategy 289
7.3 Service Reception Strategies 290
   7.3.1 Service Reception Strategies for a Two-person Service
       Reception Formation, which Utilises Two Service Reception
       Specialists with or without a Libero 292

CONTENTS

    7.3.2 Service Reception Strategies for a Two-person Service Reception Formation, which Utilises One Service Reception Specialist and Libero 295
    7.3.3 Service Reception Strategies for a Three/Four-person Service Reception Formation, which Utilises Three or Four Service Reception Athletes 296
    7.3.4 Service Reception Strategies During a Tiebreak 296
    7.3.5 General Principles for the Service Reception Strategy 297
7.4 Setting Strategies 299
    7.4.1 Setting Strategies that Take into Consideration the Opposition's Offensive Combinations 301
    7.4.2 Setting Strategies that Take into Consideration the Starting Positions of the Blockers and the Defensive Athletes 302
    7.4.3 Setting Strategies that Take into Consideration the Actions of the Middle Blocker 303
    7.4.4 Setting Strategies that Take into Consideration the Weaknesses of a Blocker 305
    7.4.5 Setting Strategies that Take into Consideration Your Own Team's Attackers 305
7.5 Offensive Strategies 307
7.6 Defensive Strategies 310
    7.6.1 Defensive Strategies in Association with Serving Strategies ...313
    7.6.2 Defensive Strategies that Take into Consideration the Actions of the Quick Hitter 314
    7.6.3 Defensive Strategies According to the Actions of the Offence ..315
    7.6.4 Defensive Strategies for Block and Defence 319
    7.6.5 Determining Factors in the Men's and Women's Game 327

8 Specific Principles for the Training of the Sport of Volleyball ..334
  8.1 Principles for a Volleyball-related Warm-up 335
  8.2 Principles for the Organisation and Use of Practice Drills in Volleyball 338
  8.3 Principles for Training under Psychological Pressure in Volleyball 342
  8.4 Principles Related to Coaching/Managing a Volleyball Practice ...346
  8.5 Principles Related to Coaching/Managing a Volleyball Match ...348

1 The Goals and Teaching Concept of this Book

The main objective of this book is to increase the opportunities for coaches and instructors of volleyball to develop and train high-level volleyball players by taking into account the ability of each individual players.[1] This includes the **training of specialised volleyball** players (i.e. positional **specialists**). In this book the term player is used but it must be understood from the outset that volleyball players are athletes in the true sense of the word.

A volleyball player is called a **specialist** when s/he focuses on a certain function in the game system. This function is based on the players's technical and tactical skills and their athletic ability. If it is assumed that each volleyball player, including the **specialist**, must be able to attack, defend, block, hit, pass, serve, and set the ball, it is quite obvious that the main focus of practice must be on **a universal and all-around training and development programme for each players,** even at the highest level. The following volleyball match scenarios clearly demonstrate the need for universal and all-around training and development of specialised players. For example, if the setter is forced to defend a ball or if the pass from the service reception is away from the setter, then everyone else on the team must possess the skills to be able to set the second ball.

A second example may include the adjustment of a service reception formation and strategy against an opposition's serve. If the opposition has a difficult jump serve to handle then the service reception strategy may change from a two-person passing unit into a three-person passing unit (or from a three-person passing unit to a four-person passing unit, or from a four-person passing unit to a five-person passing unit, etc.) depending on the type of service reception strategy the team is using and at what level of play that the team is at. Therefore, it is evident that the training of a **specialist** should not only be aimed at increasing and improving his/her specialised function in the game, but also to develop his/her wide-ranging and universal skills in general. For example, the libero, whose primary function is in playing back-row defence, needs to be an all-around player to do their job with maximum efficiency. A good all-around and universal training

---

[1] Thoughts an effects referring to the rule changes of 1996 to 2000 are highlighted in the text with a green background.

programme enables the libero to anticipate the net actions of his/her teammates and the opposition ahead of time, even though his/her function in the game is limited to service reception, defence, and coverage. All-around training of the **specialist** not only improves their specialised skills more rapidly, it also helps them to develop **a personality** as a volleyball player.

Furthermore, a specialised player who has been exposed to an all-around training programme gives the coach a variety of tactical possibilities. For example, if the outside hitter is able to change and take over the position of the middle hitter, it will be much more difficult for his/her opponents to analyse his/her net play strategy, thus, making it more difficult for them to prepare their own match plan. In addition, players who have been exposed to a more universal training programme are able to adjust quicker to situations that differ from the known standard.

Their team can then play much more efficiently making them more successful. It is the *dream* of many high level coaches to have a team which consists of **'universalists'** (all-around, utility players), who are service reception, defensive, serve, setting, outside hitting, middle hitting, outside blocking, and middle blocking specialists all rolled into one. The advantages are unbeatable!

The required basic components to achieve the goals of this book are the skills and the universal training features discussed in the first book – *Volleyball – A Handbook for Coaches and Players*.[2] In that book, universal patterns of behavior concerning the sport of volleyball were taught. The focus was on specific actions that are demanded by the ball, space, target, partner (teammate), and the opposition.

These specific actions shall be improved, expanded, and practiced to complete the development of an all-around specialised player. To accomplish this, the player's practice and training has to be adapted. For this reason, the first basic step of differentiation was introduced in the last chapter of the first volume (*Volleyball – A Handbook for Coaches and Players*). To differentiate between the setter and a universal players is the beginning of developing the universal players into a specialist.

---

[2] Papageorgiou & Spitzley: Volleyball – *A Handbook for Coaches and Players*, Oxford, 2002.

THE GOALS AND TEACHING CONCEPT

The primary focus of this book is to develop an all-around/universal player into a specialised player (specialist). This progression is discussed with references to setting, outside hitting, middle hitting, back-row hitting, serving, outside blocking, middle blocking, defence, coverage, and service reception and will be connected to related service reception, offensive, and defensive formations. Another major focus is to design and practice match systems. Strategies and counter-strategies in serving, service reception, offence, and defence will be dealt with.

Special aspects of individual, group, and team tactics will be discussed. In addition, we will look at the development of counter-strategies to an opposition's match plan and give examples of ways to cover a hitter in certain offensive formations. Furthermore, we will deal with solid ways of developing the most efficient and effective game system that would bring out the strengths of a team, including the use of the libero. The problem faced is that all of these issues are not completely or sufficiently covered in the existing literature. This poses a problem **with drawing up profiles** for specialised volleyball players, which must be associated with the highest level of volleyball.

The **training of a specialist** must be very carefully prepared and done in small steps to properly develop the players. Consequently, the main focus in lower levels of volleyball must be on an all-around/universal training programme. It is very important to give the players the opportunity to develop and improve all of their skills and work on their weaknesses before focusing on their specialised position and skills. This can be done in practice or in games against weaker opponents. For example, a middle hitter can be placed into the libero position to focus on improving their defensive skills.

The **basic skills and techniques** in setting and service reception (i.e. overhead or forearm passing, jump setting, etc.), in hitting (i.e. power hits, roll shots, tips, etc.), in blocking and defence (i.e. single block, double block, Japanese rolls, etc.), and serving (i.e. jump, float, underhand, etc.) are required. Also, service reception formations (i.e. six-person, five-person, etc.), offensive strategies (i.e. outside high ball, middle quick, back row, etc.), defensive and coverage formations (i.e. six-up, six-back, etc.), and match systems (i.e. 6-0, 5-1, 4-2, etc.) are assumed to be known.

The whole spectrum of **individual, group, and team tactical actions,** starting with the basic skills mentioned above, shall be expanded and optimised. Because of the great number and many variations of these actions, they must be differentiated and dealt with according to the structure of the match. For example, there can be no service reception formation and strategy without a serve; therefore, the interdependence of both elements is evident. Thus, to improve and train a service reception player we must respectively combine the use of a service reception formation (i.e. two-person, three-person, etc.) with the training of an individual service skill and tactic (i.e. float, jump, specific target/location, etc.). This synthesis of individual, group, and team tactical actions will be assigned and ordered to connected game situations and discussed. The complexity of the subject does not allow for detailed descriptions, but the new main ideas will be pointed out and similarities of related actions will be shown. The main goal is to make the practice as close as possible to a competitive match situation.

Three levels of volleyball will be differentiated: **a low, middle, and a high level.** The contents of each **learning component or stage** will be assigned to the corresponding level. The importance of certain factors in men's and women's volleyball will also be stressed. The main factors that distinguish the levels are the quality of players on hand and/or the amount of "time" a team practices. A team that practices once or twice a week, up to a maximum of four hours a week, is considered to belong to the **low level** (i.e. certain club teams).

A team that practices three or four times a week, up to a maximum of eight hours a week, is considered to belong to the **middle level** (i.e. Division 2 and 3 college teams). To be considered as a team in the **high level** category, the team must train more than five times a week for a minimum total of ten hours in length (i.e. Division 1 and 2 college teams). This includes only the time that the players train with a volleyball. High-level and some middle-level teams spend additional time on their conditioning and in the weightlifting room. If important differences appear between **mens' and womens' volleyball**, it will be dealt with in separate paragraphs. Reasons for the differences will be given and arguments discussed. If there is no further detail or information given, then the content is relevant and the same for both sexes.

The **introduction and order** of the *learning parts* follow the same structure as the game, but within the *learning parts* the order and teaching of the material will follow didactic guidelines. This method not only takes into account the complexity of the game, but it also makes the management of this book easier for the user. To utilise this concept most efficiently, two recommendations should be followed:

1) Service reception and defensive techniques, tactics, and strategies must be introduced before the corresponding offensive techniques, tactics, and strategies. This should be considered in the planning and designing of the training sessions and practices for the entire year.

The rationale behind this is that the current structure of the game of volleyball clearly reveals the dominance of the offence over the defence. A closer look at the 1999 Men's and Women's European Volleyball Championships showed a further increase in offensive power, despite the possibility and opportunity for teams to use their libero. Because of this, the training of the individual skill and strategy of the service reception players has to be stressed more than the training of the individual skill and strategy of the server, even though both should be done at the same time. Service reception must be developed first and then the serve itself.

The same can be said for the training of the individual skills and tactics of the middle blocker. The main focus must be placed on developing the players's blocking skills and tactics. First, the middle blocker must be able to block both the offside and outside hitters. The moment s/he solves that issue we can add the skill of middle hitting. This not only means that the players must cope with three offensive threats, but also marks the beginning of the individual offensive tactics of the middle hitter. Once again, the didactic method advocates moving from defence (blocking) to offence (hitting) and from easy to difficult.

2) The training progression of the players must always be from easy to difficult and from a lower lever to a higher level. In other words, the content of all match situations in the lower level must first be taught and practiced before the progression to the next level (middle or high) can be started. For example, a player should not move directly from a five-person service reception formation to a two-person service reception formation. The player should move sequentially through all of the phases of each service reception formation preceding the desired outcome. Therefore, in this instance, the player must first learn and master the skills, tactics, and variations of a four-person service reception formation, then progress to a three-person service reception formation, before ultimately achieving and moving to the final goal of a two-person service reception formation.

14 THE GOALS AND TEACHING CONCEPT

> 1. **Learning Part** Service reception formations, including the individual tactics of the service reception players and the server. (Photo 1)
>
> 2. **Learning Part** Offence development, offensive strategies, and coverage in combination with the individual skills and tactics of the setter and the hitter. (Photo 2)
>
> 3. **Learning Part** Defensive formations, including the development of an offence and coverage in combination with the individual skills and tactics of the blocking and defensive players. (Photo 3)

Photo 1 (DW)   *Photo 2 (Willi Zeimer)*

In addition to the **contents** of each learning part, a detailed **analysis of the facts** as they relate to the structure of the game of volleyball will be given. When conditions and profiles of learning, patterns of action, and their variations appear, didactic and methodical suggestions and general hints on how to prepare

Photo 3 (Steffen Marquardt)

a practice will be given and discussed. This will be followed by an introduction of **selected methods of practice** with detailed instructions of how to run them and what to look for in them. Here, **half-court and/or small-court games** play an important role. Small-court games that are played together prepare a learning process, whereas small-court games played against each other are more part of the practice process.

The information provided in each analysis of the facts is based on scientific examinations, personal observations, and on personal experiences. As well, graduate students' theses and projects from students majoring in the sport of volleyball from the Sports University of Cologne, Germany, have been used to compile information for this book. Papers have also been used from members of the A-License Coaching Instruction Course of the German and Austrian Volleyball Associations and from students attending the internationally known Coaching Academy in Cologne, Germany.

The assignment of a learning part to a certain level (low, middle, or high) is not necessary because the progressions of the skills are always flowing. There are also elements from the high level of volleyball at the low level of volleyball and vice-versa. The main reason for this is that the match system of a team is clearly dependent on the individual abilities of its players. Therefore, the technical and tactical abilities of a high-level player, who plays at a low or middle level of volleyball, will have an influence on the match system. For example, a very good service reception player will allow a team the possibility of employing a three-person service reception formation instead of a four-person service reception formation or a very good hitter can give a team the opportunity to use the important element of a back-row attack in their match system.

An attempt is made in the analysis of facts to outline the order of the technical and tactical contents and components in a practice. This order is justified by didactic and methodical guidelines.

Finally, it is important to restate the fact that this book does not solely focus on the introduction and teaching of new techniques and tactics, but also on their correct and efficient usage in match situations. Therefore, drills and games will not be given, but practice sequences based on certain practice methodologies will be presented as they relate to the structure of the game of volleyball and match situations in the sport.

1.1 The New Rules and their Effect on Practice and Matches

The rule changes that occurred in 1996-97 have had a significant impact on the sport of volleyball. The effects on the structure of the sport and the resulting consequences for the practice and training process need to be discussed. Generally, all former rule changes mostly aimed at strengthening the block and defensive situation (K2) and consequently to break the dominance of the attack out of the service reception formation. The intention was to prolong the rallies to make the match more attractive to all of the fans of volleyball, especially the live spectators and the media. Examinations of the rule changes have shown that this goal has not been achieved. There are two main reasons for this:

1) Coaches have successfully developed strategies to counter the new rule changes and maintain the dominance of the attack, and
2) some of the new rules have neutralised each other.

For example, the service reception has clearly not been weakened by the rule change, which allows the server to extend his/her service zone from three meters to the entire backcourt line (nine meters). The reason for this is that even though the server is given more autonomy from where they can serve the ball from, the players in service reception were also supported by a rule change, which allowed them to use the overhand pass to play the ball.

Since the latest rule changes do not achieve the same goals as stated above, they will be discussed separately and their impact on the sport will be dealt with in the following paragraphs.

1.1.1 The All Rally-Point Scoring System

The rule change to allow the entire volleyball match to be played using the rally-point scoring system was designed to better predict the length of time it takes to complete a match. This can be done because the average time of each set will be shorter and more calculable, thus allowing for the length of the match to also be more predictable. This change has also helped to make the sport of volleyball more attractive to the media, who in turn can assist in increasing the popularity of the sport through their coverage. There is no change to the inner structure of the sport; only the outer structure has been modified. Currently, the average time of a volleyball set is 19 minutes and there are approximately 44 points played. Before the rule change, the average time of a volleyball set was roughly 30 minutes. Is one team much stronger than their opposition, if the set only takes about 15 minutes? Are the teams evenly matched when the set lasts nearly 22 minutes? A comparison between the new and old scoring systems in both men's and women's Professional Division 1 leagues shows that the length of time for each set is shorter in the new system.

25:23	equals	11:10
25:18	equals	11: 4
25:23	equals	11: 8
25:16	equals	11: 9
36:34	equals	13: 5
25:19	equals	12: 6
26:24	equals	10: 8
25:23	equals	6: 5

Teams that play at higher levels of volleyball score fewer points when using the old scoring system. For example, in the 1996 Olympic Volleyball Final between Italy and the Netherlands, the score in the 5th tiebreak set was 17-15 for the Netherlands. If the teams had played using the old scoring system, the score of 17-15 would only have been 2-1 for the Netherlands (keep in mind, in the old scoring system only the serving team could score points).

Further examinations of National level (low, middle, and high) and International level (European Championships and World Junior Championships for both men and women) confirm the notion that the higher the quality and level of play that a team is and competes at, the less points they will score using the old scoring system. It is quite evident, that the better a team's attack out of their service reception formation is then the higher the level that they are at. Therefore, it is clear that when using the old scoring system, the teams at the highest levels play the longest sets. Before the all rally-point scoring system took effect, players went through their rotations approximately 4–4.5 times a set. Under the influence of the new scoring system, players rotate approximately 2.3 times a set and roughly 3.5 times a set when 50 or so points are played. Furthermore, an interesting

THE NEW RULES AND THEIR EFFECT

observation has been noted. The time that it usually takes to play a set is equivalent to the same amount of points scored by the losing team. Other results show that under the new scoring system, there are fewer matches being won by scores of 3-0 (38 % as compared to 52 % under the old scoring system). On the other hand, there are more matches ending with 3-1 and 3-2 results (28 % as compared to only 18 % under the old scoring system). The average time of a match under the old scoring system was 122 minute; under the new scoring system it is 106 minutes. Although the difference in match times between the old scoring system and the new scoring system is 16 minutes, we must keep in mind that more sets are being played during the matches.

The gap in the duration of match times would be even greater if we compared set-to-set times. In contrast to the high National and International levels of volleyball, the all rally-point scoring system has had almost no impact on the duration of matches in the low and middle levels of play. The reason for this is that the high level teams take more risks and chances in every play. At the high levels of play, the duration of the rallies is almost the same in either scoring system. At the low and middle levels of volleyball, where the focus is on "safe play", the rallies are even longer than before.

The new rules that have been implemented will have a positive impact on the introduction and teaching of the game of volleyball. Beginners and low-level players will put all of their efforts in trying to keep the ball in play by trying to omit errors, because their errors can mean points for their opponents. As a result, the rallies will be longer and the ball will cross over the net more often. The goal of all experts has always been to obtain longer rallies from their players by using didactical and methodical measures.

The reason for this is that longer rallies represent the potential for each players to have more touches and individual feedback on their personal achievements! This is perfect motivation for beginners and students. Surveys taken amongst spectators have showed the following interesting results: spectators who have never played volleyball before loved the new rules, especially the rally-point scoring system. Even spectators who play volleyball showed favorable opinions of the new rule changes and described the sport as much more exciting. Outside of Germany, there are signs that fans from other sports are getting more and more interested and attracted to the sport of volleyball.

The rally-point scoring system does not influence the inner structure of the game of volleyball. This means that individual, group, and team strategies and tactics in offence and defence, service and service reception, and in the technical and athletic requirements of volleyball do not change. Since the K1 and K2 situation did not change, there are no changes in the match strategy of the high-level volleyball players. Before the new rules were implemented, only the team serving the ball could score points (except during the 5th set where the rally-point method was used for scoring).

This means that two consecutive successful offensive actions were required to score at least one point (i.e. a side-out followed by a point on the serve). Under the new scoring system, the same situation would give a team two points (one from the side-out and the other from the serve) and provide them with a small advantage – a so-called "mini-break". The rally-point scoring system will have a different impact on the responsibilities of the specialists, even though all of the players, except for the libero, are potential scoring players.

For example, the server will first have to deal with the new situation of refraining from using high-risk serves, because a service error will directly add a point to the opposition's score. In time, the server will learn that the less risk s/he takes on his/her serve, the easier it will be for his/her opposition to score from their service reception formation. Therefore, the server is forced to revert to his/her old service strategy and begin using higher risk serves again. The only situation in which a server should use a lower risk serve is when his/her team has a commanding lead and s/he wants to put the pressure on his/her opposition to make a successful attack. Alternatively, when a team is losing it might be an effective strategy to use higher risk serves to try and get some "mini-breaks" and score while in possession of the serve. The condition of the players in the service reception formation does not change at all in these circumstances.

They were and always will be under the greatest psychological pressure to make a perfect pass up to the setter because a service reception error is a direct score and point for their opposition. The same can be said for the setter and the hitters. The K1 situation (service reception situation) does not change for them, because any mistake can mean a point for their opposition. It is the same idea as trying to score a point from the attack out of the K2 situation (block and defence situation); in the old scoring system, when a team was serving, a successful block

THE NEW RULES AND THEIR EFFECT

and defensive action by them scored them a point, but under the new scoring system, this successful action will score a team two points in a row (one from the initial side-out and the other from the block or defensive action), therefore, giving them a "mini-break".

In the beginning, the setter and the attackers face the same situation as the server. They will try and omit mistakes by taking fewer risks. When a team takes fewer risks in their offensive match strategy it gives their opposition an easier time in reading their offence and, therefore, putting in place proper defensive measures to counter the attack. Eventually, the setter and attackers will realise this and revert to their old match strategy and style of play. The blockers and defensive players also have to deal with similar predicaments, as do the other specialists.

If we compare the K1 and K2 situations under the rally-point scoring system, it may be concluded that the K1 situation may have increased in importance. It can be correctly suggested that from the K1 situation not only are points scored, but also more points can be scored out of this situation than out of the K2 situation. In the old scoring system, points could only be scored out of the K2 situation. This might give the impression that the new scoring system emphasises the K1 situation more than the K2 situation. This is partially true since the team that makes the least errors in the K1 situation wins! Nevertheless, the points scored from the block and defence (K2) situations are key points in the match, because it is from these points that a team can get "mini-breaks". It is evident that the new rule changes did not have any major effect on the importance of either the K1 or K2 situations for scoring points in the match.

In the sport of volleyball, it is very difficult to come from behind and catch a team when trailing by seven or more points in a game, but it was easier to do it under the old scoring system because only the serving team could score points and it was much more difficult to close out a game. This allowed the trailing team more opportunities to win points and potentially win the game. It is much more difficult and rarely now does a team trailing by several points come from behind and win a game. This is because every successful side-out enables the teams to keep their scoring differential. This is especially true at high levels of volleyball, where it is becoming more and more difficult to come back and win a game when trailing, even by only a few points.

One of the rare comeback exceptions took place on the international stage during the 1999 Men's European Championships between Italy and Yugoslavia. In the fourth set Yugoslavia led Italy by a score of 9-2, but Italy managed to come back and win the set. It must be stated though, that nearing the end of a set, when a team reaches the final two points needed to close out the set, it is almost impossible to make a comeback when trailing by a big point differential.

Because of the facts discussed in the previous paragraphs, the following important conclusions can be drawn for the daily practice routine:

1. The training of individual tactics is becoming more significant. Since every action on the court has the potential for being a scoring point, every player has to learn to cope with more responsibility. As well, the middle hitters must be trained to score in point scoring situations. It is no longer enough to use the middle hitter mainly as a "decoy" to try and regain the service. The players must be able to perform individually at a high technical and tactical level. They must be willing to take necessary risks and make no unforced errors. This high standard of performance must not only be executed in matches, but also during practices.

2. Psychological training must be included and stressed more in every practice session. Under the new scoring system psychological stability has become even more important to the players, because the focus of volleyball has become the elimination of errors, while still playing at the same high level. For example, if a player does not serve the ball with great power because he/she is afraid of making a mistake, it makes it much more difficult to defend the opposition's attack, get the ball back, and try to counterattack to attempt to get a "mini-break". All of the players will have the same experience now as they had ten years ago when the tiebreak rule was introduced. At first, all of the players will have to deal with greater psychological pressure. Once the players get used to it, the pressure will lessen. But there are expectations, at least at the international level that a higher psychological standard will be reached. The players' training has to adapt to the facts as they are. Therefore, every practice must contain psychological stress training. Until now, tiebreak games were a good method of putting psychological pressure on players, but now new methods of training, complex in structure, with concrete problems to deal with need to be used. For example, an attack out of the service reception

formation must be performed successfully 3-5 times to score a "Big Point" and move on, but if the players fail to do this they must start all over again. These methods of training must be designed in such a way that the players practice the omission of errors in stressful situations, while still keeping up the high technical and tactical demand levels of the sport. The players have to be trained and taught more than ever to continue to stay completely focused all of the time. The basic training principles under psychological pressure must be taken into account even more now than before. The reason for this is that until now a team had only two "go-to" or "point-scoring" players, but in today's game at least four players must be trained to be "point-scoring" players.

3. The rhythm that is followed in practice has to be adapted to the same rhythm played in matches. This requirement takes into account the following characteristics:
    - From the very beginning of practice, the players should be absolutely focused, attentive, and motivated. This means that they should be practicing their level of competitiveness because the very first point at the beginning of a game can be decisive at setting the tone for the rest of the set and the entire match. This is especially important under the new rules because it has become much more difficult to catch an opposition when trailing on points. A nice, easy start to a game, where opponents can slowly feel each other out, is no longer possible. The demands mentioned above require a properly planned and well-directed warm-up. To achieve the best possible start to a match and to get an advantage over an opposition every coach should focus on the strengths and weaknesses of his/her own team and not of his/her oppositions when preparing the starting line-up.
    - The shorter time frame of the sets, in combination with the four one-minute time-outs (or in international play – the two technical time-outs at the scores of 8 and 16 points) suggests shorter time frames in practice. The time to perform a drill or work on a training unit should get shorter to coincide with the shorter length of time it takes to play a set, but the quality of the work must be better. The national and international ten-minute break rule after the second and fourth sets must be included in our training programme. The breaks must be simulated in practice, therefore, it is important to take one-minute breaks and/or, if necessary, a ten-minute break in-between two drills. To practice a ten-minute break only makes sense when it is designed correctly into the practice. After a short

talk, the focus must be on keeping the tension of the players high. This means that the players have to stay mentally and physically "warm", therefore, it is crucial that the rhythm of the practice is not ruined by the break. The amount of weekly and time of daily practices organised should not be affected by the time frames of the sets and matches. Volleyball still requires the highest amount of accuracy in movement and action, and depends on the optimal combined performance of the players in the shortest possible time. This can only be achieved through a lot of practice.

1.1.2 The Libero-Player Rule

The rally-point scoring system has had a strong impact on the outer structure of the sport of volleyball, whereas the introduction of the libero-player has had a strong influence on the tactics and strategy of the sport (see Chapter 3.2.1 "The Libero as a Service Reception Player").

The addition of the libero has led to an increase in offensive actions out of the service reception formation (K1) by more than eight percent in men's volleyball. This is a definite support to the K1 situation, therefore, contradicting all of the former rule changes that were intended to strengthen the K2 situation to break the dominance of the attack in volleyball.

The libero as a defensive specialist has not shown any considerable results to improve the defensive performance of a team so far. Several possible reasons are:

1. The libero is only used when s/he can give a team a stronger and better service reception. This simple situation improves the efficiency of the setting and attacking actions and tactics of a team immensely.
2. The use of the libero allows the players at the net to exclusively concentrate on their attack, because in most situations they can be taken out of the service reception formation.
3. By removing the players at the net from the service reception formation, it permits the setter to play a faster offensive system, thus allowing for lower and faster sets.
4. It allows a team to use more quick attacks and combination plays to get their opposition into trouble by not allowing them the time to form as many double-blocks as they would like.
5. A weakening of a team's block means a weakening of their defence and this is why the libero, as the team's best defensive players, does not bring, in general, any major improvement to a team's defensive performance.

THE NEW RULES AND THEIR EFFECT

6. The libero rule supports an even further specialisation of the net players. For example, at least two players from the starting line-up only have to play back-row defence in one rotation. As well, five players from the starting line-up, at most, do not have any function in the service reception formation. This means that those five players can concentrate on their positions as net and service players.
7. The intention of giving shorter players an opportunity to play at higher levels of the sport has now been diminished to playing the libero position. For other players the opposite is the case. Because of the libero rule, even bigger and taller players will be chosen as net specialists.
8. The opportunities and possibilities that the libero rule offers have not yet been completely exhausted, because at this time the players chosen for the libero position have not been systematically recruited for the position. At present, an existing player on the team is usually the one chosen to play the libero position, but there are signs and intentions to start training the libero as a specialised player (specialist). A specialised recruitment and training for the libero position only makes sense when done in combination with specialised recruitment and training with the net players. This will definitely increase the average size of the top teams.

At the top level, the libero will have a positive influence on the K1 situation and a negative impact on the K2 situation. This tendency will also be true for the middle level, but almost none at all at the low level because at this level a universal training programme must be the main priority. There will be further information given about the libero as a service reception, defensive, and coverage player in chapter 3.2.1.

1.1.3 Rule Changes for the Service

There are three changes concerning the service:
1. The server has only one attempt to toss the ball in the air in preparation for their serve instead of two. This has an influence on the individual tactic of the server. Before, the server could intentionally delay the game by using both opportunities to toss the ball up in the air, but now this is no longer an option.
2. The amount of time in which the server has to execute the serve has increased. The five-second rule has been changed to an eight-second rule. Obviously, this change neutralises the above rule because it opens up another possibility of

delaying the game, and thereby breaking the rhythm of the opposition. The only positive effect of these two changes is the fact that the interruption caused by the two whistles from the referee to restart the game disappears.

3. The third and most important rule change is the legalisation of a serve in which the ball touches the net. This change is now being tested for its efficiency. It will definitely influence the flow of a match. At the top level, the match will be positively affected by the change because when the ball from a serve used to barely touch the top of the net it was difficult for the referee to see and almost impossible for the spectators to see. This will no longer be a factor since the ball is still "live" after it touches the net. As well, the servers can take more risks on their serves. If the libero is supposed to be support for the service reception formation, this rule slightly weakens the K1 situation and will create longer rallies? This aside, the attack sequence out of the service reception formation will be even more difficult to execute because balls that touch the net are harder and/or impossible to read at all for the service reception players. At the middle and low levels, the new rule will not have such a big impact on sport. A rule that creates less interruptions in the match will be welcomed to a point where the introduction of the sport and a universal training programme are the main objectives.

1.1.4 The New Rules and their Impact on Coaching

The new rules and the introduction of a coaching zone influence the style of coaching in different ways:
The rally-point scoring system forces the coach to use the strengths of all of his/her substitute players more effectively to support possible weaknesses of the starters, even for a single play if necessary. Under the new scoring system, a single action has greater chances of deciding a win or a loss of a set or the match. As mentioned previously, it is much more difficult to come from behind to win a game, therefore, it is important to use time-outs and substitutions earlier than before.

The information discussed earlier supports the necessity for the coach to perfectly prepare his/her team against their opponents. Therefore, scouting and analysis of oppositions must be intensified. The coach must determine his/her starting line-up depending on his/her players' strengths. It is inevitable in selecting the starting line-up based on the team's best serve and service reception unit. Of course, this does not mean to neglect the opposition's strengths and weaknesses, but the first priority must be to take care of the needs and strategies of your team.

Until now, the coach has had two main "assistants" on the court to support him/her. The setter is one, who is responsible for the offensive strategy, while the other is the middle blocker, who is responsible for the blocking strategy. Now, the coach gets an additional "assistant" on the court by way of the libero, who is responsible for the service reception and defensive strategy. As well, with the introduction of the "coaching zone", it is possible during a match to coach a team in almost the same manner as in practice. The new rules allow the coaches to participate more during competitions and intensify their coaching style within the guidelines allowed. The coach has more influence on his/her players because he/she can now address them individually before, during, and after rallies. As well, the coach can advise the libero of service reception and defensive formations and strategies when they are on the bench, and then, when the libero replaces the net players, the coach can advise those players of any changes to blocking and offensive strategies.

The use of the libero suggests that the coach must have at least two match systems in place and that their team must know both of them instinctively. The team must be capable of playing with or without the libero so they will always be able to instantly react to different match situations.

The libero position allows a former service reception player and outside hitter to use this newly created position to play on and coach a team at the same time. The combination of coach and players into one person should be avoided and is impossible at the top level, but if absolutely necessary the libero Position is the best method of combining both functions on the court. It is also better than having the setter perform both functions because the libero has less on-court match time, therefore, they can focus more on the coaching responsibilities than would be possible for the setter to do.

2 ORGANISATION AND SYMBOLS

---▶	Volleyball trajectory	⟹	Spike
⟶	Running path and direction	|	Single block
⟶	Running path and direction of the hitter	⟨	Double block
===▶	Flight of hit volleyball	⚃	Basket of volleyballs
◯•	Players with volleyball	△	Hitter, middle blocker with service reception function
◯	Service reception players	▲	Main hitter, back-court hitter with service reception function
◯L	Libero	⊖	Service reception players with function as a quick hitter
△	Hitter, quick hitter, middle blocker	▲	Quick hitter with a middle blocking function
⌒	Setter, supporting setter	▲	Middle blocker with a quick hitting and back-court hitting function
⌒	Main setter	⊖	Setter with a service reception function
▲	Main hitter, back-court hitter	Rule changes 1996-2000	

Fig. 1

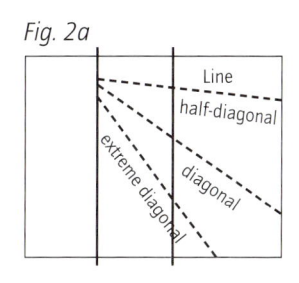

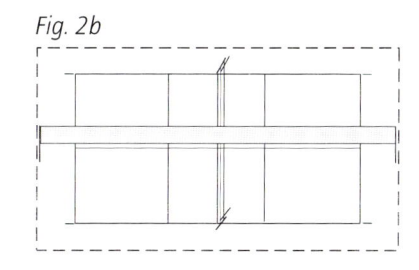

Fig. 2a

Line
half-diagonal
diagonal
extreme diagonal

Fig. 2b

28 ORGANISATION AND SYMBOLS

Fig. 2c
a = 3 x 6m
b = 3 x 9m

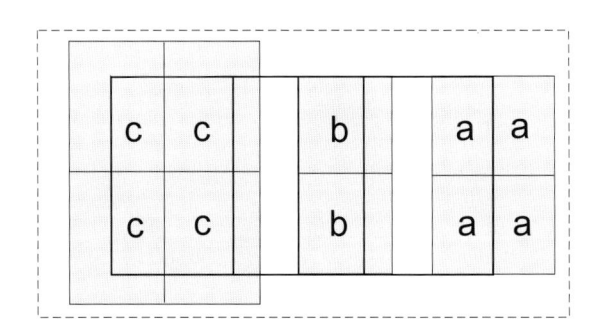

Fig. 2d
a = 4,5 x 3m
b = 4,5 x 4,5m
c = 4,5 x 6m

Fig. 2e
a = 4,5 x 6m
b = 4,5 x 9m

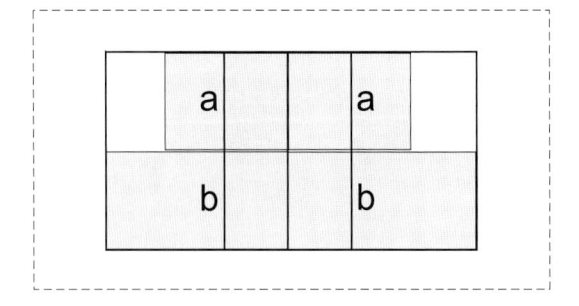

Fig. 2f
a = 6 x 3m
b = 6 x 4,5m
c = 6 x 6m

Fig. 2g
a = 6 x 6m
b = 6 x 9m

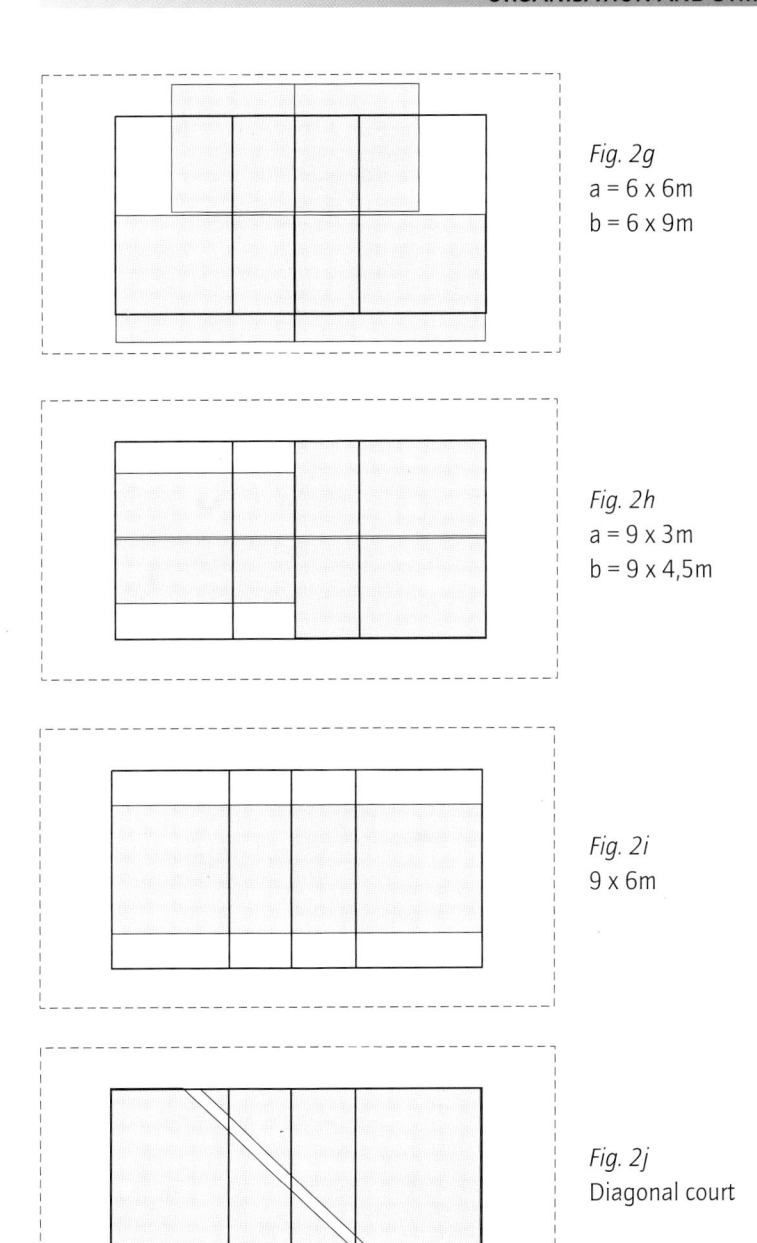

Fig. 2h
a = 9 x 3m
b = 9 x 4,5m

Fig. 2i
9 x 6m

Fig. 2j
Diagonal court

3 Learning Part 1:

Service Reception Formations and Individual Tactics of the Server and the Service Reception Players

The presentation and order of the contents of all of the Learning Parts is put together from a teaching method, factual, and purely practical point of view:

- **Team** tactics, in this case the service reception formations; will be discussed before the **individual and group** tactics. This approach takes into account that individual tactical actions are always a part of a team's own and an opposition's group and team tactical actions. For example, a server needs to know the strengths and weaknesses of a three-person service reception formation and its variations to be able to serve tactically effective.
- The individual tactic of the service reception players will precede the tactic of the server, because his/her position amongst the specialists is significant. An optimal service reception unit is the only precondition needed for ensuing actions, such as setting and attacking, to take place.
- In the development of the Learning Parts mentioned above, the server only has a supporting function and, in the beginning, practices serving at a particular target, which is the first step to an individual tactic action. The actual practice of the individual tactic of the server is the last learning progression, because it depends on the different characteristics of the service reception players and on the different varieties of service reception formations.

3.1 Service Reception Formations

ANALYSIS OF THE FACTS

The ensuing paragraph requires the following knowledge from the first volume *Volleyball – A Handbook for Coaches and Players*, especially learning part 2 (six-person service reception formations with a front-court setter), learning part 4 (six-person service reception formations with a back-court setter), learning part 7 (five-person service reception formations with a setter in position III), learning part 9 (five-person service reception formations with a setter from position II), and learning part 12 (five-person service reception formations with the setting being done by a back-court player). These learning parts are the basis of this paragraph.

To omit repetitions and overlap, these actions and their methodical introduction and development will not be discussed here. The focus of the service reception

SERVICE RECEPTION FORMATIONS

formations examined here will only be on any changes made and these changes will be discussed. For the service reception formations discussed there will mainly be practice methods offered, since match methods to introduce them can be taken from the book mentioned above.

To omit countless sketches of service reception formations, most of the figures of service reception formations are based on a serve from positions VI and I.

The question of **which service reception formation to use** depends on two factors:
- the level at which the team competes
- the sex of the players.

A team needs fewer players to take on a service reception role when they compete at a higher level. At the international men's level, service reception is almost exclusively played in a two-person service reception formation. Only when an opposition uses a jump-serve does a team switch to a three-person, and sometimes even to a four-person, service reception formation.

At the 1984 Summer Olympics Men's Volleyball competition, the two-person service reception formation was used in 73 % of the service reception situations, and in the other 27 % of the situations a three-person service reception formation was used. In men's volleyball, the tendency to use a two-person service reception formation is growing even stronger now with the introduction of the libero players. These observations are completely true **for the top-level men's national teams**.

At **the women's international level**, only very few teams use a two-person service reception formation. The main service reception formations used are three-person and four-person (and rarely even a five-person). **At the women's national level**, we find a dominant shifting to a three-person, four-person, and in some circumstances even a five-person service reception formation. **At the middle and low levels** mostly four-person and five-person service reception formations are used, and only rarely is a three-person service reception formation used.

> It can be said that, at almost all levels, a systematic and accurate usage of the libero will result in a service reception formation with fewer players.

Fig. 3a   *Fig. 3b*   *Fig. 3c*

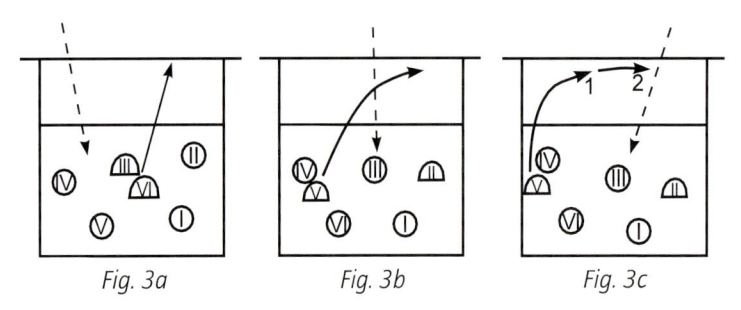

3.1.1 Five-person Service Reception Formation

The five-person service reception formation with the setter penetrating from positions VI and V is in its basic formation identical to the setter penetrating from Position 1. The only changes are in the positioning of the backcourt line-up and the running path of the penetrating setter. When the setter penetrates from position VI, s/he is standing directly behind the front-court player in position 3. When the setter penetrates from position V, s/he stands behind the front-court player in position IV (Figs. 3a and 3c).

Depending on the position from which the service is coming, the entire service reception formation is constantly changing and adjusting its position to get both the front-court and back-court players the same distance away from the server. The running path of the setter penetrating from position VI to his/her setting position is short and, therefore, causes no problems. This is different as to when the setter is penetrating from position V. Since the running path is quite distant from this position and, depending from which location the serve is coming, the running lane mostly crosses the flight path of the ball and can obstruct the service reception players. For example, the service reception players in position VI and/or III will be obstructed by the setter penetrating from position V, that is when the serve is coming from the middle (position VI) or from the right half of the court (position V) (Figs. 3b and 3c). Therefore, it is reasonable to move from a covered running path of the setter to a non-covered running path of the setter by taking into account the line-up rules (Fig. 3b). In this situation, *"not covered"* means that the setter penetrating from position V positions him/herself as far inside the court as possible, but still keeping to the left of position VI and behind position IV. This variation is a good method of covering the opposition's short serves from the baseline and is also a good tactical choice for the low- and middle-level teams. Observations of teams competing have shown a lack of technical knowledge, especially at the lower levels of volleyball. In these levels, the selected formations make the running path of the setter extremely long (Fig. 3c/running path 2).

SERVICE RECEPTION FORMATIONS   33

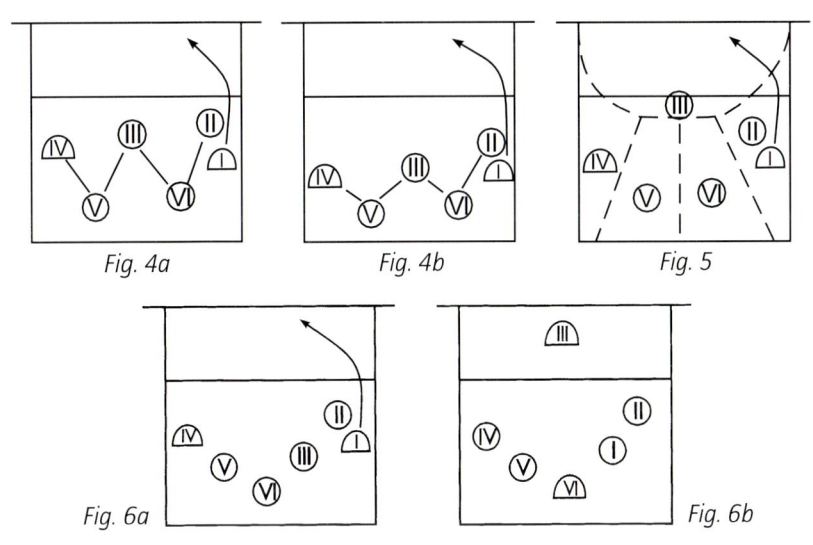

Fig. 4a   *Fig. 4b*   *Fig. 5*

Fig. 6a   *Fig. 6b*

It makes sense to send the setter outside and around the front-court players to position III/IV (Fig. 3c/running path 1), especially when you have at least one "lefty" attacking in position II or III and when the service reception players are able to vary their passing from positions II/III and III/IV.

Variations of Five-person Service Reception Formations

Besides the recognised service reception formations of the five-person service reception formation (Fig. 4a – W-formation and Fig. 4b – line-formation) there are further variations that can be used. Their use is dependent on a team's abilities, their opposition's abilities, and the location where the serve is coming from (Figs. 4-6). A useful alternative to a line-formation can be a half-circle or a U-formation (Figs. 6a and 6b). The U-formation combines the advantages of a Line-formation with a better transition to attack since at least two of the front-court service reception players are positioned at a shorter distance to the net. Furthermore, the U-formation is a useful method of reacting to a server who is serving the ball from the middle of the service zone deep to position VI. The W-formation is a good method of receiving varying and reasonably uncontrolled serves, and the line-formation is a method of receiving hard and deep serves, therefore, a five-person formation with one player covering the ten-foot zone will

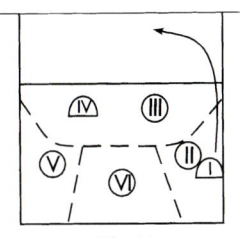

Fig. 7

be an effective formation to receive serves that are aimed at the front-court/ten-foot zone area and deep to the back-court (Fig. 5). If one player is not enough to cover the front-court, a second player can be added (Fig. 7 – M-formation). The service reception zones marked by the lines in Figs. 5 and 7 are just general guidelines. These lines are only indicating the center of the overlapping service reception zones. Systematic observations of men's and women's low and middle levels show that teams play the same unspecialised service reception formation in all six service reception rotations.

This formation is independent of the server, the position from where s/he is serving from, and of the team's individual service reception abilities. In this situation, the service reception formation is dictated by rotation. This is a major shortfall of the coaches and the training of the coaches and needs to be changed. This change will be forced with the introduction and use of the libero. There is a differentiation between the main attacker and a supporting attacker, the main setter and a supporting setter, and there must be a differentiation between the libero, **main service reception player, and a supporting service reception player.** This means that the main service reception players and/or libero must take more responsibility by covering a larger zone. The same is also true in a five-person service reception formation. The following photos show *special types of five-person service reception formations with* **two main service reception players:** the stronger service reception player is in position VI (Fig. 8), in position V (Fig. 9), in position IV (Fig. 10), in position III (Fig. 11), in position II (Fig. 12), and in position I (Fig. 13). There are many special types of five-person service reception formations depending on the position that the opposition is serving from, the position of the setter, and the choice of service reception formation that is being used. If a team has two strong service reception players, but does not use a libero, the team will be able to place the players in either position opposite to each other independent of the match system being used. It is done in the same manner as it is done with two setters or two middle blockers. The photos of the five-person service reception formations show the stronger service reception players in positions IV and I (Fig. 14), in positions III and VI (Fig. 15), and in positions II and V (Fig. 16).

Considering the fact that no team, with or without a libero, has five equally good service reception players, the variations of a five-person service reception formation mentioned above should be used as the general rule, not as the exception. This is not only true for mens' and womens' **low and middle levels**, but for most of the **women's high level** as well. If the main goal of the coach is to make his/her players all-around players, it only makes sense to use specialised

SERVICE RECEPTION FORMATIONS   35

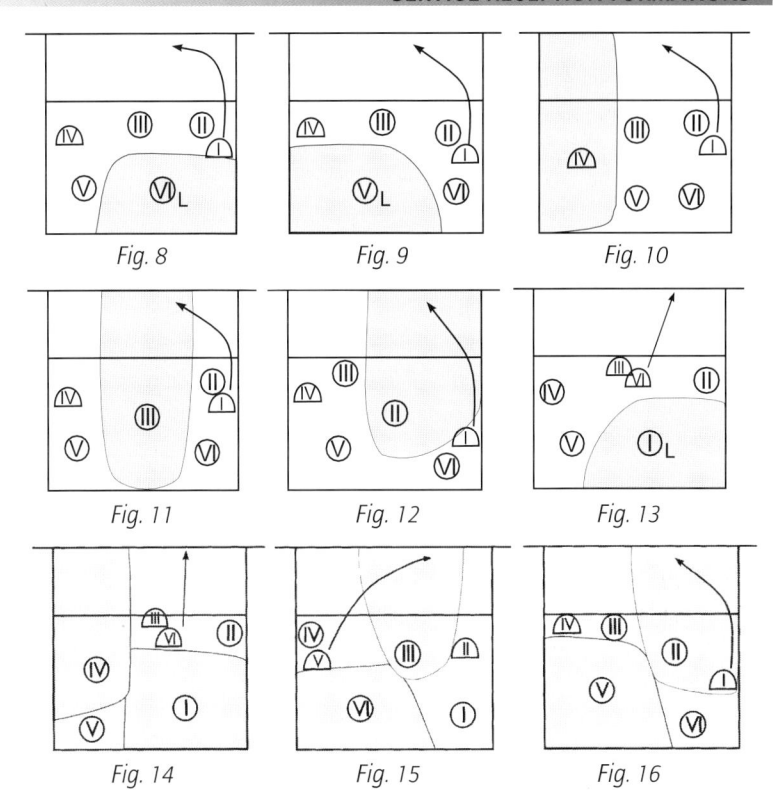

Fig. 8   *Fig. 9*   *Fig. 10*

Fig. 11   *Fig. 12*   *Fig. 13*

Fig. 14   *Fig. 15*   *Fig. 16*

service reception formations, and the use of the libero, when the opposition's service strategy puts a lot of pressure on the service reception players or the service reception players makes many mistakes consecutively. The use of specialised service reception formations in certain situations has the same effect as using a specialised service reception formation with a strong service reception players/libero (Figs. 8-13). The service reception zone has been getting smaller and smaller for certain players on the court, and because of this it can result in complete coverage of certain zones on the court.

The introduction of the libero-player rule has allowed the coach, for instructional and educational reasons, to use the libero to cover up weaknesses in a team's defence and service reception formations.

All variations of a five-person service reception formation aim at **improving the service reception** and prepare for a progression to **a four-person service reception formation**.

3.1.2 Four-person Service Reception Formation

*Changing a service reception formation from a five-person service reception formation to a four-person service reception formation or vice-versa only makes sense when the change does not weaken the current service reception formation being used. Each change to a service reception formation must bring **at least the same, if not improved, efficiency and effectiveness to the new formation**. It is for this reason that a change of a particular formation to improve the efficiency of the attack should be rejected, if at the same time the efficiency and effectiveness of the new service reception formation is weakened.* Taking into consideration the explanations mentioned earlier, the following reasons support the use of a four-person service reception unit:

- Hiding a weak front-court service reception player (Figs. 17 and 18) and hiding a weak back-court service reception player (Figs. 19 and 20) in a service reception formation.
  The front-court players are moved up to the net or, if they have an attacking role, the players are moved to the 3-meter line. The back-court players are moved to the baseline. It is the responsibility of one of the non-service reception backcourt players to signal to his/her teammates if a service is going out of bounds. Also, if a team is using a libero, it will not be necessary for them to remove or hide a weak service reception back-court player from their service reception formation.

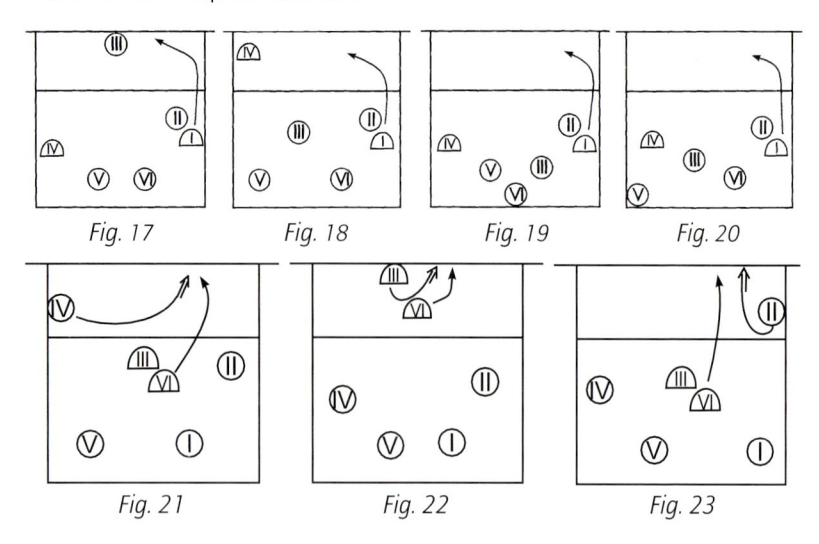

Fig. 17   Fig. 18   Fig. 19   Fig. 20

Fig. 21   Fig. 22   Fig. 23

SERVICE RECEPTION FORMATIONS   37

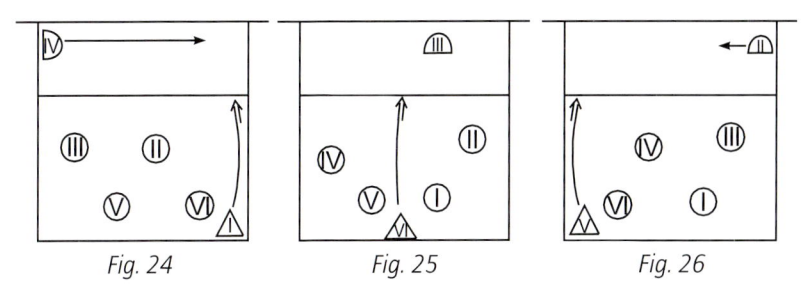

Fig. 24   *Fig. 25*   *Fig. 26*

- **Moving a middle hitter** out of the service reception formation to enable him/her to fulfill his/her role without any interference by the opposition's service strategy (Figs. 21-23).

- **Moving a back-court offside** hitter out of the service reception formation to give him/her more time to prepare for his/her back-row attack, especially when s/he is one of the main offensive options (Figs. 24-26).

- **Moving the setter** in the service reception formation when s/he must penetrate from the back-court to shorten the distance that s/he must run to get into his/her setting position (Figs. 27-28 and compare to Fig. 22)

- **Moving both setters** out of the service reception formation to enable a team to run their offence, depending on the situation at the time, by either the front-court or back-court setter (Figs. 29-30 and compare to Fig. 22).

If two of the above situations occur, the efficiency of a four-person service reception formation will be higher because of the greater number of service reception formations possible and the increase in total offensive power. For example, a weak service reception player can be used as a middle hitter or a back-court attacker depending on the situation.

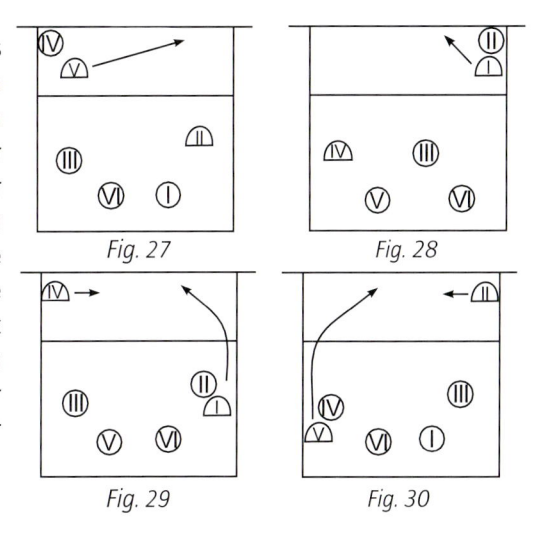

Fig. 27   *Fig. 28*

Fig. 29   *Fig. 30*

Possible Course of Action

In a four-person service reception formation, the four service-receiving players must cover different areas of the court. These areas rely on the formation designed, the strategy of the offence, and on the position of the front-court and back-court service reception players.

The following **types of four-person service reception formations** exist:
1. The **half-circle formation** (deep echelon or line) (Figs. 31-32).
2. The **zigzag formation** with the front players shifting to position II or VI (Figs. 33-35).
3. The **arrowhead formation** with one front-court players covering the front-court area (Fig. 36).

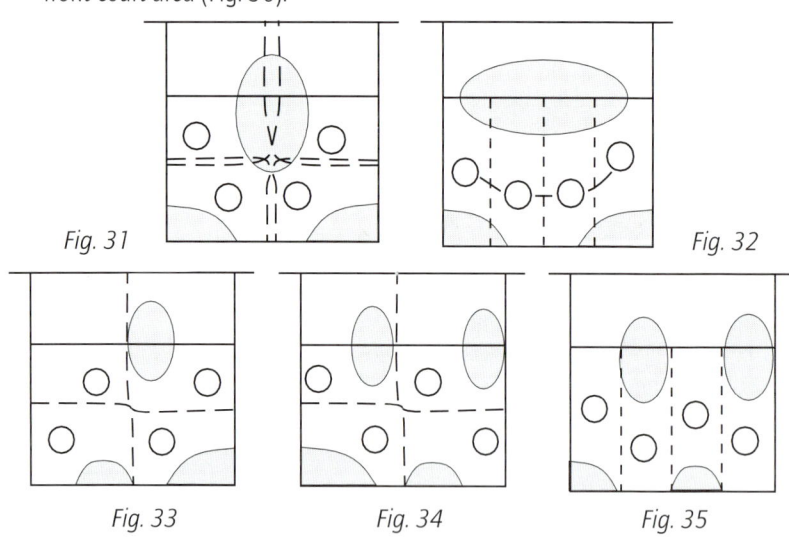

Fig. 31   *Fig. 32*

Fig. 33   *Fig. 34*   *Fig. 35*

The Half-Circle Formation

Each of the service reception players has different areas of the court to cover, depending on the design of their **half-circle formation**. The colored areas mark the most vulnerable areas of the formation. At these positions, the service reception coverage areas overlap, thus sometimes causing confusion as to which player's responsibility it is to play the ball. As the photos indicate, both variations of this formation have trouble passing short, strategic serves from the baseline, especially when the serve originates from the middle of the service area. **The deep echelon design of this four-person service reception formation** is a good strategic response to varying or unpredictable serves. The **line formation** helps in passing serves that are fast and low and are served deep into the back-court area.

SERVICE RECEPTION FORMATIONS

Studies and observations of these two formations show that they are frequently used in all levels of volleyball, except in men's national and international volleyball. **The half-circle formation** is the most commonly used service reception formation in national and international women's volleyball.

The Zigzag Formation

The zigzag formation, like the half-circle formation, can also be set up in a deep echelon design. The coloured areas mark the vulnerable areas of the formation. In comparison to the zigzag formation, it can be seen that the half-circle formations have larger exposed areas of the court to defend, thus making them easier targets to serve to. The zigzag formation is a good alternative to the half-circle formation because the closer two front-court players can completely protect the front-court area against any short, tactical serves. This rarely used formation is the preferred formation of eastern Asian women's volleyball teams. Also, this formation allows a more adaptable offensive formation and strategy, because the main offensive threat can be easily repositioned by a simple shift of the front-court and back-court players to positions II and IV.

The Arrowhead Formation

The arrowhead formation is another alternative to the formations described above. It is one in which has a four-person service reception formation with one front-court player in the middle of the court at the ten-foot line, covering the front-court area, and three back-court players positioned in a line deep in the court (Fig. 36). Although this service reception formation combines the advantages of the zigzag and line formations, which makes it a legitimately useful formation, it is rarely used or seen in any level of volleyball.

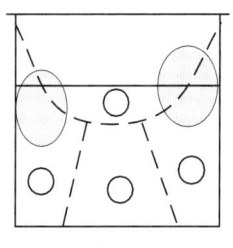

Fig. 36

The extension of the service area to the entire 30-foot baseline, and the recent rule change allowing for net contact by the volleyball during a serve, have had the following impacts on the performance of the four-person service reception formation and its variations:

1. The line formations (Figs. 32-35) have prevailed against the half-circle formations because with the implementing of the overhand service reception rule, the service reception players have the opportunity to move closer to the net during a serve. As a result, their service reception coverage areas are also shifting closer to the net and not to the sidelines. This is especially useful when covering strategic serves from the baseline.

2. The new rule changes also further accentuate the weaknesses of a four-person service reception formation and its variations because the server can position him/herself anywhere along the baseline. This allows the server the opportunity to choose a position directly opposite a weak coverage area of the opposition's court. The server can then serve a volleyball that has a shorter path and flight to that court area, thus making it more difficult for the service reception players to play the volleyball.
3. The weak coverage areas in the back-court are still vulnerable by straight-on frontal serves and by diagonal serves, especially diagonal serves coming from position V.

Studies show that the reasons for using a four-person service reception formation are often incorrect. A four-person service reception formation should be used to maintain or improve upon a team's service reception. Unfortunately, many teams use this formation to improve their offence, especially the setter's position on the court. For example, many teams move the setter from position V to position VI to shorten the setter's approach to his/her setting position. This does not provide a team with any real advantage except to shorten the setter's approach. In this instance, the service reception and attacking skills of the rest of the front-court players and what effect this change will have on them has not been taken into account. It would make more sense to move a front-court player out of the service reception formation if they had poor service reception skills, but were good middle hitters. Therefore, a team's priority should be to choose a service reception formation which optimises their first contact – the pass off of the service reception! Since the set is a team's second contact, the next step should be to improve the setter's positioning and approach patterns to the net. Finally, a team can look at improving the positioning and approach patterns of the hitters.

The contents mentioned above can be summed up in the following principle: *"The higher the quality of the first and/or previous contact (in this case the service reception), then the higher the quality of each subsequent contact."*

If there exists the possibility to choose between two or more equally strong service reception formations, then the one with the best transition to offence should be used. If there are still two or more equally strong service reception formations to choose from, then the offensive strategy will determine which service reception formation to use. Taking this information into account, the strategic reasoning behind the women's "Bundesliga", the German Professional Volleyball Association for Women, is not understood. The women's teams in this league are almost exclusively using the same four-person service reception formation, not just for one match but for the entire season. This means that the teams are always using the same service reception formation (the half-circle), with the same weaknesses

SERVICE RECEPTION FORMATIONS   41

and serving targets throughout the season, without taking into consideration the service reception skills and abilities of each player. Given the fact that four or more players *rarely* have the same service reception skills and strengths, a team should adapt its service reception formation according to the strengths and weaknesses of its own service reception players (as described above when dealing with a five-person service reception formation). *Therefore, when assigning each player with their position and role on the team, the coach must not only differentiate and assign players to the attacker, blocker, and setter positions, but also to the service reception and libero positions.* **All positions, including the main (i.e. attacker and setter) and supporting (i.e. service reception) roles, must be allocated.**

This means that the libero, the main service reception player, must take more responsibility during the service reception and cover a larger area of the volleyball court.

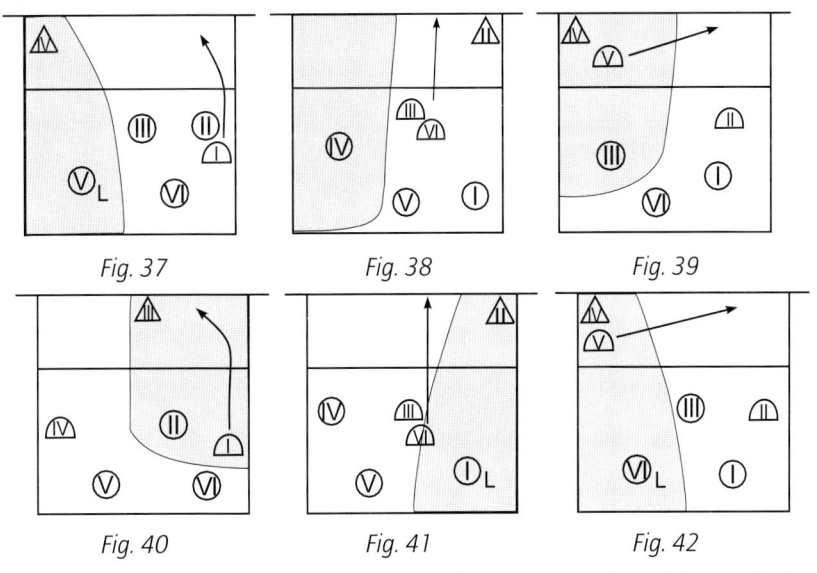

Fig. 37   *Fig. 38*   *Fig. 39*

Fig. 40   *Fig. 41*   *Fig. 42*

If a team has two strong service reception players, does not need to use their libero as one of their main service reception players, and uses the 5-1 match system (one setter and five specialists), then the two service reception players should not be lined up next to or positioned diagonally to the setter if at all possible (Figs. 37-38). If a team uses a 4-2 match system, the setters are in positions II and IV and there is one good service reception players, then the service reception players should be in position V (Fig. 37). If a team uses a 4-2 match system, the setters are in positions II and IV, and there are two good service reception players, then the service reception players should be in a diagonal

LEARNING PART 1

position to each other in positions II and V (Fig. 47). The design of this formation enables the stronger service reception players to cover a much larger area on the volleyball court without interfering with the running path of the setter. Figs. 37-42 show examples of one main service reception players in all six service reception rotations. The charts show the stronger service reception players covering approximately half of the volleyball court as a back-court service reception players, and approximately one-third of the volleyball court as a front-court service reception players. Figs. 43-46 show examples of two main service reception players that are not lined up diagonally to each other or to the setter. Figs. 47-49 show examples of two main service reception players lined up diagonally to each other (see Chapter 7 – Match Systems). In this situation, two of the service reception players cover approximately two-thirds of the volleyball court, whereas the back-court service reception players must cover the largest area of the volleyball court.

If a team has a libero with strong service reception skills, the examples above still hold true with the following additional details:
- After considering all of the information, if a team has two weak service reception players they should be lined up diagonally to each other in the rotation. This way both of the players can be replaced by the team's libero when they rotate into the back-court.
- If a team has only one weak service reception player then their position on the volleyball court should be exclusively determined by all of the other match information such as the attack, block, serve, etc.

Figs. 37, 41-43, and 45-49 show the service reception areas of the libero in different formations as one of the main service reception players.

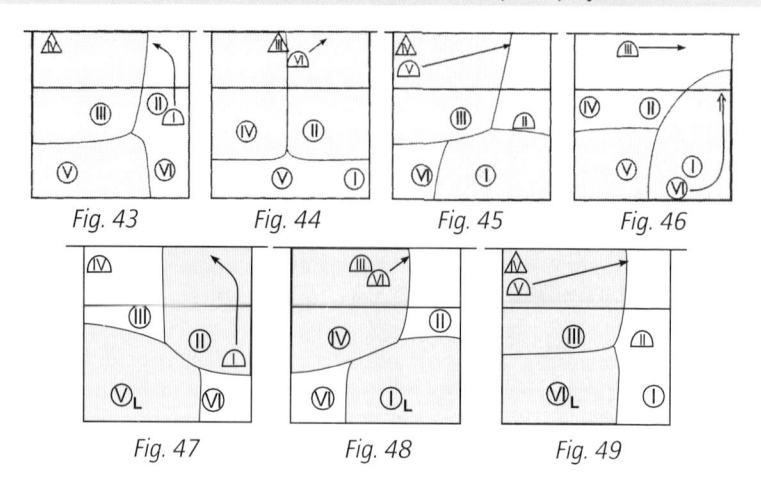

Fig. 43   *Fig. 44*   *Fig. 45*   *Fig. 46*

Fig. 47   *Fig. 48*   *Fig. 49*

SERVICE RECEPTION FORMATIONS   43

The four-person service reception formation, in which four players in a line or with three players in a line and the other pushed up in the volleyball court (Figs. 32 and 36), have purposely not been discussed because the use of either one of these formations is exclusively dependent on the opposition's service strategy.

When the four-person service reception formations mentioned above are examined, what differentiates the stronger and weaker service reception players is that the service reception formation being used is a zigzag formation. The fact that these types of service reception formations are almost exclusively used by the top-level Asian teams leads to the conclusion that their coaches know about the importance of the service reception, but are not willing to take full advantage of all of the options available to them.

Taking into account that the four-person service reception formation is the most commonly used service reception formation, it is difficult to understand the reason as to why teams do not take advantage of differentiating between their service reception players for the purpose of using them in a four-person service reception formation. Except for the coaches of top level men's volleyball teams, all other volleyball coaches and persons responsible for the education and training of volleyball coaches should deal more seriously, more intensely, and more consistently with the four-person service reception formation, especially with the addition of the new libero-player rule.

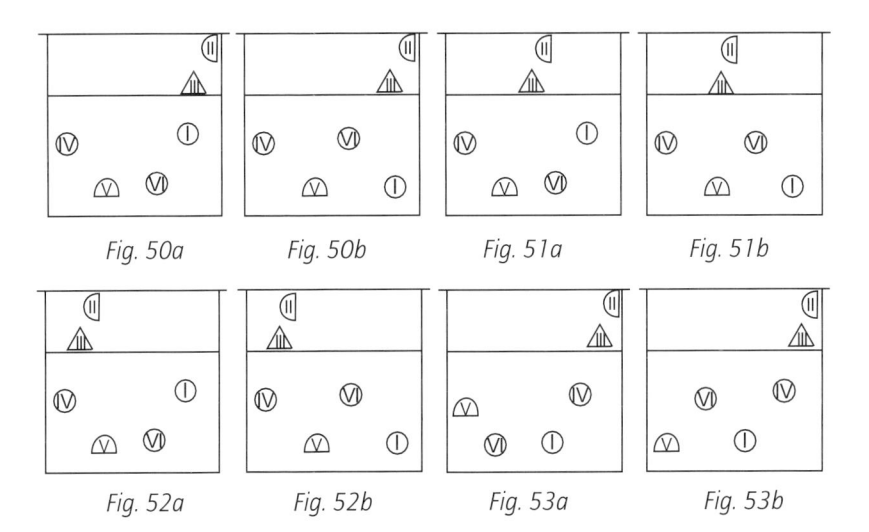

Fig. 50a   *Fig. 50b*   *Fig. 51a*   *Fig. 51b*

Fig. 52a   *Fig. 52b*   *Fig. 53a*   *Fig. 53b*

44 LEARNING PART 1

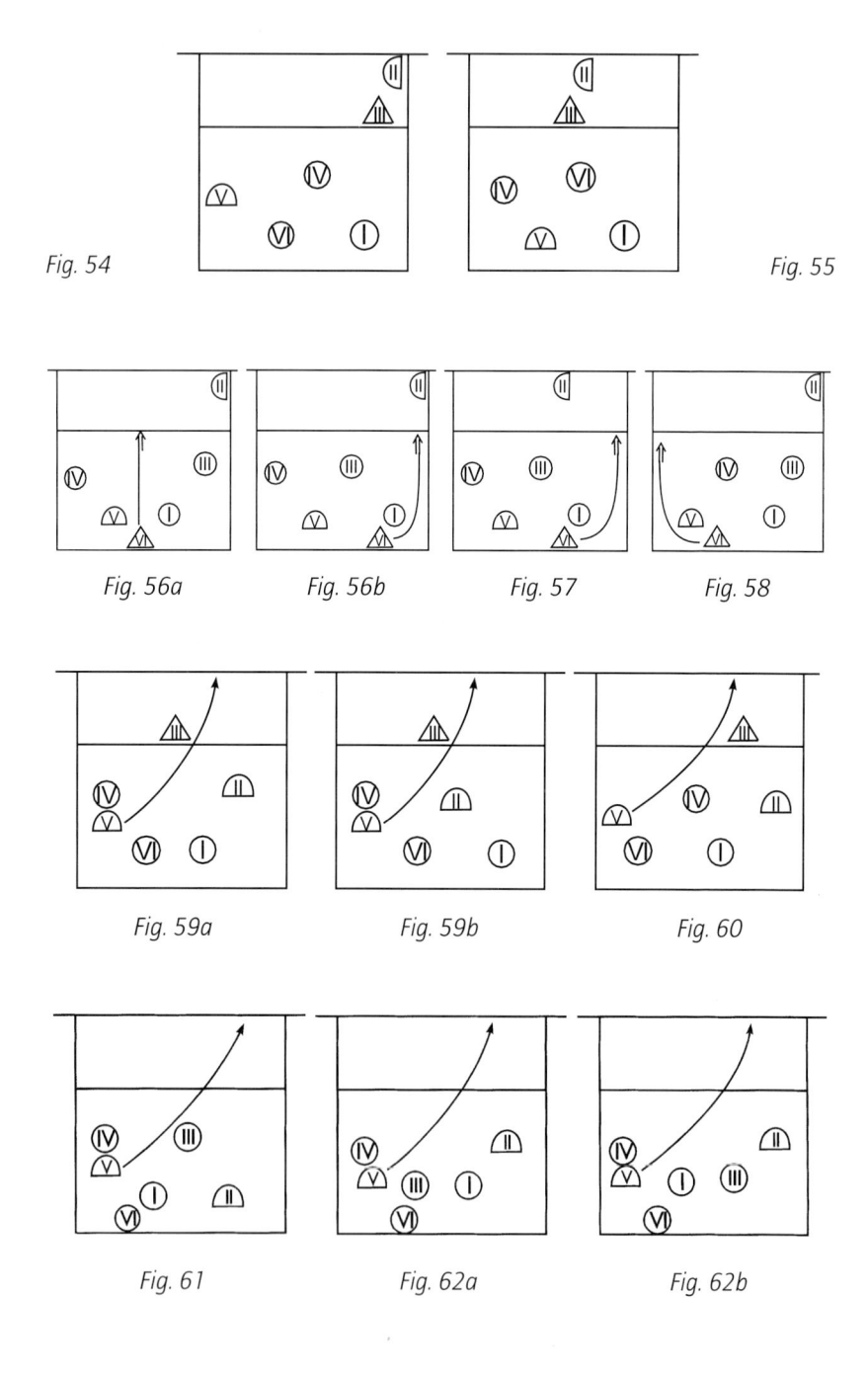

Fig. 54

Fig. 55

Fig. 56a

Fig. 56b

Fig. 57

Fig. 58

Fig. 59a

Fig. 59b

Fig. 60

Fig. 61

Fig. 62a

Fig. 62b

SERVICE RECEPTION FORMATIONS 45

Running the Offence out of the Four-person Service Reception Formation

A front-court and/or back-court setter can run the offence out of a four-person service reception formation. To clearly demonstrate this point, only one example from the following paragraphs will be chosen. The front-court setter setting from position II and the backcourt setter penetrating to the net from position V will only be shown. Figs. 50-55 show the set from position II with the front-court player in position III moved out of the formation as a middle hitter and/or weak service reception player. Figs. 56-58 show the back-court player in position VI moved out of the formation as a back-court attacker and/or weak service reception player. Finally, Figs. 59-60 show the setter penetrating to the net from position V with the front-court player in position III and the back-court player in position VI moved out of the service reception formation (Figs. 61-62).

In the previous diagrams, the individual abilities of the service reception players and the transition to offence with all the various possibilities that can be performed have been purposely left out because there would be too many variations to list. It is the responsibility of each coach to evaluate all the different variations and options to find the perfect match for each service reception situation, by knowing the individual technical and tactical abilities of the players and their physical and psychological strengths and/or weaknesses. This is where coaches can demonstrate their knowledge and competence of the sport of volleyball. Further views about running an offence and the related offensive strategies that accompany a particular offence can be obtained in chapter 5 and also in the explanations of the match systems in chapter 7.

3.1.3 Three-person Service Reception Formation

All variations of a four-person service reception formation, which improve a team's service reception, are the starting transitions to the three-person service reception formations.

> **The advantageous and efficient use of a libero with strong service reception skills in matches makes the introduction and implementation of a three-person service reception formation smoother and easier.**

To switch from a four-person service reception formation to a three-person service reception formation is only logical when the change does not weaken the new service reception. The change should also be carried out in small steps. In other words, not all six service reception rotations should be changed at once. The change should begin with one, two, or three rotations and then progress to the rest. The crucial factor in determining this is the way in which the service reception players are in relation to each other in the rotation. For example, there will not be a problem in changing to a three-person service reception formation if there is one of the two main service reception players and the libero in the back row. Taking into account the following basic concept that any changes to the service reception formation must not weaken the quality of the service reception as a whole, the use of a **three-person service reception formation,** with the addition of the libero player, offers the following advantages:

1. It removes the setter from the service reception formation.
2. Two weak service reception players can be removed from the service reception formation.
3. One hitter and a weak service reception player can be removed from the service reception formation.
4. Two hitters can be removed from the service reception formation:
a. Middle & outside hitter
b. Middle & back-court hitter
c. Both middle hitters

Possible Course of Action
a) In a three-person service reception formation, the three service reception players each cover one-third of the service reception area if they are in the back-court (Fig. 63). This type of a service reception situation may occur if a team has four or five service reception players in their line-up, but uses a three-person service reception formation

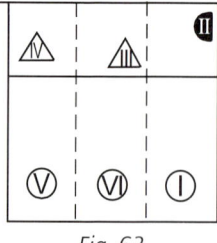

Fig. 63

b) If there are one front-court and two back-court players receiving the serve, the use of a line formation will only be possible if the front-court player meets the following conditions: S/he must be able to receive a deep serve, yet still be fast enough to get to his/her position to hit a second tempo/wave ball and/or be the best service reception player on the team and the opposition is serving deep balls (Fig. 64).

SERVICE RECEPTION FORMATIONS

c) If a front-court player does not meet the conditions outlined above and/or the opposition is serving short balls, the possibility exists to use an arrowhead formation with two back-court players covering deep positions and one front-court player covering short serves at the ten-foot line (Fig. 65).

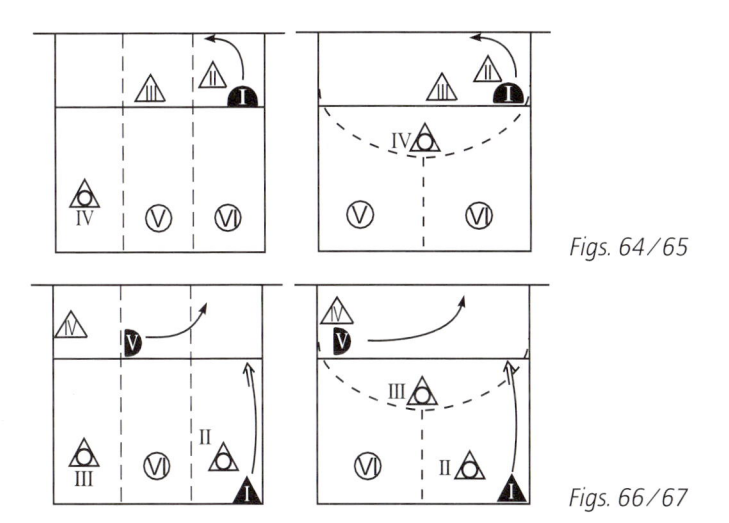

Figs. 64/65

Figs. 66/67

d) If there are two front-court players and one back-court player in the three service reception formations then the following service reception formations are possible;
  1. If the front-court players are strong service reception players and strong hitters, a line formation can be used (Fig. 66).
  2. If one of the front-court players is not a strong service reception player, an arrowhead formation can be used with one of the front-court players covering short serves at the ten-foot line (Fig. 67).

e) If a team has **four service reception players** and they **do not** use a libero, but still use a three-person service reception formation, they can choose a service reception line-up according to the attacking and blocking abilities of the players, and position them diagonally to each other. For example, if two of the service reception players are also middle hitters, their roles as middle hitters can be made easier by allowing them to only receive serve while they are in the back-court. In this case, the service reception formation will always be used with two back-court players and only one front-court player. In all six

48 LEARNING PART 1

service reception rotations, the three-person service reception formation can be set up as it is shown in Figs. 63-67. The decision of which service reception formation to use will depend upon the position of the setter and which of the two front-court service reception players has been chosen to receive the serve.

f) If a team always uses **the same three service reception players** and they **do not** use a libero, the following starting line-up with the setter penetrating from position I can be used: It is useful to always line up two of the service reception players with equal attacking and blocking abilities diagonally to each other (e.g. Positions II & IV). The third service reception player should be in position III. Also, a service reception player should never be placed diagonally to the setter in position IV or next to the setter in position VI because the distance that the setter will have to cover when penetrating from either positions V and/or VI will be extremely long, thus causing the offence to weaken and suffer (Fig. 68).

Fig. 68

Using this basic starting line-up, the following service reception formation alternatives can be used while going through each rotation (Figs. 69-74).

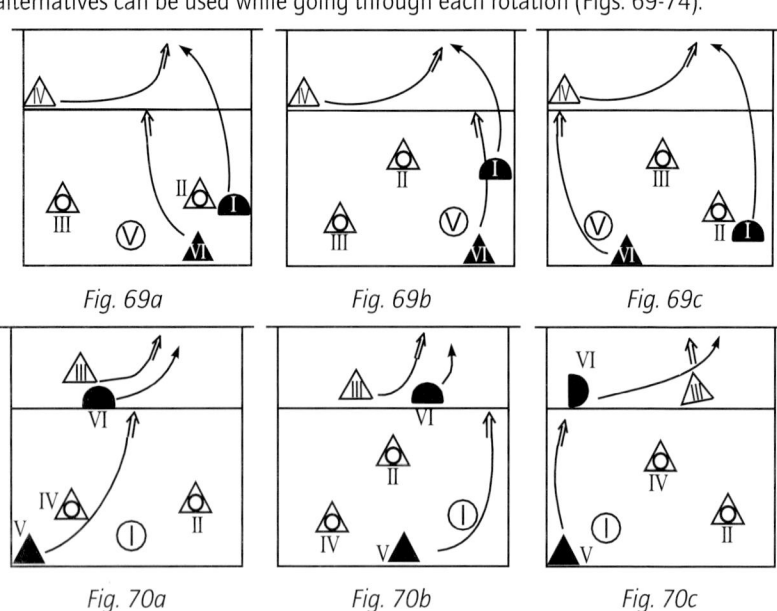

Fig. 69a   *Fig. 69b*   *Fig. 69c*

Fig. 70a   *Fig. 70b*   *Fig. 70c*

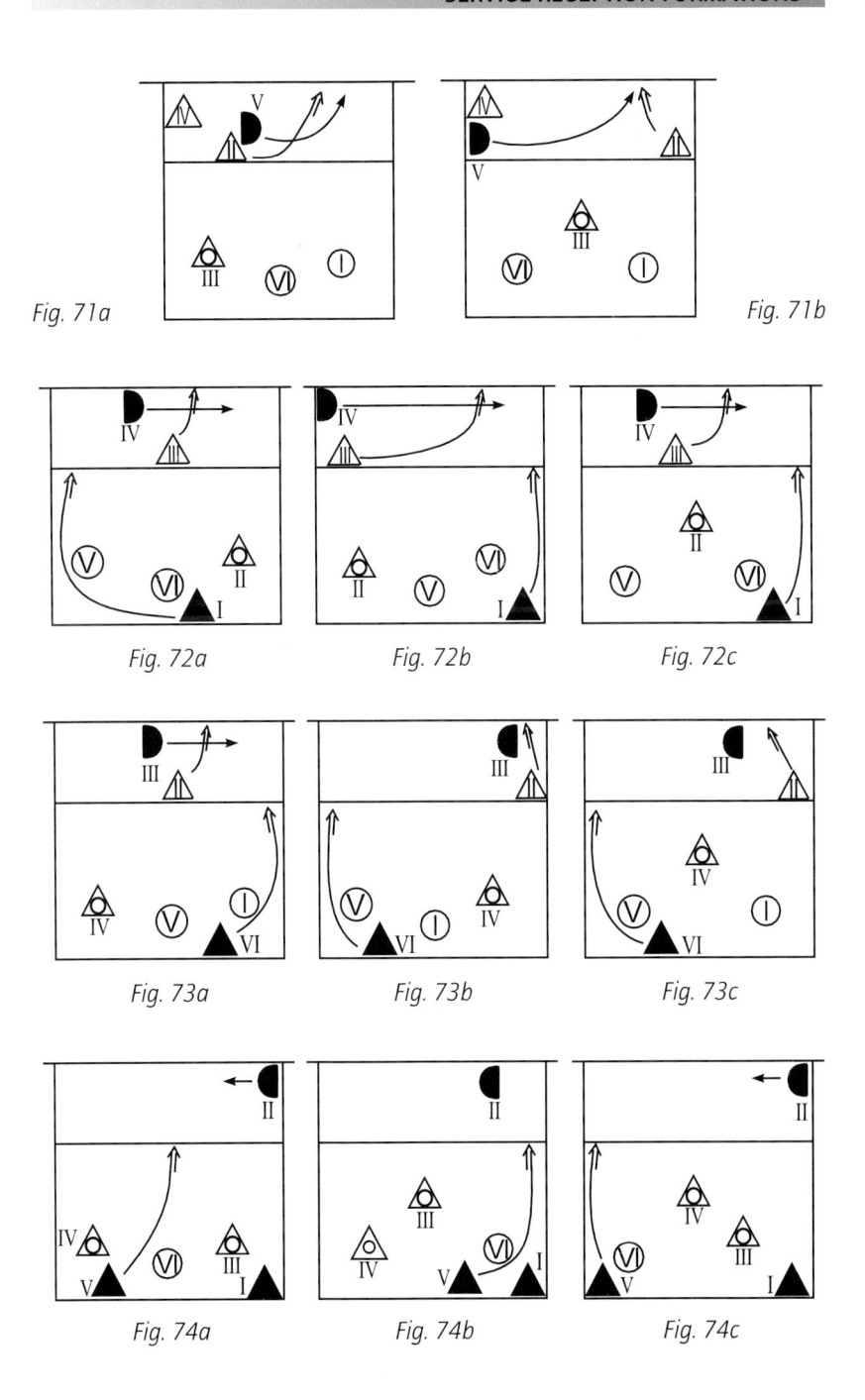

SERVICE RECEPTION FORMATIONS 49

Fig. 71a *Fig. 71b*

Fig. 72a *Fig. 72b* *Fig. 72c*

Fig. 73a *Fig. 73b* *Fig. 73c*

Fig. 74a *Fig. 74b* *Fig. 74c*

50   LEARNING PART 1

g) If a team a **does not use a libero,** but has one extraordinarily good service reception player, who is also a great attacker out of the service reception formation, for tactical reasons it only makes sense to start the player in position III (or position V). This player should be covering half the court, especially when playing in the back-court (Figs. 75-80).

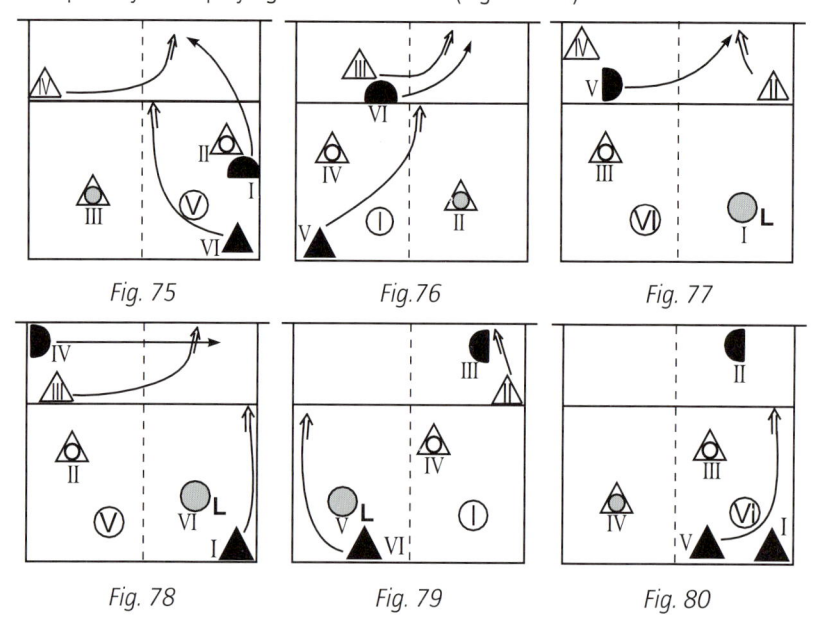

Fig. 75   *Fig. 76*   *Fig. 77*

Fig. 78   *Fig. 79*   *Fig. 80*

h) If a team **does use** a libero, but only occasionally, then all of the points mentioned from e) to g) still apply.

i) If a team uses a libero and s/he qualifies for the position with outstanding service reception abilities in such a manner that s/he is used as the main service reception player, the following points concerning the line-up for the rest of the team are important:

- If a team has four supporting service reception players and they are using a three-person service reception formation, then the main focus of the line-up will be to consider each player's abilities at the net and then place them diagonally to each other in the formation. In this system, the libero will always replace the weakest supporting service reception player when they rotate into the back-court. The libero should be covering one of the largest service reception areas on the court, up to his/her own half of the volleyball court (Figs. 77-79).

SERVICE RECEPTION FORMATIONS

- If a team has only three supporting service reception players, each with different offensive qualities out of the service reception formation, the weakest service reception player should be lined up next to the setter and the next weakest service reception player should be lined up diagonally to that player. This line-up allows a team to move one of the two weaker players out of the service reception formation while they are in the front-court, and allows that player to solely focus on his/her offence skills. It also makes it possible to replace each of those players with the libero when they rotate into a back-court position. This concept must be followed with the principle that the strongest supporting service reception player must never be positioned diagonally to the other supporting service reception player and that they should be positioned either directly behind or in front of the setter, depending on where the weakest supporting service reception player is positioned.

Depending on the level of volleyball being played, the **intended use of the three-person service reception formation** can differ greatly:
- In **men's international** and **national** volleyball, it is almost exclusively used to receive jump serves.
- In **women's international** volleyball, one uses this as a shift from a four-person service reception formation and/or even to a two-person service reception formation;
- In **women's national** or **men's mid-level** volleyball, there is a strong tendency to use this service reception formation.

In the circumstances mentioned above, the intended use of the three-person service reception formation, especially when a libero is used, is to simplify and give more options to the offence without weakening the service reception. In **women's mid- and low-level** volleyball, the three-person service reception formation is used more often with the introduction of the libero player. The efficiency of the three-person service reception formation is still underrated since the possibility of removing two weak service reception players from the formation, immediately strengthens the service reception of the team. The only argument against this is the support for the development and training of the all-around volleyball players. It is for this reason that the use of the three-person service reception formation in junior teams and at low levels of volleyball, where the main focus is the development and training of the all-around volleyball players, should be disallowed. Of course, top-level junior teams and junior national teams are exceptions to this rule.

3.1.4 Two-person Service Reception Formation

The two-person service reception formation is the introduction of a specialised service reception formation and offence to volleyball players. The three-person service reception formation is a further progression of these skills and specialisations. The **two-person service reception formation is the completion** of these skills. The moving of four, or five players if the libero is used, in the service reception formation, makes the optimisation of the offence possible on the premise that the service reception formation is played by the best service reception players. The following examples make it clear that the first priority should be on the service reception. The use of a two-person service reception formation allows the opportunity to use a double-quick attack after the pass is made. This is having two hitters in the air simultaneously waiting for a first tempo ball, but it is only possible to execute when the first pass is perfect. Another advantage is that there is only one overlapping zone on the court for the two service reception players to cover, therefore the amount of communication errors is reduced to a minimum.

The transition of a three-person service reception formation to a two-person service reception formation should be no problem if a team has three service reception specialists, allowing one to be free to execute a combination and/or a second tempo attack. This player will be the main service reception player, receiving the service in all six rotations. S/he will start in position III in a 5-1 match system, with the setter penetrating from position I (Fig. 68). The other two service reception players are positioned diagonally to each other in positions II and IV, and they only receive the ball when they are playing in the back-court. Given that they are not involved in the service reception when they are front-court players, they can be used to execute quick or combination attacks (Figs. 81-86).

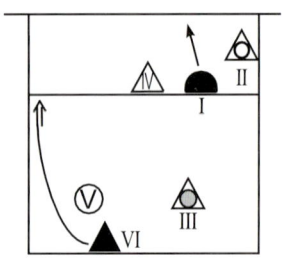

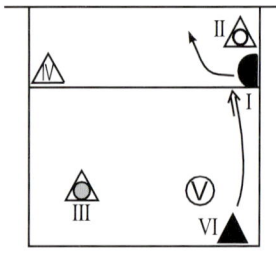

Fig. 81a

Fig. 81b

SERVICE RECEPTION FORMATIONS 53

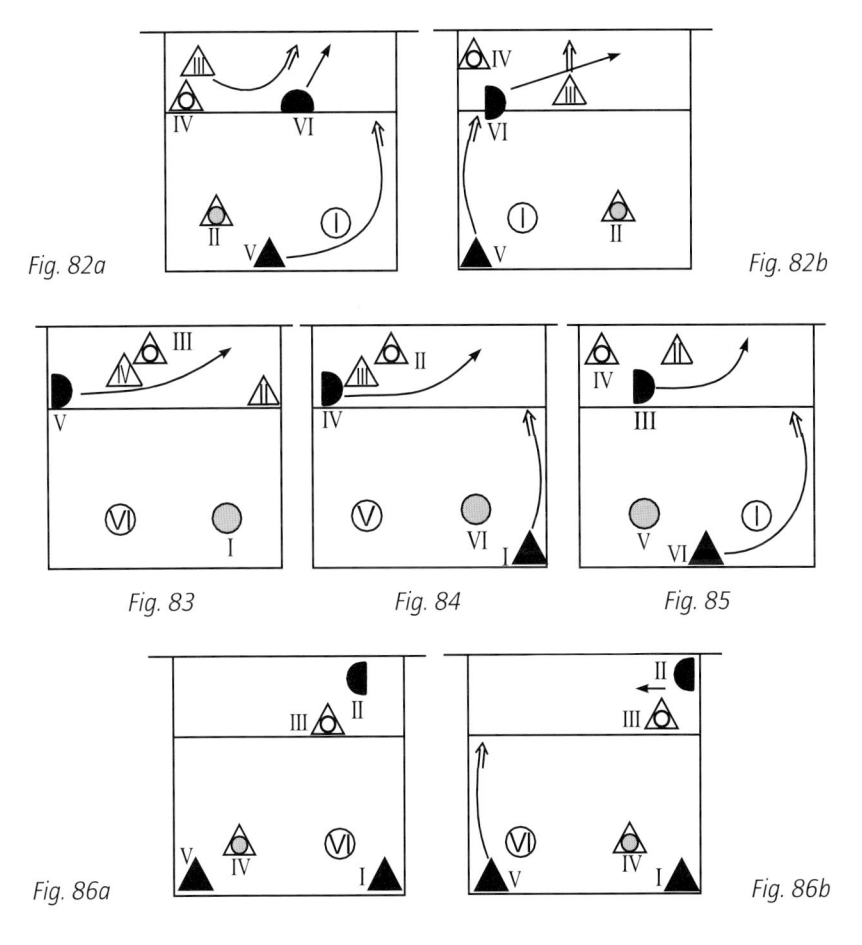

Fig. 82a *Fig. 82b*

Fig. 83 *Fig. 84* *Fig. 85*

Fig. 86a *Fig. 86b*

This starting line-up allows a coach to take advantage of the strengths of the main service reception players. The players can receive in either five out of the six rotations from the right half of the volleyball court (position I), or in four out of the six rotations from the left half of the volleyball court (position V).

The points mentioned previously do not apply if a team is using a libero as their main service reception player. In this situation, the libero is taking over the function of the main service reception player. This would leave the net and serving abilities of each player as the only criteria in determining the starting line-up of a team.

54 LEARNING PART 1

If a coach is fortunate enough to have two main service reception players, who are both able to perform a combination attack immediately following the service reception, s/he will be able to manage the service reception with only two players in all six service reception rotations. There are three main possibilities of a starting line-up when the setter is penetrating from position I, that do not complicate the transition from service reception to offence and do not infringe on the running path of the setter:
1. Player 1 in position II and player 2 in position V (Fig. 87).
2. Player 1 in position III and player 2 in position V (Fig. 88).
3. Player 1 in position II and player 2 in position III (Fig. 89).

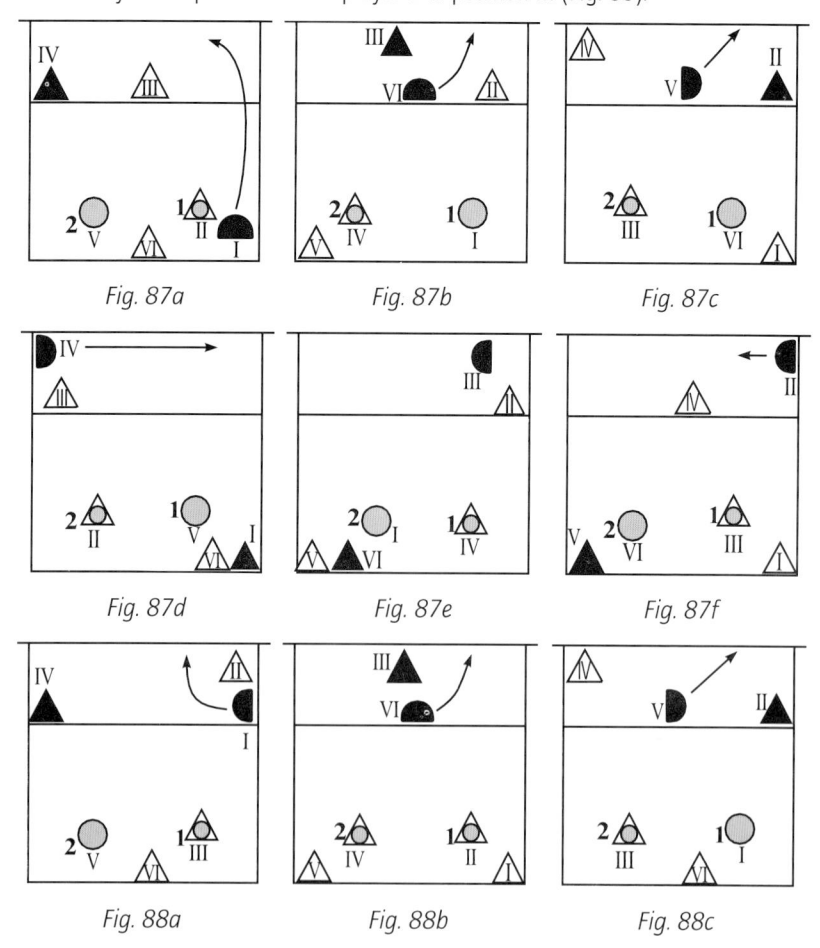

Fig. 87a   *Fig. 87b*   *Fig. 87c*

Fig. 87d   *Fig. 87e*   *Fig. 87f*

Fig. 88a   *Fig. 88b*   *Fig. 88c*

SERVICE RECEPTION FORMATIONS   55

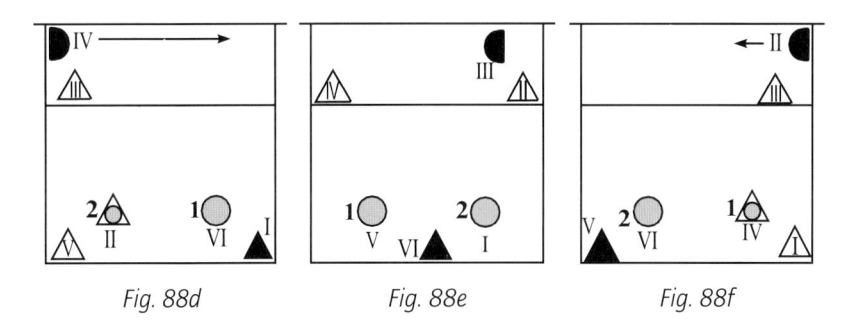

Fig. 88d   *Fig. 88e*   *Fig. 88f*

The positioning of the service reception players in situation 1 allows them to stay in the same half of the volleyball court and receive serve in all six service reception rotations. The positioning of the service reception players in situation 2 allows them to stay in the same half of the volleyball court and receive serve in up to five of the service reception rotations. The positioning of the service reception players in situation 3 allows them to stay in the same half of the volleyball court and receive serve in up to four of the service reception rotations. The diagonal positioning of the service reception players indicates that in all six service reception formations, one of the service reception players will be in the frontcourt and the other one will be in the back-court (Fig. 87). In situation 2, there is one rotation when the service reception players are both in the front-court and one rotation when the service reception players are both in the back-court. That leaves four rotations when one of the service reception players will be in the front-court and the other in the back-court (Fig. 88).

In situation 3, there are two rotations when the service reception players are both in the front-court, two rotations when both service receptions players are in the back-court, and two rotations when one of the service reception players is playing in the front-court and the other is playing in the back-court (Fig. 89). These factors are important considerations to remember, just as are the individual tactical abilities of the other and the whole concept of the sport of volleyball. The photos indicate that the three different methods of positioning the service reception players allow a coach to always have an opportunity to let one of the service reception players cover one-half of the volleyball court when they are playing in the front-court and the other half of the volleyball court when they are playing in the back-court.

56 LEARNING PART 1

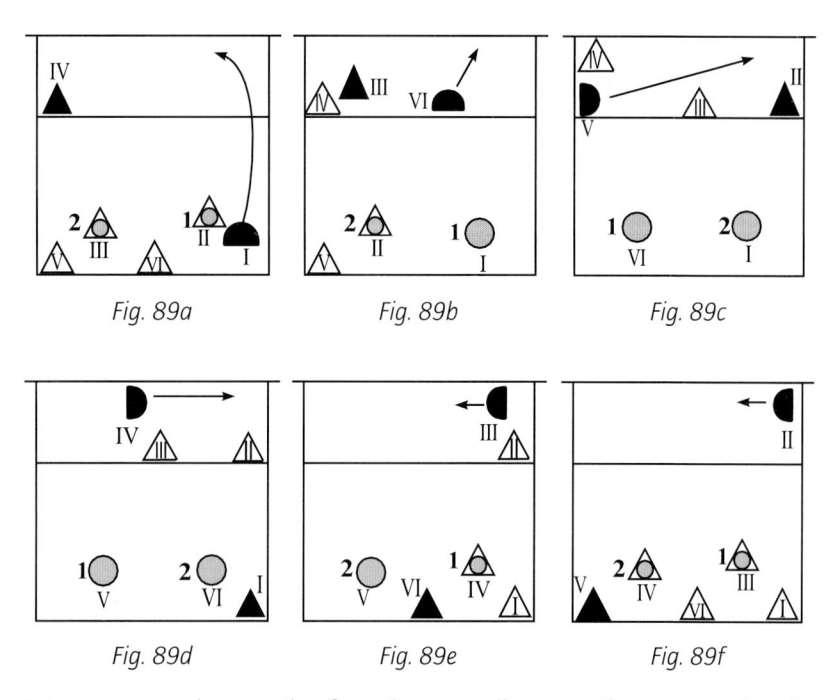

Fig. 89a   *Fig. 89b*   *Fig. 89c*

Fig. 89d   *Fig. 89e*   *Fig. 89f*

A two-person service reception formation generally means that two equal service reception players will each have to cover one-half of the volleyball court. If one of the two service reception players is in the front-court and the other is in the back-court, the back-court players can cover a larger area of the volleyball court since they only have to focus on their service reception duties and have no offensive obligations to fulfill. Currently, at the international level of volleyball, there are only a few service reception players that can also be used as back-court hitters (Fig. 90a).

If one of the service reception players is tactically and psychologically stronger than the other service reception player, then the service reception area will change

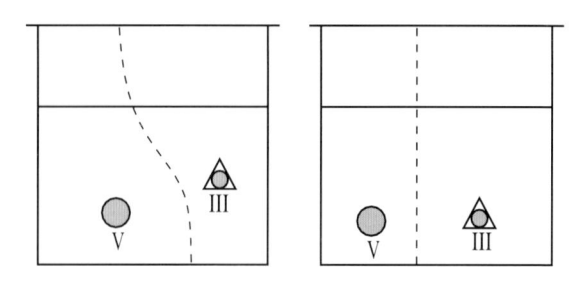

Fig. 90a   *Fig. 90b*

SERVICE RECEPTION FORMATIONS

(Fig. 90). In such a situation, it is recommended to consider using a three-person service reception formation instead of a two-person service reception formation, if such a change would be more efficient and productive.

If a team has a libero as their main service reception player and two other service reception players, the two service reception players should be positioned diagonally to each other to enable one of them to always play in the front-court without any service reception duties. When they are in the back-court, they form a two-person service reception formation with the libero. If the libero is the stronger service reception player, s/he should take over the responsibility of covering more than half of the volleyball court (photo 90a). If a team has a main service reception player, other than the libero, who is also a strong offensive threat from the service reception position, then all of the same principles of setting up a service reception formation that have been previously stated still apply. In this situation, the two-person service reception formation is not particularly engaged.

The use of a **one-person service reception formation** implies that only one player is covering the entire volleyball court during the service reception. Such a choice of service reception formation may be useful in the following situations for tactical reasons:

If the opposition's servers are serving from deep behind their baseline (more than 22 feet), then the psychologically stronger service reception player, usually the libero, will assume the responsibility of covering the entire volleyball court. This is only possible since the distance that the volleyball must travel from the initial point of service contact to the opposition's area of the volleyball court, allows enough time for the service reception player to move quickly into the necessary position to pass the volleyball.

The following outlines the steps taken to complete this action (Figs. 90a & 90b): Simultaneously, as the server is tossing the volleyball into the air the service reception player is moving, depending on the server's actions, either forward, backward, or sideways from his/her main position in the middle of the volleyball court.

The following observations have been made concerning the use of a **two-person service reception formation:**

- Currently, there is no team that uses a libero and only one main service reception player, but it is expected that this will change soon.

- The two-person service reception formation, using only two service reception players and the libero in all six rotations, is currently only used in **men's international and national volleyball**. Teams which use such a match concept, usually have one supporting service reception player, who will turn their two-person service reception formation into a three-person service reception formation for the purposes of receiving an opposition's jump serve.
- The two-person service reception formation, where two service reception players and a libero are used, is utilised primarily in **men and women's international volleyball** and in **men's top-level national volleyball**.
- In women's international volleyball, two-person service reception formations are created by using three service reception players and the libero. In this situation the service reception formation is created by always using the two back-court service reception players. The reasoning behind this is that very few female player at high levels of volleyball are able to, as front-court players, receive volleyballs served deep into the last one-third area of the volleyball court and are still fast enough to execute a second tempo offence at the net.
- In women's top-level national volleyball, three-person and four-person service reception formations are the preferred choice. The reason for this is that by using these service reception formations, over two-thirds of the service reception is performed by the back-court players, respectively the libero, thus the service reception formation resembles more of a two-person service reception formation. In women's volleyball a back-court player is removed from the service reception formation because she is a weak service reception player, and, as is done in the men's game, to use her as a back-court attacker.

3.1.5 Fake/Trick Formations

When we discuss fake/trick formations, we mean a service reception formation that does not immediately allow the opposition to figure out which of your players are playing in the front-court and which are playing in the back-court. At the very least, the role of each player is disguised as much as possible. By doing this, we try to "fake" the opposition as to what action our offence will try to perform and what defence we are playing.

The participation of the libero reduces the opportunities of using a fake formation, because s/he is immediately identified as a back-court player by the different color of uniform that s/he must wear.

The following are the main objectives:
1. Fake penetrating setter (the setter fakes that s/he is penetrating from the back-court).
   The front-court setter acts and runs as if s/he is penetrating from the back-court (i.e. penetrating from positions I, V, and VI). This fake enables the setter, depending on the quality of the service reception, to attack the first pass by hitting, tipping, or dumping the volleyball over the net.
2. Fake hitter (the back-court players fakes a front-court attack).
   A back-court player acts as if s/he is in the front-court and pretends to be a middle or offside hitter to fake the opposition's blockers.
3. Fake penetrating setter combined with a fake hitter.
4. Fake blocker.
   When his/her team is serving, a back-court player acts if s/he is blocking in the front-court to distract the opposition's setter and make him/her think that there is a blocker in that position so as to cause him/her to set the ball to another position.

In **international and national volleyball, fake formations** have lost their importance because advanced scouting has given teams a detailed and systematic analysis of their opponents ahead of time. Observation shows that fake formations are only used against certain oppositions and in certain situations, such as at the end of a set or in particular psychologically difficult condition for a team's opposition. However, at **low** and **middle** levels of volleyball, the use and efficiency of fake formations is still quite high.

Absolutely necessary conditions that must be established to make fake formations work are:
1. Using a fake penetrating setter.
   - A perfect pass to the setter's position enables him/her to do the following action in the air – jump set and/or attack.
   - The ability of the fake penetrating setter to be able to switch from setting to attacking and vice-versa. In other words, s/he must be able to jump set, attack, and/or tip or dump the first ball.
2. Using a fake hitter.
   - A perfect first pass to the setter's position.
   - An excellent temporal-spatial behavior from the middle and/or second hitter (in other words being in a position to hit a second tempo ball).

LEARNING PART 1

3. Using a fake penetrating setter with a fake hitter.
   - Possibly all of the previously mentioned conditions, but definitely the ones relating to a fake hitter.
4. Using a fake blocker.
   - A very good temporal-spatial behavior of the players, while they are changing their positions (Figs. 95g-95j).

These formations possess the danger of line-up errors, because the fake penetrating setter, the fake hitter, and the fake blocker have to directly interact with the players in front of them, behind them, and the front-court players.

If there is a line-up error purposely set up to fake the opposition, it has to be sorted out the moment that the server tosses the ball in the air and before s/he makes contact with it. In the photos this is shown with the zigzag running method.

Different possibilities of fake formations will be shown using the example of a five-person service reception formation (Figs. 91-93). Since the transfer from this to the other types of service reception formations is easily done, they will not be shown here.

Setter 2 (fake penetrating):

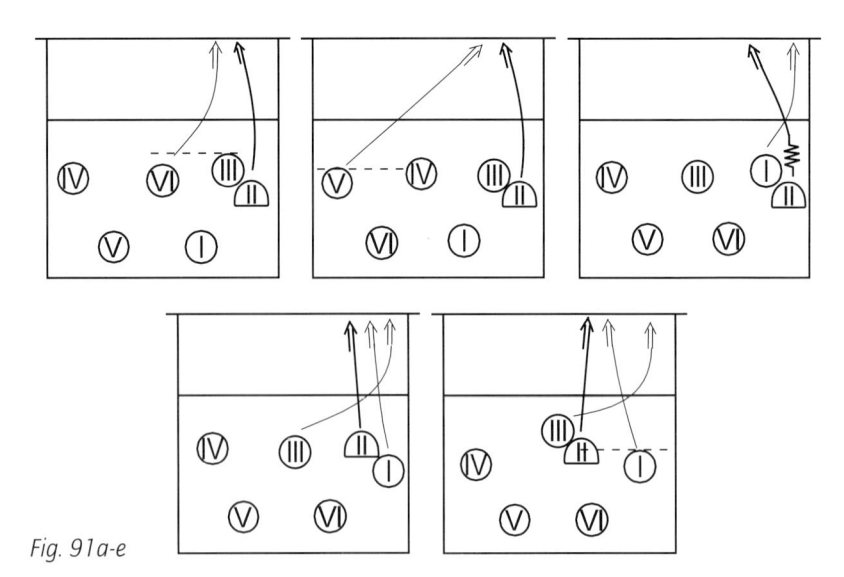

Fig. 91a-e

SERVICE RECEPTION FORMATIONS

Setter 3 (fake penetrating):

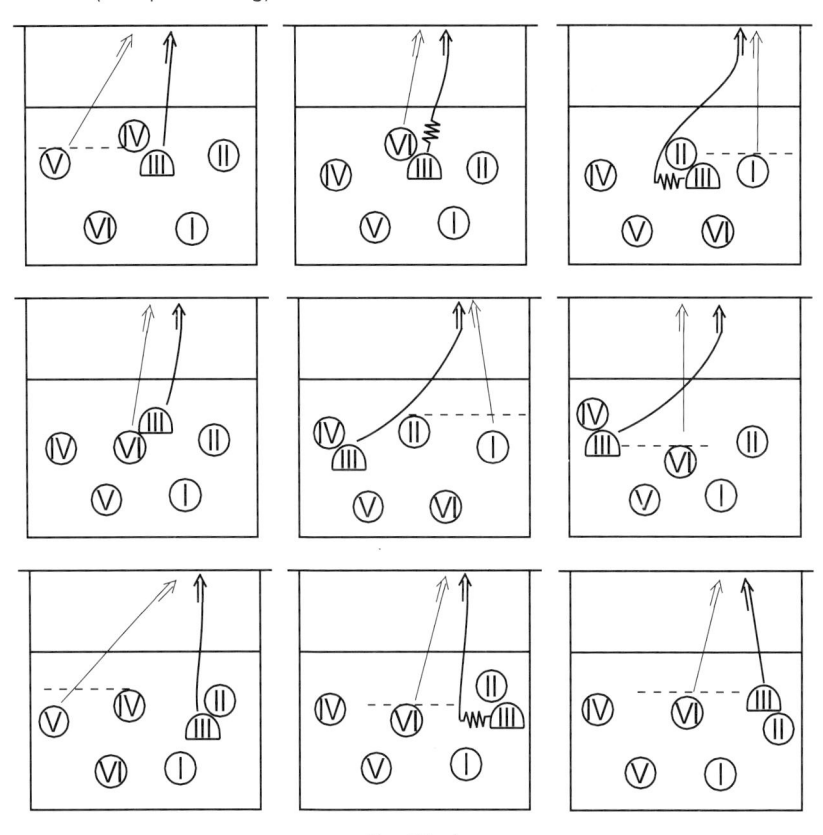

Fig. 92a-h

Setter 4 (fake penetrating):

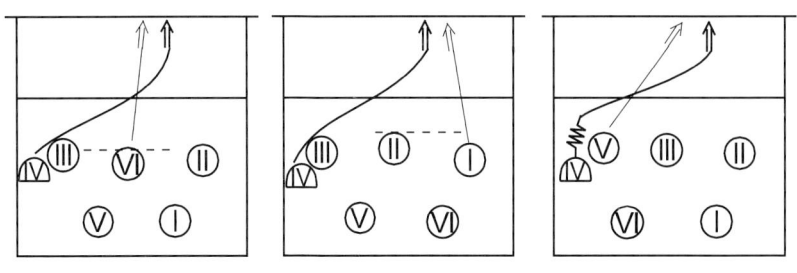

Fig. 93a-c

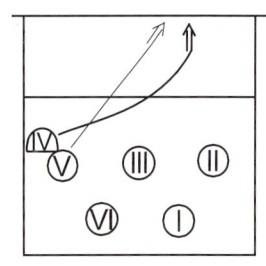

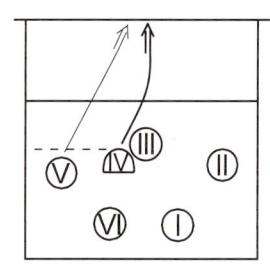

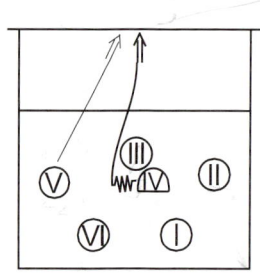

Fig. 93d-f

Fake Formation Principles

The following paragraph will be a summary of important criteria and thoughts that must be met and addressed to use fake formations (FF) in an efficient way:

- The decision to introduce a FF into a team's match system is dependent on the technical and tactical skills of the players and also on the decision of why to use a FF. In other words, *do not use a FF just for the sake of using it to fake your opponent!*
- *The service reception formation of a team must not weaken because of the FF,* because an accurate service reception is one of the most important conditions to be able to run an efficient FF!
- When the setter is in the front-court (positions II, III, and IV), the possible number of FFs for each situation increases, therefore *the FF that guarantees the highest service reception efficiency, not the one that promises the best offence, should be used!*
- If there are two equal FFs that can be selected, and neither will weaken the service reception, *it is only logical to use the one that offers the stronger offence!*
- *The efficiency of a FF relies upon the strong individual tactical skills of the setter!* Necessary are: **Tactical knowledge** (especially knowledge of different service reception formations, and the transition to offence – including offensive strategies such as different attacking combinations), and **technical skills** (especially jump sets and the ability to hit or tip/dump the first pass). The ideal situation would be, if the fake penetrating setter is able to, depending on the match situation, switch in the air from setting to attacking the volleyball and vice-versa.
- *The choice of what FF to use should be determined by the offensive capabilities of the fake penetrating setter!* If the setter is right-handed and s/he is supposed to hit the first ball, FF's with the fake setter penetrating from position V and setting from position II/IV will be a successful option because this is the

SERVICE RECEPTION FORMATIONS

perfect position for a right-handed setter to hit from. If the goal is to have the setter tip/dump the ball, FFs with the fake setter penetrating from position VI or I and setting from position II/III will be an option. If the fake penetrating setter is left-handed the ideal setting and attacking position II/III.

- *A FF that only uses a fake penetrating setter must get a perfect service reception!* Whereas FFs that use a fake hitter or a fake hitter and a fake penetrating setter do not necessarily require a perfect service reception.
- *It only makes sense to use a fake hitter, if the same hitter was offensively successful with the same attack that they are trying to fake (i.e. hitting a quick ball or shot) when they were in the front-court!*
- *FFs are more successful when they look like the real setter is managing a service reception formation!* For example, Figs. 94a and 94b show the same service reception situation, the same service reception formation, the same pair with the setter penetrating, the same running path of the setter, the same setting position, and the same offensive combination. Since both line-ups follow each other, they might be quite confusing for the opposition (Figs. 94a and 94b).

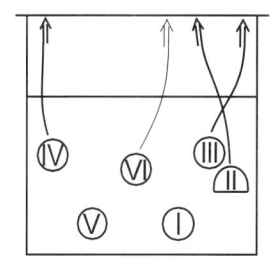

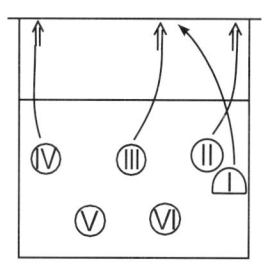

Fig. 94a/b

- *FFs must not negatively influence the feeling and understanding of the team on the volleyball court!* There must be perfect teamwork, especially between the service reception players and the fake penetrating setter or the setter, fake hitter, and all of the other hitters. The more that the FF itself, and/or the setters penetrating strategy is varied, and/or the more precisely the offence is the better and more flexible that the teamwork must be and the tactical actions of the individual players, group, and team must be.
- If the opposition realises that there is a fake penetrating setter and/or fake hitter, but the service reception is perfect then a team should do without the fake hitter but not without the fake penetrating setter because s/he is still an offensive threat and freezes the opposition's blocker! *With a poor first pass one should do without a FF, at least until the service reception improves, or do without a FF if the service reception does not improve at all!*

64 LEARNING PART 1

- *The efficiency of the FF is highly dependent on the opposition!* The greater that the opponent tactically knows and is informed about your match system, the less success you will have using a FF. If the opposition's tactical knowledge of your team is small and they do not recognise the FFs, then it is your choice of whether or not to keep them.

Figs. 94c-94h show a **4-2 offensive match system, with two setters penetrating** out of a four-person service reception formation.

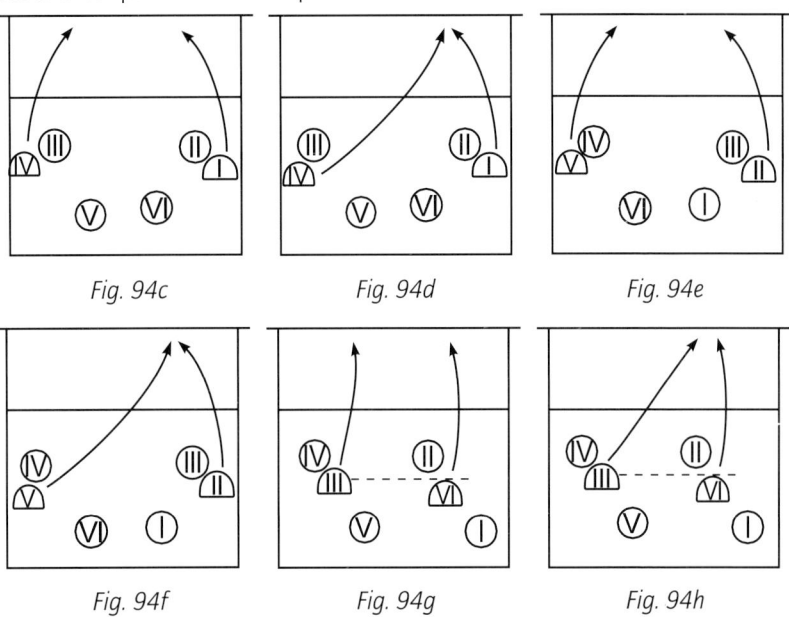

Fig. 94c   *Fig. 94d*   *Fig. 94e*

Fig. 94f   *Fig. 94g*   *Fig. 94h*

Two setters penetrating allows the offence, in the same match situations, two options of running the offence – either with the penetrating back-court setter or with the fake penetrating setter. If you use the fake penetrating setter then the other setter should take over the role of the fake hitter. Without a perfect first pass the penetrating setter should be the one to set. To be in a position to use all of the possible offensive strategies available, and not to be easily detectable then a team should switch between using each setter as well as adapting to any situation. This variant on the one hand implies that there must be very good teamwork between the service reception players and the setters, and also between the setters themselves especially when the setting is in position II/III.

With the examples given, it becomes clear that all six rotations can be carried out with two setters penetrating out of a four-person service reception formation.

SERVICE RECEPTION FORMATIONS

With the setters in positions II and V and in positions IV and I the service reception formations and the running paths of the setters (penetrating setter and fake penetrating setter) are identical. The result is that four out of the six service reception rotations are alike. By doing this, and the planned switching of who is setting, makes it difficult for the opposition to read the match situation and it also makes using a two setter system very efficient.

The following example shows a 5-1 offensive match system where all six service reception rotations use a two-person service reception formation and the setter penetrating from position VI (Figs. 95a-95f). The fooling of the opposition is supported with the use of fake hitters.

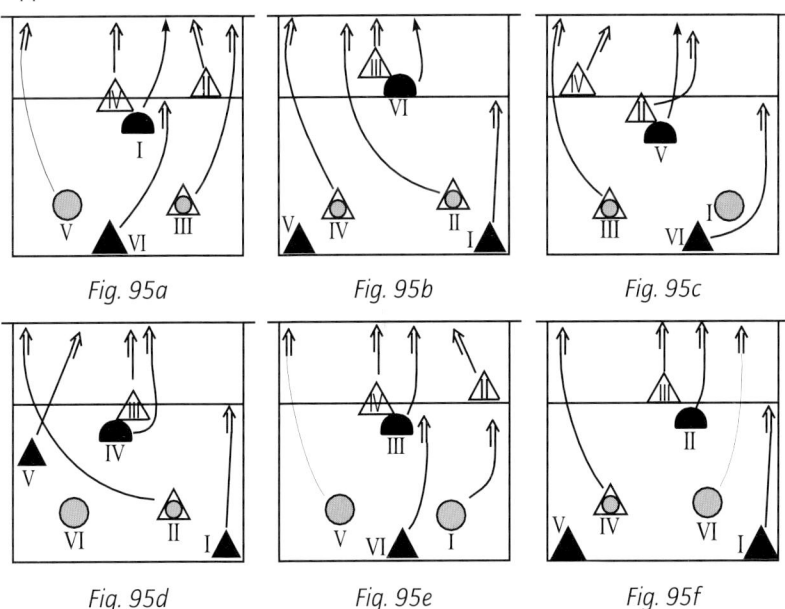

Fig. 95a   *Fig. 95b*   *Fig. 95c*

Fig. 95d   *Fig. 95e*   *Fig. 95f*

The fake formations with the use of a fake blocker aim to achieve two points:
1. To put a weak blocker in the back-court and to use a much better blocking back-court player as a fake blocker at the net hoping that the opposition's setter will be "faked out" by the move and not set the volleyball to the position of the stronger blocker.
2. To put weak blocking back-court player up to the net and use them as a fake blocker so as to invite the opposition's setter to set the blocking area of this fake blocker. The purpose of this is to convince the opposition to set to this area and then surprise them by using a hidden strong blocker.

Figs. 95g-95h show the actions of an FF with the use of a fake blocker, and Figs. 95i-95j show further possibilities by doing this action. The line-ups and the execution of the actions to fake a weak or strong blocking opposition are the same.

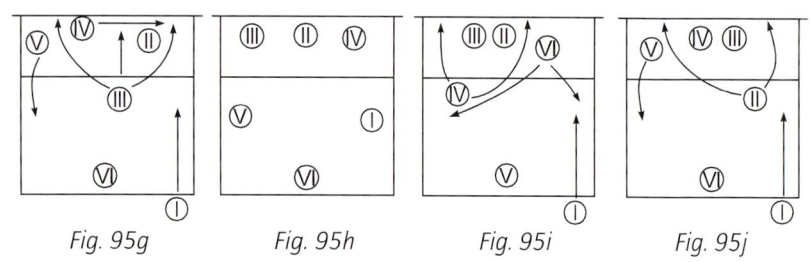

Fig. 95g   *Fig. 95h*   *Fig. 95i*   *Fig. 95j*

Finally, it must be stated that the successful use of fake formations requires hard work and many hours of practice.

3.2 Individual Tactics of the Service Reception Players

Analysis of the facts

Service reception is approximately 16 % of a volleyball match and since all of the succeeding actions depend upon the quality of the pass, it makes service reception one of the most crucial factors for a team's success in a match. Since the service reception itself is not very complicated (it occurs after a stoppage in play and it is a relatively simple execution of a technical action from a concrete position), it is the **service reception player** who has to deal with the **most psychological pressure** compared to the other players.

Male service reception players perform approximately 77 % positive actions (very good and good) per match and their quota of errors is below 5 %. Female service reception players average approximately 5-10 % less positive actions and they have approximately 3-5 % more errors.

> At this time it is important to mention that the introduction of the libero has increased the number of positive actions by approximately 8 %.

If we take a closer glance at the service reception actions of middle and low levels of volleyball we see that the quality of the service reception worsens proportionally to the level of volleyball being played. It is no surprise that men and women get worse the lower the level of volleyball that they are playing. The results at higher levels of volleyball reflect that the expectations of the coach, teammates, and spectators are much greater. A stoppage of play before the service reception action increases the fear of failure and, therefore, also increases the **psychological pressure** of most service reception players (Photo 4).

An error directly related to the service reception, which results in a point for the opposition, signifies the importance of the service reception in general. Since the goal of the service reception is clearly defined as passing the volleyball to the setter's position, bad and inaccurate passes will be easily recognised by all players involved in the play, therefore making the situation and stress level of the service receiver more demanding. Another effect of a bad first pass is that a team's offence would be negatively affected, thus allowing the opposition to be more successful with their blocking and defence. It is always on a service reception player's mind that they are the first players to touch the volleyball after an error by their team since the serve changes to the opposition and they must be in a service reception mode again. This task is even more difficult if it was them who were the cause of the original error that caused the opposition to gain possession of the serve.

Photo 4 (Steffen Marquardt)

All of these points underline the extraordinarily high psychological pressure that is placed on the service reception players and the appropriate **behavior** that is required of them:

- *The coach must train his/her service reception players in a positive manner, both in practices and in matches.* This is especially true if the players are just learning the role of a service reception player. The coach needs to teach the player that the technical skills of receiving serve are quite easy, but the tactical effects are extremely valuable.
- *The coach and teammates must always positively support a service reception player in practices and matches.* This is especially true for the setter and the hitters that are actively involved in the action following a service reception.
- *Omit the following errors by the setter and the hitter after a bad first pass.* Both the setter and hitter should try to compensate and do their best to save the bad first pass, but not at the expense of taking risky actions that could jeopardise their or their teammate's safety.

For these reasons, the training of the service reception player must replicate a match situation as closely as possible. This means that psychological pressure and possible stressful match situations must be introduced. Thus, a conscientious service reception player must learn at least one ***technique of psychological management.***

The Movement Sequence of a Service Reception Forearm Pass

The use of float serves being served from different distances and positions from the baseline. Jump serves being hit with different degrees of force, and the specialisation of the service reception (i.e. two-person, three-person, etc.), requires the service reception player to be able to use different service reception techniques depending on the situation that they are faced with. Research on different variations of service reception techniques has shown *that approximately 60 % of the serves are received while in a standing position (Photo 5), 25 % while in motion (Photo 6), and 15 % while falling (Photo 7).* Regarding the positioning relative to the volleyball, the sideward forearm pass (51 %) is preferred slightly more than the frontal forearm pass (49 %).

Photo 5 (Steffen Marquardt)

Photo 6 (Martin)

Photo 7 (Steffen Marquardt)

INDIVIDUAL TACTICS OF THE SERVICE RECEPTION PLAYERS

Training the basic skills of passing to the service reception player ensures that the forearm pass is mastered standing sideward and frontal, as well as falling forward, backward, and sideways – although the final ones are more defensive techniques. The following characteristics of movement should be observed, analysed, and improved upon in practice (Photos 5-7):

- The ready position must allow for quick changes of direction and positioning. It is for this reason that the muscles should be loose and relaxed. The shoulders should be slightly pushed forward in front and above the knees. The knees should be slightly ahead and above the toes. As a result, the weight of the body is resting on the balls of the feet. The arms are held slightly open in front of the body. This is an active ready position and it is necessary because a service reception player never knows ahead of time where the flight of the volleyball off of a serve will travel. This is especially true for float serves. Furthermore, a service reception player must be aware of any changes to the ball's flight path until the very moment of contact. This is particularly important since no one can predict where over 90 % of the serves will land in the volleyball court.
- At the instant of contact, a service reception platform can be achieved by pushing the shoulders forward and at the same time bending the wrists down. This results in an "over-stretching" of the arms and makes the forearms move closer together.
- There are many different hand positions that can be used to pass a volleyball, but one tends to stand out more than the rest. One of the hands rests in the palm of the other hand with both thumbs parallel to each other. As mentioned earlier, with an over-stretching of the arms, the inner sides of the forearms create a large platform. The stronger hand should be holding the weaker hand in its palm because by doing this the stronger hand can lead the whole movement of the pass.

Photo 8 (Köhler)

- To understand the importance of the accuracy of the service reception pass, we must pay close attention to the relationship between the service reception spot and the volleyball-body relation to the target (the setting spot). Depending on the flight path of the volleyball (direction, height, and speed) and on the service reception player's position relative to the setter target several different passing techniques must be used. For example, the service reception players must be conscious of the angle to bend their knees, the angle to position their arms, and the amount of force to use to pass the volleyball.

With the sideward forearm pass from a standing position the shoulders must be pushed higher and further forward to eliminate a "breaking away" of the volleyball (Photo 8).

Photo 9

- The basic principle for the service reception is *"the angle of incidence = the angle of reflection"*.
- The main **force** is given by the legs and resembles a **thrust movement.**
- Hard hit and low trajectory serves often force the service reception player to pass the volleyball while falling backwards or sideways (Photo 9). Using this technique allows the service reception player to position his/her arms at the correct angle to the volleyball and to reduce some of the force generated by moving out of the way and falling backwards. Float serves have a tendency to suddenly drop to the court at the end of their "flight", therefore, often the only solution for the service reception player is to dive forward to pass the volleyball (Photo 9).
- Taking a step backwards and using a sideward forearm pass will pass serves coming in at shoulder height.
- It is important to keep in mind that the service reception player's movement to the volleyball, with regards to footwork, is to always start and finish with the leg closest to the volleyball. The in-between step can be a side step or better yet a cross-step. The main goal of the service reception player is to anticipate the serve and pass the volleyball in a standing position and, if possible, face the setter target.

The service reception player must be trained hard and educated in such a way that allows him/her to react in match situations to the speed, trajectory, location, type of serve (i.e. jump or float). Also to spin of the volleyball by using the correct service reception technique (i.e. frontal, sideward, falling, defensive, overhand, etc.).

INDIVIDUAL TACTICS OF THE SERVICE RECEPTION PLAYERS

Observations concerning the service reception using an overhand pass show that in the men's Professional National League less than 5 % of the serves are passed using the overhand pass technique. This statistic is even less in the Women's National Professional League.

In international volleyball, especially in eastern Asian junior national teams, it is evident that they are using, under the correct circumstances, the overhand pass technique to receive serves.

This leads to the conclusion that the skill of overhand passing as part of the service reception has to be systematically trained in players and then used in matches. The use of the overhand pass as part of the service reception during practice and in matches requires additional focus in the general training process. A selective and guided training of the arm, hand, and especially the finger muscles must be included as part of the general training process.

The training of the service reception player is aimed at enabling him/her to use one of the following alternatives depending on his/her abilities and on the service reception situation:

1. To pass the volleyball perfectly to the setter target to meet the concept of the match (Fig. 96 – zone A).
2. To pass a good, but not perfect, volleyball to the setter target with the intention to omit a service reception error and/or to omit any other succeeding errors (zone B).
3. To not pass a good volleyball in favor of making a safety service reception pass (high ball) in the middle of the volleyball court (zone C) to at least allow the volleyball to be set and to omit a direct service reception error (Fig. 96).

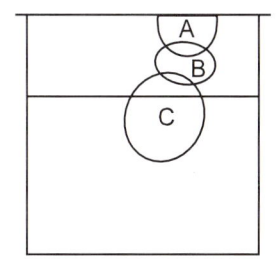

Fig. 96

It is important to keep in mind that the setting zones A, B, and C (Fig. 96) are overlapping and, therefore, the transitions are not clearly marked, but are different for each individual service reception player depending on their service reception skills.

An improvement of a service reception player is shown by the fact that his/her direct errors in relation to digs, his/her digs in relation to good service receptions, and his/her good service receptions in relation to perfect passes gets reduced season by season and possibly even month by month.

Individual Tactical Training
The goal of training the service reception player is to make him/her look at the inner and outer factors in every match situation. After judging the situation, s/he should be able to decide as to where to pass the volleyball – zone A, B, or C.

The *inner factors* are closely related with the service reception player. They are his/her athletic and tactical abilities and even more importantly his/her technical and psychological abilities. As with the **outer factors,** the service reception player is influenced by his/her teammates, opponents, and his/her surroundings. The crucial factors are:
- The precise knowledge that his/her teammates have of the service reception formation, and their psychological strengths and weaknesses.
- The precise knowledge of the setter, especially their athletic and technical skills.
- The knowledge of the server. In other words, early recognition of the spot where the server serves from, the kind of serve s/he will use, and the trajectory, direction, spin, and speed of the volleyball that s/he will employ.
- The accountability of his/her teammate's and opposition's psychological condition, especially in relation to the success/failure rate of their previous actions.
- The awareness of the development of the match, especially the score of each set, the reactions of the spectators, and the quality of the officiating.

Training a service reception player is the same as training the whole team. It requires that the types of training/drills are adapted to the level of the players and/or the team. The key to a successful practice is the right choice of drills, but keep in mind that these drills must be combined and linked to the overall goal of the training session. Another important factor is the coach and his/her ability to simplify or complicate the drills without changing the structure of the practice and without changing the intended outcome and intention of the match-related drills.

The first step to a successful training of the individual tactics of a service reception player is to do a **detailed analysis** of his/her service reception statistics. This analysis must be carried out during a competitive match situation because this is the only time that a complete and whole picture of the player, with all of his/her strengths and weaknesses under match conditions, can be seen and analysed.

The observations have to contain the following pieces of information:
- Does the player have a weaker service reception side? For example, for a left-handed player his/her right side.
- Does the player display any weaknesses when s/he must pass the volleyball while s/he is motion (i.e. changing his/her direction or position forwards, backwards, or sideways)?

INDIVIDUAL TACTICS OF THE SERVICE RECEPTION PLAYERS

- Does the player have any trouble when s/he must pass a volleyball served above or below his/her hips?
- Does the player show any weaknesses when s/he must use the overhand pass to play a volleyball that is served at or above his/her shoulder height?
- Does the player have any difficulty playing in certain positions on the volleyball court or with the distance that the first pass must travel to the setter target?
- Does the player have any difficulty passing certain types of serves (i.e. jump serves or float serves)?
- Does the player show any weaknesses that are related to the trajectory and distance of the serve?
- Does the player reveal any weaknesses that are related to the location of where the volleyball is served (i.e. serves from position V or Position 1)?
- Does the player show any weaknesses based upon his/her position as a back-court and/or front-court player?
- Do the front-court players reveal any weaknesses in the service reception formation and/or in the offence, especially after a long first pass by the service reception player?
- Do the front-court service reception players have time to run an efficient second tempo offence and/or certain combination plays after a very short and/or a very deep serve?
- Does the player reveal any weaknesses when s/he must communicate with his/her teammates?
- Does the player show any weaknesses in critical match situations or is s/he able to take upon more responsibility in those critical service reception and/or offensive situations?
- Does the player reveal any weaknesses in his/her service reception after s/he or his/her teammates have committed an unforced error?
- Does a service reception player show any weaknesses after big mistakes and/or errors by his/her teammates or after the official has made a bad call?

These observations and analysis have to be completed in the **men and women's top levels of volleyball** during the pre-season. This is also true for the middle and low levels of volleyball, but usually they do not have the same time advantages to complete these same observations as they do in the professional levels. If observations and analysis are done in the middle and low levels, it should be carried out in a different manner. The analysis should only focus on certain main factors that are important at these levels. The principle followed here should be "less is more". It is crucial to keep an eye on the volleyball-specific principles (see Chapter 8) regardless of what methods of training will be used. For example, training a service reception player should also include the training of a server and all of the players that are involved in the following actions – attack (front-court and/or back-court players) or the coverage of a team's own offence.

Observations of weaknesses and mistakes by service reception players have resulted in the following **preferred actions for a helpful practice:**

Example 1
- *The service reception gets worse the moment the opposition's server varies his/her serving spot or the service reception player must use a sideward passing technique to his/her right or left side!*

1. The service reception player is choosing his/her service reception Position in such a manner that his/her stronger passing side is covering more court space (i.e. covering 2/3 of their area with their one side while only covering 1/3 of their area with their other side).
2. If the service reception player must pass using his/her weaker passing side, s/he should focus on passing the volleyball to zone B as the passing target, therefore eliminating any errors due to an inaccurate pass.
3. If poor technical skills are responsible for a weak service reception:
- Check the angle of the outstretched arms in relation to the incoming trajectory of the volleyball and the setting target;
- Check to see if the arms are turned in such a manner as to move the platform in the direction of the setting target to omit a "breaking away" of the volleyball to the outside.
- Check if the outer shoulder is pushed higher and further forward than the inner one.
- Check if the service reception player is trying to move his/her outer foot forward a little to position his/her upper body more in the direction of the setter's target.

The first two hints mentioned above offer a short-term solution to deal with service reception weaknesses. The third hint is more of a long-term solution since the problem is purely a technical issue and technical improvements take a much longer time to correct. The following types of practice deal with the third opinion above. It is important to show players the causes of their mistakes and to watch their progress because their training has to be continually adapted to monitor their improvement.

Types of Training
1. The service reception player must use the sideward forearm pass to play the volleyball to the setter at the net; therefore s/he is receiving a series of

INDIVIDUAL TACTICS OF THE SERVICE RECEPTION PLAYERS

volleyballs tossed to them from the front zone of the volleyball court. When doing this, the player who tosses the ball should always be changing his/her position at the net to simulate a match-related volleyball movement.
2. Similar to 1, but the volleyball is now hit as a roll shot by the player who tosses the ball while s/he are in a standing position.
3. Similar to 2, but the volleyball is now hit from the opposite side of the volleyball net.
4. Similar to 3, but the volleyball is now served and the service reception player, after a given number of service receptions, changes to the other half of the volleyball court to continue to pass volleyballs.
5. Similar to 4, but the serve and the spot from where the volleyball is served will be varied.
6. Types of drills and/or small court games, where the service reception player must work as a front-court and/or back-court player. As a front-court player s/he can be used to hit the volleyball against a blocker. If s/he does not hit the volleyball s/he must go and cover the other hitter's attack. As a back-court player s/he must always cover the hitter.

Note
The service reception player must be trained hard on his/her weaker passing side to get him/her to the point that his/her sideward forearm pass is improving from zone B & C to the setting zone A.

Example 2
- *The service reception gets worse the moment that the player has to move to pass the volleyball.*
1. The service reception player should always try to hustle to the volleyball and then try and pass the volleyball from a standing position. By doing this, s/he should omit using cross-steps at the moment of contact because cross-steps make the center of gravity change. The change that it makes to the position of the body increases the difficulty in anticipating and/or observing the incoming trajectory of the volleyball. Movements to the volleyball should begin and end with the leg that is closer to the volleyball. If larger distances need to be covered, cross-steps and sidesteps should be used.
2. By knowing and understanding service reception weaknesses after movements in certain directions to the volleyball, the player should compensate and try to correct these weaknesses by initiating a change in his/her position. For example, with weaknesses in moving backwards, the player should move his/her initial starting position further back.

Types of Training
All types of training that improve the sideward forearm pass can be used. It must be noted that the serves must force the service reception player to move. If the service reception player needs to improve his/her movement backwards to pass the volleyball, then start him/her in a closer position to the volleyball net and have him/her move backwards to pass the volleyball. It must be noted that the volleyballs must then be served deep for the player to have any training effect. The drills can be varied and made more complex by incorporating additional work for the player. For example, make the service reception player lie on the volleyball court, then stand up and move backwards to his/her correct position, and then pass the volleyball, etc.

Example 3
- *The service reception gets worse when the trajectory of the volleyball is high or low.*
1. Check the technical execution of the player, especially if s/he is making a large step sideward to lower his/her center of gravity to try and get a better angle position of his/her arms to the setter target.
2. With a high trajectory volleyball from the side, it must be observed to see if the player is getting quickly behind and under the volleyball to be in a position to pass the volleyball with an overhand pass. Alternately is the player extending his/her leg that is closer to the volleyball and turning his/her arms to open up and form a good angle for the platform to the setter. With high trajectory serves, the service reception player should use the overhand pass to play the volleyball.
3. The use of supporting help techniques such as a single-handed pass or a tomahawk defence should only be allowed and used in extraordinary situations.

Training Drills
All the drills mentioned earlier, especially the drills that include additional effort by the player, are useful. The types of drills that are important in this case are the ones that involve tossed volleyballs and/or off-speed hits. Drills that reduce the reaction time of the service reception player should not be used in the training of this player because these types of drills are not typical for the sport of volleyball. It is also inappropriate to use mats and blankets to block the sight of the server. The opposite is the case for the service reception player because this player needs

to watch the server as closely as possible to try and anticipate or predict where the serve is going to. This is very important because it is the only time in the match where the player can prepare for the next play of the match.

3.2.1 The Libero as a Service Reception Player

The libero will be discussed in his/her role as a service reception player rather than in his/her other role as a defensive specialist. All explanations in chapter 3.2 regarding the individual tactics and strategies of the service reception player also apply to the libero. Only an extraordinary all-around volleyball player can be developed into the role of a very good libero. This theory confirms a belief that applies to all players that play the sport of volleyball that states that the specialisation of a player should be started as late as possible. The decision to specialise, train, and develop a libero should not be selected any earlier than the moment the decision is made to specialise a quick hitter or a middle blocker. It is much more difficult for the libero to predict the actions of his/her own teammates and the actions of the opposition's players at the volleyball net without any sufficient experience as a blocker or a hitter. This will impede and stagnate his/her development as a good volleyball player. Therefore, the libero must be a good all-around player. S/he must continue to work on his/her hitting, serving, and blocking skills to develop his/her ability to anticipate the next actions that may occur in a match. Particularly with the development of junior volleyball players, it may be sensible for the coach for instructive and developmental training purposes to put a player who is a strong net volleyball player but weak in his/her defensive skills in the role of the libero.

At high levels of volleyball, the importance of a specialisation will generally increase with the use of a libero because it allows for a weaker defensive player to be replaced when s/he rotate into the back-court. The only instance that this player would have to remain in the back-court and play defence is for the time that s/he must serve.

Systematic examinations of the 1999 Men's European Championship showed that the service reception improved immensely as indicated by two factors: the addition of the libero and the willingness to take risks while serving declined. In more than 70 % of the offensive actions out of the service reception, quick hitters could be used.

When the libero played constantly, his share of the service reception duties amounted to 24-29 %. It was evident that the effectiveness of the libero was, at that moment, 10 % less than the effectiveness of the other service reception players. However, it can be expected that in the future this figure will turn in favor of the libero and then the number of service reception actions that he must perform will decline. Furthermore, it was clearly evident that the libero always replaced quick hitters/middle blockers, even if those players had good skills as back-court hitters.

An analysis of the 1999 Women's European Championship revealed the following results:
1. The libero was used differently than in the Men's Championships. The libero would replace one, two, or even three different players in match.
2. Similar to the men's results, the quality of the service reception of the libero was as much as 20 % below the quality of the best service reception players on their own team. Therefore, the share of the service reception duties of the libero was as much as 47 %.

In contrast to the international men's and women's senior teams, assessment of the 1999 Junior World Championships revealed that the use of the libero had been better understood and taken advantage of.
The quality of the service reception of the libero was approximately 5-10 % better than the service reception of the other players on their team. Consequently, the share of the libero in the service reception was between 20-28 %.

For the choice of the libero, the following characteristics and features apply:
1. The players must identify themselves with the role of the libero, especially in situations where they only have a very few volleyball contacts. This reveals that the opposition has recognised his/her intensity and strengths as a specialist and that the options of the opposition, especially when serving, have been reduced.
2. The libero should be an emotionally positive player. S/he should bring a psychological and moral support to the whole team when s/he is introduced and inserted into the match, but this also requires a very positive attitude from the team towards the libero.
3. It only makes sense to insert the libero into a match if s/he is the better service reception/defensive player than the player that s/he will be replacing

or, even though it is a rare circumstance, if a player is psychologically overtaxed and needs a break.
4. The libero will be indispensable if s/he is the team's best and psychologically strongest player.
5. If the use of the libero only slightly increases the effectiveness of only one service reception/defensive situation, then his/her use is still justified.
6. The perfect libero should be as good if not better in the service reception formation as the other main service reception players.
7. The libero, after the service reception, will cover the hitters and be as good as the main defensive coverage players, because s/he cannot execute any offensive manoeuvres and, therefore, cannot perform any subsequent actions.
8. The libero must be able to execute a very good "safety set" from the back-court.
9. The libero is the coordinator of the service reception and defensive formations and of the team's counter strategies on the volleyball court.
10. The libero should be trained and specialised in passing very long serves in such a manner as to be able to play them as a one-person service reception formation.
11. The use of the libero makes it possible to move the front-court service reception players or a back-court attacker out of the service reception formation. The decision as to who the libero will replace will depend upon the type of serve and the location of the serve of the opposition.
12. The use of the libero to replace a back-court hitter will on the one hand weaken the back-court attack, but on the other hand strengthen the front-court offence.

Further thoughts regarding the libero as a defensive specialist will be discussed in Learning Part 3, Chapter 5.5.1.

3.3 Individual Tactics of the Server

The effectiveness of the serve and its impact on the match is very high; therefore, it is a very important component in the training of beginner and advanced volleyball players. This is based on the fact that the serve is a relatively quick and easy skill to learn, whereas to learn the skill of service reception is much more difficult.

At the top levels of volleyball, the training and development of service reception specialists was started by the fact that the server had lost his/her effectiveness.

The new rules with the introduction of the rally-point scoring system and the libero player support this concept. The fact that every service error now results in a point for the opposition has a negative impact on the willingness of the server to take more risk while serving. Currently, there is a rule change that is being tested that may stop this trend and development. If the legalisation of a "net contact" by the volleyball during the serve will be implemented then this will definitely move towards strengthening the serve again (comp. Chapter 1.1 about "effects of the rules").

While the serve can be overlooked during the training and teaching of the basic skills, it cannot be omitted from a single practice at the top levels of volleyball. Studies of the 1992 Olympics in Barcelona, the 1996 in Atlanta, and of the 1999 European Championships prove that the service reception dominated the serve and that the offence dominated the block and defence. This was a result of an increase in the segment of the match that involved the service reception relative to the portion of the match that involved defence. Jump serves are even not as effective as they were in previous years because the use of a third or fourth service reception specialist during jump serves has reduced their effectiveness.

Nevertheless, observations from the above competitions still showed a dominance of the jump serve. This is a result due to the fact that the best men's teams have more than three starters that use a jump serve. This development can also be seen in the top women's teams.

Individual tactics of the server should correspond with the following minimum standards depending on the level of volleyball that s/he plays at:

Low level: The players should be able to hit an overhand serve from just behind the center of the end line (baseline) accurately to the target in the last third of the volleyball court, especially in the zones which include positions V and I because this makes it much more difficult for the setter to run a good offence. Furthermore, the server should be able to serve short and deep volleyballs from at least two different service positions and by standing near the end line. This will increase the running distance of the front-court service reception player and/or the setter who must penetrate from the back-court.

Middle level: The server should be able to serve from just behind the end line and from three different service positions (zones). The server should be able to serve short volleyballs to the opposition's front-court service reception areas (position II,

III, and IV), especially between positions III-IV and positions I-II. By being able to accomplish this, it gives the server two options: it gives him/her the ability to serve to weak areas of the opposition's service reception formation and it allows him/her to serve the volleyball to the opposition's front-court players. This would make the opposition's transition to offence, especially the quick attack, much more difficult to execute. Furthermore, the player should be able to serve from approximately 5 meters behind the end line to the target position in the last third of the opposition's side of the volleyball court.

High level: The players should be able to serve tactical serves from all of the service positions near the end line to all areas of the volleyball court, especially positions II, III, and IV. Variations of the types of tactical serves used should be possible without any changes to service technique. A different amount of force used on the volleyball or a different method of using the wrist should be enough of a change to "place" or position the volleyball to any service target. Furthermore, the server must be able to serve the volleyball from at least 5 meters behind the end line to the opposition's front-court. This serve should be able to be carried out from longer distances (7 meters or more from behind the end line) to cover any forward or diagonal direction concerned. It would be the perfect serve if, from this greater distance to the end line, the distance that the volleyball is served can also be varied.

An important key to the effectiveness of a serve is the trajectory of the volleyball. For example, serves originating from "middle distances" behind the end line should not be any higher than 2 meters above the volleyball net. Volleyballs served from "short distances" behind the end line should not be higher than the antennae if their target is the opposition's backcourt. The exception would be if it were a short serve with the opposition's front-court as the target.

If net contact by a volleyball from the serve are legalised, then serves originating from "middle distances" should not be higher than the antennae and serves from "short distances" should be as close to the top of the volleyball net as possible.

In high levels of volleyball it is invaluable for a team's strategy to have at least three jump serve specialists. In addition, they must be able to serve from all three distances (short, middle, and long) from the end line. Without these jump serve specialists, specific service reception training against a jump serve is not possible, therefore, it is important from a training perspective to make this mandatory and a part of a team's strategy.

The following tendencies can be found as a part of service strategies:
1. The jump serve is the "match deciding" element in the men's game and it is constantly gaining in importance in the women's game.
2. From all of the different types of serves, the jump serve is the most effective one. The goal is to score points and to break the dominance of the opposition's offence out of their service reception formation. This can be achieved with the use of a high-risk, hard, and powerful jump serve. The favorite target position using this serve is position VI (60 %).
3. The willingness to take risks with the service strategy is documented by the number of errors that are made from the serve: At international and national levels of volleyball the men have up to 9 service errors per match per team and the women have up to 7 service errors per match per team.

The latest observations have revealed that teams that fall behind in the score continue to serve high-risk volleyballs, while their opponent's slightly reduce the risk with their serves when they are ahead by two or more points.

1. The latest technical variant is the jump-float serve, which is mostly used in critical match situations. It can be expected that the jump-float serve just as the jump serve will be used more often. This tendency is clearly seen with the new rally-point scoring system and the use of the libero player.

A jump serve and/or a jump-float serve is supposed to force the opposition to change their two-person service reception formation into a three-person service reception formation or a three-person service reception formation into a four-person service reception formation. This will force a front-court player to pass and begin their attack out of a service reception formation.

2. Float serves from "middle and long distances" lose their effectiveness, especially in the men's game.
3. Tactical serves used randomly and on target gained importance until 1994 because they caused major problems for the service reception players in a two-person service reception formation. When the rule to allow overhand passing as part of the service reception was introduced it weakened the effectiveness of tactical serves because the front-court service reception player could no longer be easily pushed back by deep serves because s/he could pass the volleyball using the overhand passing technique. Only tactical

serves, hit low and aggressively right above the top of the volleyball net, to the side or in-between service reception players will maintain and even possibly increase their effectiveness.

4. In the women's game, a float serve from a middle distance behind the end line served to one-half of the opposition's volleyball court is dominating. A tactical serve from the end line is rarely used.

Legalisation of the rule that will allow the volleyball to contact the top of the volleyball net will definitely reintroduce more tactical serves from the end line.

LEARNING PART 1

Movement Patterns of the Serves
The following principles have to be taken into account regarding a float serve:

1. A short toss of the volleyball (Photo 10-11).
2. A quick contact (hitting) action.
3. The middle (center) portion of the hand must contact the middle (center) portion of the volleyball.
4. The wrist of the serving arm must be in a fixed and tight position when the volleyball is contacted.
5. There is a sudden stop of the follow-through at the moment when the volleyball is contacted during the serving motion.

If the principles mentioned above are met, in theory all volleyballs can be served as floaters and, as recent observations show, jump serves (Photo 11-13).

Photo 10 (Felgner)

Photo 11 (Th. Martin)   *Photo 12 (Eisenring)*    *Photo 13 (Martin)*

The following principles have to be taken into account regarding a jump serve:
1. There must be coordination between the approach/toss phase and the jump/hitting phase.
2. One or two-handed toss of the volleyball.
3. An aggressive jump serve includes a high and long jump and landing position in the volleyball court.
4. A low risk and/or tactical jump serve includes a high jump and landing position close to the takeoff position.

If we look at the movement patterns of a jump serve, it can be stated that a high risk jump serve (Photo 12) can be compared to a normal spike, whereas a low risk jump serve (Photo 13) can be compared to a roll shot.

An aggressive jump serve will add one or two more initial steps to the approach to generate more power. A less aggressive jump serve is usually carried out with just the initial portion of the approach.

Individual Tactical Factors
Generally, the fact of the matter is that the server should receive immediate information from the coach about what, where, and/or who to serve the volleyball to and then carry out his/her instructions and duty. This fact must not be an excuse for neglecting the individual tactical training of the server. It should have the opposite effect. Immediate information that is provided by the coach to the server should also be intensively included in the practice process. Only if the player acquires and realises a sense of purpose and importance from the information will s/he identify him/herself with the necessity to successfully carry out his/her duty. The effectiveness of the server is dependent on several factors. The first and most important factor is the technical and psychological abilities of the player, but the effectiveness of the players is also dependent to a high degree on his/her tactical knowledge of service reception formations and how the offence is executed from them.

Immediately before and during the season, the server should only be allowed to practise serves that s/he would use in matches. This will increase the consistency of the serve and, therefore, the player's individual tactical actions. This statement is especially true when discussing the serving location of the server. In other words, the player should always serve from the same distance to the end line and from the same service zone (area). By doing this, the player's error quota is minimised and at the same time optimised his/her serving target skills and effectiveness. This also applies to the training of the service reception by taking into account the opposition's serving style. The substitute players should mainly do the imitation of the opposition's serves.

At the low and middle levels of volleyball the probability of success of the offence after the service reception is not very high. Therefore, it is left up to the judgment of the server to decide whether or not to make a high risk serve or to make a safe, low risk serve.

At the high levels of volleyball the serves must be high risk because the offence out of the service reception is very effective. Therefore, it must be differentiated at this level between high risk powerful and float serves and high risk serves to a particular target and/or location. High risk powerful and float serves aim for a direct score, but at the very least a poor pass by the opposition. High risk serves to a particular target aim at disturbing the planned offence of the opposition.

All serves made from the end line (except aggressive jump serves) to the middle distance from the end line are regarded as being high risk serves to a particular target. All serves made from the long distance, as well as aggressive jump serves are regarded as belonging to the high risk powerful and float serves group. Each high-level player must know how to execute a serve from both groups – one high risk serve to a particular target and either a high risk powerful or float serve.

The following are goals for tactical serves from the end line:
1. To serve the volleyball to the weaker side of the service reception players.
2. To choose a service spot opposite an overlapping service reception area and serve the overlapping zone of the service reception players.
3. To push the front-court service reception player deeper into his/her back-court and particularly to the side that would make his/her transition from passing to offence much more difficult.
4. To serve into the area of the psychologically weaker service reception player (s. points 1-3).
5. To serve into the area of the weaker service reception player (s. points 1-4).
6. To serve into the endangered and weaker areas of the opposition's service reception formation.
7. To serve into the area of the quick hitter to disturb his/her preparation for the transition to offence, especially if s/he shows any weaknesses in the use of the overhand pass.
8. To serve into the running path of the setter.

INDIVIDUAL TACTICS OF THE SERVER

9. To serve into the running path of the second hitter or back-court hitter.
10. To serve to position I (more specifically position I/II) to force the setter to turn his/her back to his/her main hitters and then must use a backset to play the volleyball to them.
11. To serve as close as possible to the setter's position (position II/III) to make the preparation time for the hitters shorter because of a short first pass.
12. To choose a service spot close to the end line and opposite to the position where the setter is penetrating from. By using serves that force him/her to move deep into the back-court, will make the distance and penetrating path of the setter will be made longer.
13. To serve from the service zone V diagonally to the service reception area IV/V because this will change the service reception situation as far as the service reception areas are concerned.
14. To serve in the area of the libero if s/he has not passed a volleyball in some time.

At the international level, the goals of the serve are the same as mentioned in the points above with the addition of the service strategy in relation to blocking and defence. For serves from the middle distance points 2, 3, 4, 5, 10, 13, and 14 apply. For serves from the long distance points 2, 4, 5, and 10 apply. To be included is the goal to force a poor first pass or even directly score a point.

The following are goals for jump serves:
1. To directly score a point or force a poor first pass.
2. To move the starting position of the front-court service reception player as far back as possible.
3. To make the running distance of the setter longer.
4. To allow the hitters less time to prepare for their attack.
5. To force the opposition to change their service reception formation because the opposition has to add an additional service reception player into the formation.
6. To make the preparation time shorter for the additional service reception player in the opposition's offence, even if s/he is a front-court or a back-court hitter.

The ability to perform individual tactical actions depends mainly on the psychological preparation and condition of the players. After the service reception players, the setter, and the hitter, the server has to deal with the most psychological pressure. For this reason, the training of the server has to be physically and psychologically demanding. It is extremely important to practise the ability to concentrate, especially for long periods of time, because the server is always involved in starting the next play after every point. The coach must pay particular attention to situations in which the player who is about to serve was responsible for making a spectacular offensive or blocking action that returned or maintained the service for his/her team. Such a situation can serve to break up a player's concentration relative to the following action. The simple concept of not giving a server a second chance/opportunity after a serving error during practice will improve the player's ability to concentrate.

> It is recommended to use the entire time of eight seconds before the serve must be made, to not only improve the player's concentration but to also invoke some insecurity in the opposition's service reception player.

To cause stressful situations for the server during practice (see Chapter 3.4), the principle of positive and negative intensification should be used for both the server and his/her teammates. During practice, situations of psychological pressure, such as at the end of a set or a match under the new rally-point scoring system must also be taken into account (see Chapter 1 – "The effects of the new rules").

3.4 Selected Drills to Train the Individual Tactics of the Server and the Service Reception Players, and the Training of the Service Reception Formation

These drills are based on the complexity of the game and are kept as close and as similar as possible to the match/game situation. Their main goal is to improve on the points mentioned above. All of the following drills will be presented as small court, half-court, or full-court games that all obey the rules of the sport of volleyball. With that said, the coach still has the opportunity to make changes in the organisation and structure of the practices and drills depending on what skills, techniques, and areas that s/he wants to train:

1. Rotation based on the time factor (3-5 minutes).
2. Rotation after both teams have reached a certain score (3 or 5 points).
3. Rotation after a series of serves (i.e. one team serves 5-10 times before the serve change.

4. Rotation of a team after it has managed to complete a certain amount of successful actions (5 or more).
5. Rotation of a team after it has managed to complete a certain amount of consecutive successful actions (i.e. two, three, four, or more).

The last drill (#5) is especially good in helping the players adapt to the new rally-point scoring system and to complete the main goals of the training process.

All drills must be performed in a competitive manner! During these rotations points can be earned by what is called "big points". A "big point" is given to the team that completes a multiple task/point/action. For example, gets two side-outs in a row. Also, certain actions can be credited with additional points (i.e. a serve that causes a direct error by the opposition = +2 points) or be deducted additional points (i.e. a service error = -2 points). The points can be awarded using either the old or new scoring systems.

With 5 vs. 5 or 6 vs. 6 games, two or three volleyballs should always be used. The first volleyball is introduced into the game by a serve and the other volleyballs are tossed in, by the coach, as free-balls. This is very important because it helps in getting the necessary changes in the players' positions in the front and back rows. Thus making the service reception players attack from a block and/or defensive situation, and to keep the intensity of the practice at least the same as in a match. The new rally-point scoring system is used to keep score and the team that first scores two points in a row receives one "big point".

If there is only one volleyball court available and there are more players than necessary to form one game in practice, then the following setup ("Israel Game") will solve the problem. Players and/or a group of players are replaced after they make any errors. By doing this it allows two groups of players on each side of the volleyball court with one group playing and the other waiting to rotate in. If an error occurs then the group waiting outside of the volleyball court will replace the group inside of the volleyball court.

The team that rotates into the game will then start the new game by serving (Fig. 97). Every time a new team rotates into the game a new player must also be chosen to serve because in this manner it ensures that there is also a change in the roles of the group of players on the volleyball court. The winner is the team

Fig. 97

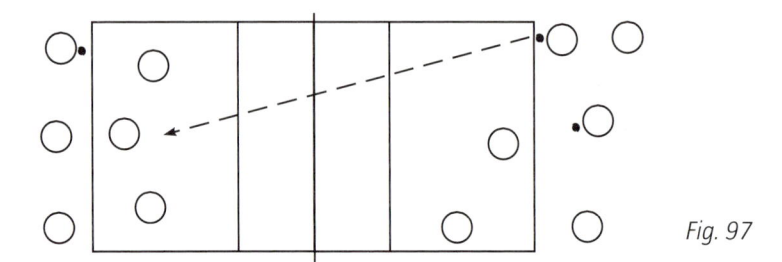

that first wins a game or reaches a certain score first. All of the opposition's errors will count as a point. If there are not enough players to use the "Israel Game" described above, then there is the possibility to change the teams on only one side of the volleyball court whilst the team on the other side remains unchanged. If there are not enough players to play 6:6 then the game can be modified to have an unequal amount of players (i.e. 3 or 4 vs. 6). If the smaller team is much weaker than the other team then the first offensive action by the larger team is restricted to a roll shot or a jump set and/or the weaker team will receive more free-balls.

Another possible solution is to add more "Volleyballs to the Game". By doing this a two, three, or four-person team is playing against a complete team. The smaller team gets to serve five or more times in a row and after a service reception error the six-person team must rotate as quickly as possible because they must also have the right to immediately continue with their serve. It is true that this type of training is not designed to create a specific match situation, but it is a great opportunity to observe the automatic responses to the service reception formations. The serving group changes after a series of serves and the new rally-point scoring system is used.

1. **Game 1 vs. 1 with two setters (later only one setter for both players)!**
[On a volleyball court 4.5 x 9 meters (later 3 x 9 meters)]

Server:
- The volleyball is served deep into the back of the volleyball court and especially to the side of the service reception players!
- The serve should be hit very quickly and low above the net.

Service Reception Players:
- The first pass is played up high (to zone B) and safely to the setter to allow for enough time to get ready for your own attack!

SELECTED DRILLS

- Serves that are at or above the height of the service reception player's shoulders should be played using the overhand pass if the players can get in front of the volleyball.

Server:
- Use a short serve if the service reception player is standing deep in the volleyball court and a deep serve if the service reception player is standing close to the volleyball net.

Service Reception Player:
- Watch the arm motion of the server and you might be able to guess ahead of time how hard the serve might be. This may also give a clue as to how long the serve will be (i.e. the harder the serve the longer the volleyball will travel).

Variation 1: The setter is allowed to tip/dump the volleyball!

Server:
- Get to your defensive role in position 1 or 5 (4 meter off of the volleyball net) as quickly as possible.

Service Reception Player:
- Depending on the difficulty with the service reception, either perfectly pass the volleyball to the setter to allow him/her to jump-set or to dump the volleyball, or to play a safety pass first in such a manner as to allow the setter to set a good volleyball from a standing position.
- Pass the volleyball purposely higher using the overhand pass than when using the forearm pass to have enough time as a service reception hitting player to prepare yourself for your own offensive attack.

Variation 2: Game 1 vs. 1 with two touches allowed in a 3 x 9 meter volleyball court (later 4.5 x 9 meter volleyball court).

Server:
- Force the service reception player to move forward or laterally backwards!

Service Reception Player:
- Play the first pass in an easy service reception situation, regardless of if you use a forearm pass or an overhand pass, high and in front of yourself to be in a position to attack the volleyball. In difficult situations, play the volleyball just high (in the middle of the volleyball court) to be able to continue to the play.

LEARNING PART 1

Server:
- Use the depth in a narrow volleyball court and the width with a larger volleyball court!

Observational Hints with 1 and 2
If this is expecting too much from the service reception players, then make the size of the volleyball courts smaller (i.e. shorten the length of the volleyball court (remove the front zone – photo 98). In games without front zones, attacks from the front zone are only allowed from a standing position but not from a jumping action. Offensive actions in the opposition's front zone are not allowed either. On the other hand, if this is not asking enough of the service reception player then the size of the volleyball court can be increased and/or the server may be given individual tactical hints on how to serve with increased difficulty (Fig. 98).

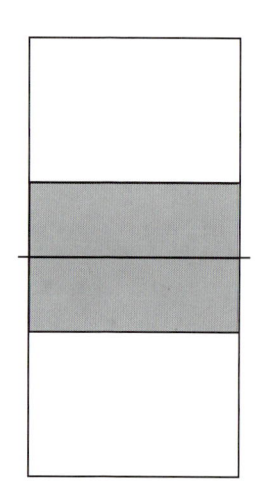

Fig. 98

2. Game 2 vs. 2 With one setter for both teams as an introduction to a four-person service reception formation!
[On a 3 x 9 meter volleyball court (later a 4.5 x 9 meter volleyball court – Figs. 99a-99b)]

Both players are service reception players. One of the players is playing in the front row and the other is playing in the back row. In a defensive situation, the front-court player is blocking and the other one is playing defence. The setter is playing as if s/he was a back-court players (Figs. 99a and 99b).

Server:
- Serve to the overlapping areas between the service reception players! Pick a serving spot exactly opposite this zone!

Fig. 99a/99b

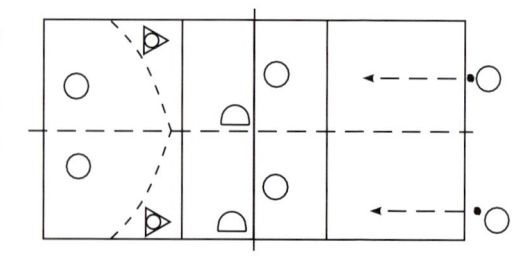

SELECTED DRILLS

- *Purposely serve the volleyball low above the volleyball net and take the chance of the serve touching the top of the volleyball net.*

Service Reception Player:
- Start your action early!
- Move in the direction of the setting spot and/or get your stronger side in the service reception position (the passer with the stronger side in relation to the volleyball should be the one to pass it).
- Both of the service reception players must communicate (i.e. "My ball", "Got it", etc.).
- The player who moves first or who calls out first is the one who takes the volleyball.

Server:
- Serve the front-court service reception player laterally high or above his/her shoulders to make the transition to offence more difficult!

Service Reception Player:
- Note the principle that says that the service reception is ahead in priority than the offence!
- Make the service reception areas clear again with your back-court players!

Server:
- Continue to help your blocker by serving laterally to the front-court player to move him/her to the side and force the back-court player to move forward. By doing this it will make the preparation time of the hitters shorter!

Service Reception Player:
- Play the volleyball high off of the service reception to the setter (zone B) to allow for some extra time for the transition to the offence!
- Use the overhand pass as much as possible!

Variation 1: *The setter is now in the front row and is allowed to attack.*

Server:
- Serve the volleyball close to the setting position to make it harder to set the second ball!

3. Game 3 vs. 3 with two service reception players and a setter!
[On a 4.5 x 9 meter volleyball court]
It will be played with two front-court and one back-court players.

Server:
- Watch the opposition's line-up. Choose with both of the service reception players in the front-court and the setter penetrating one of the options provided in Figs. 100a-100b.

Service Reception Player:
- With the formation shown in Fig. 100a, choose your position as close as possible to the volleyball net so that you are able to use an overhand pass to play deep served volleyballs.
- Switch between the formations provided in Figs. 100a-100b.

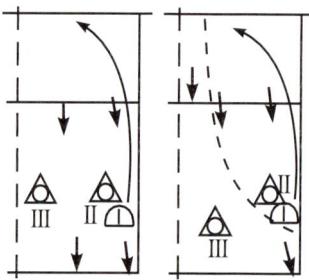

Fig. 100a/b

Server:
- Constantly serve the technically or psychologically weaker service reception players.
- Use the new eight-second rule every so often!

Service Reception Player:
- The stronger service reception players should take on more responsibility and cover more court space (Fig. 101).

Server:
- In service reception situations, with front and back row players, proceed as shown in Figs. 102-103!

Variation 1: *Game 3 vs. 3 without rotation*

SELECTED DRILLS

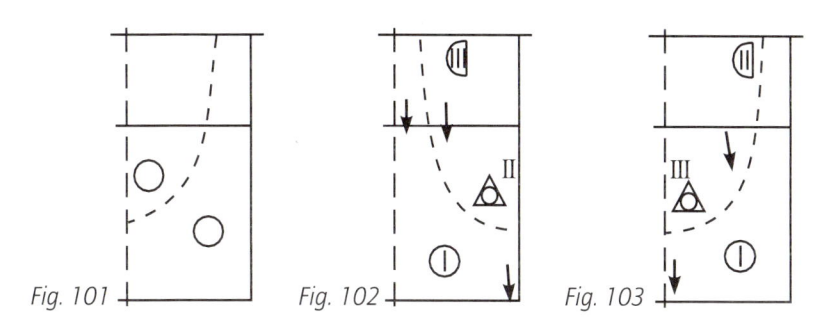

Fig. 101   *Fig. 102*   *Fig. 103*

a) With the service reception player playing in the frontcourt and the setter in the back-court (Figs. 100a-100b).
b) With one of the service reception players playing in the front-court and the other playing in the back-court and the setter in the front-court (Figs. 102-103).

Observational Hint
This variation can be used before the game described above to give the server and the service reception players the opportunity to check their individual tactical decisions repeatedly.

4. **Game 4 vs. 4 With one setter for both teams or two setters as a development for the four-person service reception formation!**
   [On a 9 x 9 meter volleyball court]

Server:
- Remember the different strengths and weaknesses of the four-person service reception formations (see Chapter 3.1.2)!

Service Reception Player:
- Keep an eye on the different service reception areas of the four-person service reception formations, including the transition to offence (see Chapter 3.1.2).

Server:
- Instead of a tactical serve from the baseline, hit a float serve from the middle or long distance zones to the baseline!

Variation 1: *Game 4 vs. 4 with a setter, middle hitter, and two service reception players on a 4.5 x 9 meter volleyball court (Figs. 104a-104d).*

Fig. 104a-d

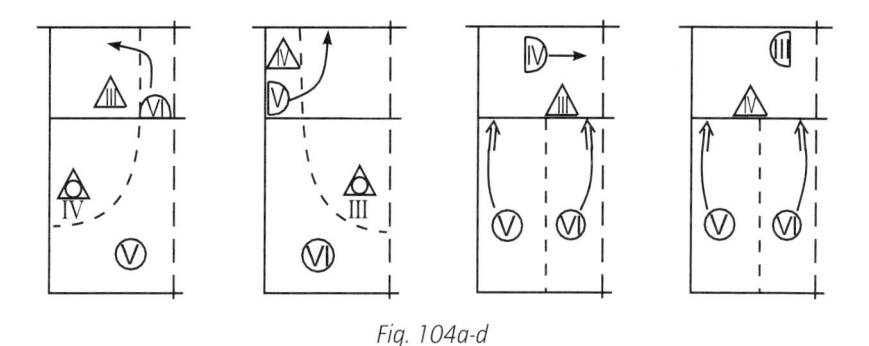

Server:
- Besides the individual tactical clues mentioned above, serve the volleyball to the area of the middle hitter!
- Serve the volleyball to the back of the setter to make it more difficult to use the middle attack!

Service Reception Player:
- Pass the volleyball higher to the setting spot, especially when using the overhand pass, to give the setter and middle hitter more time for an offensive play from this transitional phase.

Middle Hitter:
- Talk to your service reception players if you will be passing the volleyball coming into your area or not! If you pass the volleyball, then pass the first ball high enough to enable yourself to be in a position to execute a first tempo attack!

Variation 2: The same as variation 1, but the different service reception situations from Figs. 104a-104d will be practiced based upon time, a certain amount of points, and/or with a different series of serves.

Variation 3: The serving team will continue to play with two front row and two back row players. The service reception team will use three front-court and one back-court players, with the condition that there is always a middle hitter and a second hitter that can be used. The setter stays with the middle hitter at the net to block while the second hitter plays defence. If the setter is in the back row, then the second hitter will move back to play defence.

SELECTED DRILLS

5. Game 6 vs. 6!
[On a 9 x 9 meter volleyball court]
A four-person service reception formation will be used.

The following points can be the main goals of the game:
1) The service reception formation and the transition to offence must be practiced! The server hits different types of serves from different serving spots to different targets. Create different and changing situations for the service reception players and the setter. The coach observes and analyses the service reception formations and decides if a change in the service reception formation is necessary (see Chapter 3.1.2).
2) The coach observes the passing and offensive performances of the service reception players to make sure that they are assigned the proper areas to cover. The coach may also change these areas so the players can practice covering different zones (see Chapter 3.2.1 "Special Drills for the Main and Supporting Service Reception Players").
3) The individual tactics of the server against a four-person service reception formation must be practiced because a change to this type of service reception formation will also change the serving strategy that is used. The coach will control and support the individual tactics of the server.

The main points mentioned above must be executed during the season as follows: If focusing on points 1 & 2, the server should imitate the serving strategy of the upcoming opposition. If focusing on point 3, the team must imitate the opposition's service reception formations and their offensive strategies.

6. Game 3 vs. 3 As an introduction to the two/three-person service reception formation!
[On a 3 x 9 meter volleyball court, later 4.5 x 9 meter volleyball court]

One back row setter, a middle hitter/blocker, and a service reception player as a second hitter/outside blocker are playing. The middle blocker's main responsibility is to cover the opposite middle hitter and the second/outside hitter/blocker.

Variation 1: *Only the service reception player is in the back row and hitting back row.*

Variation 2: *Only the middle hitter is in the back row and hitting back row.*

Variation 3: *All three players are front-court players. In block and defensive situations they all switch around and cover behind the player that is playing defence.*

Variation 4: *Players obey all the rules using two front-court and two back-court players.*

Server:
- Watch to see if the service reception player is playing in the front or back row!
- Decide if changes in the type of serve being used or the serving spot will be helpful!
- After serving, return to your proper defensive position as quickly as possible!

Service Reception Player:
- Take into consideration if the setter is in the front or back row!
- Pass the first volleyball in such a manner as to allow the setter enough time to jump-set!
- Keep in mind that a service reception pass over the net to the opposition is worse than a safety pass up to the ten-foot line!
- Focus on service reception first, then on offence!
- Cover your offensive hitter if you are not being used as the second hitter!

7. **Game 5 vs. 5 With three front-court players and two back-court players as a development and introduction to the three-person service reception formation!**

[On a 9 x 9 meter volleyball court]

Three service reception players, a middle hitter, and a setter are playing: the setter and one service reception player are in the back row.

Variation 1: Two service reception players are playing in the backcourt.

Variation 2: The middle hitter and a service reception player are playing in the back-court.

Server:
- Take into consideration the strengths and weaknesses of the service reception formations and of the service reception players!
- Choose your serving spot based upon your serving target.

Service Reception Players:
- The libero should be prepared to help his/her teammates, especially when s/he feels strong in his/her service reception skills!
- The libero is responsible for the organisation of the service reception formation!

8. **Game 6 vs. 6 With a three-person service reception formation!**
   [On a 9 x 9 meter volleyball court]
One possible line-up can be to use three service reception players, two middle blockers/hitters, and a setter. Another possible line-up can be to use four service reception players (one having the qualities of a middle hitter), a middle blocker/hitter, and a setter. Keep in mind the explanations provided in chapter 3.1.3 when deciding what starting line-up to use and what strengths and weaknesses of the three-person service reception formation to observe.

Server:
- Increase your tactical knowledge regarding the three-person service reception formation!
- Following a successful high-risk jump serve, perform a tactical jump serve!

Service Reception Players:
- Try to recognise and analyse your strengths and weaknesses and look for solutions regarding showing and exercising your strengths and covering up your weaknesses!
- Is it necessary to change to a four-person service reception formation?
- Is the libero being substituted properly according to the rules?

9. **Game 3 vs. 3 With one setter for both sides or 4 vs. 4 with two setters!**
   [On a 9 x 9 meter volleyball court]
The setter, middle hitter, and service reception player are front-court players.

Variation 1: The middle hitter and both service reception players are playing front row!

Variation 2: The setter and both service reception players are playing front row!

Server:
- Performing quick and low tactical serves away from the service reception players is very effective because these serves force the service reception players to move!
- Remember that jump serves are highly efficient and effective against a two-person service reception formation!
- Always observe and analyse the two service reception players regarding their technical, psychological and athletic framework!
- Remember that float serves and tactical jump serves can be used with varying degrees of *risk*!

Service Reception Players:
- Observe the position (axis of the shoulder) of the server and his/her serving spot in relation to the service reception formation to be able to better anticipate the direction of the serve!
- Observe the arm of the server when s/he is getting ready to hit the volleyball and the hitting motion to be able to better predict how hard and how deep the volleyball will be hit!
- The libero should be ready to take over the main responsibility for the offensive coverage.
- A strong service reception libero should always be prepared to take upon themselves more responsibility and to cover more volleyball court area.

10. Game 6 vs. 6 With a two-person service reception formation!
[On a 9 x 9 meter volleyball court]

The team consists of three service reception players, two middle blockers/hitters, and the setter or of two service reception players, two middle blockers/hitters, one offside/power hitter, and the setter.

Again keep in mind the explanations provided in chapter 3.1.4 when deciding what starting line-up to use and what strengths and weaknesses of the two-person service reception formation to observe.

Server:
- Watch to see if both service reception players are in the front-court and, in this situation, try to serve the overlapping area in-between them to disturb their offensive action!
- Vary the risk that you take when jump-serving!
- Remember that the two-person service reception formation always reveals weaknesses against jump serves!

- Remember that jump serves increase the number of service reception players in the formation!
- Always keep the score in mind: if you have a big lead then you will not need to take many high risk serves anymore, whereas if you are down by a lot of points then you should increase the risk of your serves.

Service Reception Player:
- Always be positive with your service reception teammate!
- If the service reception is getting worse, then the service reception areas must be adjusted!
- Are there hints that it would make sense to switch from the two-person service reception formation to a three-person service reception formation?
- Position yourself closer to the volleyball net if your service reception area is narrow and deep so you can use an overhand pass to play any incoming high volleyballs!
- Position yourself further back if your service reception area is broad!

11. Play practice/friendly/exhibition matches to train:
a) *The individual tactics of the server/serve strategy.*
b) *The individual tactics of the service reception player and the service* reception strategy.
c) The different types of service reception formations.

12. Participate in preparation tournaments and competitions:
a) To observe and analyse, therefore, being able to control the observational points mentioned under 11.
b) To observe that the libero and serving rules will be used in the correct manner in a match situation.
c) To observe if the players that are replaced by the libero will have more service errors.

13. The game for the service reception specialists!
There are three players playing 1 vs. 1 with one of them setting for both sides on a 4.5 x 9 meter volleyball court. The game is played up to 21 points. Only the player who is serving can score a point. The service reception player who makes an error becomes the setter and the setter takes over that player's place as a service reception player and now has the opportunity to also score points. The rallies must be played using three touches. Setting errors count against the service reception player.

LEARNING PART 1

At higher levels, the game should be played without a front zone. In other words, all offensive actions must be back-row attacks. If there are four service reception players available, the game can be played with a "waiting position/player".

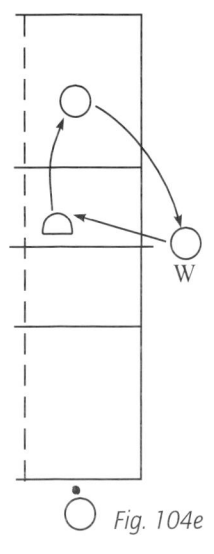

Fig. 104e

In other words, the service reception player who makes an error leaves the volleyball court and becomes the "waiting player". The player that was just the "waiting players" now becomes the setter and the setter becomes the new service reception player (Fig. 104e).

If the serve is more effective than the service reception then the volleyball court should be made smaller to a 3 x 9 meter volleyball court size.

Photo 14 (Willi Zeimer)

4 Learning Part II –

Offence: Setting, Offensive Combinations, Offensive Coverage, and the Individual Tactics of the Setter and the Hitters

4.1 Analysis of the Facts

The transition from a situation/position-oriented offence to a person-oriented offence is the beginning of specialisation. A differentiation exists between the setter and the hitter even at the low levels of volleyball. A greater differentiation exists at the middle levels of volleyball between the main and supporting hitter and even further differences at the high levels of volleyball between the back-court, middle, offside, outside, and combination (swing) hitters.

Usually, at the low level of volleyball two setters play diagonally to each other and at the middle level of volleyball the second setter only has a supporting role and, therefore, acts as a supporting setter. At the high level of volleyball the supporting setter disappears altogether and is replaced by a main power/offside hitter.

The offence can be run by a front-court athlete, a back-court athlete, by an emergency set (only after a bad pass), and the first pass can also be attacked. At the low levels of volleyball the percentage of the offence that is run by a front-court athlete out of the service reception formation is approximately 30 %. This number significantly drops at the middle levels of volleyball to approximately 10 %. Interestingly enough, at the high levels of volleyball, the percentage of the offence that is run by a front-court and back-court athlete is equally balanced at 50 %. This is because at the high levels of volleyball the teams use a 5-1 match system. A planned attack off of the first pass – usually a setter's tip/dump – is only used as an offensive option at the high levels, while at the low and middle levels of volleyball it is used to solve the problem of poor passing. Not very surprising, the case is reversed when it comes to executing an emergency set, which is only necessary after a poor first pass. Whereas at the low levels of volleyball the emergency set has a high percentage of use because of the poor first passing, the percentage drops more and more being closely related to the increasing quality of the service reception and reaches less than 10 % at the high levels of volleyball.

With regards to the offence out of different service reception formations, it will be referred to chapters 3.1.1 – 3.1.5 and 3.4. Service reception formations and the way that the offence is run and completed are forming a unity and common front that can be called the first basic actions of the sport of volleyball. This situation will be referred to in the following pages as Complex 1 (C1). Complex 2 (C2) defines the other basic action, which is the manner in which the offence is run and completed out of the block and defensive situation.

The domination of C1 over C2 has led and still leads to changes of the rules of the sport of volleyball that aim to support C2 (see Chapter 1.1 "The Effects of the New Rules"). Some examples are the moving in of the antennas, the penetration of the block, the legalisation of three touches after the volleyball has touched the block, and to remove the option of being able to directly block the serve just to name a few. Some changes have led to the result that the offensive spots have moved from the outside to the inside and to the development of certain combination plays in a narrow area, but improved blocking and defensive strategies on the technical, athletic, individual, group, and team level have successfully stopped this development. For example, the use of the switch-block (see Chapter 5.2.1) has been a direct help in stopping some of this development. Due to the dominance of the offence, further specialisation was developed:
a) On the service reception level (two-person service reception formation), and
b) On the offensive level by the use of the offside hitter as the main power hitter in position IV and as a back row hitter.

The purpose of moving the offence to the outside positions was not to eliminate the block (0-block), but rather to be successful against a one-person block.

This development was connected with the introduction of the stopper/shoot (with or without a change of direction), flyers or fade away hits, all to irritate or fake the middle blocker (see Chapter 4.5.1).

With women, the one-legged take-off to hit an A-quick/first tempo/short ball or short first tempo/B-quick behind the setter became popular and successful.

Again, the answer was not only an improvement of the group tactics in the front and/or back row of the defence, but especially in an improvement of the cooperation between the blockers and the defensive athletes. This was accomplished by using new block and defence formations and a much more detailed observation and analysis of the opposition.

The results of the examinations of the 1992 and 1993 Olympic Games show that the relationship between the percentages of the involvement of the C1 and C2 have shifted in favor of C1. This is equally true for men and women with a percentage of approximately 8-10 % each. This result can be explained using different factors: the use of four or five hitters out of the service reception formation with two middle hitters that are in the air at the same time and/or back row attackers that are also to be used as combination hitters and a continuing development of the setter and the offside hitter. Almost all of the points mentioned above concern the men's top professional level (see Chapter 1.1).

The women's game cannot keep up with the development of C1, especially with the offensive development. Major differences are shown in the offensive actions in general (i.e. in power and variability of the types of hits used, in speed of the game, in the use of special offensive combination plays involving the back row hitter, and the number of hitters that are able to go for a combination play).

The final consequences of the rule changes from 1994 are still to be seen: examinations have shown at the low, middle, and high levels of volleyball that:

1. There is no recognisable increase in the efficiency of the serve despite the increase of the serving zone.
2. Position I in the serving zone is still the favored spot by most of the athletes at the top level and, especially, by the women. In the men's Bundesliga (German Professional League) approximately 40 % of the serves are served from position I, approximately 38 % are served from position VI, and approximately 22 % are served from position V. In the women's Bundesliga, serves from position I dominate with an approximate 48 % use, approximately 31 % are served from position VI, and approximately 21 % are served from position V.
   At the low and middle levels of volleyball, the volleyball is served from all three positions about equally. This makes it clear that coaches and athletes like the new rule and have already tried it in the first season to take advantage of the rule.
3. Approximately 80 % of the tactical serves in the men's Bundesliga have been served from the right side of the volleyball court, which means that the serving zone in position V has not yet been included in the serving strategies. This allows for the conclusion that the coaches at the high levels of volleyball have not yet dealt with the new rules and have relied too much on the innovations and the impact of the individual athletes instead.
4. Concerning the direction of the serve, independent of the serving spot and what type of serve is used, two-thirds of the serves in the men's game are hit diagonally while two-thirds of the women's serves are hit frontally.
5. The overhand pass is still not used very often, especially by the women's Bundesliga, but observations of international juniors reveals that this variant of the service reception is being used more often and in a smart, tactical manner (Photo 14a).

It might be expected that in the near future a better tactical use of the increased serving zone will occur and as a result a better serving strategy will be implemented, especially when the serve being allowed to touch the volleyball net is legalised and used. Of course, this will lead to a further change of the service reception formations and the use of the overhand pass will increase (Photo 14a).

Photo 14a (Thomas Maibom)

4.2 Offensive Combinations

In general, there are two types of offensive combinations (OC) – general offensive combinations (GOC) and special offensive combinations (SOC). A GOC is a combination where the setter is telling the hitter at what time, what space, and what type of set s/he is going to receive. For example, the hitter in position III is going to receive an A-quick first tempo set while the hitter in position II will receive a medium second tempo or a high third tempo set. With a SOC, the time-spatial understanding of the hitters is added because their running patterns for their approaches are crossing over or they have to perform their play in a very narrow space next to each other or behind each other (Fig. 105).

Photo 15

OFFENSIVE COMBINATIONS

The set is divided into four categories depending on its height, distance, and especially on its speed (Fig. 106).

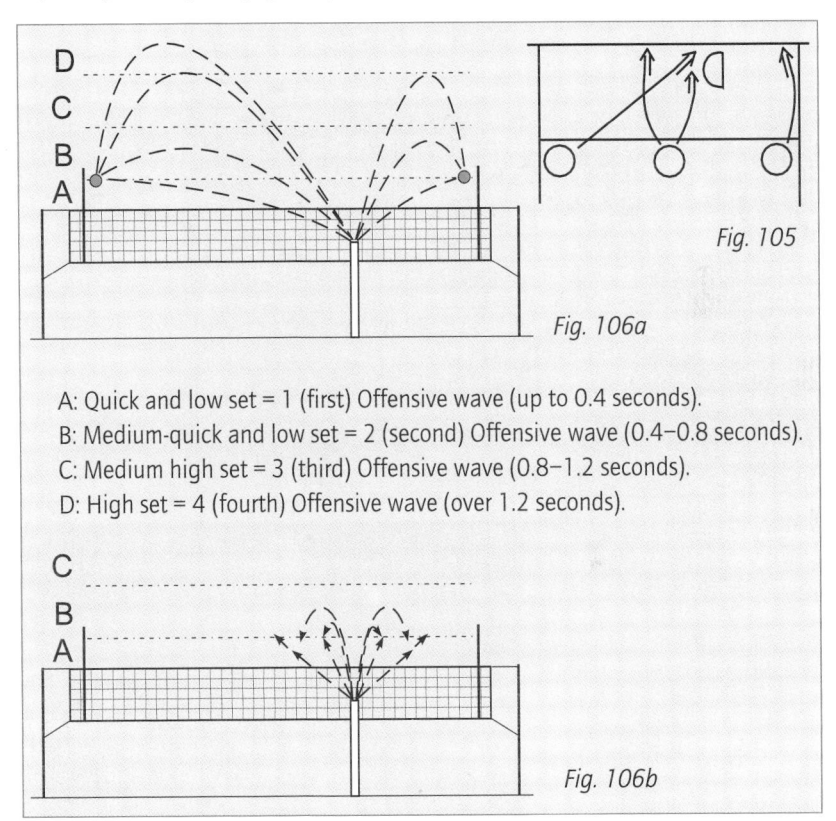

Fig. 105

Fig. 106a

A: Quick and low set = 1 (first) Offensive wave (up to 0.4 seconds).
B: Medium-quick and low set = 2 (second) Offensive wave (0.4–0.8 seconds).
C: Medium high set = 3 (third) Offensive wave (0.8–1.2 seconds).
D: High set = 4 (fourth) Offensive wave (over 1.2 seconds).

Fig. 106b

There are two methods of using quick sets:
1. The hitter jumps before the setter and is ready to hit an A-quick (Photo 16) or a B-quick (short set 1-2 meters away from the setter) (Photo 17).
2. The hitter jumps at the same time as the setter (not a real A-quick = a short ball or a short set 2-3 meters away from the setter) (Photo 18).

The four offensive waves require different times that the hitters must begin their approach:
- First offensive wave: The hitter approaches and jumps before the volleyball is set.
- Second offensive wave: The hitter starts his/her approach the moment that the setter sets the volleyball.

108 LEARNING PART 2

Photo 17 (Friese)

Photo 16

Photo 18 (Steffen Marquardt)

Photo 19 (Steffen Marquardt)

OFFENSIVE COMBINATIONS 109

Photo 20 (Martin)

Photo 21 (Martin)

Photo 22

- Third offensive wave: The hitter starts his/her approach after the setter has set the volleyball
- Fourth offensive wave: The hitter starts his/her approach after the setter has set the volleyball but not before the volleyball has reached its peak in the air.

The height of the set is dependent on the jumping reach height of the hitter. At the men's international level this height is usually 60 centimeters and higher above the top of the volleyball net and at the women's international level this height is usually 60 centimeters or lower from the top of the volleyball net (Photo 19). Quick attacks (first wave attacks) are A-quicks in front of the setter (Photo 20) and behind the setter (Photo 21). They are short balls set 1 meter away from and in front of or behind the setter. Also, they can be a short ball set in front of or behind the setter but a little higher than an A-quick or a B-quick which is a short set 2 meters away from the setter, or a shoot by the setter (Photo 22). Second wave attacks are short balls that are set 2 meters away and behind the setter, a "two" ball in front of the setter or a "two" ball behind the setter, a short ball set 3 meters away from the setter, a shoot to the outside in position IV, or a "shadow combination". A "shadow combination" is where the middle hitter attempts an A-quick and immediately behind him/her another hitter is attempting to hit a "two" ball. The idea behind this is to keep the opposition's middle blocker occupied with the first hitter, thus, setting up the second hitter with a clear kill. As well, a shoot set (with a one-legged or two-legged take-off) or a shoot set with or without a change of direction. The height of the set varies between 1-2 meters above the top of the net.

All sets that are two-three meters above the height of the net are considered third wave attacks. Finally, it is evident that all sets that are higher than 4 meters above the top of the net belong to the category of fourth wave attacks. The transition between the different waves concerns the height, speed, and the time of the set. This sometimes makes it difficult to identify which set belongs to which category.

The width of the volleyball net can be divided into nine zones, each zone relating to the length of a set and to the attacking spot. Each zone is one meter wide. Zone 0 is the setter's spot. A, B, and C are the attacking zones behind the setter and 1-5 are the attacking zones in front of the setter (*Fig. 107*).

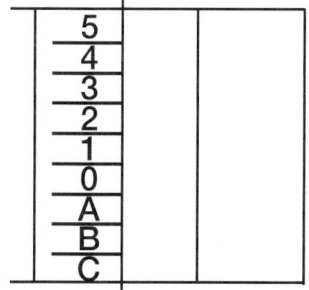

Fig. 107

A definition of the different sets and of the attacking zones makes quick and precise communication between the setter and the hitters. Since the pass is not always to the setting spot 0 there must be some rules that must be kept in mind:
1. The attack spot always remains the same independent of the setting spot. For example, a short set 2 meters away from the setter must always remain in zone 2!
2. As a second option, the attack spot shifts depending on the setting spot. For example, a B-quick is hit from zone 0 because the setting spot shifted to zone B.

The first rule puts the main responsibility on the setter. To use this rule makes sense when the setter is very experienced and/or the hitters are not. The second rule shares the responsibility with both athletes and should be used with experienced hitters and a less experienced setter.

OFFENSIVE COMBINATIONS 111

The communication between the setter and the hitter can be managed by a number/letter combination. The first number/letter is signaling the attack spot to use and the second number of the combination is always related to the set/wave of the volleyball. For example, A1 signifies an A-quick behind the setter, a 53 signifies a medium-high set in position IV, and a B1 signifies a "two" ball set behind the setter in zone B. This definition is clear and easy to understand when you see it on paper, but it can cause problems when in practical use. The little zones require incredibly accurate setting skills and this leaves the main responsibility exclusively with the setter. This is especially true with longer distance sets.

Outside	2 m
4	2 m
3 ⓩ	1,5 m
2	1,5 m
Outside	2 m

Fig. 108

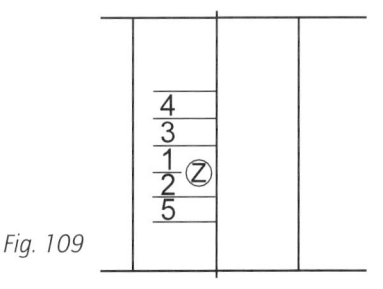

Fig. 109

Another definition of the attacking zones is shown in Fig. 108. This gives part of the responsibility to the second hitter since there are less attacking zones and, therefore, they are bigger ones.

The attacking spots for the first hitter can be defined as follows (Fig. 109):
1 = A quick in front of the setter.
2 = A quick behind the setter.
3 = A short ball 1 meter away from the setter.
4 = A short ball 2 meters away from the setter.
5 = A short ball 1 meter away and behind the setter.

- A third option for a communication system is that all the sets have numbers and each hitter receives a set according to what number s/he has been given (Photo 23). Most teams use this method of communication.

Photo 23 (Martin)

In the following paragraph offensive combinations will be shown and discussed in relation to the number of athletes that are involved: As well, it can be said that the setter, as a front-court athlete, must be seen as an offensive threat (i.e. tips, dumps, first pass attack, etc.).

1. **Setter with a Quick/Middle Hitter and an Outside Hitter!**
   No special OC should be used because this would mean that there is no hitter available for a safety set. To get the opposition's middle blocker away from your own outside hitter, your own middle hitter must be used a large distance away from your own outside hitter to make it difficult for the opposition to be fast enough to move over and form a double-block. The following are some methods in which this can be accomplished: if the outside hitter is in position IV the middle hitter will come in for an A-quick in front or behind the setter. If the outside hitter is in position II then the middle hitter must go for a B-quick in front of the setter.

2. **Setter with a Quick/Middle Hitter and Two Outside Hitters!**
   In this situation, the offensive spot in which the middle hitter is set to attack is not as important as before because the setter has available an outside hitter on both sides of him/her in which to set a safety set if need be. The same situation can be accomplished if instead of a second outside hitter the setter has a back row hitter in which the volleyball can be set to.

With the first two examples, where no combination hitter is available, it is important to have an individual tactically well trained as a middle hitter. If this middle hitter is able to play a shoot (with or without a change of direction) s/he will still be able to keep the opposition's blockers occupied.

3. **Setter with a Quick/Middle Hitter, a Combination Hitter and an Outside or a Back Row Hitter for a Safety Set!**
   In this situation, it would be a smart move to use combination plays that move the combination hitter away from the attacking spot with 3-4 wave sets (positions II and IV) to keep the opposition's middle blocker focused on the middle with the help of your middle hitter (Figs. 110a-110b).

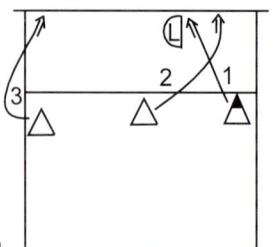

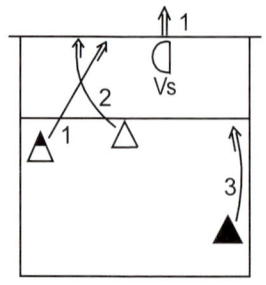

Figs. 110a/b

OFFENSIVE COMBINATIONS 113

4. **Setter with a Quick/Middle Hitter, a Combination Hitter, an Outside Hitter, and a Back Row Hitter!**
   Once again, it is the intention of the middle and combination hitters to fake the opposition's middle blocker and/or to keep him/her occupied long enough to create an offensive opportunity for their other teammates (Figs. 111a-111b).

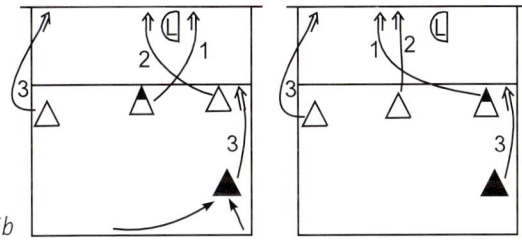

   Figs. 111a/b

5. **Setter with a Quick/Middle Hitter, two Combination Hitters (one of them can be a back row hitter), and an Outside Hitter (Fig. 112a) or a Back Row Hitter (Fig. 112b)!**

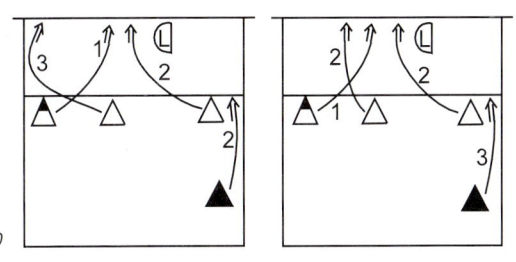

   Figs. 112a/b

6. **Setter (front-court) with a Quick/Middle Hitter, Combination Hitter, and Two Back Row Hitters (Fig. 113a) (one of which can be a combination hitter) (Fig. 113b)!**

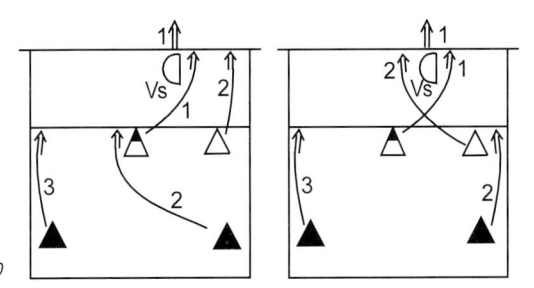

   Fig. 113a/b

If it is taken into account that the setter is in the front row then there will be five athletes involved in the offence.

LEARNING PART 2

7. Setter with two Quick Hitters, a Combination Hitter, and a Back Row Hitter (Figs. 114a-114b)!

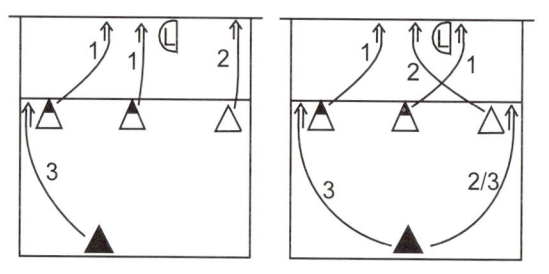

Figs. 114a/b

8. Setter with two Quick Hitters and Two Back Row Hitters (one of them is able to be the second hitter) (Figs. 115a-115b)!

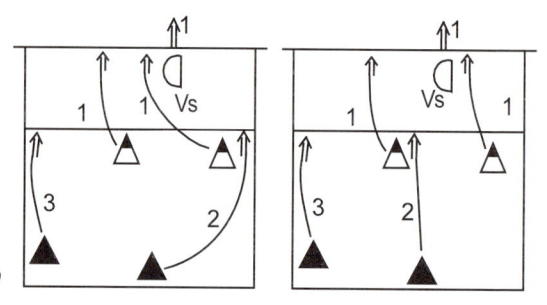

Figs. 115a/b

9. Setter with a Quick/Middle Hitter, Two Combination Hitters, and One Back Row Hitter (Figs. 116a-116b)!

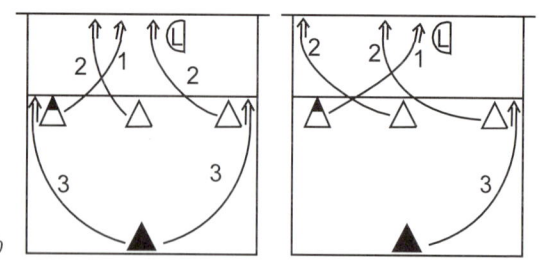

Figs. 116a/b

10. Setter with a Quick/Middle Hitter, Two combination Hitters, and Two Back Row Hitters (Figs. 117a-117b)!

OFFENSIVE COMBINATIONS   115

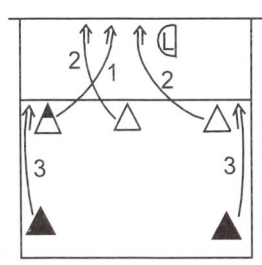

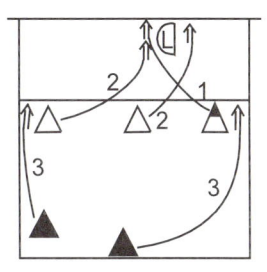

Figs. 117a/b

11. **Setter with Three Quick Hitters and One or Two Back Row Hitters (photos 118a-118b)** – Played by the Olympic Champions Brazil in the 1992 Barcelona Olympics!

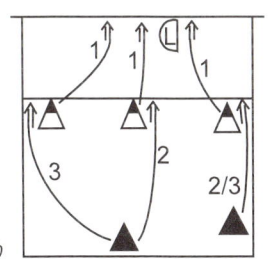

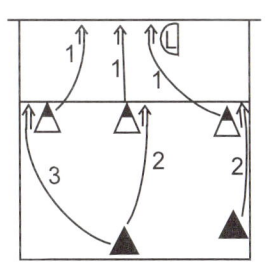

Figs. 118a/b

Tendencies can be seen in the men's game where the back row attack is performed as a quick attack, where the set used is an A-quick, which is a short ball that is set away from the net. In the women's game, the back row attack is mostly used as a safety set (3-4 wave) and only rarely used as a combination set (second wave), but a shoot set with a one-legged fade away take-off (Photo 24) is very effective and used very often as an A-quick and/or B-quick attack behind the setter (Fig. 119). This play is rarely in the men's game. In this situation, a shoot set with a two-legged take-off in front of or behind the setter is predominantly used.

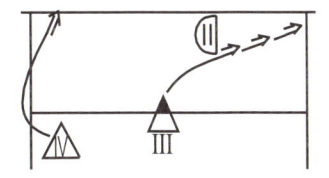

Fig. 118

Photo 24

Service reception has considerably improved with the introduction of the libero. This makes special offensive combination plays, using two quick hitters in the air simultaneously, possible and, therefore, the use of these plays will increase.

It is quite obvious that most of the OC's shown above are only used at the men's national and international levels of volleyball. Some may be used at the women's top levels, but not all of them.

At the low levels of volleyball only general offensive combinations should be used. The quick hitter plays as if s/he is a second wave hitter and hits "two" balls or short balls as a middle hitter. It only makes sense to use the quick hitter as a first wave hitter if the quality of the first pass is relatively good and the setter is penetrating from the back row. In this way, with a bad service reception pass the setter still has two hitters at the outside positions that can still have the volleyball set to them. To make the opposition believe and focus on the threat of the quick hitter, the setter, with short sets and not real A-quicks because the volleyball is set slightly higher, should use the quick hitter. This is also true for the women's middle levels of volleyball.

At the men's middle levels of volleyball they use too many difficult special offensive combinations and as a result they get quantity as opposed to quality of attacks. This match tactic is incorrect because the efficiency is simply not there! Too often developments and plays/tactics of the higher levels of volleyball are copied, but individually, as a group, and as a team the athletes are not tactically capable of performing these skills. Their main focus is not on the service reception and the setting, as it should be, but rather on the execution of offensive plays and hitting the volleyball.

General offensive combinations should be the main focus at this level, combined with a slow transition to simple special offensive combinations (i.e. cross or shadow plays). If the setter is in the front-court the offence should be played with one quick hitter and one outside hitter in case a safety set is needed and, with the setter penetrating from the back row, the offence should be played with one quick hitter, one combination hitter, and an outside hitter who is ready for a 3-4 wave set.

4.3 Covering Offensive Combinations

In this section, different coverage formations will be discussed. Firstly, the coverage is dependent on the number of athletes that are involved in the combination play. All information regarding the coverage of a medium-high and high set (3-4 wave sets) are covered in *Volleyball – A Handbook for Coaches and Players* (Photo 25).

Depending on their role and position, athletes that are involved in an offensive combination with the set being a 1-2 carry out the following actions:

a) The quick/middle hitter is the only athlete who is never involved in the coverage because s/he is either still in the air or in the process of landing after the jump.
b) If the setter is playing the volleyball from a standing position s/he will then become the coverage athlete at the setting spot. Immediately after the set, s/he will take up a deep defensive position to cover the hitter. If the setter is jump-setting then s/he will "try" to get into a coverage position as soon as s/he lands.

Photo 25 (Martin)

c) The combination hitter, depending on the combination play, has almost no coverage function, but at the moment that s/he realises that the setter is going to set the volleyball to the middle hitter s/he tries to stop his/her approach and become a coverage athlete right at the spot where s/he is.
d) If the quick hitter is receiving the set, the hitter who is attacking a 3-4 wave set tries to cover the area away from the attacking spot where s/he currently is. If the combination hitter is used then s/he will move one or two steps closer in the direction of the attacking spot and take up a distant coverage position.

LEARNING PART 2

e) If the back row hitter is attacking a 3-4 wave set then s/he will cover in the same manner as the outside hitter in d). Also, if s/he is hitting a second wave attack as part of a combination play then s/he will follow the details outlined in c).

f) The only athletes that can cover in an organised manner are the libero and the back row athletes that are not involved in the offence. These athletes are the coverage specialists and take upon themselves most of the responsibility for the defensive cover, especially the libero who is not allowed to perform any attack options after the service reception or a defensive play.

> The libero is the main coverage athlete and is always a part of any close coverage of the attacker.

The non-attacking and non-service reception back row athletes must cover but the non-attacking service reception back-court athletes must also participate in the coverage. It is an easy principle to remember that if the athlete is not involved in the hitting then that athlete will be the most important part of the offensive coverage.

The following examples will explain and make clear the coverage formations:
1. OC with two hitters and the setter is in the front row (Figs. 120a-120b).
2. OC with three hitters and the setter penetrating (Figs. 121a-121b).
3. OC with three hitters and the setter is in the front row (Figs. 122a-122b).
4. OC with four hitters and the setter penetrating (Figs. 123a-123b).
5. OC with four hitters and the setter in the front row (Figs. 124a-124b).
6. OC with five hitters (Fig. 125).

1. Out of a four-person service reception formation:
a) Position III: A-quick behind the setter.
b) Position IV: Medium-high.

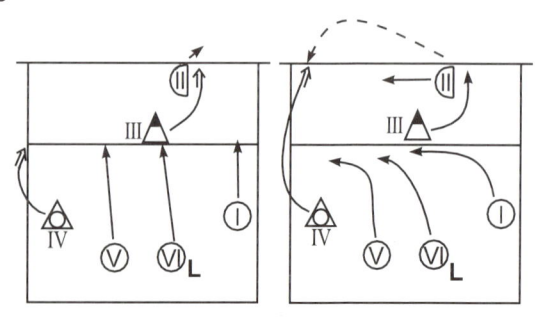

Figs. 120a-120b

COVERING OFFENSIVE COMBINATIONS 119

2. Out of a three-person service reception formation:
a) Position II: A-quick.
   Position III: A short ball 1 meter behind the setter.
b) Position IV: Medium-high.

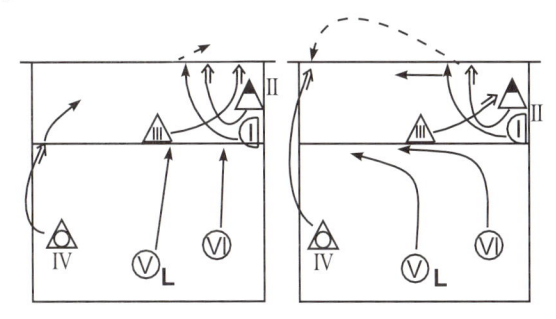

Figs. 121a-121b

3. Out of a two-person service reception formation:
a) Position II: B-quick.
   Position IV: A short ball 1 meter in front of the setter.
b) Position VI: Back attack.

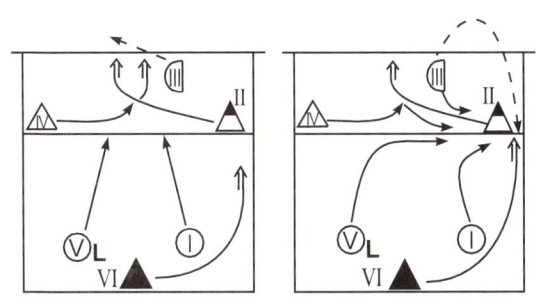

Figs. 122a-122b

4. Out of a two-person service reception formation:
a) Position II: B-quick.
   Position IV: A short ball 1 meter
b) Position I: Back attack.
   Position III: Medium-high/medium-quick.

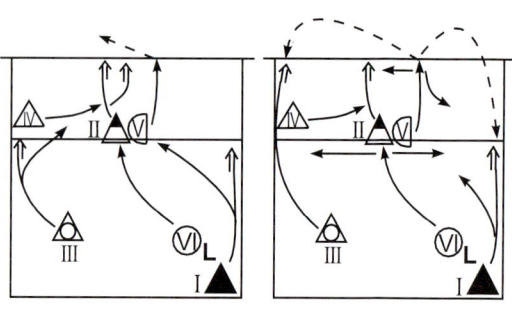

Figs. 123a-123b

5. Out of a two-person service reception formation:
a) Position II: A-quick behind the setter.
   Position IV: B-quick.
b) Position I: Back attack.
   Position VI: Back attack.

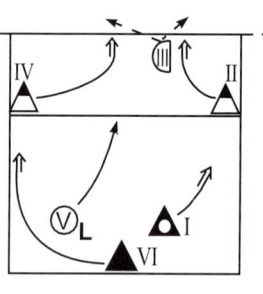

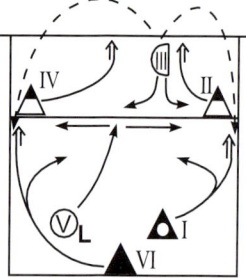

Figs. 124a-124b

6. Out of a two-person service reception formation:
a) Position I: Back attack.
   Position II: A-quick behind the setter.
   Position III: B-quick in front of the setter.
   Position IV: A short ball 1 meter in front of the setter.
   Position V: Back attack.

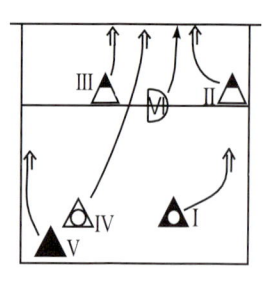

Fig. 125

COVERING OFFENSIVE COMBINATIONS

The following is important information regarding the coverage specialists and the libero:

- As a back-court hitter, who is not receiving the serve, move quickly to the starting position of your offensive action. At the same time, watch the length of the flight of the volleyball off of the serve to communicate to your serve receiving teammates if the volleyball is going out!
- As a back-court athlete, who is not receiving the serve and not hitting from the back row, watch the serve and communicate to your serve receiving teammates if the volleyball is going out!
- Always be prepared to play poor first passes back into the volleyball court (save the volleyball) even if you are not a service reception athlete. In other words, you are covering the service reception athletes.
- As a service reception specialist you should be covering your service reception teammates!
- After the service reception move quickly to the ten-foot line: if you are one of the main coverage athletes cover one-half of the front zone. Always move to the attacking zone after the set. If you are the only main coverage athlete then move immediately to the front middle of the volleyball court and after the set to the side of the attacking spot!
- Volleyballs that are touched by the block and easy to defend should be played to the setting spot. Volleyballs that are touched by the block and difficult to reach should be played high to the middle of the volleyball court!
- Use the overhand pass to play any volleyballs that come off of the block and that are above your shoulders!

The execution of the coverage is the most neglected tactical area of volleyball. The reason for this is that coaches and athletes are equally persuaded of the necessity of covering their own offence, but they are not asking to do it in practice and consequently they are not doing it in their training drills. This can be explained but not excused by the expectations that lie in the dominance of the offence, especially out of the C1 situation. If we take into consideration the fact that sometimes one or two points are important and decisive in a game, it is not understandable and irresponsible to ignore and refuse the opportunities that occur from a well-organised coverage. Again, remember the principle that only what is systematically practiced and trained in game-oriented situations will be successfully carried over and used in an actual game/match situation.

4.4 Individual Tactics of the Setter

The setter is the connecting link between the service reception/defensive athletes and the hitters. S/he is involved in almost every play and has the decisive role in how the offence is to be run. The setter has the opportunity to compensate for a poor pass with a good set. Also, the setter can use the strengths of his/her hitters against the weaknesses of the opposition's blockers and defensive specialists. However, one condition for the setter being able to do this is that s/he must have the skills to perform all types of sets (ie. overhand pass/set, forearm pass, etc.) and to precisely use the correct set in each match/game situation. *The higher the quality of the set and the amount of different sets that the setter can perform then the more individual and tactical options that the setter will have at his/her disposal.* The setter's tactical knowledge, physical strengths, and psychological state of mind are all tactical factors. The quality of these factors will determine how good the individual tactical decisions and actions of the setter will be. The importance of the individual tactical abilities of the setter depends on the level that s/he is playing at.

At the low levels of volleyball the abilities and skills of the setter and his/her teammates dominate what individual tactics can be used. A minimal condition for the setter's individual tactics is that s/he must able to perform at least three different types of sets from a good service reception pass. The setter should be able to set a high ball, a medium-high ball, and a "two" or short ball (between 1 and 2 meters above the height of the volleyball net).

At the middle levels of volleyball the setter should be able to act accordingly depending on the quality of the first pass and at the same time the setter should be able to keep in mind the actions of the opposition's middle blockers when choosing what set to execute. In addition, the setter should be able to make up for a bad service reception pass and to set medium-quick and quick short balls. From a perfect pass the setter should be able to jump-set and use setter fakes and/or tips if possible. Tactically, the setter's role is to initiate reasonable and effective offensive combinations.

At the high levels of volleyball the setter should be able to take advantage of the individual tactical weaknesses of the opposition's blockers, especially the middle blocker. This should be possible thanks to the results from an intensive analysis

INDIVIDUAL TACTICS OF THE SETTER   123

and scouting report on the opposition that has been provided before each match. Technically, the setter must be able to make up for a bad pass with a good set and with a good service reception pass the setter must be able to set the volleyball perfectly. The setter should only perform a jump-set to speed up the setting, thus hiding the type of set that will be used. In this manner, the opposition never knows if the setter will set the volleyball or attack the volleyball. The setter should be able to set the volleyball frontally, to the back, and laterally using the **jump set.** Out of the same arm and hand position and the same body (neutral) position to the volleyball the setter should be able to set the volleyball at different heights and distances right to the target in the attacking zones (Photo 26).

Photo 26 (Sabraz)

Furthermore, the setter should be able to speed up or slow down the set according the situation at hand to convincingly fake the opposition's middle blocker and to disguise the direction of the set. The setter's peripheral view must be well trained because s/he must be able to see the volleyball, his/her service reception athletes, his/her attacking teammates, and the opposition's blockers, especially the middle blocker and then, at the same time, make the correct setting decision. Additionally, the setter must be able to perfectly perform the **forearm pass** to set poor service reception passes to hitters who are attacking 3-4 wave sets. The setter must be able to execute a **one-handed overhand pass** to properly set volleyballs that are very high and tightly passed to the volleyball net and set these volleyballs to the outside (Photo 27).

Photo 27 (Köhler)

Especially with the new rules that allow the setter to use the overhand pass out of difficult positions, it will bring a much higher focus to the overhand pass in comparison to the one-handed set or the forearm pass. This also means that a set out of a falling body position will gain importance and, therefore, must be included in the training (see Photo 18).

Generally, it can be stated that the **setter** needs to have a quiet and non-violent tempered character. S/he must be intelligent and have an understanding of the sport of volleyball because s/he is like an assistant coach on the volleyball court who executes the match plan of the coach. The setter runs and organises the offensive strategy and must be able to decide and act accordingly to the situation at hand. S/he must be able to save and evaluate his/her actions so as to be able to take the decisions/actions made into account and use the results appropriately in any future reoccurring situations when making any individual tactical decisions. To do this the setter must talk to his/her hitters and exchange information.

At the professional and international levels of volleyball there is a tendency to use tall setters (i.e. In men's volleyball they are 1.90 meters in height or taller). The reason for this is because if there is no difference in the quality of sets, it only makes sense to use a taller setter so as to take advantage of his/her blocking and offensive strengths and skills. It offers no advantage to a team to have a setter whose sets are marginally better but who is also a weak blocker. In this situation, size does matter!

One athletic requirement of the setter is the ability to quickly cover short distances. For this to occur, s/he must have a perfect orientation of the volleyball court. S/he should also have good jumping ability and good jumping endurance and s/he must be very well coordinated. At the *international women's level of volleyball* the setter performs 65 *jumping actions* per hour of match time. In the *men's Bundesliga*, observations show that the setter jumps 90 % of the time, of which only 5 % are offensive actions and 14 % are blocking actions. These two actions account for approximately 20 % of all the setter's jumping actions in a match. If we break this down statistically into an hour match time it means that the setter jumps 85 times, which is equal to performing the following actions: 53.3 % jump sets, 36.5 % blocks, and 10.2 % of offensive actions. *Internationally*, the results are different. In an hour match, the setter jump sets

63.7 % of the time, blocks 27 % of the time, performs an offensive action 5.3 % of the time, and jump serves 4 % of the time.

Chart 1 shows **the average and extreme physical resilience of the setter** per rotation. It is divided into a front-court/net sequence and a back-court sequence. The time that passes by from one jumping action to the next is measured in seconds and is defined as density:

Jumps	
Front-court/net sequence average	= 5 jumps – Density 31 seconds
Front-court/net sequence extreme	= 10 jumps in 144 seconds – Density 14.4 seconds
Back-court sequence average	= 2 jumps – Density 84 seconds
Back-court sequence extreme	= 6 jumps in 168 seconds – Density 28 seconds

Chart 1a

Dashes/Sprints	
Front-court/net sequence average	= 7 dashes/sprints – Density 23 seconds
Front-court/net sequence extreme	= 15 dashes in 134 seconds – Density 8.9 seconds
Back-court sequence average	= 12 dashes – Density 14 seconds
Back-court sequence extreme	= 21 dashes in 169 seconds – Density 8 seconds

Chart 1b

These results from the German Bundesliga are supposed to assist the coach in choosing the correct physical pressure to put on the setter during practice to get the setter as close as possible to the real match situation.

In summary, the characterisation of the ideal setter would be:

The setter is the brain and the soul of the offence. S/he is a servant of the team, disciplined, creative, and always focused on the success of the team. The setter must show leadership and the ability to integrate people. S/he must be quick and intelligent and s/he must be mentally and psychologically strong. Metaphorically speaking, this means that the setter must be connected with the hitters through an invisible string.

The Setting Action

The following kinds of **jump sets** should be trained in practice: one-handed and two-handed jump sets to the front, to the back, and laterally (to the side). These jump sets should be practiced out of a standing position and out of a penetrating/moving situation and without a turn in the body. It is important to make the setter play the volleyball out of the same body/arm-hand position and the same position to the volleyball. The setter should also be setting the volleyball when s/he is at the peak point in his/her jump (photo 28).

Once the setter has mastered this then s/he can begin working on delaying the moment of the set or to set at an earlier moment to irritate the blockers. The irritation can be supported by the setter intentionally misleading the opposition with fake movements before the moment of the set (photo 28).

Photo 28 (Steffen Marquardt)

The **impulse**, especially with long distance sets, is performed at **the middle levels of volleyball** by a strong extension of the arms. At the **high levels of volleyball** the impulse is performed completely by the wrists. By performing this action, the setter is able to hide the direction of the set until the last possible moment and is still capable of setting the volleyball to all the different attacking zones. The same is true for the performance of a lateral or one-handed set.

The **setter's tip/dump** is the most important offensive action of the setter. Every setter's clinic should also focus on this skill (photo 29). There are two different kinds of tips/dumps:
- The **aggressive** tip/dump, which is when the volleyball is directly "dumped", especially when there is no block and,
- The **conservative** tip/dump. This is where the volleyball is pushed over the block into the ten-foot zone or deep into the back-court area.

The tip/dump is executed with the right or the left hand (Fig. 126). At the **middle levels of volleyball** it can be also carried out with both hands. To use the setter's tip/dump in an effective manner the setter must observe or "feel" the actions of the blockers, then by knowing the opposition's blocking and defensive formations, s/he must strike without revealing any hints of his/her intention (photo 29).

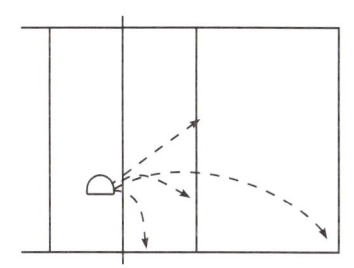

Fig. 126

A discussion of the most important individual tactical factors and special training drills regarding the setter's tip/dump will be provided later in the chapter dealing with selected training drills for the individual tactics of the setter's tip/dump.

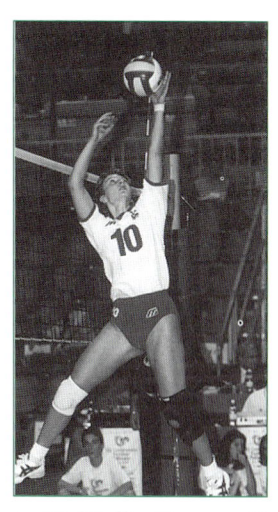

Photo 29 (Steffen Marquardt)

4.5 Individual Tactics of the Hitter

Observations at the **women's national level of volleyball** show the following data regarding the **physical jumping resilience of the athletes.** The intensity of the physical resilience in competition (density = time between one jump to the next in seconds) reveals the following for different athletes:

> 36.8 seconds for the outside hitters
> 24.6 seconds for the quick hitters/middle blockers
> 56.0 seconds for the setter.
> > The degree of the physical resilience in a competition
> > (jumping actions per hour) show:
>
> 49.4 jumps for the outside hitters
> 76.7 jumps for the quick hitters/middle blockers
> 52.5 jumps for the setter.

Data concerning the off-side/back-court hitters are missing because at the national women's level of volleyball there are no specialists in these positions. At the **women's international level of volleyball** at least 15 % of the jumps must be added and the main/offside/back-court hitters have to be included as well.

At the *men's national level of volleyball the following* average and extreme results for *running and jumping resilience* have been found (Chart 2a and Chart 2b):

Offside/main Hitter	
Front-court/net sequence average	= 5 jumps – Density 32 seconds
	= 10 dashes – Density 16 seconds
Front-court/net sequence extreme	= 9 jumps – Density 15.9 seconds
	= 26 dashes – Density 9.0 seconds
Back-court sequence average	= 10 dashes – Density 16 seconds
Back-court sequence extreme	= 20 dashes – Density 8.1 seconds

Quick Hitter/middle Blocker	
Front-court/net sequence average	= 8 jumps – Density 20 seconds
	= 9 dashes – Density 18 seconds
Front-court/net sequence extreme	= 14 jumps – Density 11.3 seconds
	= 27 dashes – Density 9.5 seconds
Back-court sequence average	= 8 dashes – Density 20 seconds
Back-court sequence extreme	= 11 dashes – Density 8.5 seconds

Chart 2a

Outside/combination Hitter	
Front-court/net sequence average	= 5 jumps – Density 31 seconds
	= 11 dashes – Density 14 seconds
Front-court/net sequence extreme	= 16 jumps – Density 15.9 seconds
	= 28 dashes – Density 9.1 seconds
Back-court sequence average	= 8 dashes – Density 20 seconds
Back-court sequence extreme	= 11 dashes – Density 8.5 seconds

Chart 2b

The distribution of the jumping actions per match and athlete shows a relation of 16 blocking actions to 13 hitting actions to 3 jump sets. These figures do not include the back row hitting actions that average 8.2 % per match. This percentage can be added to the one athlete (the offside hitter) or to two athletes if the back-court attack is shared.

INDIVIDUAL TACTICS OF THE HITTER

At the **men's international level of volleyball** there are at least 10 % more jumping actions due to more jump sets, more jump serves, and more back-court attacks, as well as to a higher amount of blocking actions because of the use of more two-person and/or three-person blocking formations.

4.5.1 The Quick Hitter

The quick hitter is the most important offensive athlete because all offensive combinations begin and are designed around him/her. *S/he must have exemplary fighting spirit and must not measure his/her importance on the team by the frequency of his/her own offensive actions, but also by the successful offensive actions by his/her teammates who only have to deal with one blocker thanks to him/her.* S/he has the **serving role** on his/her team in the offence.

There is a reason as to why the quick hitter is called a "decoy". This is because s/he is tempting the opposition's middle blocker to jump with him/her or at least keep them busy long enough to make it difficult for them to get to the outside to set up a double-block (Photo 30). The quick hitter especially needs to have a good positive attitude towards the setter and must provide the setter with positive hints to help with the setting.

Photo 30 (Tom Schulte)

The middle hitter must be taken seriously by the setter regarding his/her individual tactical observations and/or hints otherwise these points will not be considered and performed by the setter (Photo 30).

The second hitters must be aware of the decoy role of the quick hitter and must positively communicate with him/her and the setter after any successful attacks against only one blocker. Most of the time the quick hitter is fulfilling the role of a middle blocker (see the explanations regarding middle blocking in chapter 5).

The quick hitter in the men's game is approximately 2 meters tall and in the women's game is approximately 1.85 meters tall. The reach height for the men when they are jumping is approximately 3.6 meters and approximately 3.30 meters for the women.

Athletically, quick hitters must be able to cover short distances of approximately 2-3 meters very quickly. They must have very good reactive jumping skills and enough power and endurance to keep this up over the course of an entire match. Technically, the quick hitters must demonstrate the following *qualities:*
- Execute a perfect quick attack in front of and behind the setter with a solid and dynamic approach rhythm to help the setter out.
- S/he must be highly effective against only one blocker.
- S/he must be successful against a double-block without any direct mistakes.
- S/he must be able to perform an aggressive tip/dump from their position out of a credible hitting movement.
- S/he must be able to hit in and against the power line. By doing this s/he must be able to use hits using his/her wrist action as well as hits using an over the shoulder action.

A well-trained quick hitter *at the high national and international levels of volleyball* also knows the following techniques:
- "Stopper" with or without a change in direction (faking an A-quick and hitting a short ball)
- Shoots/"flyers" (you approach towards one attacking zone and then after the take-off you jump/fly to another) played as:
a) Jumping from the attacking zone for a B-quick towards the setter to hit an A-quick/short ball.
b) Jumping from an A-quick in front of the setter to hit an A-quick behind the setter.
c) Jumping from an A-quick behind the setter to hit an A-quick in front of the setter.
d) Jumping away from the attacking zone of an A-quick behind the setter to a B-quick behind the setter.
e) Jumping away from an A-quick behind the setter to a ball set 1 meter in front of the setter (1 meter set).
f) Jumping away from an A-quick to a 1 meter set or a B-quick.

INDIVIDUAL TACTICS OF THE HITTER

Figs. 127a and 127b show two different take-off spots.
The credibility of the quick hitter, which means the effect of his/her fake on the blocker, will only be successful if the whole movement of his/her action including the take-off spot is not changed and different quick attacks are being performed. This so called *"neutral" take-off position* makes it difficult to anticipate which quick attack will be used and from what position. The quick hitter is able to act with the setter in the front-court at the setting spot as if s/he would be running combinations with him/herself (Figs. 127a and 127b).

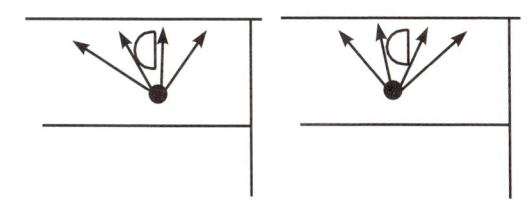

Fig. 127a *Fig. 127b*

At **the women's national and international level of volleyball** the shoots/"flyers" mentioned above are rarely used. On the other hand, the women, in contrast to the men, perform one-legged shoots/"flyers" such as:
   a) Starting in front of the setter and jumping away for an A-quick behind the setter.
   b) Same as in a) but jumping away for a 1 meter short ball behind the setter.
   c) Same as in a) but jumping away for a B-quick behind the setter.
   d) Jumping away for a 1 meter short ball in front of the setter.
   e) Jumping away for a B-quick in front of the setter.

The shoots/"flyers" in front of the setter are only used with left-handed hitters.

The typical mark for a **short set without a change of direction** is the same approach as for an A-quick, but then you stop and delay the take-off and hit a short ball/1 meter above the volleyball net. For a **short set with a change of direction** following the fake there is an additional step to the real attacking spot (ie. from an A-quick in front of the setter to a short ball/1 meter above the volleyball net behind the setter or from a B-quick to a short ball right at the setter).

Characteristically, **offensive "flying" actions** (jumping away from or to the setter) require a take-off up into the air and to the front and to the side to respectively "fly" from the fake to the real attacking spot. Of course, good jumping ability and some "hang-time" would help.

A main feature of the ***one-legged attack*** is that the expected two-legged take-off is replaced by a one-legged take-off up into the air and to the front to get as quickly as possible to the desired attacking spot. The second non-jumping swinging leg is used to get more energy for the jump and is supported by an active use of the arms. All this is done to reach high enough to be in a position to hit the volleyball at an earlier and/or delayed moment depending on the block.

The ability to switch immediately from a quick attack to blocking and from blocking to a quick attack is one of the most important conditions in becoming a quick hitter/middle blocker. With these fast switches all of the actions are taking place in the front zone (ten-foot zone). This means that the approach of the quick hitter is rarely vertical to the volleyball net, but mostly diagonal and even parallel to the volleyball net. This approach gives the quick hitter a larger field of vision to watch the volleyball and to see the direction, speed, and quality of the pass and to use all of this information to quickly calculate and adapt his/her time-spatial behavior according to the match situation. Since the quick hitter is principally never leaving the front zone and is performing attacking and blocking actions throughout the entire offensive zone his/her nicknames are "ruler of the front zone" and "king of the air". These nicknames seem to fit quite nicely (Photo 31).

Photo 31 (Martin)

It is important for an efficient use of teamwork with the setter to have the ability to choose an attacking position not too close to the setter so as to be able to, depending on the quality of the first pass, use a quick attack by making tiny adjustments in timing if necessary.

There are different methods used to approach and jump for the attack. The typical approach is he left-right-left approach. Here, the first left step is a long ***stemming step*** that puts the athlete in position for the final two quick take-off

INDIVIDUAL TACTICS OF THE HITTER

steps. Usually, there are even some preparation steps before this typical left-right-left sequence, but sometimes the middle hitter does not have the time for such an approach, especially since s/he does not leave the front zone. If the time factor is more important than the spatial factor (perfect positioning in the correct attacking zone) there is a second method of jumping. It is called the ***stem jump.*** Simply, this means that the athlete is using a reactive "punch" jump where both feet are touching the court at the same time and deliver the energy for a quick take-off together. All preparation steps are left out. This is not the standard situation, but since time is the crucial factor the athlete has to try anything that might make him/her quicker to be in a position to execute a first tempo attack at any time.

The arm swing or the hitting motion of a quick hitter must be developed in such a manner that enables him/her, depending on the opposition's block, to speed up his swing or to delay it. Furthermore, s/he should be able to hit past the block to the left and to the right by the active use of his/her wrist. This is also true for aggressive tips/dumps (past the block) or delayed tips/dumps (fake hitting motion).

All of this information regarding the quick hitter makes it clear that no successful offensive strategy is possible without the quick hitter at ***the top levels of volleyball.*** ***At the lower levels of volleyball*** the function of the middle hitter does not exist because of the lack of technical and tactical abilities of the athletes. The quick hitter is the first hitter but he is only hitting short balls that are 1 meter above the volleyball net.

At the middle levels of volleyball the importance of the quick hitter is realised, but the use of this athlete is often ineffective because the requested standards are set too high for the setter and the quick hitter. The main reason for this is that they do not have enough practice time to work on the necessary fine tuning between the service reception, setting, and hitting.

Coaches at this level very often tend to copy developments at the higher levels of volleyball without critically analysing the individual abilities of his/her own athletes to see if this is even possible. A typical scenario for this is that athletes, teams, and coaches are all excited about one spectacular B-quick by the quick hitter and forget that the 20 B-quicks before were all useless or resulted in direct errors and that the last two games/matches have been lost. Here, the relation between effectiveness and frequency is turned upside down. Instead, it makes sense to be using fake quick attacks or short balls because they do not require as much practice to work and be effective in a match situation. Another positive by-product is that the responsibility is equally shared between the setter and the quick hitter. In this case, it should not necessarily be the goal of the *middle hitter* to make the middle blocker jump, but to make the middle blocker stay with the middle hitter throughout his/her offensive action as long as possible.

Furthermore, *individual tactical thoughts* are:
- The quick hitter (QH) must adapt his/her own actions to the quality of the first pass and the abilities of the setter.
- The QH must be successful against a single block since half of his/her attacks are against a single block.
- The QH must be effective against a double block because one-third of his/her actions are against a double block, especially with a fake quick attack.
- The QH should always analyse the actions of the middle blocker. It should be seen if the blocker is fully jumping, passively blocking, or faking the block and the QH should then pass along these hints to the setter.
- The QH should show his/her variability to force the middle blocker to always deal and cope with new situations.
- The QH must watch the defence especially positions I and V to find uncovered areas.
- The QH must come to a "blind" understanding with the setter, even in unusual situations that are not common.
- The QH and setter must be involved in all offensive actions and must feel that it is because of their own success that a teammate has a single block to hit against.
- The QH must be a fighter by nature (ie. request the set even when it is the opposition's match point).
- The QH should be a role model in the offence, should show leadership, and always be ready to take over responsibility when needed.
- The QH should play tactical serves in his/her area by using the overhand pass and play them high enough so that the setter has enough time and space to get to the volleyball and prepare to be able to set a quick attack.
- **The QH should especially take serves that touch the volleyball net and drop into the front zone.**

The teamwork of the quick hitter, setter, and the service reception athletes must be a part of each practice. This is especially true during the preseason and the season phases. During these times these skills must be a part of the planning and preparation of each practice.

4.5.2 The Offside/Main Hitter

In the past, the athlete who was put diagonally to the setter in the starting line-up was a very good all-around athlete with the role as the back-up setter on the volleyball court. Today, the offside/diagonal hitter is the main hitter and has the highest share, approximately 25 %, of the offence regardless of whether s/he is playing in the front row or back row. S/he is almost pushed out of the service reception and is playing as an outside hitter of the 3-4 waves. S/he is less frequently used as a combination hitter or as a quick hitter. On most teams s/he is the only main back-court hitter (see Chapter 4.5.3 regarding the back-court hitter). One quality is to have a great jumping ability and, therefore, have a long reach height in the offence, and is, in contrast to the quick hitter, a true power hitter who can hit the volleyball hard. S/he needs these qualities because most of the time s/he must work against a double block or even a triple block. S/he must be able to hit extreme diagonal, half-diagonal, and long line (Photos 32 and 33). His/her power is to force the defence to push back into the volleyball court and thus giving him/her the opportunity to be successful will a good fake followed by an offensive tip/dump.

Photo 32 (Martin)   Photo 33 (Martin)

A defining point for a **turning spike** is that the upper body is turning in the air and, by doing so, the result is a change in the hitting direction which is different from the direction of the approach **(jump-turn spike)**. Everything else is identical to a frontal hit.

With the women the **use of the outside block** is dominating, whereas with the **men** the **use of the top of the block** is an absolutely necessary condition for the diagonal hitter. The reason for this is that after a poor pass this hitter usually gets most of the sets and then s/he must deal with a well-positioned double block or triple block and s/he must score (Photo 34). *Therefore, s/he must have a high physical and psychological stability and an extraordinary self-confidence.* S/he must quickly get over any unforced errors and inefficient actions. This should motivate him/her for an even more aggressive play. S/he must be able to make up for slightly inaccurate sets and must feel responsible for any errors following a 3-4 wave attack. This is especially true in critical situations where s/he must request the volleyball and by doing so support the setter. The diagonal hitter is not only attacking as an outside hitter, but also as a second/combination hitter and rarely as a quick hitter (Photo 34).

The information regarding the diagonal hitter at the high levels of volleyball mentioned above is not true for the low and middle levels of volleyball. The athlete in the diagonal position at the **low levels of volleyball** is most of the time a second setter (4-2 match system) or a supporting setter. At the **middle levels of volleyball** this athlete is a setter, supporting setter, or a good all-around athlete.

Photo 34

4.5.3 The Back-court Hitter

Everything mentioned above regarding the diagonal hitter is also true for the back-court hitter, since it is the diagonal hitter who usually also has this role. With the setter in the front row s/he is the third attacker. This is why s/he has to be able to run back row attacks of the second wave and also of the 3-4 waves.

The set for a back row attack of the fourth wave is a medium-high/high set approximately 3 meters away from the volleyball net. The set for a back row attack of the third wave is a medium-high approximately 2-2.5 meters away from the volleyball net. Finally, a back row attack of the second wave (combination attacks) is set 1 meter above the height of the volleyball net or a medium-quick and approximately 1.5-2 meters away from the volleyball net. There are

INDIVIDUAL TACTICS OF THE HITTER

tendencies during the actual development to play the back row attack at a distance of 1-1.5 meters away from the volleyball net as a fake A-quick or a short ball, even with a one-legged take-off.

Back row attacks of the second wave are exclusively hit from positions I and VI back row attacks of the 3-4 wave are hit from positions I and V, and rarely from position VI (see Chapter 4.2 regarding offensive combinations).

Regarding *the attacking spot of the back-court hitter and the communication with the setter* there are, just as with the quick hitter, two possibilities:
1) The attacking spot remains the same no matter what type of first pass is completed and what setting spot the volleyball has been passed to. This is a good solution for attacks of the 3-4 waves.
2) The back-court hitter adjusts to the service reception and setting situation and is, for example, hitting from position I sidewards behind the setter.

The following differences are given in the **course of movement** as compared to the front-court attack:
- The approach is quicker.
- The left stemming step is quicker and, therefore, the stemming phase is shorter.
- The coordination is much more difficult since the approach is quicker and the take-off is up to the front and the landing is without any net contact (Photo 35).

Similar to the diagonal hitter, the back-court hitter must be able to make up for any inaccurate sets. This is difficult because from the back row the antennas are missing as orientation points. As well,

Photo 35 (Martin)

one advantage of the back row hitter in comparison to the front row hitter is that s/he can see the block better and observe it for a longer period of time. This is why the main requirement for the back-court hitter is to hit past the block hard enough to fool the defence.

At the ***international women's level of volleyball*** the back row attack is finally accepted, but only with one athlete per team. It is used more as a 3-4 wave attack. At ***the men's national and international levels of volleyball*** there is more than one back-court hitter, which means that, especially internationally, there are two back-court hitters involved in the offence.

> With the use of the libero, the number of back-court attacks is definitely going down and the use of two back-court hitters in the same formation will become rarer.

At the ***national level of women's volleyball*** there are only a few teams that are using back-court hitters as part of their offensive strategy.

At the ***low levels of volleyball*** back-court attacks are usually "stopgaps" and at the ***middle levels of volleyball,*** especially with the men, there are tendencies to use an organised back-court attack of the 3-4 waves.

4.5.4 The Service Reception Outside Hitter

Idealistically, the outside hitter is combining the abilities of a diagonal and a second/combination hitter. This means that everything mentioned above regarding the diagonal hitter is also true for the outside hitter, especially concerning the psychological aspects of the sport of volleyball. S/he is not only dealing with a great psychological pressure when s/he is receiving the service but also when s/he must attack. Everything that has been said regarding service reception athletes (see Chapter 3.2) is also true for the service reception outside hitter, especially the demand that s/he must be able to run an offensive combination out of the service reception formation. This means that s/he must be able to perform a second wave attack. From this the conclusion can be drawn that s/he must be a very good all-around athlete (see the following information regarding the combination hitter).

At the ***low levels of volleyball*** the outside hitter, who is part of a four-person or five-person service reception formation, should be able to hit the frontal direction and the diagonal direction, as well as perform an attack tip/dump. This is necessary to omit successive errors after one or two poor passes.

At the ***middle levels of volleyball*** the outside hitter should be able to make up for inaccurate sets and be able to take into consideration the opposition's blocking actions for his/her own offensive actions. S/he should be able to hit sets out of the 2-3 waves from his/her attacking position as well as combination balls at the setter's position. Here it helps to perform turning spikes and hits using the wrist action.

INDIVIDUAL TACTICS OF THE HITTER 139

4.5.5 The Second/Combination Hitter

In comparison to the diagonal and outside hitters it is the role of the combination hitter, who is not receiving the service, to perform all types of attacks after a change of direction and/or after a long approach. To be able to successfully fake the opposition, s/he must be able to hit short and 1 meter volleyballs in front of and behind the setter. Of course, this requires high coordinative abilities. When tactical serves and serves that touch the volleyball net are coming into the area of the combination hitter s/he should, like the quick hitter, play the volleyball using the overhand pass and play the volleyball high to the setting position to get enough time and space to prepare for his/her attack.

Since the combination hitter is mostly attacking against a single-block in the complex 1 situation and after a good first pass s/he must successfully solve this dilemma/problem. S/he should know the exact abilities, characteristics, and behaviors of the setter and the quick hitter because as a combination hitter s/he must closely interact with them in a tight space. Figs. 128a-128c show **the time-spatial behavior of the combination hitter** in relation to the quick hitter and the setter. The coloured zone marks the true starting position for the planned combination play. It is approximately 3 meters behind the quick hitter's starting position (Figs. 128a-128c).

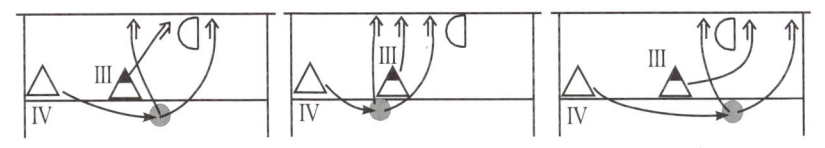

Figs. 128a-c

Depending on the situation in the game/match, the second hitter must get to his/her exact starting position because it is a decisive condition for good teamwork and understanding to occur between him/her and the setter. At the ***international levels of volleyball*** the second hitter is calling their own set depending on their observations regarding the opposition's blocking strategy. The combination hitter must develop a good emotional relationship with the quick hitter. S/he must always be aware of the fact that all of his/her actions against a single-block or no-block are a result of the effective behavior and actions of the quick hitter and the setter's intelligent sets. In the **men's game**, the combination hitter is the only hitter who can use the one-legged hit with or without a change of direction. To summarise the characteristics of the combination hitter one might say that s/he is quick, agile, recognises and knows when to use a lot of different variants, and is able to hit the volleyball hard if necessary.

4.5.6 Individual Tactical Factors/Strategies

The following individual tactical factors/strategies are important for all **offensive specialists**. Besides having little time to realise what possible influences can affect your own offence the following points are also important for the attacker to pay attention to before each play:

1. *Before the opposition serves pay attention to the following:*
- The gym and the lights.
- The score, behavior of the referee, the linesmen, and the spectators.
- The opposition's starting line-up.
- Planned changes of positioning and distribution of the blockers.
- Any communication by the setter concerning offensive combinations.
- The strengths and weaknesses of the opposition's blockers in relation to the plays previously executed.
- Your own psychological and physical condition.
- The psychological and physical condition of your teammates, especially the setter.
- The defensive formation and any intended changes of positions.
- The effectiveness of the server and the prediction of the type of serve and the direction of the serve that is about to be received.
- The psychological and physical condition of the opposition.

2. *At the moment right after the opposition serves pay attention to the following:*
- The spot, type, and direction of the serve.
- The degree of difficulty of the serve in relation to the service reception formation and setter's position.
- The strengths and weaknesses of the service reception athletes and the anticipation of the quality of the first pass.
- The readiness and starting position of your own offensive teammates.
- Any changes in positioning of the opposition, especially the blockers.

3. *After the service reception pay attention to the following:*
- The quality of the first pass in relation to the height, distance to the volleyball net, and the setting spot.
- The time-spatial behavior of the quick hitter.

INDIVIDUAL TACTICS OF THE HITTER

- The time-spatial behavior of the middle blocker.
- Take into consideration the individual tactical abilities of the setter and anticipate the setting action.

4. *After the set pay attention to the following:*
- The quality of the set in relation to the height, speed, and distance to the volleyball net and the attacking spot.
- The starting position of the directly opposite blocker and the prediction of his/her spatial behavior.
- The behavior of the middle blocker and the prediction of the blocking formation and the spatial behavior of the defensive athletes.

5. *Before the attack pay attention to the following:*
- The quality of the block in relation to the aggressiveness, arm-ball relationship, and timing and closing of the block.
- The quality of the setting action in relation to your own timing.
- The choice of the offence.

6. *After the attack pay attention to the following:*
- The effectiveness of your own individual tactical actions and successive actions.
- The prediction of the development of the game situation after the attack in relation to your own/opposition's possession of the volleyball.
- The immediate transition to blocking or to a second offensive action.
- The effects of the play on the attacker, his/her teammates, and the opposition.

7. *After the coverage and your team's possession of the volleyball pay attention to the following:*
- Generally, all of the same factors mentioned in points 3-5 also apply here again.

8. *After the defensive actions and the possession of the volleyball by the opposition pay attention to the following:*
- Your own blocking and defensive formations.
- Changes in positioning of your teammates, especially of the athletes at the volleyball net.
- As well as to all of the same factors mentioned in points 1-6 also apply to this situation in a transferred sense.

All of the observations and thoughts mentioned above apply to all athletes from the server to the defensive specialist with only some slight changes in the main focus depending on which athlete is at question. Generally, it must be stated that depending on the level and situation of the game/match, not all factors may occur.

The higher the individual tactical training of the athlete, then the more factors that s/he can observe, realise, analyse, and take into consideration in their own game.

At the **higher levels of volleyball** there is a large amount of factors already given to the athletes due to a close analysis and scouting report of the opponent ahead of the match. For the athletes this means that they only have to check during the match if there have been any changes that they must adjust to. The greatest ability of a good coach is to find out the most important points and factors in a match or even in a particular situation, which may decide the outcome of a game/match. The ability of a good athlete is to take this information into account with his/her own individual tactical actions.

"The higher the quantity and the quality of the computed factors, the higher degree of maturity that an athlete needs to have regarding himself/herself and his/her own individual tactical actions."

The importance of the **individual tactics** should not be underrated. For this reason, each practice must be designed in such a manner that each athlete is forced to make observations and decisions in each training drill. The only exception is a practice that focuses on technical skills training. These decisions are not only related to each athlete's own abilities but also on the technical, tactical, physical, and psychological abilities of his/her teammates and on the opponent.

Observations show that at the **low levels of volleyball** the individual tactical training is almost non-existent, at the **middle levels of volleyball** individual tactics are only discussed in practice, and at the **national levels of volleyball** the individual tactical training needs to be much more intensified. The level of the individual tactical abilities of many athletes is too low since you can only effectively use a skill in a match that has been previously practised.

4.6 Selected Training Drills for the Individual Tactics of the Setter, the Outside Hitter, the Diagonal Hitter, the Back-court Hitter, and the Quick Hitter

4.6.1 Preliminary Thoughts

The concept of this training is step by step putting the main emphasis on the following points:
- Training the athlete's peripheral view.
- The setting depending on the quality of the first pass.
- The setting depending on the quality of the first pass and the willingness of the attacker.
- The setting and attack against a single block.
- The setting and attack depending on the opposition's blockers.
- The setting and attack depending on the action of the middle blocker.
- The setting and attack depending on the block and defensive formations.

The individual tactical actions of the setter and the attacker are not only dependent on the quantity of the captured/scouted points, but also on the ability to recognise and select them and to draw the correct conclusions. By doing this it will help the setter to include the most important influences and factors in a particular game/match in his/her setting decision-making process.

For the planning and organisation of a practice session it is important to know the number of jumping actions per hour in a match situation. For example, the setter jumps approximately 85 times, the middle blocker/quick hitter jumps approximately 80 times, and the outside/diagonal hitter jumps approximately 75 times. By knowing this information, a two-three hour practice must include, along with the main goal of the component, at least two-three times the number of required jumps to get onto a competitive level. *With that said it is still important to maintain the typical sequence of the skills/techniques as they occur in a match: the setter performs a blocking action after every two or three jump sets, the middle blocker executes one or two quick attacks after every two or three blocks, and the diagonal hitter is switching between blocking and attack or performs two blocks and then two attacks.*

This makes the structure of the game clearer and the roles of the athletes must be the same during practice as it would be in a match situation. The training drills concerning the server and the service reception athletes discussed in chapter 3.4 are still true in these and the following training drills.

The following training drills aim at generally improving the peripheral view of the athletes and are especially designed for athletes at the low and middle levels of volleyball.

A: Two-person (Pairs) Drills
1. Back row athlete A and front row athlete B are passing the volleyball. After the volleyball leaves the hands/arms of the athlete, athlete A changes his/her position. Later only athlete B changes his/her position.
2. Same as 1 but both athletes are moving.
3. Athlete A (later athlete B) shows his/her partner after the set a signal of what type of pass (i.e. overhand or forearm) to be played.
4. Same as 3 but both athletes show signals of what type of pass is to be played.
5. Same as 3 but one athlete is also changing his/her position in addition to the signals that are shown.
6. Same as 5 but both athletes show signals and change their positions.
7. The athletes now signal numbers to determine what type of pass is to be used – first athlete A, then athlete B, and finally both athletes A and B.
8. Athlete B attacks or sets the volleyball depending on the position of the baseline athlete (in a setting or a defensive position).
9. Both athletes with a volleyball: Shadow game (overhand or forearm passes) – the second athlete imitates the actions of the first athlete.
10. Imitate the actions of your partner: Athlete A is performing an additional movement after s/he releases the volleyball. Athlete B must copy this movement after s/he double-plays the volleyball.
11. Set with a change of direction around/over/below obstacles.

B: Three-person Drills
1. Line formation: Athlete A is setting the volleyball back and forth with athlete C over athlete B. Athlete B changes his/her position and sets the next pass (Fig. 129a).

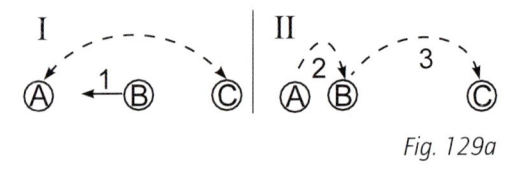

Fig. 129a

2. Triangle game: One of the three athletes is sitting down before the next volleyball is played and must not be passed the volleyball.

3. Triangle game with the same drills that were discussed in points A1-A10 above.
4. Triangle game with two athletes (Fig. 129b). The volleyball will always be played against each athlete's own running direction. In this drill, mostly the backwards-overhand pass should be used.

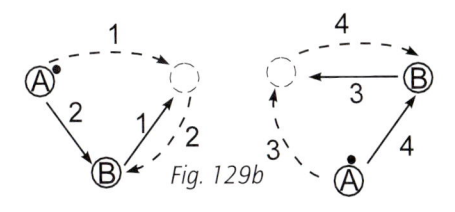

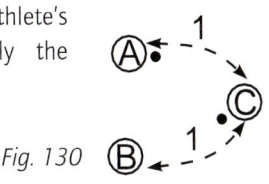

Fig. 129b

Fig. 130

C: Drills with More than One Volleyball

1. Playing in pairs with two volleyballs: At first without a change of direction, but later with a change of direction to the side.
2. A group of three athletes with two volleyballs: At the beginning without a change of direction, then with a change of direction, and then with an increased angle, and culminating in a change of direction or with the introduction of signals to determine what type of pass should be used (Fig. 130).
3. Triangle game with starting with two volleyballs and then adding a third volleyball (Fig. 131a).
4. Triangle game with three volleyballs: All athletes set the volleyball vertically up into the air and if one decides to continue to pass the volleyball the other athletes must follow. At first, the playing direction is given – later it is free (Fig. 131b).

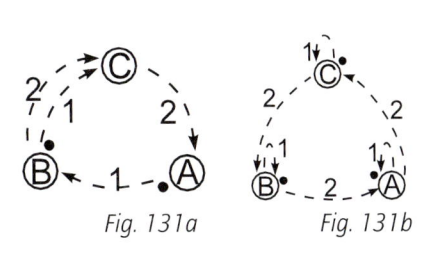

Fig. 131a   *Fig. 131b*

5. Quadrangular game with four athletes:
   a) A group of four athletes playing with two volleyballs (parallel changes of passing direction) (Fig. 131c). The pair of athletes A and B and the other pair of athletes C and D are each playing the volleyballs using overhand and forearm passes. It is important that both pairs of athletes are synchronised in their actions because each time that they release the volleyball they must change their positions (athlete A with athlete C, and athlete B with athlete D).

b) A group of four athletes playing with two volleyballs (diagonal changes of passing direction) (Fig. 131d). The volleyballs are set around the outside and after each release the athletes change their positions diagonally through the inside of the "four-sided" formation that they are in.

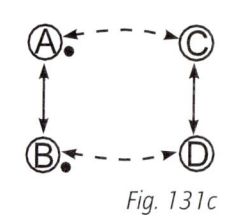

Fig. 131c

c) A group of eight athletes with two volleyballs (Fig. 131e). The volleyballs are set around the outside of the four-sided formation that the athletes are in and the athletes are performing changes in their positions inside of the formation with their diagonally opposite teammate.

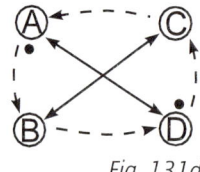

Fig. 131d

d) A group of two athletes with one volleyball (Fig. 131f). The volleyball is set around the outside of a four-sided formation. This means after each release there must be a diagonal change of position. Athlete A is always changing from the upper left side to the lower right side and athlete B from the lower left to the upper right side. It is the only way to play the volleyball around a four-sided formation with only two athletes performing the drill.

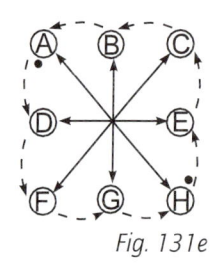

Fig. 131e

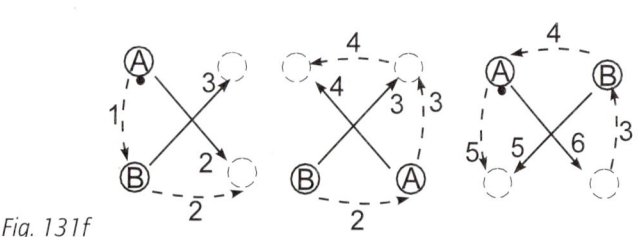

Fig. 131f

- To improve the coordinative abilities, especially the footwork of the setter, all training drills that involve coordinative runs, one or two-legged coordination jumps with different changes of direction, and with or without the use of obstacles are useful. To improve technical skills training drills that include the use of more than one volleyball are extremely helpful.

4.6.2. Sequence of Training to Improve upon Individual and Group/Team Tactics

1. **Game 3 vs. 3!**
   [On a 9 x 6 meter volleyball court]
   The setter is always in setting position II/III. The other two front-court athletes are receiving the serve and attack from the outside positions (beginning with jump sets, roll shots, and hits aimed at a specific target). The hitters are verbally commentating on the quality of the sets (i.e. higher, too tight, good, etc.).

   Variations to Drill 1:
   a) The setter is receiving good first passes and tries to perfectly set the volleyball to the attacker in front of him/her.
   b) The setter is only executing backsets.
   c) The setter is receiving good first passes and only performs medium-high sets.
   d) The setter is intentionally receiving first passes of different levels of quality. With a perfect and/or good pass the setter should set the volleyball medium-high and with a poor pass the setter should set a high volleyball to the outside.
   e) The hitters can switch their positions after each attack and it is the job of the setter to find the same attacker three–five times in a row.
   f) One of the attackers is intentionally taking him/herself out of play (i.e. sits down, turns around, etc.) and cannot be used as an offensive option. This forces the setter to use the other attacker to execute the play.
   g) The hitters request a particular set by calling it out loud and then prepare for this set. It is the job of the setter, depending on the first pass and his/her own abilities, to perform a perfect set.
   h) The same as in g) but without the players verbally communicating to the setter.
   i) The two hitters must prepare themselves for one of three different types of sets to the outside position (medium-quick, medium-high, and high).
   j) The non-service reception athlete is positioning him/herself for a 1 meter set in position III.

2. **Game 3 vs. 3!**
   [On a 9 x 6 meter volleyball court]
   The hitters are in positions III/IV and the setter is in position II. With this training drill the main focus is the long sets to outside position IV, as well as 1 meter sets in front of and behind the setter with the hitter in position III. Since it is pretty much the same as Drill 1 above, all of the variables mentioned then can be used with only minor adjustments.

3. **Same Points as Drills 1 and 2!**
   The only change is that the setter must now jump set.

4. **Game 4 vs. 4!**
   [On a 9 x 6 meter volleyball court]
   The same training points can be used as in drills 2 and 3, but a back-court hitter is added (position I). The setter must jump set from this point on after every good first pass.

   Setter:
   - If the setting is inaccurate, then it will have to be practiced separately!

   Attacker:
   - Only ask for sets that the setter is able to execute depending on the quality of the first pass!

5. **Game 5 vs. 5!**
   [On a 9 x 6 meter volleyball court]
   The setter is always penetrating and the hitter in position III is always performing a quick attack. The hitter starts at the volleyball net and then moves back to make room for his/her attack after the opposition's offensive action. The quick hitter always tries to be on time so as to be there for a quick attack (A-quick/short ball). At the volleyball net when the opposition is receiving the volleyball, the quick hitter is playing the role of the middle blocker and moves as early as possible, depending on the set, to the left or to the right or simply stays at that position. It is the job of the setter to now use one of the hitters who is away from the middle blocker. All variations of Drill 1 may be used.

   Attacker:
   - If the hitter's attacking spot is occupied by the setter then the hitter needs to make a quick decision closely related to the match situation at hand of whether to go for an attack in front of the setter or behind the setter!

   Quick Hitter:
   - No matter how poor the passing may be, always try to be there for a quick attack!

SELECTED TRAINING DRILLS   149

- If the service reception is poor or far off the net then choose your attacking spot to be not too close to the setter but with the correct timing to remain credible for the opponent. Otherwise, try to perform a fake quick attack (a short ball set 1 meter above the height of the volleyball net)!
- Play serves that are hit directly at you by using an overhand pass!
- Be prepared to pass serves that touch the volleyball net!

6. **Game 3 vs. 3 with One Setter for Both Teams!**
   [On a 9 x 9 meter volleyball court (Fig. 132)]
   The serves are hit in the service reception area of the back row athlete in position VI. The setter is focusing on using one of the outside hitters as long as the pass permits him/her to do so. The blockers on the outside are strictly covering the cross-court/diagonal hit or the line hit. The athlete who does not have to block moves back from the volleyball net to play defence. The server, depending on the game/match situation, defends and starts his/her block in position VI. The setter covers the hitter first and then moves across to the other side of the volleyball net to set for the other team. Since the setter is covering close to the hitter the other two athletes (the service reception athlete and the other hitter) are covering deep and away from the hitter before they must move into their defensive positions.

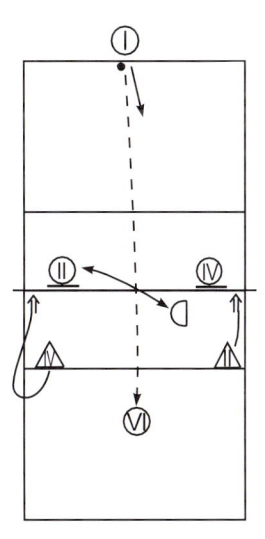

   Fig. 132

   After ten serves the serve changes and the athletes rotate.

Attacker:
- Hit in the zone that is not covered by the block and commentate to the setter on the quality of the sets.

Variations to Drill 6:
a) The outside hitter in position IV (later position II) is moving into and becoming a part of the service reception formation.

Outside Hitter:
- **Note** – The service reception is the first priority in this drill – not the offence!
- Try to pass all high incoming serves using an overhand pass!
- **As a combination hitter, be prepared to pass serves that touch the volleyball net!**

Setter:
- Pay attention to the service receiving outside hitter!
- Always keep an eye on the volleyball!

a) All three athletes are receiving the serve! The serve is hit the same as it would be in a match!

b) Only the front-court athletes are receiving the serve. The hitter in position II is attacking in the middle zone and the athlete in position VI is preparing for a back row attack in position I.

c) The same as in point c) but the athlete in position II is hitting outside and the athlete in position IV is hitting in the middle.

7. **Game 4 vs. 4!**
   [On a 9 x 9 meter volleyball court]
   The same as Drill 1, but with a setter and a middle blocker on the serving side of the volleyball court. Before each set, the middle blocker is in his/her normal starting blocking position and then s/he

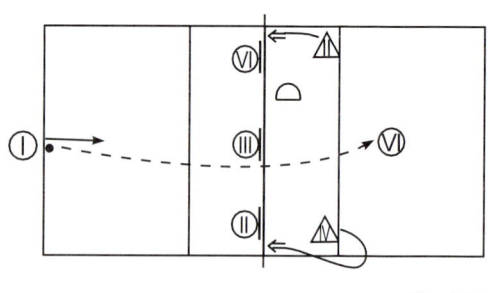

Fig. 133

tries to get into position to form a double-block in the outside position that the set is going to (Fig. 133).

Outside Hitter:
- Watch to see if the middle blocker is able to close the block!
- Hit the cross-court/diagonal shot if the middle blocker is late in closing the block!
- Hit at the "seam" (where the hands of the two blockers meet) of the block or just through it if it is open!
- Try to use the top or the outside of the block if it is perfectly positioned!
- If the set is too tight and the block is perfectly positioned try to hit the volleyball straight into the block in such a manner that the rebounding

volleyball does not go straight down but rather comes off of the block high enough to give you or your covering teammates an opportunity to play the volleyball and attempt another attack!
- Hit past the block if it is closing on just one side!
- Always hit over the weaker of the two blockers!

Setter:
- Watch the middle blocker and use the hitter who is furthest away from him/her. In other words, use the hitter where the middle blocker must travel a greater distance to form and close a double block!
- If the pass is perfect, then set a medium-quick volleyball to the outside position. This does not allow enough time for the middle blocker to form and close a double block!

Variations to Drill 7:
a) The same as the variations that were mentioned in drill 6 a) to d) except that it is now 4 vs. 4!
b) Practice drill 7 and variation a) as mentioned above, but the middle blocker is no longer forced to jump before each set. Play as if it was a true game/match situation.

Setter:
- Watch the middle blocker, keep jump setting, and use the best offensive option depending on the game/match situation!
- Remember that a medium-quick jump set makes it really difficult for the middle blocker to get to the outside position in time to close a double block!

Outside Hitter:
- Watch the middle blocker before you jump to predict if you have to deal with a single or a double block!
- Watch after your take-off if the block is shutting down the line or the cross-court/diagonal zone!
- Vary your hitting timing: Hit quickly if the blockers are not immediately penetrating with their hands and delay your hit if the blockers are penetrating early!
- Use the outside of the block on a passive blocking athlete!

Observational Help!
See if the outside hitter needs to work separately on his/her turning spike or a hit using his/her wrist to be able to effectively use those shots in the correct game/match situation!

8. Power Volleyball – Game 4 vs. 4 with Two Front-court and Two Back-court Athletes!

[On a 9 x 9 meter volleyball court (Fig. 134)]

There must be three touches before the volleyball crosses the volleyball net. The coach and/or the assistant coach are alternatively tossing free balls onto each side of the volleyball court. The setter is in position II and is always setting medium-high or high sets to the outside hitter in position IV. The defending team forms a double-block ahead of time and the defence is in positions V and I. An attack tip/dump is not allowed! Every error counts and the team that reaches six points first score one "big" point. After every "big" point all the athletes rotate except for the setter.

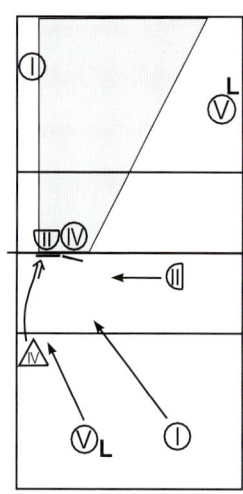

Fig. 134

Athletes:
- If your team is attacking then all of the athletes, excluding the hitter, are covering the offensive action either close or deep in the volleyball court.

Outside Hitter:
- After blocking, move quickly to your starting position for an outside attack in position IV!
- After the attack, move quickly to position II to form a double-block!

Libero:
- Always cover the hitters at a close distance!
- Remember that you have the main responsibility for your own team's offensive coverage!

Variations to Drill 8:
a) The same points as described in drill 8 but this time the set is coming from position IV and the attack from position II.
b) The same as point a) but the attack is now coming from the back row in positions I and then V.
c) Drill 8 with all of the variations mentioned above but there is no fixed setter. Everyone rotates and the hitters can also set.

Outside/Back-court Hitters:
- Always be prepared for a poor set and try to make up for it without committing any errors!

d) Drill 8 with the same variations that have already been mentioned but a game of 5 vs. 5 with two front-court and three back-court athletes!

Outside/Back-court Hitters:
- Always keep the opponent's blocking and defensive formations in mind when you are about to attack and use an attack tip/dump if necessary!

9. **Power Volleyball – Game 4 vs. 4 with one setter for both teams!**
   [On a 9 x 9 meter volleyball court]
   The execution is the same as that described for drill 8 but the difference is that the setter is now allowed to use two outside hitters. This will make it more difficult for the teams to set up and use a double-block!

Observational Help!
The coach designs the rules of the game in such a manner as to prevent his front-court athletes from being overpowering. They must not cross their physical limits!

Variations to Drill 9:
a) The offence is run from position IV and position I: Outside and back-court hitter.
b) The offence is run from position II and position V: Offside and back-court hitter.
c) After determining which attacking zones can be used all of the athletes are allowed to attack.

10. **Power Volleyball – Game 6 vs. 6 with One Setter for Both Teams!**
    [On a 9 x 9 meter volleyball court]
    The execution can be organised in the same manner as in drill 8 and its variants (with only one hitter) and then later in the same manner as in drill 9 and all of its variants (with two hitters).

Attacker:
- The attack tip/dump can be used!

Athletes:
- Know ahead of time who is setting after any defensive actions because the setter is playing for both teams and might not be there in time to set in some circumstances!

Variations to Drill 10:
- The same drill but with a fixed setter in position II and also that the setter can tip/dump the volleyball now.

Setter:
- Jump and, instead of setting the volleyball, attack the volleyball! Also, fake the attack and then set the volleyball!

- Watch the opposition's block and defensive formations after your setting action to see how and when a setter's tip/dump can be effectively used!
- Watch the actions of your opposite blocker while you are setting!

Observational Help!
- The setter's tip/dump must be separately practised because if the technical skills are not developed enough it will not be able to be used successfully in a match/game situation.
- Does the setter use the forearm pass often to set? Does the setter need to practise overhand setting from a falling position?
- Are the offensive actions of the setter too obvious? Does the setter get blocked often? Does the setter need to work on disguising his/her sets?
- Does the setter need to be separately trained so s/he can learn to "feel" and see the opponent's blockers, in particular the blocker that is covering him/her?

Coach:
- Choose drills that can be done with or without a block. Use mats as targets on the volleyball court to practice the setter's tips/dumps.
- Vary the position from where you toss the volleyballs to the setter (i.e. positions V/VI/I)!
- Have the setter work against a single block. The setter must fake a tip/dump and then set the volleyball. Later, the setter must tip/dump the volleyball past or over the blocker to the mats and if there is no blocker the setter must aggressively power tip/dump the volleyball to the target.

Observational Help!
- If the athletes are specialists, then they should switch to their specialised positions!
- After a "big" point, one, two, or three athletes can be rotated to avoid them overtaxing themselves.

11. The Power Volleyball Games Mentioned Above in Relation to the Level of the Team and the Goals of the Training Session!
a) The volleyball is always tossed to the team that made the error!
b) The volleyball is always tossed to the team that scored the point!
c) The volleyball is always tossed differently and hard to create different defensive situations for the athletes to cope with!

SELECTED TRAINING DRILLS   155

12. **The Power Volleyball Games Mentioned Above in Relation to the Level of the Team and the Goals of the Training Session!**

The volleyball is served just as it would be in a match/game situation. In other words, the server is using all of his/her individual serving skills and tactics (Fig. 135).

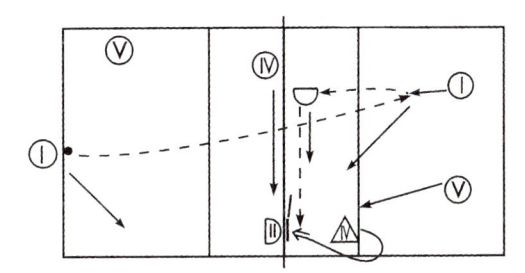

Fig. 135

The following small court games create difficult situations for the setter and the hitter and their main focus is the training of the specialised hitter. These games can be easily involved in the sequences of training that have been mentioned previously.

13. **Game 3 vs. 3 with One Back-court Service Reception Athlete, and the Setter and the Diagonal Hitter are Playing in the Front-court!**
    [On a 4.5 x 9 meter volleyball court]

Outside/Back-court Hitter:
- Remember that you must attack against a well-positioned double block and that only half of the volleyball court is available!
- Remember that you can use the top or the outside of the block or that you can tip/dump the volleyball!
- Make sure that you disguise your attack tip/dump with a good fake attack hitting motion!

Service Reception Athlete:
- Cover along with the setter the hitter at a close distance.

Variations to Drill 13:
a) The diagonal hitter is a back-court athlete who also hits back row.
b) The same drill mentioned above and its variations but the setter is allowed to tip/dump the volleyball.

Setter:
- Try to keep the opponent's blocker that is covering you with you as long as possible!
- Make the sets quicker so that it becomes more difficult for the opponent to set up a double block!

c) The setter is in the back row and the front-court athletes are receiving the serve. The athlete who is not receiving the serve is always attempting to hit a 1 meter ball against a double block.

d) The same as before but both of the service reception athletes are attacking. The one who is receiving the serve is attempting to hit an outside set.

e) The same as before but now the same service reception athlete, independent of the service reception, is always attempting to hit a 1 meter ball.

f) The setter and the service reception athlete are in the front-court and the back row athlete is also a back-court hitter. All three of them can attack the volleyball.

14. **Game 3 vs. 3 with the Setter Penetrating, a Quick Hitter, and a Front-court Service Reception Athlete!**
    [On a 4.5 x 9 meter volleyball court]
    The setter is using both hitters in combinations. The quick hitter is going for an A-quick in front of the setter and later behind the setter. By the end, they are free to use whichever quick attack they choose.

Setter:
- If there is no block set up and there is a good pass, always use the quick hitter!
- Always use the second hitter at a distance from the quick hitter to make it more difficult for the opposition to set up a double block.
- If the blocker is often/always jumping with the quick hitter, then use one of the special offensive combination plays (i.e. shadow or cross step or behind the setter).
- Always check and evaluate the efficiency of your actions.

Quick Hitter:
- Provide the setter with feedback regarding the sets and ask for information about your particular time-spatial orientation!
- No matter what kind of pass is made, perform a quick attack!
- Immediately following your blocking actions, release from the volleyball net to prepare yourself for a quick attack in time!

SELECTED TRAINING DRILLS   157

Second Hitter:
- After your attack inform the setter about the blocking actions of the opponent.
- Provide the setter with some hints about the opponent's blocking action before the set was made.

Coach:
- Does there need to be any special training regarding the teamwork and communication/understanding between the setter and the quick hitter?
- Is the quick hitter only able to hit power-line? Does the hitter need to learn to hit using just their wrist action?
- Is it possible for the quick hitter to get past the block with an aggressive tip/dump?
- An aggressive tip/dump is extremely effective against the approaching direction!
- Watch to see if the libero is organising the coverage of the offence and if s/he is always covering at a close distance!

Variations to Drill 14:
a) The same drill as above but the quick hitter is only allowed to attack B-quicks!

Setter:
- If the outside blocker is covering his/her own opposite quick hitter, then use your second hitter on this blocker's original blocking position with a medium-quick set.
- If the middle blocker is covering the quick hitter, then use the second hitter with a 1 meter ball set between the setter and the quick hitter (this combination is called a "Moscow") or use him/her with a 1 meter ball set behind the setter!
- Judge your setting actions by their tactical and true effectiveness! In other words, if your second hitter must attack against a double block or your quick hitter must deal with a full jumping single block then your tactical effectiveness is very poor! On the other hand, if your combination hitter is able to attack against a single block then your tactical effectiveness is very good. A perfect set would be if your hitter has no block to go up against at all.

b) The same thing as before but the quick hitter is used with an A-quick (in front of or behind the setter) or a B-quick.

c) The same drill with the quick hitter being his/her own combination hitter:

1. A stopper, with or without a change of direction, in combination with an A-quick in front of the setter or behind the setter.
2. A flyer jumped towards or away from the setter (i.e. a combination starting from a B-quick but ending with an A-quick right at the setter or starting with an A-quick and resulting in a B-quick or faking an A-quick behind the setter and "flying" to a short set 1 meter away from and in front of the setter).

Coach:
- Do the "flyers" need to be particularly trained because the teamwork between the setter and the quick hitter is not perfect?
- Remember that "flyers" are only effective with athletes that have great jumping ability!
- Stoppers and one-legged actions do not require as much great jumping ability!
- "Flyers" and stoppers are only useful if the actions that they are supposed to fake have been used successfully more than once before.
- The quick hitter and combination hitters need to be reminded that any serves that touch the volleyball net and come into the front zone are their responsibility!

15. Game 3 vs. 3 with the Setter and the Quick Hitter as Front-court Athletes and the Back-court Athlete as a Back-court Service Reception/Hitter (3-4 Wave)!
    [On a 4.5 x 9 meter volleyball court]
    The setter tries to keep the opponent's blockers with him/her as long as possible to give the quick hitter the opportunity to attack against a single block.

Setter:
- If the blocker is often jumping with the setting action, then use an A-quick behind the setter and/or one-legged attacks!
- Start with B-quicks to separate the blockers!
- Increase the distance that the blockers must cover to set up a double block by using the back-court hitter as far away from the quick hitter as possible.
- Use "flyers", stoppers, and one-legged attacks more often.

16. Game 4 vs. 4!
    [On a 4.5 x 9 meter volleyball court]
    The same points as in drill 14 but with all of the variations described in drill 15. The only change is that a fourth back row service reception athlete is added.

Coverage Athlete:
- As a back row service reception athlete without any offensive functions or as a libero you are always responsible for the close distance coverage.
- Remember that with certain offensive combinations you are the only coverage athlete and that this means that you must move up to the ten-foot line immediately after the service reception so as to be in a position to cover at a close distance.

17. Power Volleyball – Game 4 vs. 4!
[On a 9 x 9 meter volleyball court]
The setter is penetrating from the back row, one of the three front-court athletes is a quick hitter, one of the front-court athletes is a second hitter without any service reception duties, and the other front-court athlete is a service reception athlete and attacker of the 3-4 wave sets. The organisation and the execution is the same as mentioned in power volleyball games in drills 8 and 11. Of course, there is one main difference. This time all of the front-court net positions remain occupied. The course of action/offensive combinations of drills 13–16 should be more intensely used here.

Variations to Drill 17:
a) The setter is in the front row and is using combinations with the quick hitter and the second hitter. The back-court athlete is receiving the serve and gets the safety set out of a 3-4 wave attack.
b) *Game 5 vs. 5.*
   The setter is penetrating from the back row and is setting combinations to the quick hitter and the two outside hitters. One of the combination hitters is running his/her offence out of the service reception formation. The service reception athlete in the back-court is attacking a safety set (see the discussion regarding offensive combinations in chapter 4.1).
c) The same as in point b) but the setter is now in the front-court. The back-court hitter who is not receiving the serve is involved in the combinations with sets of the 2-3 waves.

18. Power Volleyball – Game 6 vs. 6!
[On a 9 x 9 meter volleyball court]
The same as drill 17 with all of its variations.

Variations to Drill 18:
a) The setter is penetrating and setting combinations with four hitters:
1. Two quick hitters, a second hitter as a front-court athlete, and the back-court hitter with 3-4 wave sets.

2. Two quick hitters, a back-court athlete as a second hitter, and a front row athlete as an outside hitter for 3-4 wave sets.
a) The is playing in the front row and is using combinations with two quick hitters, a back-court hitter as a second hitter, and a back-court hitter as an attacker of 3-4 wave sets.

4.6.3 Drills for Training Offensive Tactics

The following drills can be involved in the sequence of training that was described earlier depending on the level of the team and the main goals of the training session. The main target of these drills is to deal with known strengths and weaknesses of certain opponent's athletes and strengths and weaknesses of the opponent's blocking and defensive formations. It is important to train how to take advantage of certain deficiencies of future opponents.

A. Game 4 vs. 4 – Later 6 vs. 6!
   [On a 9 x 9 meter volleyball court]
   The organisation of this training drill is just like power volleyball with serves and two tossed volleyballs. All the net positions are occupied. In the opponent's front row line-up there is a small and weak blocker who:
   - After the serve, is at a predetermined volleyball net position.
   - Later is serve receiving first and then performing any other duties.
   - Finally, s/he is faking different blocking positions and waiting until shortly before the setter's touch before s/he is switching into his/her true blocking position.

Setter:
- Watch where the weakest blocker is going to and then set the volleyball to the hitter opposite him on your team.

Attacker:
- Hit over or "use" the opponent's weakest blocker!

Setter/Attacker:
- If the setter is not able to see the switching of the opposition's weakest blocker because s/he is faking and/or switching very late, then the second hitter, in the attacking zone of the opposition's weakest blocker, will call and receive the set. Another possibility is that the service reception athlete is generally informing the setter regarding the whereabouts of the opposition's weakest blocker.

Setter:
- Try to always use the hitter who is opposite the opposition's weakest blocker, even out of a defensive situation.
- Know any changes by the opposition thanks to preliminary information discovered from an analysis and study of a scouting report on them. Run your offensive combination in a manner that the strongest second hitter is attacking against the opposition's weakest blocker.

Attacker:
- If the opponent's middle blocker is trying to back up their weakest blocker by reaching over him/her and covering his/her zone, then hit the volleyball hard and diagonally!

B. Game 6 vs. 6 – Played like Power Volleyball with Serves and Two Tossed Volleyballs!
[On a 9 x 9 meter volleyball court]
The setter is in the front row! The team receiving the serve is playing according to their match system. The defending team is playing for a short time (5-10 minutes) using different blocking and defensive formations (see Chapter 5):
- Without any coverage at a close distance behind your own team's block (see Figs. 143a-143g).
- With coverage of the area behind the block by the athlete who is not blocking (see Figs. 144a-144b).
- With coverage of the area behind the block by the direct back-court athlete (see Figs. 145a-145c).
- With double-coverage of the area close behind the block by the non-blocking net athlete and the direct back-court athlete (see Figs. 148a-148b).

Setter/Attacker:
- Know each of the opposition's block and defensive formations and use the setter's tip/dump in the opposition's uncovered zones.

Variations to B:
a) The defending team is varying its defensive system in shorter time frames.
b) The defending team is adjusting its actions according to the situation.

Attacker:
- Look for changes in the opposition's blocking and defensive formations before and after each attack!

Setter/Attacker:
- Support the attacker by calling directions concerning the weaknesses of the opposition's defence (i.e. cut, line, deep, etc.)!

C. Practice and Exhibition/Friendly Games/Matches!
It is important to systematically analyse the setting and offensive actions of the athletes in each preparation game/match. It is especially important to see and check the effectiveness of the offensive combinations and offensive covering formations that are being used. Furthermore, a close examination and observation of the individual tactical strategies by the specialists helps to optimise the following training process.

D. Competitive Games/Matches!
The measurements mentioned above are necessary to control the offensive strategy in relation to the individual, group, and team tactical strategies. Among other things, a comparison of practice and exhibition/friendly games/matches with competitive games/matches will allow the coach to draw conclusions about the psychological constitution and stability of the athletes. In the end, this is only a check to see if the training is creating enough situations of physical and psychological pressure and stress to prepare the athletes for the actual game/match situation (see Chapter 8 – "Specific Principles for the Training of the Sport of Volleyball").

4.6.4. Special Training Drills for the Setter and the Attacker

The following selected practice drills are supposed to train the ability to adjust to new situations (i.e. the transition from service reception to offence, etc.). Another important factor is to include the volleyball in the training when working on the quickness/speed of each attacking specialist. By doing this you train typical chains of actions that occur in a game/match situation, which should not take longer than six to ten seconds (see Chapter 8). Depending on the chain of action, one to three repetitions seems to be appropriate. After that, the athlete is stacking volleyballs and is taking over a supporting role for the other athletes. The phase of an active rest should not be shorter than two minutes. It is also important to put these training drills at the beginning of practice when the athletes are rested and after a very good warm-up. If the athletes show signs of fatigue, the training drills must be stopped. They can also be used as

SELECTED TRAINING DRILLS

interruptions in-between practice drills. A perfect time to use these training drills would be during the special preparation period during the pre-season and during the special competition period.

It is also important to pay attention to the fact that the overhand service reception is not neglected.

Service Receiving Second or Outside Hitter:
- Attack three times against the double block after serve receiving.
- Attack against a double block after receiving the serve, then perform a blocking action, then release from the volleyball net and attack again.
- Perform a blocking action, defend the volleyball at a close coverage distance, then attack a 1 meter ball by the setter or on the outside.
- After receiving the serve attack against a double block, perform a blocking action, release from the volleyball net to a defensive position, and again attack against a double block.
- Perform a blocking action, release to your defensive position, attack, and then perform a blocking action again.
- Perform a blocking action in position IV, then a blocking action in position II, and then attack from position IV.
- After receiving the serve attack in position IV against a double block, then a blocking action in position III, then play defence against an offensive tip/dump in position II, and then attack again from position I/V.
- After receiving the serve attack against a double block and then perform two more attacks against a double block.

Combination/Second Hitter:
If the service reception/outside hitter is attacking as a combination hitter, then the following training drills must be used:
- All training drills mentioned above can also be used here. Attacks against a single block or a double block can be performed but not out of the service reception formation.
- Two attacks in a row from the same position with a change of direction before reaching the attacking zone.
- Two attacks in a row from different positions after faking another attacking zone.
- Two attacks in a row with long approaches to get into the attacking zone (positions IV-II/II-IV).

- Three attacks in a row of a 1 meter ball in the same position.
- Three attacks in a row in position IV with medium-quick sets.
- Three attacks in a row: medium-quick sets in position IV/1 meter ball set in position III and in position II.
- Three attacks in a row: medium-quick sets in position IV/two 1 meter balls set in position III with a change of direction before.
- One-legged attack in position II after a long approach and a second medium-quick set in position II.
- Two one-legged attacks in position II and in-between a 1 meter ball set in front of the setter in position III.

Diagonal/Main Hitter:
- Three attacks of the 3-4 wave in position IV against a triple block and a complete defensive formation.
- Two attacks against a triple block in position IV after a defensive action.
- Two attacks in position IV against a triple block each after a coverage action or an action in-between.
- All training drills mentioned above but in position II.
- All training drills regarding 1) the service reception/outside hitter and 2) the combination hitter can also be used here.

Back-court Hitter:
- Three attacks of the second wave in a row in positions VI or I.
- Two attacks of the second wave in a row in positions VI or I with a long approach against a single block.
- Three attacks of the third wave in a row in positions V or I against a double block.
- Two attacks of the third wave in a row in positions V or I after a long approach against a triple block and defence.
- One attack of the third wave in position V and then two attacks of the second wave in positions VI and I.
- Two attacks of the third or fourth waves in a row in positions V or I after a defensive action.
- Two attacks of the third or fourth waves in a row in positions V or I after a defensive action at a close distance to the volleyball net.
- Two attacks of the third or fourth waves in a row in different attacking positions after taking a spot in position VI close to the baseline as a starting position for the attacks.

Quick Hitter:
- Three A-quicks in a row against a single block.

- Three A-quicks in a row behind the setter against a single block.
- Three B-quicks in a row against a single block.
- Three "flyers" in a row against a single block.
- One quick attack in-between two blocking actions.
- Two blocking actions in a row and a quick attack.
- A quick attack and then two blocking actions.
- Two quick attacks after an offensive coverage at a close distance.
- Two stoppers in a row with/without a change of direction.
- Two quick attacks out of the defence of a free ball.
- Two quick attacks out of the service reception of a short serve.
- Three different quick attacks in a row.
- Two quick attacks with a blocking action in-between.
- A quick attack out of coverage and then a blocking action.

Setter:
- With all of the training drills for the offensive specialist mentioned above, the setter should either jump-set, set out of a standing position, or set out of a falling position but s/he should always do an additional action before each set.
- Depending on the training drill, the setter should be purposely made to set like s/he is receiving a perfect, a good, or a bad first pass.
- The setter penetrating from the back row should also be included in these training drills. This means that the setter must move quickly before setting.
- As a front-court athlete, the setter should perform some blocking actions in-between each set.
- In a non-practice drill, the setter is allowed to neglect the covering of the hitters.

The following training drills aim at the training of the ability of the setter to adjust to new situations and to improve the quickness of the setter:
- Block/set/cover.
- Set/play defence/set.
- Set/cover/set.
- Set an A-quick/block/set a medium-high ball.
- Set or tip-dump/block/tip-dump.
- Set the volleyball three times medium-high to the outside and cover in-between the sets.
- The same as before but the set is dependent on the quality of the first pass (i.e. jump-set, falling, standing).
- Set a quick attack, then a back-court safety set, cover the hitter, and perform a blocking action.

- Three safety sets using the forearm pass and then cover the hitters.
- Three sets to the same position from different qualities of first passes.
- Three sets to different positions after receiving different qualities of first passes.
- Four setting actions in a row in the same position. Later to different positions and intentionally changing the distance of the sets to the volleyball net from tight to further off.
- Three different sets in a row. For example:
  a) An A-quick/1 meter ball/medium-high set.
  b) B-quick/A-quick behind the setter/high ball to position I.
  c) 1 meter in front of the setter/1 meter behind the setter/1 meter to back-court position VI.
  d) High back-court/high to position IV/high to position II using the forearm pass.
  e) Safety set from different positions to the same position. Later change attacking positions, etc.
- Three first passes right to the top of the volleyball net to train the setter's tip/dump or a one-handed set.
- Three first passes to the top of the volleyball net or over the volleyball net to train the setter's tip/dump or a single-block against an attack by the opponent.
- Three first passes from the opponent to the top of the volleyball net or over it to initiate an offensive, blocking, or a setting action.

All of the training drills for the offensive specialists or the setter mentioned above can be varied and should be adjusted to the level of the team and of the individual athletes (Photo 36).

Photo 36
(Steffen Marquardt)

5 Learning Part III:

Blocking and Defensive Formations and the Individual Tactics of the Blocking and Defensive Athlete!

Photo 37 (Martin)

5.1 Analysis of the Facts

The blocking and defensive portion of the game has developed and improved immensely over the last decade. In the beginning, this was a result of the extensive and systematic analysis of the opponent, which is a precondition for a successful defensive strategy, but the observation (scouting) of matches and athletes has also created strategies that have changed how the game is played. For example, the starting positions of the blocking and defensive athletes can be changed with each play and can be adjusted to fit your own team's strengths and weaknesses and/or adjusted to fit your opposition's strengths and weaknesses. With the addition of the new rules, techniques that are a part of the sport of beach volleyball, especially the overhand defensive techniques, have now become a major factor in the indoor sport of volleyball. This has led to the effect of the defensive coverage positions being pushed forward, closer to the volleyball net (see Chapter 1.1 – "The New Rules and their Effect on Practice and Matches").

This development can be seen at the international levels of volleyball, only in its initial stages of development in the national levels of volleyball, but not at any other levels of volleyball. At the low and middle levels of volleyball it still has to be seen if one defensive formation can be played for an entire season, not for just one game or match. Unfortunately, one can also see that at the high levels of volleyball there is only one defensive formation used/played most of the time. At least they use/play more than one blocking strategy.

A ***defensive formation/strategy*** can only effectively work if the following points are met:
- Adjustments to the different skills, abilities, and strengths of the opposition's offence.
- Omit long penetrating/approaching/switching runs in favor of shorter ones because this will result in more economical actions. This is primarily true for the entire match strategy/situations and its transitions, especially when it is in regards to returning to the starting defensive positions.
- Change your team's blocking and defensive strategy to make it more difficult for the opponent to read your defensive formation and system.
- Hide your own team's defensive weaknesses.

The ***goal*** of the defending team must be:
- To hold/win your team's serve and score a point through a block.
- Perfect teamwork by the blocking and defensive athletes. The volleyball must not be allowed to directly touch the court!
- Successful transition into a counter-attack out of the defensive situation and score a "mini-break".

Studies of ***men's international levels of volleyball*** regarding the frequency of ***defensive actions related to the type of block*** reveal:
- Approximately 7 % defence with the use of a triple block.
- Approximately 55 % defence with the use of a double block.
- Approximately 35 % defence with the use of a single block (see sections 1.1, 3.2.1, and 5.5.1).

Recent observations support the trend that thanks to the improved C1 situation, single-block situations are increasing and double-block situations are becoming more infrequent.

The **main blocking spot** is in the area of position II (approximately 40 %) followed by the areas of positions III and IV (approximately 30 % each). This is not surprising if we take into consideration that the back-court attack from position I has become much more important and prevalent at the international levels of volleyball.

> At this time, the rally-point scoring system and the use of the libero are causing a shift of the attacking spots and consequently the blocking spots in the outside positions, but it is to be expected that these changes will turn around again in the future and, therefore, by doing so get closer to the numbers mentioned above.

Furthermore, international tournaments have shown that the top three teams all have much better results as far as the effectiveness of their block is concerned than the other teams. This clearly stresses the importance of the block as the decisive factor in the sport of volleyball today. *The effectiveness of the defence is closely related to the effectiveness of the block, since the defensive areas that are not covered by the block are becoming much smaller, therefore, increasing the chances for a successful defence.*

5.2 Blocking and Defensive Formations

In the following paragraphs the contents of the Learning Objectives 3, 8, 10, and 13 from the first volume, "Book of Volleyball – Basic Training" is assumed to be known. In these objectives, the basic formations for a **defence without a block and with a single block and/or double block with position VI playing up or back** is developed. They are mainly relevant for the low levels of volleyball.

At the **high levels of volleyball** a defence with position VI moved back is almost exclusively played. There are two reasons as to why this formation is used:
- A very good service reception in C1 makes a high percentage of attacks against a single block or a poorly positioned double block possible.
- The use of the quick hitter and the setter's tip/dump makes it necessary to move the outside defenders in positions V and I up.

At the **middle levels of volleyball**, although incorrectly chosen and used, most teams play their defence with position VI back. Based on the fact that most attacks take place in the outside position IV and that the middle is rarely used, the decisive factor when choosing a defensive formation should be the quality of your own team's double block. With a well-positioned double block it only makes sense to use the defence with position VI playing up.

This is even truer for the women than for the men because less athletic and individual tactical preconditions need to be met when position VI is playing up. *The use of position VI moved back only makes sense if your own team's block is much weaker compared to the opposition's offence.*
A comparison of the two defensive formations shows that the abilities of the defensive athletes are the decisive measure in choosing a defensive formation. For example, with position VI playing up every athlete has only one duty to perform, either covering the block or playing defence, but with position VI playing back every athlete has the following double role in the defence:
- Blocker – To block and to cover his/her own block.
- Defender – To play defence and to cover the block from a distance.

While the defensive areas and the defensive roles of the athletes are clearly defined when position VI is playing up, it is quite different when position VI is playing back. The defensive areas are not as clearly defined and are overlapping and this requires a very good understanding and communication (teamwork) between the defenders. With position VI playing up, the defensive athletes are able to do their job without having to meet any more difficult technical and tactical conditions. With position VI playing back, the team is losing the close coverage behind the block. This means a larger defensive area that an athlete must be able to cover especially increased open areas to the front of the volleyball court (behind the block). As a result, this requires more athletic abilities and additional defensive techniques of an athlete and, therefore, means certain demands for the individual tactical actions of the athlete.

5.2.1 Course of Action of a Defence with Position VI Playing Back

5.2.1.1 Starting Position of the Defensive Athlete

The starting position of the defensive athletes in positions V and I is, at the high levels of volleyball (Fig. 136a), close to the ten-foot line (3 meter line). The athlete in position VI is on a spot approximately 6-7 meters away from the volleyball net. This positioning must be used; especially when the opponent's setter is in the front row and when the opponent's quick hitter(s) is (are) using aggressive tips/dumps and hits (attacks of the first wave).

BLOCKING AND DEFENSIVE FORMATIONS 171

If the opponent's setter is in the back row and the quick hitters are not using any short tips/dumps and hits, then the starting position of the athletes in positions V and I can be pushed back approximately one meter (Fig. 136b). This is also true in the situation when your own team's middle blocker is jumping with the opponent's quick hitter and the hits are expected to be hit into the middle of the volleyball court or deep into the volleyball court.

At the middle and low levels of volleyball, the athletes in positions V and I should choose the starting position for their defence at a spot approximately 6-7 meters off of the volleyball net because at these levels the setter's tips/dumps are rarely used. There are also match tactical strategies and reasons for choosing this position: First, the quality of the first pass is not good enough and because of the use of a 4-2 or a 2-2-2 match system the setter is always penetrating. As well, the quick hitters do not reach high enough to force another defensive formation (Fig. 136c).

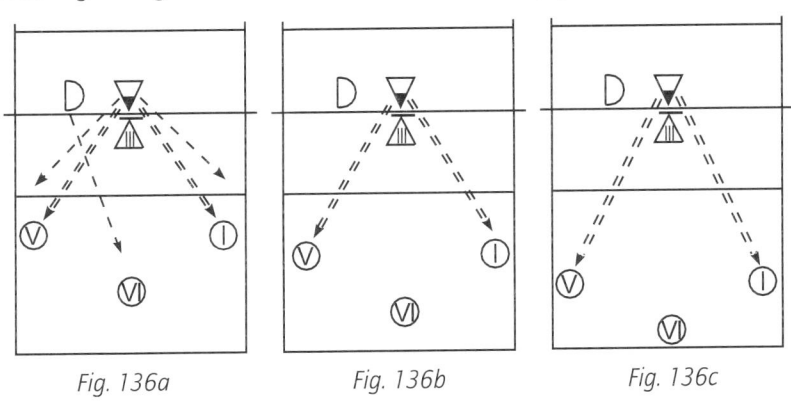

Fig. 136a   *Fig. 136b*   *Fig. 136c*

Observations of practices and matches show that coaches and athletes do not pay attention to returning to their own defensive starting positions when a rally develops and the opponent has the volleyball for a second opportunity to attack. This behavior might be explained by the fact that defenders do not expect tips/dumps or quick attacks to be performed out of a defensive situation. There is almost no opportunity to defend a short played or hit volleyball from a deep and distant defensive starting position because of the very short time of reaction and action (0.3-0.5 seconds). This is why in practice there should not only be paid close attention to the coverage of your own team's offence but also the transition from coverage to playing defence with a focus on getting into the correct defensive starting position. Practice drills that always force one team to play defence and to attack out of their defensive formations and positions are very good to develop and train these skills of getting back into position (see section 4.6.2).

The starting position of the blocking athletes is dependent upon the opponent's offensive tactics and on the individual abilities of the blockers. This will be discussed in more detail in the chapter regarding defensive strategies. At this point, a quick execution of the changes in positions (switching) is stressed with short running paths and different starting positions. These will be discussed in more detail shortly. If the opposition is attacking from all positions or if there is no analysis of the opposition (scouting report) available the blockers (at the middle and low levels of volleyball) should be lined up according to Fig. 137a. If the opposition is hardly attacking from position II and without any effect from position I it is recommended to use the line-ups (formations) shown in Fig. 137b and 137c. If the opposition is mainly using combinations in the middle and in position IV, then a starting position for the blockers so they can execute a block switch is reasonable (Fig. 137d). The last point is useful when the opposition's setter is in the front row and they perform many offensive combinations.

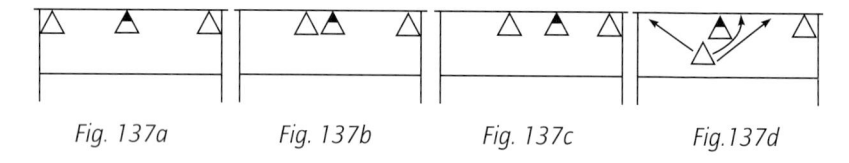

Fig. 137a   *Fig. 137b*   *Fig. 137c*   *Fig.137d*

5.2.1.2 Course of Action with a Single Block

The defensive starting formations in positions V and I are identical for the athletes and for the defensive areas (zones) that they must cover when there is a single block against an opponent's quick hitter. The athlete in position VI can choose the following positions depending on the hitting directions that have been observed by the opponent and also depending on the blocking direction of the middle blocker (Figs. 138a-138c):

- Position VI supports the defender in position V, and the middle blocker is blocking frontally (Fig. 138a).
- Position VI supports position I, and the middle blocker is blocking the half-diagonal direction (Fig. 138b).
- If the middle blocker jumps after the opponent's set and not with their quick hitter then the defender in position VI will move his/her starting and defending position a little closer to the volleyball net (Fig. 138c).

BLOCKING AND DEFENSIVE FORMATIONS 173

- If the defensive actions of the athletes in positions V and I are mainly focused on defending attacks of the first wave, then it might be an option for the athlete in position VI to concentrate on attacks of the second wave. In this case, the main hitting direction of the second hitter is decisive for the selection of the defensive position to cover. The defensive position is almost the same as shown in Figs. 138b and 138c.

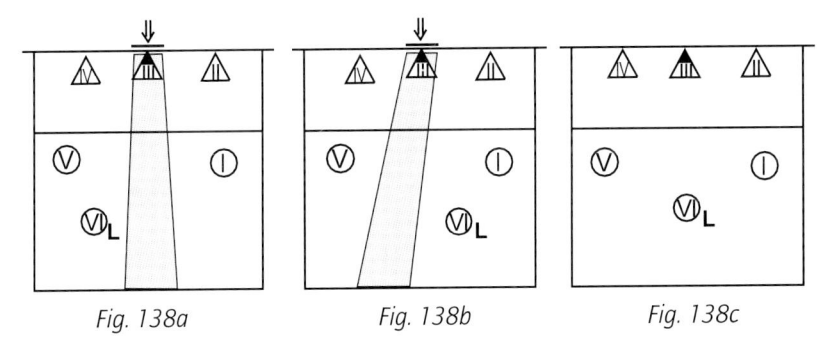

Fig. 138a   *Fig. 138b*   *Fig. 138c*

Based on the opposition's setting and the actions of the middle blocker then there are the following possibilities for the defence when there is a single-block against the outside hitter:
If the set to the outside is a medium-quick or a quick (faster then 0.7 seconds) set and leaves no opportunity for the middle blocker to get to the outside to form a double block (because it takes the middle blocker 0.8-0.9 seconds to cover a distance of three meters to get into position to do this), then the following blocking and defensive situations will be possible:

- The outside blocker covers the half-diagonal, which is the main hitting direction. The middle blocker is trying to set up a double block, which will leave him/her in neither a blocking nor a defensive role, and the non-blocking outside athlete should release from the volleyball net. The main responsibility of the defence lies in the

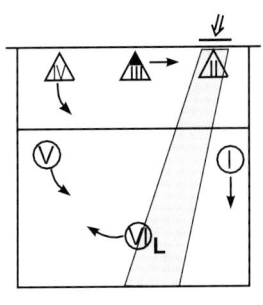

Fig. 139a

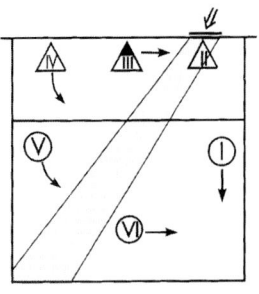

Fig. 139b

back-court athletes in positions I/V and VI. Position I is attempting to move his/her defensive area (zone) backwards before the hit, position V is attempting to move his/her defensive area (zone) inside and to the back, and position VI is attempting to move his/her defensive area (zone) out of the blocking shadow (Fig. 139a).

- If the outside blocker is covering the diagonal zone, then the athlete in position VI should be defending to the side of defensive position I (Fig. 139b).
- If there is only a single block on the outside because the middle blocker was jumping with the quick hitter and the set was a medium-quick set, then the defence and the net athlete in position IV are playing defence as shown in Figs. 140a-140b.

With a higher set, the defensive athletes gain time to move their defensive areas further back. In this case, the non-blocking net athlete also gets the opportunity to take over a role in the defensive formation.

These examples show the importance of communication amongst the athletes on the volleyball court: a) between blockers, b) between defensive athletes, and c) between blockers and defensive athletes.

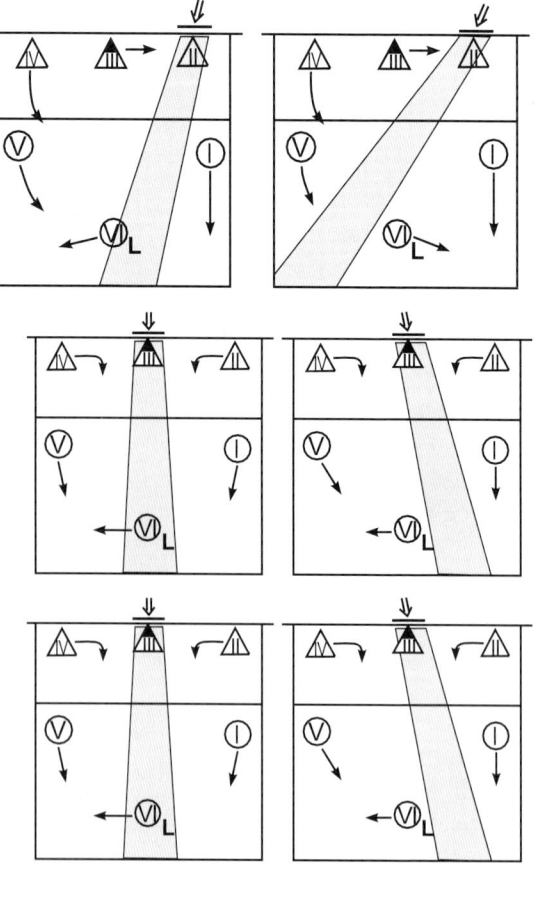

Figs. 141a-d

BLOCKING AND DEFENSIVE FORMATIONS 175

With a single block in the middle and a second wave attack, the following alternatives are possible:
- The middle blocker blocks alone.
- One of the outside blockers is blocking alone because the middle blocker jumped with the quick hitter (Figs. 141a-141d).

The movement of the defensive athlete from his/her starting position to his/her actual defensive position and from a ready position to a low defensive position must be finished before the attack. It is more useful and more effective to be ready and prepared and not in an ideal defensive position (zone) at the moment of an attack than to be caught in the middle of moving to an ideal defensive position (zone)!

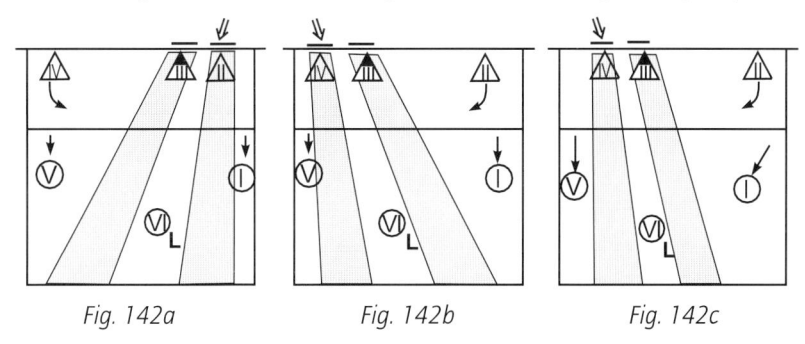

Fig. 142a   *Fig. 142b*   *Fig. 142c*

Figs. 142a-142c show an open double block that has been intentionally left open. This occurs when the middle blocker cannot close the double block because s/he was jumping with the quick hitter and/or because the set to the outside was too fast and low to enable him/her to set up and close the double block. The "open double block" is based on the following thoughts:

A closing of a double block by the middle blocker, without any immediate and active penetration, not

Photo 38 (Friese)

only makes the blocking shadow smaller but it also invites the opposition to hit off of the block and to use the block to their advantage. Another advantage of an open block is the fact that the defender can make a decision to cover a clear defensive area (zone) until the moment of the attack. The open block, respectively the intentionally not closed block, is in the end nothing else but the combination of two single blocks that form a unity relating to the communication of the blockers with each other and with the defender in position VI. This means nothing else but a group tactical strategy (photo 38). The defensive strategy is based on a very strong defensive athlete in position VI.

The formation of an open double block reiterates the principle that it is the purpose of the block to always cover the main hitting direction. This is done in favor of a better and more aggressive block and in favor of an earlier and better communication between the defensive athletes.

5.2.1.3 Two-Person Block Formation at the Outside Position

Two-person blocking formations occur thanks to a good blocking strategy, a very good middle blocking action, and/or a medium-high/high set by the opponent to the outside position. Blocking and defensive formations are able to:
- Play without covering the area close behind the block.
- Play with coverage of the area behind the block by the non-blocking net athlete (rarely seen at the women's high levels of volleyball).
- Play with close coverage by the direct back-court athlete.
- Play with a double coverage of the area behind the block (done mostly in the women's game).

The following paragraphs are directly related to Chapter 7, "Defensive and Offensive Strategies". For this reason, their use and meaning is only lightly touched upon here. In regards to the starting positions of the athletes, the same applies here as mentioned before with the single block. In the following Figures, the defensive spot (positioning) is shown that must be taken at the moment of the opponent's attack.

Figs. 143a-143g show defensive formations without a close coverage behind the block that are tactically and strategically sensible in a match when:

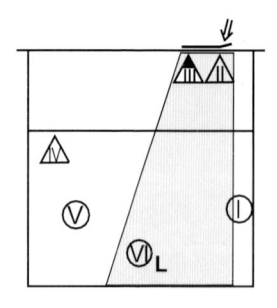

Fig. 143a

BLOCKING AND DEFENSIVE FORMATIONS   177

- The opposition, even with high sets, is not using many tips/dumps because they are offensively strong.
- The block is reaching very high, which would result in a high tip/dump by the opposition. This would allow the defenders enough time to run and cover the tip/dump (covering the block from a distance) and the blockers would also have enough time to cover it themselves (self-coverage).

The decision for this defensive formation implies that support for a defence with a fourth athlete is given priority. Fig. 143a shows a basic line-up with the athlete in position VI inside the block shadow. This is often used in the low and middle levels of volleyball. The difference in the high levels of volleyball is that the defenders in positions VI/I and V are pushed further back and it is for this reason that they are more oriented towards the volleyball net in their defensive movements. Very often this defensive formation is not very effective because the athletes do not have the abilities (tactical, technical, and athletic) to play it.

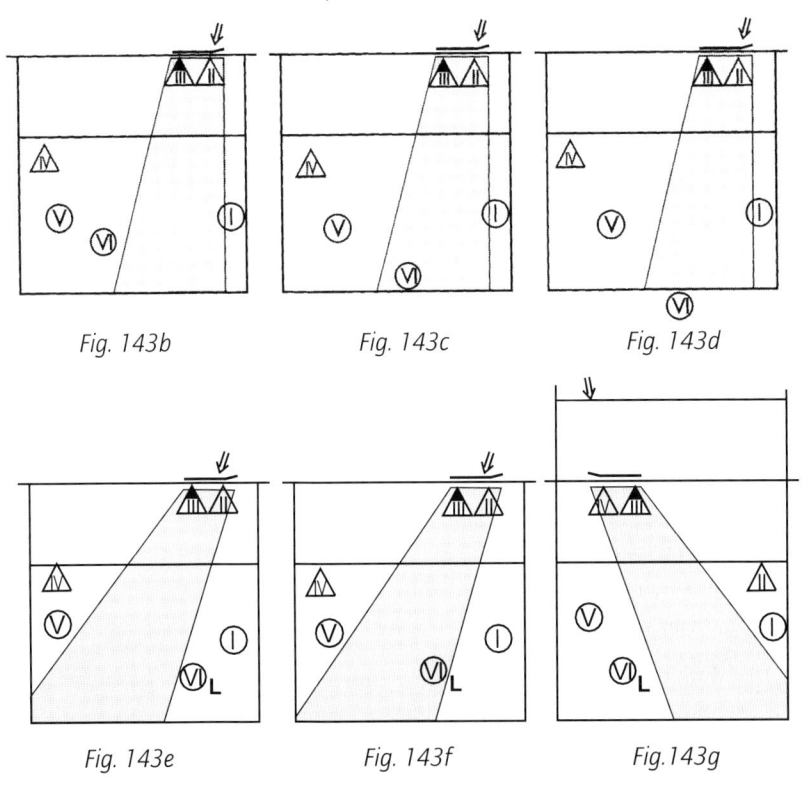

Fig. 143b   *Fig. 143c*   *Fig. 143d*

Fig. 143e   *Fig. 143f*   *Fig.143g*

178 LEARNING PART 3

Fig. 143b shows a stronger defence towards the half-diagonal direction, whereas Figs. 143c and 143d show two defensive line-ups against the hitting off of a block or the use of a block. If the block is covering the diagonal direction then the defender in position VI must move up in the frontal direction to back up the defender in position I (Figs. 143e and 143f).

These formations are recommended against attackers that mainly hit the volleyball in the diagonal direction, but especially against back-court hitters who, like in the men's top levels of volleyball, prefer to hit the volleyball in the diagonal direction as well (Fig. 143g). All of the photos can be used with their mirror images for the other outside positions. Regarding the non-blocking net athlete, it must be explicitly stated that s/he only has time to leave the front zone to play defence in the back zone when the set to the outside is one of a medium-high or higher set.

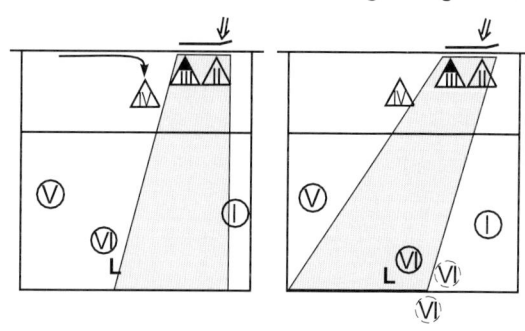

Figs. 144a/b

Figs. 144a-144b show defensive formations where the non-blocking net athlete is covering at a close distance behind the block (Photo 37).

If the main focus of the blocking strategy of a team is to form a triple block (if possible) then the final following blocker must cover closely behind the block in case s/he cannot make it time to set up a triple block. In the examples mentioned earlier, the net athlete in position IV should play like the following points state:

If the opposition is attacking over position III s/he must try to participate in a double block or, if possible, a triple block and with an attack over position IV s/he must set up a triple block. If the formation of a triple block is not possible s/he will have the main responsibility for the close coverage behind the block. Assuming that the opponent is not hitting in the extreme diagonal direction but instead using "turning spikes" and hits out of their wrist along the line and is using a very good offensive tip/dump then this formation will be a very good option for the defence.

A very important condition for the successful use of this defensive formation is the ability of the front-court coverage athlete to get to his/her attacking zone in position IV in time to be an offensive option after s/he has played defence in position II. If this is not the case, the team needs an effective back-court hitter to be able to finish the

BLOCKING AND DEFENSIVE FORMATIONS

counter-attack. These factors give an explanation as to why this formation is almost exclusively played by the men's top-level teams. The defence with close coverage by the non-blocking front-court athlete can be played in the same manner as the defensive formations without any close coverage (see Figs. 143a-143g). The only difference being that the defender in position V is not pushing as far back as before because s/he must also cover the defensive area of his/her covering front-court athlete. The defender in position I is pushed back as far as possible knowing that it is not his/her job to cover behind the block. The defender in position VI is playing a defensive position dependent on the analysis (scouting report) of the opponent and is arranged with the blockers. S/he is either defending in the diagonal direction (Fig. 143b), in the block shadow (Figs. 143a, 143c, and 143f), in the block shadow outside of the volleyball court (Fig. 143d), or in the frontal hitting direction as support for the defender in position I (Fig. 143e).

The photos and examples intentionally show only double block formations in position II to make a comparison of the different defensive situations easier. With a double-block formation in position IV, one only has to look at the mirror images of the photos to see the formations. Another variant is a close coverage behind the double block by the back-court athletes. This formation is very effective against attackers that mainly hit in the frontal or half-diagonal direction or against teams that do not hit very hard and whose attacks are relatively easy to defend. This last fact is a reason as to why this formation can very often be seen at the women's high levels of volleyball.

With all defensive formations with a close coverage behind the block it is to be expected that the opponent is effectively using offensive tips/dumps.

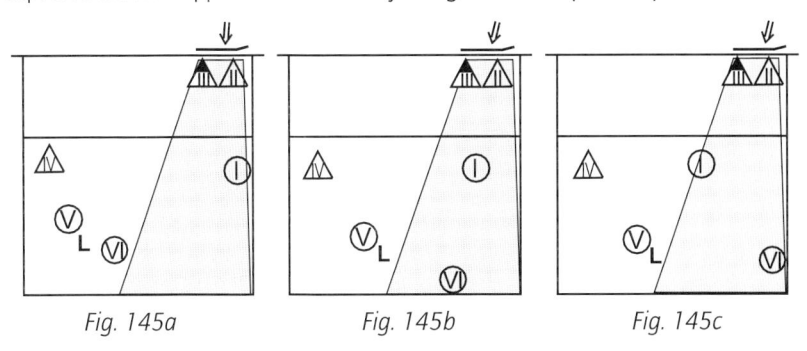

Fig. 145a   *Fig. 145b*   *Fig. 145c*

Fig. 145a shows a double-block against hits down the line and with three defenders strengthening the diagonal direction. Figs. 145b and 145c make it clear how the deep area (zone) of the block shadow can be defended against tactical hits and/or against hits off of the block. These formations are favored at the women's top levels of volleyball.

The formations in Figs. 146a-146b make sense to be used against hitters that prefer the diagonal direction as their main hitting direction and that rarely use effective tips/dumps or hit long line. They are also useful against hitters that hit off of the top of the block and try to use the block to their advantage. The defensive formation in Fig. 146c is played by women more often than by the men.

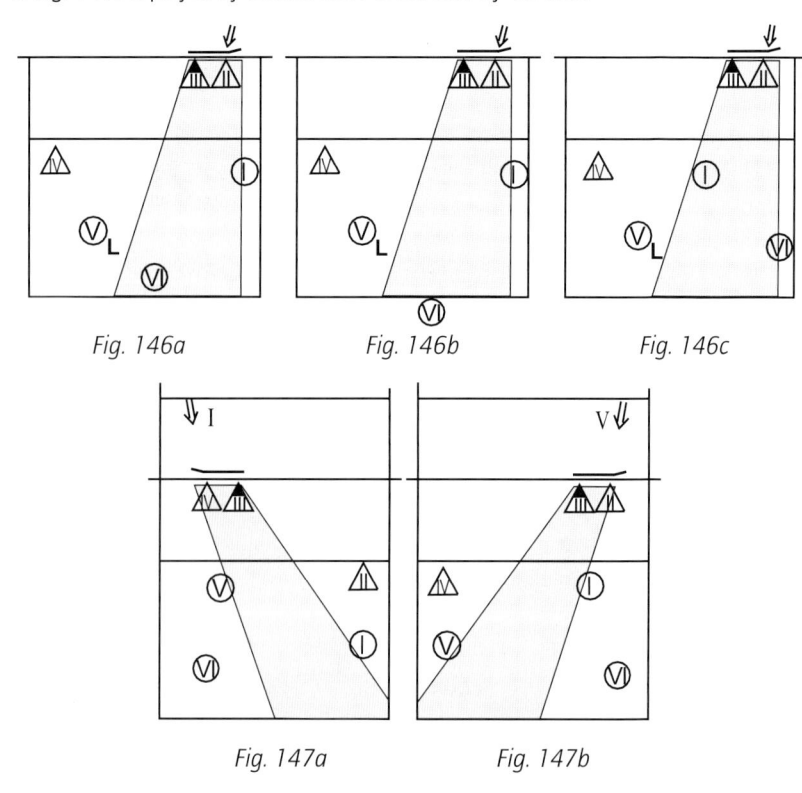

Fig. 146a   *Fig. 146b*   *Fig. 146c*

Fig. 147a   *Fig. 147b*

If the opponent is hitting hard and extremely diagonal and with back-court attacks then the formations in Figs. 147a-147b can be used.

Against attackers that know how to use a tip/dump effectively, the following formations with two athletes in close coverage are appropriate (Figs. 148a-148b). Women almost exclusively use this defensive formation.

Observations and analysis reveal that teams, including the national top level teams, only use double-block formations which they use independent of the opposition and the attacker over the entire season.

BLOCKING AND DEFENSIVE FORMATIONS

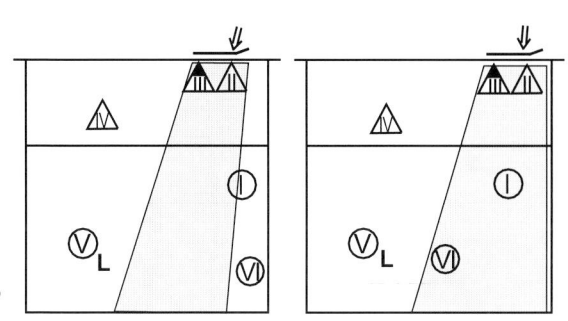

Figs. 148a/b

This procedure of choosing a defensive formation is not very reasonable. It shows the same problem that was pointed out earlier when it was discussed in regards to the choice of service reception formations. There are no strategic or tactical match reasons whatsoever to justify a procedure such as this. Of course, the choice of blocking and defensive formations must be based on your own athlete's/team's abilities, but it is just as important to take into consideration the abilities and potential weaknesses of the opponent's team in general or of certain attackers/athletes.

Consequently, this might lead to the situation that against all six of the opposition's rotations a different double-block and defensive strategy/tactic must be used (see Chapter 7, "Defensive and Offensive Strategies"). Sometimes against certain line-ups, depending on the hitting actions of the opponent, even more than one defensive strategy must be used.

In the following paragraphs, two double-block and defensive formations will be discussed that are based on finding and giving the correct answers to any newly occurring situations:

- The actions of the non-blocking net athlete (in this situation – position IV) will determine the defensive areas/zones of his/her teammates if the opponent's set is a medium-high/high set. If s/he decides to cover closely behind the block then this means that the defender in position V must move up and cover the area in position IV also. Position VI is moving out of the block shadow and supports the coverage of a diagonal direction hit and, by doing so, is supporting the athlete in position V. The defender in position I tries to push back as far as possible to cover the line since s/he is free of any close coverage duties behind the block (Fig. 149a and see Fig. 144a).

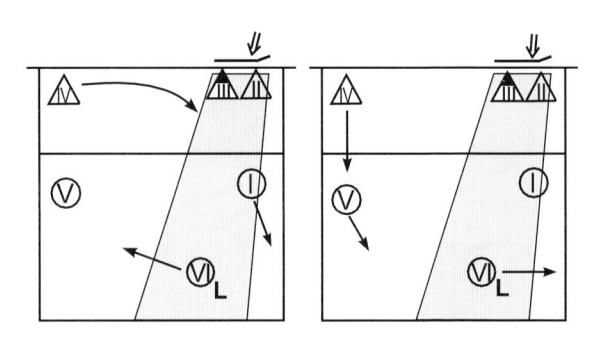

Figs. 149a/b

If the athlete in position IV takes the defensive position in the extreme diagonal hitting direction, then the athlete in position V will move further back to his/her original defensive area (zone) and the athlete in position VI will remain in the block shadow. The defender in position I is almost exclusively responsible for the distant coverage of the block and moves up slightly (Figs. 143a and 143c). If the defender in position I decides to cover closely behind the block, then the athlete in position VI must move over and cover the line (Fig. 149b and Figs. 145b-145c). With these actions, according to the situation at hand, the position of the double block and the block shadow must be watched. This is especially true for the athlete in position VI.

- The actions of the defender in position VI will determine the defensive areas (zones) of his/her teammates (i.e. block and defence with position VI playing in the middle of the volleyball court).
- Since position VI is in the middle of the volleyball court and covering closely behind the block, the non-blocking net athlete and athlete in position I must focus on the defence without any duties or worries regarding the close coverage of the block.
- Defenders in positions IV and I must, according to the situation, take a distant coverage role if the defensive coordinator in position VI decides to play in position VI back.
- The defensive coordinator in position VI, usually the libero, has at least four choices/alternatives for each double block or triple block:
- Close coverage behind the block (Fig. 150a).
- Play position VI pushed back (Fig. 150b).
- Support the line or the diagonal area (Fig. 150c and Photo 39).
- Remain in the block shadow but behind the end line (Fig. 150d).
- Note – For the teamwork of the defenders: If position VI is moving up, the

BLOCKING AND DEFENSIVE FORMATIONS 183

Photo 39 (Martin)

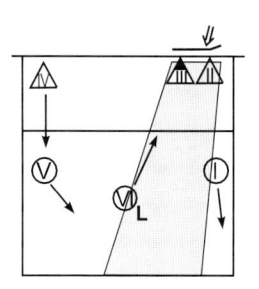

Fig. 150a

defenders in positions V and I should move back. If position VI is playing back and covers the diagonal or long line hits, then the defenders in positions V and I should move up.

- The formation with position VI playing in the middle of the volleyball court can only be effective if the defensive specialist in position VI knows his/her block, teammates, the opposition's setter, and the opposition's attackers very well and is able to predict each of their actions. S/he must also have the ability to quickly adjust to new situations.

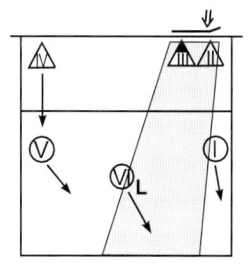

Fig. 150b

This is a perfect profile of the libero who only plays in the back-court.

With a single-block, position VI must decide if s/he is playing six-back and has decided to cover either the diagonal hitting direction or the line hit, or s/he must decide to cover the most endangered area (block shadow) behind the end line.

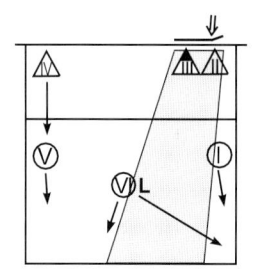

Fig. 150c

Finally, a conclusion can be drawn that a team that is using a defensive formation with position VI in the middle of the volleyball court is able to adjust to each offensive variant thanks to the formation's high flexibility. This major advantage over other defensive formations makes the position VI mid-court formation with the libero as the defensive specialist the defensive formation of the future.

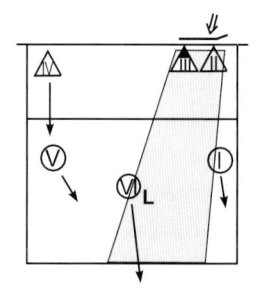

Fig. 150d

5.2.1.4 Defence with a Two-Person Blocking Formation in Position III

A double-block is rarely used against a quick hitter but is used against a combination hitter if s/he attacks in the middle position. The middle blocker is always involved:
- Because s/he did not jump with the quick hitter.
- Because the setting (set) allowed him/her to jump a second time.

Based on the assigned opposite net athletes shown in Figs. 137a-137d and on the fact that the setting is coming from position II or II/III, it can be said that the blocker in position IV is responsible for the formation of a double-block in the middle. On the one hand, s/he has the best opportunity to watch the setter and on the other hand s/he also has a shorter running distance to get to the middle as compared to the blocker in position II. For these reasons s/he will be the one forming the double-block in the middle with the middle blocker in the following situations.

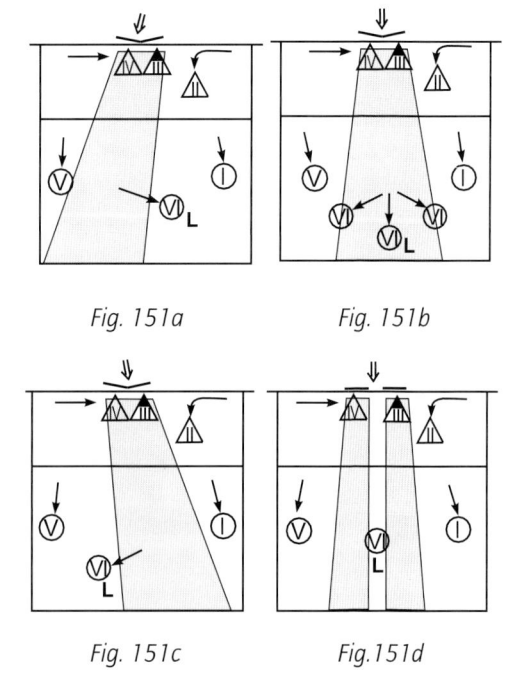

Fig. 151a

Fig. 151b

Fig. 151c

Fig. 151d

If we take into consideration that sets of the second wave or combination attacks usually take approximately 0.4-0.8 seconds it becomes quite clear how important the match tactical decision is for a practical starting position for the blockers and the defenders (Fig. 151). Generally, it should be the intention of the blocker in position II to participate in the blocking action in the middle. If s/he does not have enough time to manage this then it is his/her job to cover the block at a close distance. This forces the defenders in positions V and I to try and move back but they have to be in a low defensive position before the hitting action occurs to do this. The defender in position VI is playing his/her defence according to his/her arrangement with the blockers and depending on the block shadow shown in Figs. 151a-151d.

BLOCKING AND DEFENSIVE FORMATIONS

5.2.1.5 Defence with Three-Person Blocking Formations

It is the main goal of each offensive tactic and strategy to attack against no block or a single block but it is the opposite tactic and strategy for the block. Each blocking strategy is aimed at the formation of a triple block or at the very least a double block.

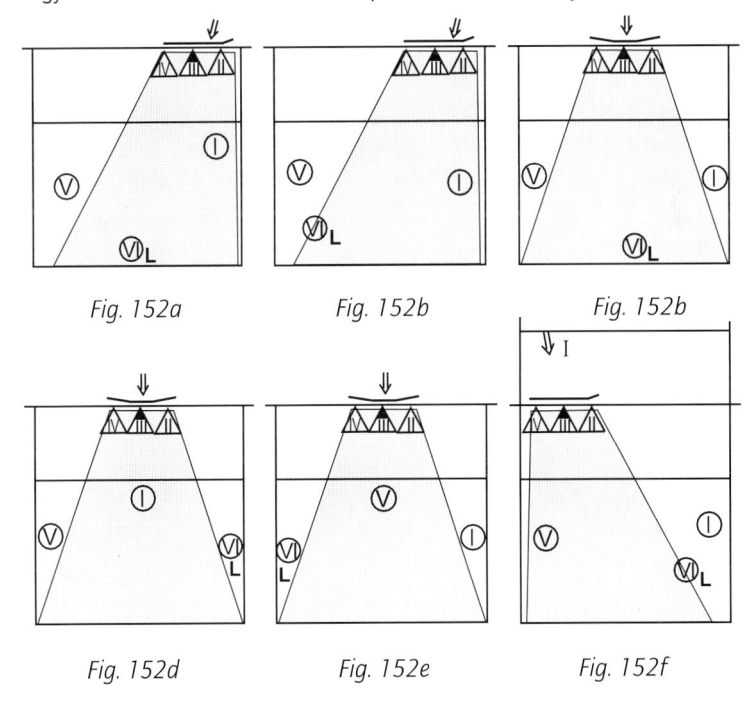

Fig. 152a *Fig. 152b* *Fig. 152b*

Fig. 152d *Fig. 152e* *Fig. 152f*

A triple block in position II only has a chance of getting formed if a safety set from the back-court to position II is played (and not set by the setter). The triple block in position IV can be used against the back-court hitter in position I after a high set. In position III a triple block can even be formed against attacks of the second wave thanks to the narrow starting positions of the blockers (photo 40). With a triple block after a high set, the three defenders have enough time to get into their perfect defensive positions. The following photos show selected defensive formations depending on the block shadow (Figs. 152a-152f).

Photo 40 (Friese)

5.2.1.6 Defensive Areas (Zones)

According to the high levels of volleyball different defensive areas (zones) will be shown and explained. It is assumed that an athlete is able to cover an area (zone) of approximately 3 meters even though the volleyballs are hit hard. By doing this s/he defends 1/3 of the area in front of him/herself and 2/3 of the area behind him/herself. The volleyball court is divided into four different areas (zones) (Figs. 153a-153b):

- The area behind the block (block shadow).
- The area in which the defender has no real chance of defending a volleyball because of the speed and power of the on-coming volleyball.
- The area in which most attacks occur and in which the defender has an approximately 40-50 % chance of defending the volleyball.
- The area which is at the greatest distance to the attacking spot and which offers the greatest chance of a successful defence because of the longer "air" time of the volleyball.

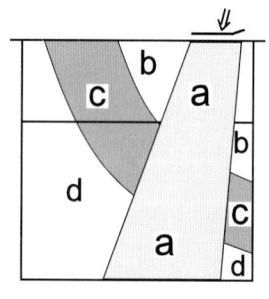

Fig. 153a
(Men) 5-8 m

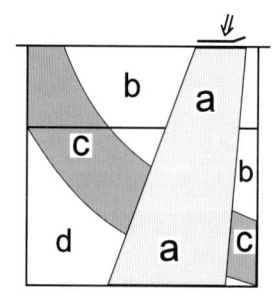

Fig. 153b
(Women) 6-9 m

The reach height and power of the attacker, in combination with the distance of the set to the volleyball net, are what mostly determines the defensive zones. It is for this reason that women move defensive area C farther back (Fig. 153b) than the men do (Fig. 153a).

- The better that the block covers the main hitting direction, the smaller the opportunity that the attacker has of hitting the volleyball in the area in which the defender has no chance of defending the volleyball (area B). This means that the blocker must always try to eliminate a hard hit attack to area B by the opponent.

BLOCKING AND DEFENSIVE FORMATIONS

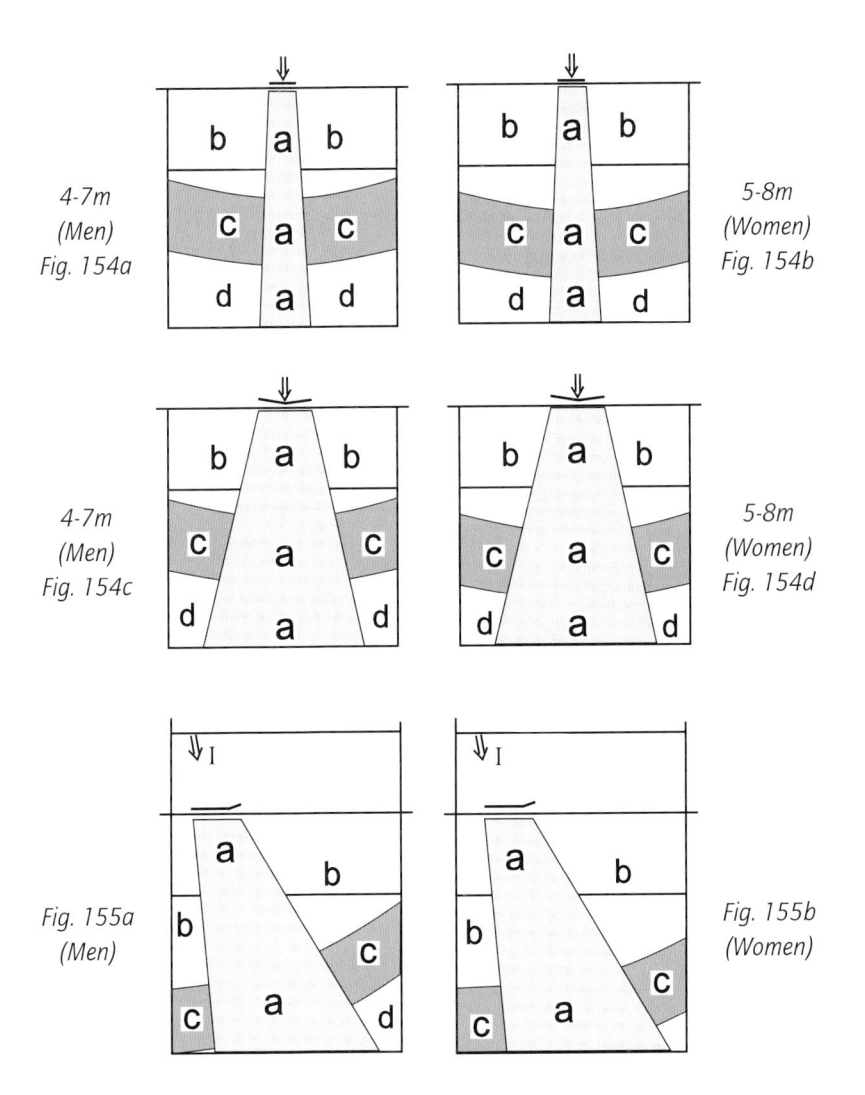

4-7m (Men) Fig. 154a

5-8m (Women) Fig. 154b

4-7m (Men) Fig. 154c

5-8m (Women) Fig. 154d

Fig. 155a (Men)

Fig. 155b (Women)

- With the defence against quick attacks (Figs. 154a-154b) the coverage of area B is easier than against second hitter attacks (Figs. 154c-154d) because the power and reach height of the quick hitter is not as strong. It is for this reason that the main defensive area is moved up.
- With back-court attacks of the third and fourth waves, area C will be moved back (Figs. 155a-155b).

The defensive zones depend on the levels of volleyball that the teams are at and they can be different from level to level. The lower the reach height of the attacker, then the more the main defensive zone moves back (area C). A defender is simply doing wrong if s/he tries to defend attacks out of this zone.

5.2.1.7 Changes of Positions (Switching) of the Front-court and Back-court Athletes

Regarding these changes of positions (switching) only your own team will be discussed. The most important criterion for the defensive tactic and strategy is what is the opposition's offensive tactic and strategy. The offensive tactic will only be shortly discussed at this time, but it will be covered in more detail in the chapter concerning offensive strategies.

The main principle regarding the ability to perform switches is an improvement in the block and the defence. This specifically means that all thoughts are focused on a successful first touch of the volleyball. Only if there are two or three equal defensive strategies, then the second touch of the volleyball (setting/offence) will decide the defensive tactic. If there are still equal alternatives, only then can the offensive advantages be involved in the decision-making process. This is based on the notion ***"Never do the second step before doing the first step!"***

The following points must be kept in mind with the changing of position (switching) of the blockers:

- The best blocker (quick in the outside positions, great reach height, very good ability to anticipate) is blocking in the middle to be able to participate in all blocking actions.
- The second best blocker, especially one who is good with blocks from a standing position, blocks in position II because the opposition's position IV is their main attacking zone.
- The weakest blocker switches to the outside position IV to have less blocking actions. This is especially true against back-court attacks from position I where s/he might be quite successful even if s/he has a low reach height.

These modified and very concentrated helpful hints do not lose their truth since there is the postulation that every blocker must be able to block in any position at the volleyball net. This is a clear tendency in the modern sport of volleyball. Simply the fact that not only the middle blocker, but also the outside blocker, must perform multiple blocking actions supports the demand for an all-around training of the blocker. For example, the outside blocker in position IV is responsible for setter's tips/dumps, the back-court attack is executed from position I, and a combination attack in the middle or an A-quick behind the setter and a 1-meter volleyball behind the setter are performed. The last two are especially true at the men's high levels of volleyball.

If the offensive actions out of C1 are not effective and lead to long rallies (such as what generally occurs at the women's low and middle levels of volleyball) the points mentioned above need to be qualified again. This also means that the second touch of the volleyball (setting/offence out of the defence) must gain more importance in the thoughts regarding the changes of position of the defenders. Therefore, it might be possible in the women's game that the setter, as the weakest blocker, can still play in position II:

- If the difference to the other blockers is not that great.
- If successful defensive actions are to be expected.
- Because as the setter she can organise the offence much better.

Thoughts/Points Regarding the Changes (Switching) of the Defenders

- For switching of the back-court athletes, the principle defence takes place and has complete priority before the setting action. This means that the strongest defender will cover the main defensive zone. If the main attacking spot is in position IV and the main hitting direction is the cross-court (diagonal), as it usually is at the men's low and middle levels of volleyball and even at the national women's level, the best defender (usually the libero) will cover defence in position V even if it means that the setter must go there.
- The worst defender switches into position I because there are the least defensive actions to be carried out in that position. The second best defender is in position VI. If the defensive formation with "six-up" is being played then the worst defender will perform the close coverage of the block and the second best defender will switch into position I.

At the men's high levels of volleyball, where the game is quick and a lot of combinations are played, there are often single-block situations that occur. The following switches are appropriate under these circumstances:

- The most experienced defender who has the best ability to anticipate and the best ability to adjust to new situations (usually the libero), will defend in position VI-back. The course of action for the blocking and defensive actions shows how big of a radius that his/her action is and how many different jobs that s/he must do and how many different situations s/he must solve. S/he

is the one defender who must always differentiate between the most possible actions, in contrast to the defenders in positions V and I who do not have as many decisions to make. Many coaches think that the middle blockers/quick hitters are the best qualified for the job because they must deal with many similar issues when they are playing in the front court.
- The technically strongest athlete must be placed in position V because s/he must defend the most difficult and hardest hit volleyballs.
- The defence in position I should be played by the quickest athlete. This means that the athlete in this position must be able to quickly cover longer running distances and areas (i.e. the setter or the back-court hitter).
- Switching in the back row might also have the goal to compensate a weakness in the front row (i.e. the strongest defender is placed behind the weakest blocker).

Studies have shown that most coaches, even at the high national levels of volleyball, only use the increased serving zone to give the server the shortest distance to get back into his/her defensive position or to make switching for the back-court athletes easier. This is strategically incorrect because by doing this it gives more importance to the defence rather than to the serve and this means that the second action is given priority over the first.

More thoughts and discussion regarding this can be found in chapter 7, "Defensive and Offensive Strategies".

5.3 Offence out of the Defence

An important criterion for the definition of the transition from defence to offence is the share and effectiveness of the volleyball-related actions:
- The defence has a share of approximately 11 % of the number of actions, which is the lowest amount compared to all of the other elements of volleyball.
- For approximately 13 % of the defensive actions the setter has to run to the volleyball and can only use one of his/her hitters.
- Someone other than the setter must set approximately 25 % of the defended volleyballs and they will end up being a safety set.
- Approximately 32 % of the defensive passes are passed perfectly to the setter's spot which enables the setter to use all of his/her hitters.

OFFENCE OUT OF THE DEFENCE

- Approximately 16 % of the setting actions are safety sets.
- Approximately 40-50 % of the defensive actions in the men's game and 30-40 % in the women's game are not successful at all. As well, approximately 25-30 % of the actions out of the defence do not score.
- Approximately 15 % of the volleyball-related actions cannot be played anymore.

These statistics are taken from the men's Bundesliga. At the international levels of volleyball, the percentage of the positive defensive actions increases by approximately 5 % thanks to a better service and a better communication between the blockers and the defence. At the women's high levels of volleyball, the positive actions increase by approximately 10 %. Some reasons for this are that most of the hits are not as hard, they use less combination hitters, and they can set a double-block more often.

The importance of a counter-attack is proven by the statistics. At the men's international levels of volleyball approximately 30 % of the mini-breaks and at the women's international levels of volleyball approximately 40 % of the mini-breaks are scored out of the defence.

From these statistics the following points can be concluded:

- Every athlete, but especially the libero, must be able to set. S/he must be able to perform a safety set, which means s/he must be able to set a high ball right on target to one of the hitters from each spot in the back-court. A safety set must always improve the quality of the first pass to initiate an effective counter-attack.
- The setter, like the libero, must also be able to play a safety set right on target using the forearm pass. This is necessary when they must run to play a poor first pass.
- The teamwork between defenders and blockers must be the focus of each practice because the communication between all of the athletes is a major precondition for a successful transition from defence to offence.

Basically, one can distinguish between an offence out of a front-court set, a back-court set, a safety set, and the first pass.

At the middle levels of volleyball most of the offence out of the defence should be set by a front-court athlete to omit one of the most frequent and crucial errors – the setter penetrating from the back-court moves too close to the volleyball net or that s/he is leaving his/her defensive zone too early. Another important point is that the training of the defence with transition to offence should be as intensely practiced as the training of the service reception with its transition to offence.

Regarding the course of action of the setting out of the defence, there are three typical basic situations that are distinguished:
- The situation in which the setter is not defending.
- The situation in which the setter is defending and playing the first pass.
- Free ball situations.

In regards to a):
- It is assumed that the setter is focusing on his/her defensive actions first and foremost, regardless if s/he is also blocking or playing defence. The setter should only be preparing and concentrating on his/her setting action (releasing from the volleyball net or leaving his/her defensive zone) when it is clear that s/he does not have to block or defend the volleyball. Remember the principle: Defence First then Setting!
- For the blockers/attackers remember the principle: Defence Before Setting/Offensive Action!
- For the defenders/backcourt attackers remember the principle: Defence Before a Safety Set and Before an Attack!

For the defenders, taking into consideration the quality of the opposition's attack and their own abilities, the following course of action applies:
- Try to keep the volleyballs that are very difficult to defend in play to give your teammates an opportunity to carry on with the play (save the volleyball)!
- Defend the volleyballs that are difficult to get, high into the middle of the volleyball court to make a safety set possible!
- Play volleyballs that are not as difficult to defend, if possible, with an overhand pass high to the ten-foot line close to the setting spot. This will enable the setter to jump set!
- Use the overhand pass with volleyballs that are easy to defend and play them high to the setting spot to give the setter the opportunity to jump set and use more than two hitters, or to attack the first pass himself!

These steps and their transitions are flowing and individually different for each athlete. If the defender is neither underrating nor overrating his/her abilities in a defensive situation s/he will do the individually and tactically correct option. Especially in difficult defensive situations, a communication between the setter and his/her teammates ahead of time is absolutely necessary to make a successful transition to the offence possible.

A further main factor for a successful transition from defence to offence is the ability to switch from a blocking action to a hitting action. This ability to adjust requires a very good time-spatial coordination between the attackers and between the attackers and the setter.

A major issue here is the action of the quick hitter who, depending on the first pass, is supposed to always be a potential offensive threat to the opposition (see section 4.5.1 regarding the quick hitter). Another major factor is the coverage of the offence. The only difference for the coverage out of the service reception as compared to coverage out of the defence is that from the defence there are many more attacks of the third and fourth waves, which allows the attacking team to use more coverage athletes.

In regards to b):
The same points mentioned before regarding the defender will apply to the defending setter if the team is using two setters or a setter and a supporting setter. If the team is only using one setter (5-1 match system) then there will be some changes in the middle and in some easy defensive situations. Generally, the following possibilities to set are used:

- Every athlete in position II is responsible for the set. This option is as well played at the middle levels of volleyball as it is at the high levels of volleyball. Internationally, very often it is not the best all-around athlete in the front row that switches to position II, but the strongest blocker. This again demonstrates the principle mentioned earlier that defence has priority over setting and offence.
- Every athlete that plays the middle blocker role in position III is also setting. This option is to be found at all levels of volleyball, including the international level. Even the non-all-around athlete is able to set a volleyball from a mid-range distance.
- It is always the same athlete who is responsible for the setting, independent of his/her position in the line-up. S/he is usually not positioned diagonally from the setter but usually next to the setter. S/he only takes over the portion of the setting that would generally be attributed to the role of the supporting setter during the time when the setter is performing some defensive duties. This last point is almost exclusively used at the men's international levels of volleyball.
- The libero must perform the safety set.

In all four situations, independent of the level of volleyball, very often the same error occurs. The supporting setter tries to execute spectacular sets (A-quicks, B-quicks, etc.) out of difficult setting situations. By doing so s/he is causing unforced errors. S/he has overrated his/her abilities thinking it would not be as difficult to complete such a complicated set because the teamwork with the quick hitter requires continuous training, which cannot be performed at any time. Therefore, it is important that the setter remains as the main organiser of the offence, even when s/he is defending the volleyball. S/he calls the where and how the volleyball is to be set and played. Without overrating his/her abilities and the abilities of his/her teammates, the setter as the organiser is able to initiate the offence after the first pass. S/he can pass the volleyball to the supporting setter or to any other attacker but this requires a systematic training of the athletes as all group and team tactical actions do.

In regards to c):
In free ball situations, mostly defensive situations where there is no block, the largest mistakes tend to be made. Following are some possible reasons for this:
- The defenders are using the overhand pass to play the volleyball but have not been setting for some time during the game/match. This might lead to an inaccurate length of the set and/or the volleyball might cross the volleyball net to the opponent's side of the volleyball court.
- Often, many athletes feel responsible for chasing down a free ball, resulting in a communication problem followed by an error.
- The offence out of a free ball situation is not practiced very often; therefore, it is not very structured in a game/match situation resulting in errors.
- Problems with passing the free ball also occur when, instead of using the overhand pass to play the volleyball, athletes prefer to use the less accurate forearm pass.

The following strategies and tactics help to minimise errors:
The offence out of a free ball situation should be the same as the offence out of a service reception situation. This means:
- Only the service reception athletes are responsible for playing the free balls.
- All other athletes must react according to their roles (i.e. setter/attackers). They should prepare for the offensive transition and get into their starting positions. They have nothing to do with the first pass unless it is a free ball that flies directly at the quick hitter and/or the combination hitter.

- The timing regarding when the athletes should go to their starting positions (i.e. the setter penetrating to the volleyball net, the blocker releasing from the volleyball net, the service reception athletes preparing to receive serve, etc.) is dependent on the game/match situation, but the latest it should occur is before the opponent touches the volleyball for the third time (contact). If all athletes react at the same time, then it is a sign of good judgment of the situation and very good communication skills between each of them. The setter making a call manages the communication at the low and middle levels of volleyball.

This possible solution can be associated at all levels of volleyball and is easy to practise. Regarding free balls at the high levels of volleyball, at least two special offensive combinations must be prepared for action according to the game/match situation.

If the setter is in the front row then the service reception athletes should allow him/her the opportunity to attack the first pass. Based on the opponent's situation, the tempo of the game/match must be increased until the hitting action (attack). This would prevent the opponent's athletes from having enough time to get into their defensive positions.

5.4 Individual Tactics of the Blocker

A comparison of the four jumping elements in the sport of volleyball and the frequency of these jumping actions shows that block jumps occur approximately 48 % of the time (thus occurring the most often), attack jumps occur approximately 35 % of the time, jump sets occur approximately 13 % of the time, and jump serves occur approximately 4 % of the time. If you compare these numbers from the international levels of volleyball to the numbers at the national levels of volleyball, you will see that there are approximately 2 % less jump sets and jump serves and approximately 1-2 % more blocking and offensive actions.

Relating this information to a one-hour game/match it means approximately 80 jumps per athlete. If we divide this information into the four jumping elements it translates into 39 blocking actions, 28 offensive actions, 10 jump sets, and 3 jump serves per athlete.

With the blocking element in the game/match it must be remembered that this action is also related to the number of athletes involved in the block during the game/match. The following differences at both the international and national levels of volleyball can be found:
- Double-block actions: 64-66 %.
- Single-block actions: 27-29 %.
- Triple-block actions: 7-10 %.

Judging by the number of blocking actions that occur, the middle blockers must be called the main blocking athletes. The setter, outside blocker, and diagonal athlete almost all have the same number of block jumps with approximately 12-14 %, thus jumping approximately half as much as what the middle blockers jump (23 %).

Detailed information regarding this profile can be found in section 4.5 – Individual Tactics of the Attacker. *Since the middle blocker usually has the role of also being the quick hitter and the outside blocker usually has the role of being the outside/diagonal hitter do the demands mentioned above and described in section 4.5 equally apply to the blockers?*

In the women's Bundesliga, studies regarding the distribution of the jumps reveals the following information:
- Blocking actions: approximately 53 %.
- Attacking actions: approximately 36 %.
- Jump sets: approximately 11 %.

If the blocking actions are further differentiated the results will show that 81.5 % of the jumps are for double blocks and 18.5 % of the jumps are for single blocks. It is evident that neither a triple block nor a jump serve is used in a game/match.
If we compare the jumping actions of the athletes, we will discover that the middle blocker/quick hitter jumps approximately 43.4 % of the time, the outside blocker/outside hitter jumps approximately 26.8 % of the time, and the setter jumps approximately 29.8 % of the time. The middle blocker has approximately 36 % attacking actions and approximately 64 % blocking actions, but she does not have any jump setting actions at all. The outside blocker has approximately 60 % attacking actions, approximately 40 % blocking actions, and approximately 0.5 % jump setting actions. The setter has approximately 14 % attacking actions, approximately 51 % blocking actions, and approximately 35 % jump setting actions (see section 5.1).

5.4.1 Individual Tactics of the Middle Blocker

At the middle levels of volleyball especially, the middle blocker can be called the "egoist" of the team because s/he neglects the formation of the double block in favor of his/her efforts to stop the directly opposite middle hitter. A check of the effectiveness of his/her blocking actions shows how often s/he is jumping in vain with the directly opposite middle hitter, who does not even receive the set. As a result s/he is not able to form a double block against the opposition's outside hitter and a single block on the outside cannot be called effective in comparison to a double block on the outside. *The middle blocker uses their "egoist" character as an excuse for jumping with the opposition's middle hitter and sacrificing the formation of the double block.* Especially at volleyball levels where the quick attack in the middle is not a "real" one (short set) the middle blocker should always be jumping after the set is made.

It is good to see the improvement and advancement of the skill of the middle blocker at the national levels of volleyball and that it is consistently improving and closing the gap to the international levels of volleyball.

A detailed analysis of the setter and of the opposition's offensive strategy is the reason for an improvement in the individual tactical game and strategies of the middle blocker. Another important factor for this development is the selection and usage of tall athletes with a great reach height as middle blockers. The effectiveness of the blockers, especially the middle blocker, is not judged by his/her personal effectiveness and success as much as it is judged by the effectiveness and success of the defence as a whole. This is because the middle blocker, as the organiser of the blocking strategy, also determines the defensive strategy. In general, an improvement of the defence is based on a good communication strategy between the blockers and the defenders (photo 41).

Photo 41 (Sabarz)

The middle blocker can provide his/her teammates the following information:
- If s/he will be jumping or not with the quick hitter when the first pass is good.
- If s/he does jump, which area will s/he be covering!
- If s/he jumps, to which side will s/he still try and go to set up a double block.
- If s/he does not jump, which area of the volleyball court is s/he going to cover.
- Whether or not s/he will perform an open double block or an open single block and whether or not the block will be passive or active.

This information makes it clear that the middle blocker must communicate with his/her teammates that are next to him/her or behind him/her. The communication is done with hand signals and/or verbal communication and feedback/confirmation is given, at the very least, by the use of eye contact (photo 42).

If the opposition's play is not different from what their expected offensive strategy is supposed to be, then it is absolutely necessary to stay with the pre-arranged defensive strategy. It should only be changed if the first pass is poor or the setting is inaccurate. If the set is too tight to the volleyball net then the volleyball must be blocked as opposed to covering a particular zone. If the set is far off the volleyball net then the diagonal (cross-court) direction must be blocked, not the line. The last point does not mean that if you are using this blocking strategy the middle blocker cannot adjust his/her position and strategy to the particular situation at hand.

Photo 42 (Köhler)

5.4.1.1 Course of Action

Generally, the middle hitter takes his/her starting position between the setter and the attacking spot. S/he is standing at the volleyball net, his/her knees are bent, and all of his/her bodyweight is on the balls of the feet so that the athlete can move quickly out of this ready position. An upright position means that time will be lost because the start of the movement will be delayed and the first step to the side will be shorter. An upright jumping position, with a stressed tension of the muscles, only makes sense if the middle blocker intends to jump twice. In other words, jump with the quick hitter and then jump with the second hitter. The first jump cannot be a full jump but a quicker landing gives him/her the opportunity to have enough time to move to the side. If the first pass is poor, s/he should immediately get into his/her "bent" starting position. The upper body should be upright and the arms should be almost completely extended to give enough time to block the quick hitter. Despite the tension of the situation, the athlete should be standing in his/her position relaxed and ready. The hands should be spread shoulder length apart and the elbows should be showing and pointing to the front. A wide spread of the hands and arms only makes sense if the athlete is able to aggressively penetrate when s/he is blocking (photo 43).

Photo 43 (Köhler)

There are two kinds of approach steps for the block. The first is a side or "gliding" step and the second is a cross-over or transition step with an adjustment step. Professional top-level athletes use both movements. There are also mixed versions of these techniques. For example, an athlete might always use the same leg for the lunging step. This means that s/he is using a cross-over step to the one side and a side step to the other. An athlete who is just learning to become a middle blocker must use speed as the main criterion to decide which foot to use. This means that s/he should compare the time that it takes to use both techniques to complete the blocking movement and use the quicker one. It is a definite advantage to learn and know both techniques and to use the appropriate one depending on the game/match situation. Both should be learned and practised at the junior levels of volleyball. If greater distances must be covered to get to a medium-high or high set, then an initial step can be added to the approach.

A jump with extended arms enables the blocker to move his/her hands and arms quickly over the volleyball net, and, by doing so, it allows them to immediately penetrate into the opponent's side of the volleyball court (photo 44). Generally, the extension of the arms must be completed, at the latest, with the jump and must never be done after the jump. This extension should be performed in front of and above the head to enable an immediate penetration (photo 45). Additional

Photo 44 (Sabarz)    *Photo 45 (Sabarz)*

hand and arm movements, especially to the side, will ultimately lead to the following blocking errors:
- The block is not a helpful orientation for the defenders anymore.
- The hands are no longer penetrating enough so the volleyball goes down between the hands and the volleyball net (Photo 46).
- A movement of the hand to the side brings one hand almost below the height of the top of the volleyball net (Photo 46).
- The blocker gets into trouble when s/he is landing.

As a result, the block must always be active, aggressive, and penetrating. A far penetration to the opposition's side of the volleyball court means that there will be a larger coverage area of the volleyball court.

Photo 46 (Steffen Marquardt)

The middle blocker should close tight to the outside blocker and time his/her approach in such a manner that s/he is jumping within an arm length away from the outside blocker and closing the block with an active penetration. It is incorrect when the middle blocker tries to close the block with an arm movement to the side at the expense of an immediate penetration. In situations like this, an open block would be a good solution but only with an aggressive penetrating blocking action (see section 5.2.1.3 regarding double-block formations).

The hands and arms need to be highly tense at the moment of contact with the volleyball to cope with the energy and power of the volleyball. The positioning and posture of the hands and arms to the incoming volleyball is a crucial element for a successful block. A general requirement is that the hands point to the end line (baseline). Only this positioning of the hands will guarantee that the volleyball is blocked back into the opponent's side of the volleyball court and not out of bounds. Very often, many middle blockers make the error of blocking an incoming volleyball against the power zone of the hitter. This is a result of poor footwork and/or poor positioning of the feet during the moment of their jump (the feet are not at the same level and parallel). The result is that after the block has touched the volleyball, the volleyball flies directly outside of the volleyball court.

A hitting clinic/lesson against a fixed block (blocker/blocking board) will demonstrate to the athletes the principle of "angle of incidence = angle of reflection" and its effect on the block.

To be in a ready state after landing from a block for a second blocking action in the same spot, the middle blocker should land with relatively extended knees. S/he should land in a broad and low position if s/he were to quickly move to the outside position to block there.

5.4.1.2 Individual Tactical Skills and Abilities

The middle blocker can only be successful if s/he has the following skills and abilities:

For his/her own actions, it is important that his/her perceptive ability is above average. S/he must have the ability to immediately adjust and relate to new situations. S/he must be able to quickly cover short distances and the endurance of his/her jumping ability must be very good. Finally, s/he must be very disciplined and psychologically strong.

S/he needs to receive the following information regarding the opposition before the match. S/he must know the setter and the methods that the setter uses to run the offence and if the setter has any peculiar characteristics. S/he needs to know the exact time-spatial behavior regarding combinations and the strengths, weaknesses, and peculiar characteristics of the quick and second hitters.

In specific match/game situations, s/he should be able to see and recognise the following:
- The quality of the first pass in connection to its impact on the quick hitter (i.e. Is a quick attack possible?).
- Incorrect timing of the quick hitter.
- Fake movements by the setter.
- A change of the opposition's offensive tactics (with the help of the coach).

Working with his/her teammates, it is important for the middle blocker to request and receive information and support for his/her actions from them.

The middle blocker must repeatedly deal with the most complex situations. In almost all of the opposition's offensive situations s/he must deal with the setter, the quick hitter, the outside and/or combination hitter, and the outside and/or backcourt hitter. S/he must watch the movements and actions of four or more athletes and must have a different defensive answer and response for each one. S/he must always carry out multiple observations and multiple tasks/actions. S/he should be the volleyball athlete with the best coordinative abilities. Relating to the physical intensity of his/her game, s/he might be call the "decathlete"/"heptathlete" of all of the volleyball athletes (see section 4.5 regarding the "quick hitter").

5.4.2 Individual Tactics of the Outside Blocker

Thanks to the many blocking strategies in the modern sport of volleyball, there is a tendency evident that every athlete must be universally trained when blocking is concerned to enable all of these athletes to block in any position. This is why most of the information mentioned above regarding the middle blocker also applies to the outside blocker.

Generally, regarding the organisation and formation of the block, the blocker who has the least movement to the blocking spot is the one responsible for organising the block.

INDIVIDUAL TACTICS OF THE BLOCKER

At the high levels of volleyball, a comparison of the profiles of the outside blockers in positions II and IV shows that the blocker in position IV has to do a more difficult and complex job:

- S/he is the one mainly responsible for the double-block in position III since his/her starting position is closer to the middle blocker and the opposition's setter.
- With the opposition's setter in the front row and with a backcourt hitter possibly attacking, s/he can support his/her middle blocker by blocking the opposition's setter in case the setter tries a tip/dump.
- With four attackers and the opponent's setter in the back row, s/he is responsible for two of the hitters: the outside hitter in position II (even if this hitter is trying to execute a quick attack (A-quick behind the setter) or a combination play in position III) and the back-court hitter.
- S/he is responsible for the formation of the triple block in position II.

The outside blocker in position II rarely has only one direct hitter of the opponent to deal with and it is not very often the quick hitter and the outside/second hitter.

If the outside blocker has only one role to do and his/her starting position is not too far inside, then s/he will jump to block like the middle blocker would out of a standing position or after a short positioning step. Internationally, it can be seen that smaller athletes are trying to increase their reach height by using an approach from the sideline or from outside of the volleyball court through the use of a stemming step and an arm swing for their block jump.

The outside blocker must position the double-block at the correct spot on the outside. Either s/he must position the block to cover the line or the half-cross-court shot depending on the preliminary tactical strategy. S/he should see ahead of time if the middle blocker is able to close in time for a double block or if s/he must cover the main hitting direction using a single block.

It is a large individual tactical error by the outside blocker to make the decision to defend or to cover the attack instead of forming a double block.

The outside blocker must watch his/her opposite athlete closely and must not fall for any fakes to be in a position to block him/her in other positions as well. The switch block is a good method of doing this. The use of the switch block requires a special blocking strategy. The blocker who is covering the opponent's quick hitter is jumping fully with the quick hitter and the outside or middle blocker is blocking or covering the second hitter (Fig. 137d).

This strategy is very difficult and only a few teams are able to use it successfully (see Chapter 7, "Defensive and Offensive Strategies").

Photo 47

Regarding the posture and positioning of the hands and arms, the important principle to remember for the outside blocker is that "the angle of incidence = the angle of reflection". It is especially important for him/her to make the following changes if the hitter's approach to the volleyball net is vertical and if the opponent is hitting multiple shots off of the outside of the block and using the block to his/her advantage:

- Push the outside shoulder forward in combination with a slight turning in of the outside hand to the inside (Photo 47).
- Abandon the blocking action by pulling the hands away.

Another error by the outside blocker is that s/he is "flying" to the outside (his/her take off spot is not the same as his/her landing spot). The reason for this is that the blocker is missing or has not developed a good stemming movement and this makes him/her "fly". It also makes it more difficult for him/her to penetrate over the volleyball net.

This causes problems for the defenders because s/he is not setting up a clearly defined blocking position, therefore, allowing his/her block to be used by the opposition's hitters and not allowing the defenders to set up a good defensive position for themselves. Additionally, the middle blocker will never be able to close the block, even if s/he has enough time to set up and form a double block. This is especially true if the outside blocker is starting at an inside position and is moving to the outside.

5.4.3 Individual Tactics of the Blocking Athletes at the Middle and Low Levels of Volleyball

At these levels of volleyball, almost exclusively the abilities of your own team are taken into consideration for the individual and the group tactics of the blocking athletes. The explanation for this is a simple one: there is no systematic analysis of the opponent. The only way of influencing the tactic/strategy and to make changes is during the actual game/match itself based upon what occurs on the volleyball court. These changes can only be coaching strategies.

The course of movement of the blocker should generally be the same at these levels as it is at the higher levels of volleyball. Only if the opposition's set is high and the jumping ability of the athlete is low, is there a possibility of allowing a two-handed arm swing as support for the blocker to get higher. The starting position of the middle blocker is in the center of the volleyball net, and the outside blocker is positioned at a distance approximately 1-1.5 meters away from the sideline at the volleyball net. If the opponent is setting from the front row and has no back-court hitter, it is possible for the outside blocker in position IV to move his/her starting position further inside the volleyball court (Figs. 137b-137c).

If we look at the middle levels of volleyball as a preparation level for the high levels of volleyball then there is a sense that an all-around training of every athlete should be done which enables each of them to block in every position. The middle blocker should almost never jump with the middle hitter but instead wait for the set before s/he begins his/her blocking action. His/her main role is to form a double block! Since the outside hitters do not hit the line shot very well at this level of volleyball, the outside blocker within a double block should cover the half-cross-court shot and as a single blocker s/he should always cover the cross-court direction or the power line of the hitter (outside hand at the volleyball).

The non-blocking net athlete in this level, as it is done at the women's high levels of volleyball, should not carry out the close coverage of the block. One reason for this is that most of the time it is impossible to include the covering athlete in the counter-attack. This is a crucial factor and point because there is also no back-court hitter to step up for him/her, which is another reason for this. Since there is no organised offence out of the defence possible, another defensive formation should be used. In this situation it is important at the low levels of volleyball not to use defensive formations that force the blocker to cover him/herself. At this level, the blocker should only have one clearly defined role. It is also more important that every blocker penetrates at the expense of a lower reach height than not penetrating but having a higher reach height.

5.5 Individual Tactics of the Defender

The running and jumping actions in combination plays with the hitters has already been discussed. In the following paragraphs, the running actions at the high levels of men's volleyball will be discussed and differentiated into the different defensive positions:
- If jumping actions, including the approach, are compared with dashes/runs, then there is a relation of 2:1 (dashes/runs – jumping actions).
- Only approximately 5 % of the dashes/runs had to cover a distance greater than 6 meters.
- Runs forward are the most used kinds of runs with approximately 53 % of them being of this nature.
- Runs with a change in direction rarely occur (2.5 %).
- Approximately 20 % of all dashes are in a backwards direction and approximately 24 % of them are to the side.
- The setter penetrating from the back row has a higher amount of dashes than any other athlete; per back-court sequence the setter averages 42 meters – 11 dashes with a density of 14 seconds.
- The defenders in position I (excluding the setter), usually diagonal hitters; per back-court sequence averages 35 meters – 10 dashes with a density of 16 seconds.
- There is almost no difference in the running actions of the athletes in positions V and VI; per back-court sequence they manage approximately 27 meters – 8 dashes with a density of 20 seconds.

These results must be taken into consideration in every practice, especially as far as the runs/dashes to the back are concerned. At the middle and low levels of volleyball, there are much more runs in a forward direction (approximately 65 %), whereas the movements in the backward direction are way below at 10 %. The most important criterion with the training of running actions, excluding approaches for jumps, should be explosive dashes over short distances and then a sudden but controlled full stop. Each run should end with a combination of stepping and straddle steps from which each movement, especially to the front and to the side, can be quickly started.

The most important condition for a successful defensive action, besides the choice of the correct defensive zone to cover and play, is a low to mid-low defensive ready position before the attack (Photo 48). The defender outside of the

INDIVIDUAL TACTICS OF THE DEFENDER 207

block shadow must be able to, out of a low forward orientated defensive position without any additional movements, dive to the front and to the side for the volleyball (Photos 49 and 50).

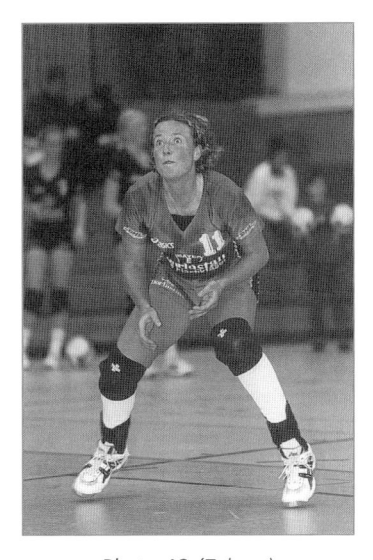

Photo 48 (Zeimer)

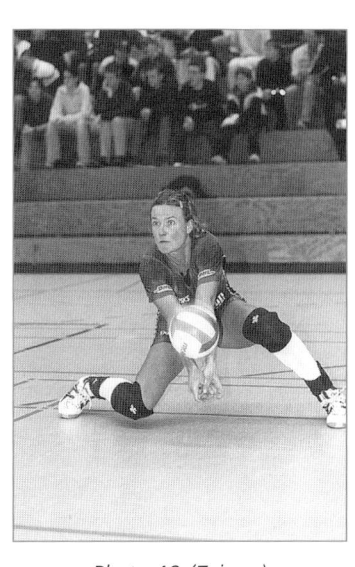

Photo 49 (Zeimer)

The defender must get into his/her defensive ready position early in order to be in a good position to start observing the attacker's hitting action before the attacker moves his/her hitting arm back. From this moment, every movement is directed to the volleyball (volleyball-centered) and not focused on getting to the correct defensive spot or into a low defensive position. It is much more effective to stand in a defensive ready position nearby the correct defensive spot before the hitting action by the opponent than to try and get into the perfect defensive zone and by doing so not being ready for the opposition's attack at all.

Photo 50 (Zeimer)

The harder that the volleyball is hit past the block, the lower the athlete must be in a defensive position to have any chance at all of successfully defending any volleyball hit at such a high speed. To be able to defend a larger defensive zone the defenders must be able to use supporting/help techniques:

- Defensive techniques above the head using one or two hands (Photos 51-54).
- Defensive techniques using one hand/arm to the side.
- Defensive techniques at or above the shoulder with one or two hands should be used, especially the overhand pass (Photo 55).

Photo 51 (Zeimer)

Photo 52 (Niemann)

Photo 53 (Niemann)

Photo 54 (Niemann)

Photo 55 (Niemann)

Examinations have proven the following results to be true that defence using the legs or feet (allowed under the new rules) does not have a share or role in the defence because it does not improve the defence and, therefore, it does not make any sense to systematically practice a "foot" defence. The principle still applies that a two-armed defence should be used before a one-armed defence and a one-armed defence should be used before a foot defence!

INDIVIDUAL TACTICS OF THE DEFENDER

At the men's high levels of volleyball there are two extreme defensive techniques used: one is to dive for the volleyball and the other is to use a one-armed sliding defence, where instead of jumping the athlete glides out of a low defensive position to the volleyball. One hand/arm, the one that is playing the volleyball, pushes forward with contact on the court to the spot where the volleyball is expected to hit the court. Depending on the distance, the athlete slides low over the upper body or with the whole body into the correct position. At the moment of contact, the hand is flat on the court like a "pancake" (Photo 56). This is the only way that the volleyball can come off of the back of the hand, as it would bounce off of the volleyball court.

At the women's high levels of volleyball a similar technique is used, but at the end of the action there is a rollover movement. In this situation, the sliding movement is more to the side and over the side of the body. The hand is pushed forward, but the back of the hand is pointing to the floor. The volleyball is then played with the inside of the hand. With a very quick sweeping movement a rollover movement is then added. If it is a less sweeping movement it will only be rolled to the side and then a getting/standing up step (Photo 57).

Photo 56 (Martin)

Photo 57 (Köhler)

The training of the defender must request willpower and strength of mind from the athlete. It also must ask for concentration, including endurance of concentration, and determination. S/he must not allow a single volleyball to drop that comes into his/her defensive zone.

An effort must be made to touch the volleyball or at the very least show a great determination in attempting to touch the volleyball. A defender is also not allowed to give away a volleyball that is defended by a teammate without having shown the greatest possible effort to reach it. It is important for the coach to keep the principles in mind for psychologically training the defenders in each practice, no matter what the main target of the practice may be. The reason for this is: Only what is successfully trained in practice can be expected to successfully occur in a competition (see Chapter 8, "Specific Principles for the Training of the Sport of Volleyball").

It is very important for the individual tactics of the defender to know the quality of his/her own team's defensive techniques and their physical and, especially, psychological abilities. The correct assessment of your own team's strength of mind and willpower is the key to each successful defensive action. Fear and the lack of self-confidence are guarantees of failure (Photo 58).

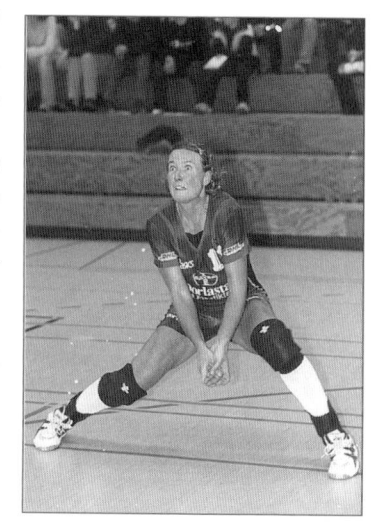

Photo 58 (Zeimer)

To simplify it for a specific match/game situation, the following factors are critical for getting into the correct defensive position:
- The quality of the first pass.
- The speed and accuracy of the set.
- Take into consideration the arranged and predicted action of the middle blocker.
- Watch and keep in mind the blocking position in relation to the volleyball.
- Observe the positioning of the attacker to the volleyball and predict the power of the volleyball.

Photo 59 (Zeimer)

- The transition from defence from a setter's tip/dump to the one from a quick hitter, or from the defence of an attack by the second hitter or to the one from the outside/back-court hitter.
- Take a defensive position that covers up your own weaknesses (i.e. give more space/room to your stronger defensive side).
- As a defender in positions V and I, always defend outside of the block shadow!
- As a defender in position VI with a single block, always defend outside of the block shadow!

5.5.1 The Libero as a Defensive Specialist

All of the information in section 5.5 regarding the individual tactics of the defender is also 100 % true for the libero as a defensive specialist. See also section 3.2.1 – The Libero as a Service Reception Specialist and section 1.1 – "The New Rules and their Effects on Practice and Matches".

Presently, at the men's top levels of volleyball (1999 European Championships), the libero, when he is used as a defensive specialist in all back row positions, has a share in all of the defensive actions totaling approximately 10-16 %. With the senior women (1999 European Championships) the share is approximately 21-27 %. With the junior women (1999 World Championships) the share is approximately 27-30 %. The effectiveness of the defence is with the men (between 23-33 %), with the women (between 19-31 %) except for Russia (51 %), and with the junior women (between 31-52 %). These statistics clearly show that the libero is used much more by the junior women in relation to the libero's share of quality defensive actions in a match.

At the women's low, middle, and high levels of volleyball the libero mostly plays the defensive position V and at the men's high levels of volleyball and at the junior women's level the libero is also used in position VI. Some coaches think that the use of a back-court hitter in the C2 situation is more important than the use of a libero.

Photo 59a (Steffen Marquardt)

Additionally, some coaches do not have a superior service reception and defensive specialist or they have not trained one yet. It is expected that soon the advantages and use of a libero will be realised and completely exploited. At the international levels of volleyball, it has been requested that the roster for teams be increased from 12 athletes to 14 athletes. The reason for this is that teams will not have to replace and/or reduce their team roster by an athlete or two because of the use of the libero.

The goals of an organised training of the libero must include:
- The libero as a back-court athlete and defensive specialist should be the organiser and enforcer of the defensive strategies.
- The libero needs to have knowledge of the offensive strategies and, especially, the characteristics of the opponent and of the opponent's main hitting directions.
- The libero must identify him/herself with the role as a defensive specialist, even with only a few contacts of the volleyball or when s/he is rarely replacing another athlete on the volleyball court.
- The libero is mainly responsible for the close coverage of the offence and for the safety set after a defensive action by the setter.
- The libero is the athlete who quickly and specifically passes on and enforces the strategies and counter-strategies of the coach.
- The libero is the perfect athlete to use the blocking and defensive strategy with position VI mid-court as the most effective defensive formation.
- The libero should be used in the training process in a planned manner. In other words, s/he should also play in the front row from time to time.
- The priority in practice for the libero is still in his/her role as the libero. Therefore, s/he must train completely in practice sessions as the libero and be trained as close to the related game/match situations that s/he will encounter in her role as the libero. S/he also needs to adjust his/her attention and ability to concentrate and focus on any continuous changes. S/he needs to learn to keep his/her concentration and focus up at all times, regardless if s/he is off of the volleyball court and especially in those time when s/he is in the backcourt.

The training of the libero as a service reception and defensive specialist requires a fundamentally sound all-around/universal preparation. For example, this means to also allow the front row athletes to play in the libero position during practices and in friendly/exhibition games/matches.

5.6 Selected Training Drills

All training drills discussed in Learning Part II (setter/attacker) can also be transferred to this learning part. To always get blocking and defensive situational types of training drills that usually start with a serve-service reception action can instead start with a setting-offensive action. For this reason, more training drills to improve the individual and group tactical actions will be offered here (see Chapter 7, "Defensive and Offensive Strategies").

5.6.1 Individual Tactics of a Single Block and the Defenders
- Single block in position II (later in positions III and IV) vs. an attack from a medium-high set!

The attackers are hitting hard in certain areas (zones). The outside blocker is covering the line (later the medium-diagonal direction and then the diagonal direction) (Fig. 138a).

Blocking Athlete:
- Jump after the attacker!
- Penetrate immediately!
- Block the volleyball to the middle of the volleyball court by using the correct posture and positioning of the hands!

Variation 1:
The attackers hit in the direction of their approach and then down the power line.

Blocking Athlete:
- Do not block directly in front of the attack but:
- Extend in the direction of his/her approach.
- Depending on his/her hitting movements and positioning, to the volleyball (outside hand at the volleyball)!

Variation 2:
The setter is intentionally setting inaccurate sets regarding the distance to the volleyball net.

Blocking Athlete:
- Jump earlier with volleyballs that are set tight and delay your jump with sets that are further away from the volleyball net!
- With tight sets block the line and with sets that are off of the volleyball net block diagonally!

Variation 3:
The attackers vary their approaches and by doing this also vary their hitting directions!

Variation 4:
The setter varies the sets as far as speed and height are concerned.

Variation 5:
All variations mentioned above either alone or in a combination depending on the first pass (after a service reception or after an "indirect" set – which means that the setter is setting a defended volleyball).
- Keep in mind the time-spatial behavior of the setter depending on the quality of the first pass.
- If the setter is far away from the volleyball net, always block the diagonal direction.
- The outside blocker is blocking out of movement!

The setter is setting volleyballs that are tossed to him/her as 1 meter sets in front and behind him/her. It is the same structure and routine as 1 above with all of its variations.

Blocking Athlete:
- Using sidesteps quickly and economically move to the next blocking position!
- Keep your hands above your head and remember that the reach height is not as important as is to immediately penetrate (photo 60)!
- Start an immediate penetration with the jump!
- Attackers vs. a single block and a defender in position VI!

The attackers can hit a variation of hits but not in the extreme diagonal (cross-court) direction (Figs. 156a-156b). The offence is run from positions II/IV and III. The blocker is covering the main hitting direction.

SELECTED TRAINING DRILLS 215

Defender in Position VI:
- Watch the opponent's approach and the position of the block and defend outside of the block shadow!

Variation 1:
This training drill using the variations outlined in drills 1 and 2 above.

Coach:
- Make sure that every defended volleyball is used in a counter-attack.
- Make sure that the defence is giving the overhand pass priority over the other defensive techniques!

Photo 60 (Köhler)

Attacker vs. a Single-Block and with Defenders in Positions VI, V, and I!
After a successful defence, initiate a back-court counter-attack.

Blocker:
- Watch the volleyballs that are hit past you while you are landing and be ready to set (Photo 61).

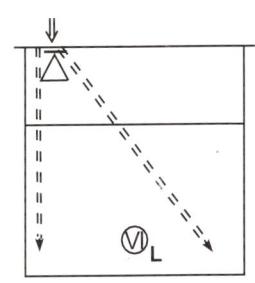

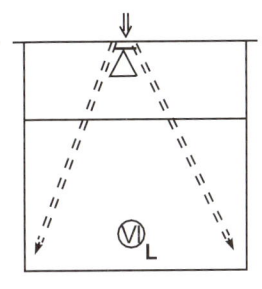

Figs. 156a/b

Defenders:
- Get out of the block shadow and move back if the volleyball is set far away from the volleyball net!

Photo 61 (Zeimer)

Variation 1:
The setter plays in the front row and is allowed to tip/dump the volleyball!

Defenders in Positions V and I:
- Be prepared and ready to defend against a setter's tip/dump after a good first pass!

Blocker:
- Give signs to your defenders regarding how you are going to block (Photo 62)!
- Make sure that your signals have been understood!
- Try to block the setter's tips/dumps!

Quick Hitter and Setter are vs. a Middle Blocker and Defenders in Positions VI, V, and I!
Start with A-quicks, then A-quicks behind the setter, then B-quicks, and then whatever you want to set!

Photo 62 (Zeimer)

Defender in Position VI:
- Always defend the diagonal direction out of the block shadow.

Variation 1:
The same but add a second hitter who receives a two-ball set behind the quick hitter (echelon combination behind each other).

Middle Blocker:
- You and the defenders in positions V and I are responsible for the setter's tips/dumps!

Defenders in Positions V and I:
- Move back as soon as the second hitter receives the set!

Variation 2:
Variation 1 but this time the quick hitter can be used as a second hitter and the setter can tip/dump the volleyball.

Middle Blocker:
- Make the following arrangements with the defenders: With a good first pass you will block the tip/dump and jump with the quick hitter, but with a poor first pass you will jump with the second hitter!

Defenders:
- With a good first pass, and knowing that the middle blocker is taking the quick hitter, move further back!

Variation 3:
The same as variation 2 but the second hitter attacks next to the quick hitter (cross-echelon combination next to each other).

Middle Blocker:
- Choose your starting position between the setting and the attacking spot!
- Do not fully jump with the quick hitter so you have time to block the second hitter also!

Defenders:
- If the middle blocker is not jumping with the quick hitter then be prepared and psychologically ready to defend a quick attack or at least to get a touch on the volleyball!

Outside Hitter vs. a Single-Block and Four Defenders!
First, the attack will be out of position IV, then position II, and finally from back-court positions V and I. The setter is in the front row.

Blocking Athlete:
- If the sets are far away from the volleyball net, choose to block in the diagonal (cross-court) direction rather than the half-diagonal or line.

Non-Blocking Athlete:
- Block (in position IV) the setter's tip/dump and move back to play defence after the set!

Variation 1:
The same as before but the setter is allowed to use two hitters: Positions IV and II, Positions IV and I, Positions V and II, and Positions V and I.

Defenders:
- With a back-court attack, move back as far as possible! Always check the quality of your defence and remember that the quality of the following action is the standard for your own action!
- Get into your defensive positions at the latest possible moment of the attack to be ready to move/fall in all directions to play the volleyball.
- Always remember that every two-handed/"armed" defence has priority over any kind of defence involving the feet/legs.
- As the libero, coordinate the defence.

5.6.2 Selected Training Drills for Block and Defence with a Special Focus on the Individual and Group Tactics of the Blocking and Defensive Athletes

Double-Block in Positions II, III, and IV vs. Attacks from a High Set!

Before the set, the middle blocker blocks in his/her starting position and then moves to the outside to form a double block. At first, the blocker covers the line, then the half-diagonal, and finally the diagonal (cross-court) and extreme-diagonal (extreme-cross-court) directions. The attackers hit to specific targets, which are the defensive zones.

Middle Blocker:
- Close the block with an immediate penetration in such a manner that your hands are pointing to the end line (Photo 63)!

Outside Blocker:
- Push your outside shoulder, more specifically your outside hand, forward to omit the hitter's use of the outside of the block (Photo 64)!

Variation 1:
The attackers hit power line in the direction of their approach, which the block is supposed to cover.

Photo 63 (Martin)

Outside Blocker:
Organise the positioning of the double-block with consideration to the set and the direction of the hitter's approach!

Variation 2:
A front-court hitter and his/her direct back-court hitter are attacking. The setter uses positions IV and V, then I and II, and finally III and VI.

Variation 3:
The attackers vary their approaches and hitting directions.

Photo 64 (Sabarz)

The Offence Alternatively Attacks 1-Meter to Medium-High Sets in Front and Behind the Setter!
The blockers move correspondingly to the offence. The organisation and routine is the same as in drill 1 and its variations!

Blocking Athletes:
- Try to move with a synchronised cross-step to the new blocking spot!
- The outside blocker is always organising and positioning the block!

Attack vs. a Double-Block and Defender in Position VI!
The attackers are allowed to vary their hits. The attack takes place in position IV, then position II, then position III, and finally in the back-court positions. The blocking athletes cover the main hitting direction. The attackers try to hit off of the top of the block and try to use the block to their advantage. The defender in position VI is moving back outside of the volleyball court to defend any volleyballs that touch the block.

Blocking Athlete:
- Use a passive "soft" block to direct the volleyball after it has touched the block, high into your own side of the volleyball court or pull your hands back to omit the block being "used" by the attacker!

Variation 1:
According to an arranged defensive strategy, the blocking athletes block a particular zone (in other words they cover a particular area of the volleyball court)!

Defender:
- Move out of the block shadow!

4. Attack vs. a Double-Block and Defenders in Positions VI, V, and I!

The counter-attack is run using a back-court hitter.
First, the block covers the main hitting direction, then, with coordination with the defenders, certain zones of the volleyball court are covered. The setter is in the front row and allowed to use tips/dumps.

Defenders:
- Be ready to chase down volleyballs that come high off of the block and to use the overhand pass to play them to the setting spot.
- Be ready to chase down poorly defended volleyballs and to bring them back into the volleyball court!
- Position VI needs to make a decision, depending on the formation of the double block, of whether to move back inside the block shadow or to leave it in favor of defending the main hitting direction!
- Defenders in positions V and I need to make a decision of whether to cover the block closely or at a distance if the zone block is covering their defensive area (zone).
- As the libero, play the safety set if the setter must defend the volleyball.

5. Two Outside Hitters (First from Positions II and IV, then Positions II and V, then Positions I and IV, and finally Positions I and V) Attack a High or Medium-High Set!

The setter is in the front row and is allowed to use tips/dumps.
The first pass may be out of the service reception or a defensive situation. The middle blocker and the defenders in positions V and I must cover the tips/dumps. The non-blocking net athlete is releasing from the volleyball net to play defence and is responsible, together with the defender directly behind the block, to cover the block from a distance (Figs. 157 and 143a).

Defender in Position VI:
- Start in the block shadow and in the extension of the seam of the block!

SELECTED TRAINING DRILLS 221

Middle Blocker:
- Watch the positioning of the setter to the volleyball to be ready to make the decision of when to move to form the correct formation for an outside block on time!

Variation 1:
The defender in position VI is covering the main hitting at the edge of the block shadow (Figs. 158 and 143b).

Variation 2:
Position VI (on the end line inside of the block shadow) is responsible for volleyballs that touch the top of the block (Figs. 159a-159b and 143c-143d).

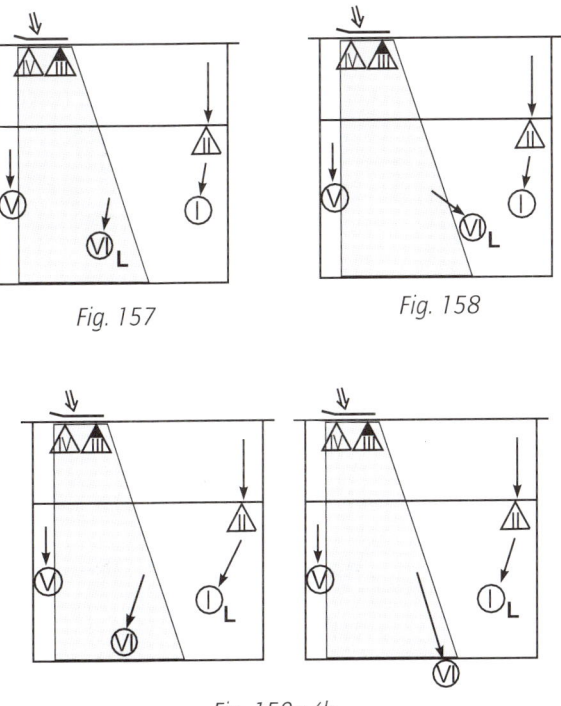

Fig. 157

Fig. 158

Fig. 159a/b

Variation 3:
The block covers the diagonal (cross-court) direction and position VI is defending the frontal direction (Figs. 160a-160c and 143e-143g).

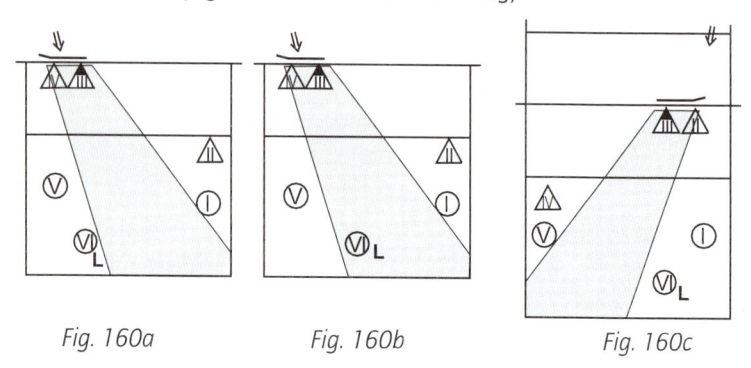

Fig. 160a　　*Fig. 160b*　　*Fig. 160c*

Variation 4:
The non-blocking net athlete covers the block at a close coverage (Figs. 161a-161b and 144a-144b).

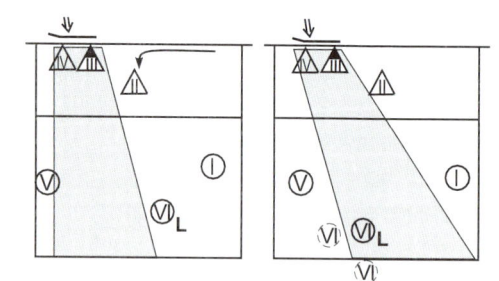

Figs. 161a/b

Variation 5:
The direct back-court athlete covers the block at a close coverage (Figs. 162a-162f, 145a-145c, and 146a-146c).

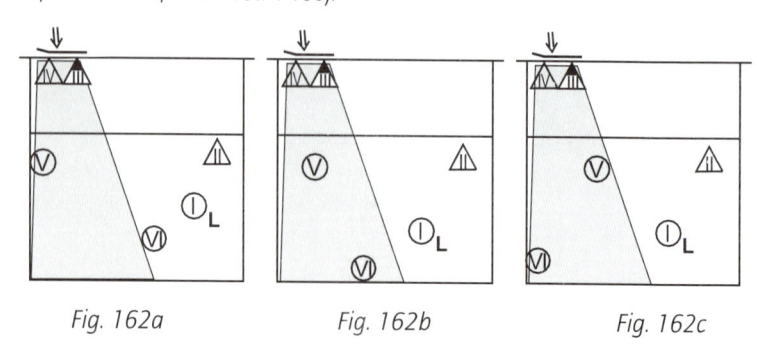

Fig. 162a　　*Fig. 162b*　　*Fig. 162c*

SELECTED TRAINING DRILLS

Fig. 162d

Fig. 162e

Fig. 162f

Variation 6:
The non-blocking net athlete and the direct back-court athlete cover the block at a close coverage (Figs. 163a-163b and 148a-148b).

Fig. 163a/b

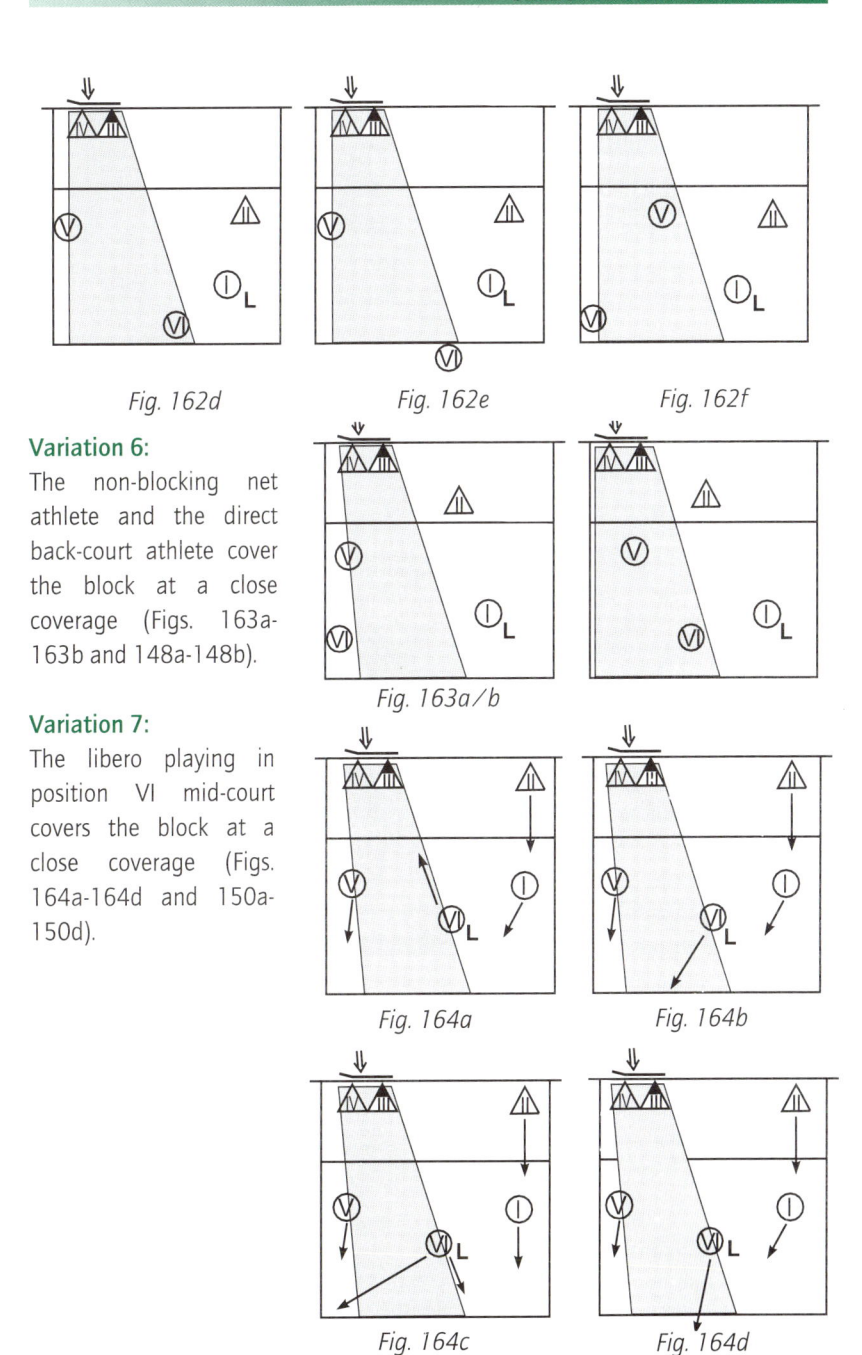

Variation 7:
The libero playing in position VI mid-court covers the block at a close coverage (Figs. 164a-164d and 150a-150d).

Fig. 164a

Fig. 164b

Fig. 164c

Fig. 164d

Three Attackers and the Setter Run Plays Vs. the Block and Defence!

The setter is either using the quick hitter (with an A-quick in front or behind the setter or with a B-quick) or the two outside hitters with medium-high sets.

Middle Blocker:
- Do not fully jump to have the chance to get to the outside and close a double block!

Defenders:
- Be ready to save the volleyball, perform a safety set, and to cover the offence!
- As the libero you are responsible for the offensive coverage!

Blocking Athletes:
- Remember to cover yourself, be aware of the setting, and the offence (especially the offensive coverage).

Training drill 5 and all of its variations can be used!

Variation 1:
Block and defence against the setter in position II, quick hitter in position IV, outside hitter in position III, and a back-court hitter in position I.

Variation 2:
Block and defence against a penetrating setter, quick hitter in position III, combination hitter in position II, and an outside hitter in position IV.

Middle Blocker:
- Communicate to your teammates your blocking actions!
- Start your blocking action after the set has been made!
- Think if it makes sense to block twice in a row. Do not fully jump against the quick hitter and fully jump against the combination or outside hitter (Figs. 151a-151d).

Variation 3:
Block and defence against the setter (front row), quick hitter in position II, combination hitter in position III, and a back-court hitter in position V.

Variation 4:
Block and defence against a penetrating setter, quick hitter in position III, combination hitter in position IV, and an outside hitter in position II.

Variation 5:

Block and defence against the setter (front row), quick hitter in position IV, combination hitter in position III, and a back-court hitter in position I.

Coach:
- Think if it would make sense to use a switch-block strategy!

Defenders:
- The higher the set the further back the defence must be!

Switch-Blocker:
- After you see the setter perform his/her setting action, move to the attacking spot.
- Neglect the approaching movement by your opponent!

Variation 6:

All variations mentioned above with the setter in the front row. The quick hitter is doing combinations by him/herself using shoot sets and "flyers".

Middle Blocker:
- In expectation of shoots and "flyers" always watch the opponent's passing and the volleyball and do not worry about the take-off spot of the quick hitter!

7. **Training Drill 6 and all of its Variations with Medium-Quick Sets to the Outside Hitters from a Good First Pass!**

Defenders:
- Be prepared for single-blocks and open double-blocks (Figs. 138a-138b, 139b-139c, 140a-140b, and 141a-14d).

- Triple-Block Formation and Defence vs. a Front-court/Back-court Hitter After a Set of the 3-4 Wave (Figs. 152a-152g)!

- Block and Defence vs. Two Quick Hitters and One Outside Hitter (Setter is Penetrating)!

Blocking Athletes:
- With a very good first pass everyone is blocking his/her direct opponent!

Variation 1:
The setter is in the front row, two quick hitters, and a back-court hitter.

Defender:
- Cover the setter's tips/dumps and one of the quick hitters!

Middle Blocker:
- Cover one of the quick hitters and the back-court hitter!

- **Block and Defence vs. the Setter, Two Quick Hitters, and Two Back-court Hitters!**

Middle Blocker:
- Watch for any setter's tips/dumps, cover one quick hitter, and always block against the back-court hitter!

5.6.3 *Selected Games for the Training of Blocking and Defensive Athletes*

All games, with appropriate "special" rules, can be played as games with and/or against each other or as power volleyball games (see the training drills # 8-12 in section 4.6.2). In the following paragraphs, the most important hints for the organisation and, if necessary, the goals of each game will be explained.

Two **special rules** apply for all games:

1 – Blocks that fall inside the normal volleyball court but outside the small court of the game will still be counted as a score. This will give the athletes the opportunity to practise the correct technique and positioning of the block.
2 – Every defended volleyball that directly crosses the volleyball net will be called as a fault. This rule will force the athletes to keep, even the volleyballs that are difficult to defend, on their own side of the volleyball court and by doing so allow a counter-attack possible.

- *Game 2 vs. 2 with One Front-court and One Back-court Athlete!*
  [On a 3 x 9 meter volleyball court]

Goal:
- The blocker is blocking the volleyball towards the volleyball court and tries to omit that his block is "used" at the side by the hitter.
- The defender is running a back row attack after s/he has defended or received serve!

Variation 1:
Both athletes are attacking as front-court athletes.

Variation 2:
Game 3 vs. 3 with two front row athletes and one back row athlete. A front row athlete handles the setting. The offence must be a front row attack against a double block.

Goal:
- The blockers should try to omit to "being used" at the side by the hitter by showing the correct arm/hand posture/technique and positioning or they should simply pull their hands away so that they cannot be "used" by the hitter.

Variation 3:
Game 3 vs. 3 but the offence must use a back-court attack against a double-block.

Variation 4:
Game 3 vs. 3 but now either a front row or a back row offence is allowed.

- **Game 2 vs. 2 with One Front-court and One Back-court Athlete, Hitting Back Row Against a Double Block!**
  [On a 4.5 x 9 meter volleyball court]

Goal:
- The defender is always outside of the block shadow.

Variation 1:
Both athletes are hitting front row.

Variation 2:
Game 3 vs. 3 with two front-court and one back-court athlete, first hitting front row then only hitting back row and finally hitting whatever they choose. A front row athlete performs the setting.

Variation 3:
Game 4 vs. 4.

Goal:
- The defender behind the block is responsible for a close coverage of the block (the offence is the same as in variation 2).

Variation 4:
Game 4 vs. 4 (the same as variation 3 but on a 6 x 9 meter volleyball court).

Goal:
- A quick transition game from defence to offence and vice-versa (offence to defence).

- **Game: Games 2 vs. 2, 3 vs. 3, and 4 vs. 4 with the Setter Allowed to Tip/Dump the Volleyball!**

Goal:
- In expectation of the setter tipping/dumping the volleyball, the defenders will take their starting positions near the ten-foot line.

- **Game: Games 3 vs. 3 and 4 vs. 4 with the Setter Allowed to Tip/Dump the Volleyball, a Quick Hitter, and a Back-court Hitter as a Combination Hitter!**

Goal:
- Each blocking athlete has two roles: either block the tip/dump and the combination hitter or block the quick hitter and the combination hitter.

Variation 1:
The offence is run by the penetrating setter, a quick hitter, a second hitter, and a safety set to the back-court hitter (fourth wave set).

- **Game 2 vs. 2 on a Diagonal Volleyball Court (Fig. 165a)!**

The volleyball court is colored! The net athletes are blocking and setting, but they only cover the half-diagonal (cross-court) direction and leave the extreme diagonal (cross-court) direction open.

SELECTED TRAINING DRILLS   229

Goal:
- A defence suitable for the game to the setting spot in position II/III.
- A defence suitable for the situation to a) the setter, b) the area around the ten-foot line, and c) the middle of the volleyball court.

Variation 1:
The same as before but change to the mirror image of the defence with the defender in position I and the setter in position II.

Variation 2:
The same game drill but with the defender in position IV then in position II. The setter is in the setting spot (Fig. 165b).

Goal:
- Defence of attacks that are hit using the wrist (wrist hits).

- **Game 3 vs. 3 on a Diagonal Volleyball Court. The Same as Drill 5 but with Two Defenders and Attackers (Positions V and VI)!**
  [On a 4.5 x 9 meter volleyball court]

The setters are allowed to tip/dump the volleyball (Fig. 165c).

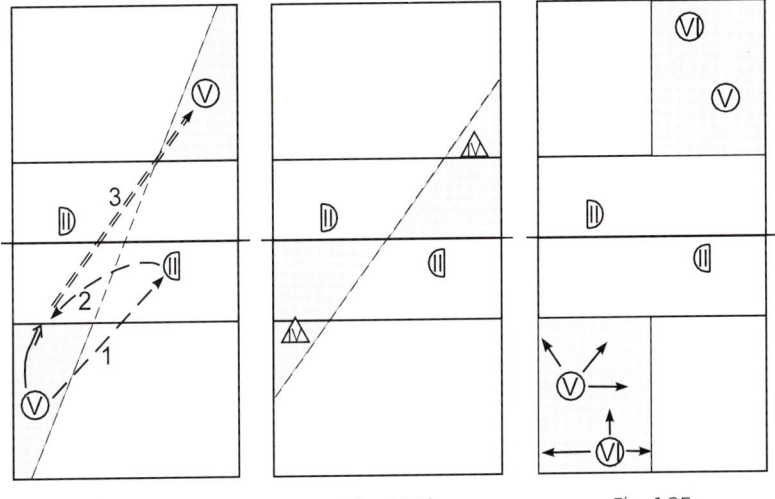

Fig. 165a   *Fig. 165b*   *Fig. 165c*

Goal:
- The starting position of the defenders allows them to defend more of a sideward direction and they are positioned at a distance to each other. Position VI is pushed further back into the volleyball court to have no overlapping defensive areas (zones).

Variation 1:
The same game drill but with the defenders in positions VI and I.

Variation 2:
Now positions V and VI are playing positions II and I. The volleyball court is almost the same as shown in Fig. 165a but includes the ten-foot zone (Fig. 165b).

- Game 4 vs. 4 on a Diagonal Volleyball Court with Athletes in Positions IV, V, and VI and a Front Row Setter!
  [On a 4.5 x 9 meter volleyball court (Fig. 165d)]

Variation 1:
With the defenders in positions VI, II, and I.

Variation 2:
The same as drill 7 but the athletes block the frontal and half-diagonal (cross-court) directions.

Variation 3:
The same as variation 2 but using the mirror image of the defence with the defenders in positions VI, II, and I.

- Game 2 vs. 2!
  [On a 4.5 x 9 meter volleyball court]

There must always be three touches and a double block (Fig. 166a)

Goal:
- The blockers must try to block a tip/dump at the highest point of their jump or to cover themselves after they land.

SELECTED TRAINING DRILLS   231

Variation 1:
Game 3 vs. 3 on a 3 x 9 meter volleyball court. There must be a high set and a double block (Fig. 166b).

Goal:
- The non-blocking net athlete must cover the whole front-court area (close coverage of the block).

Variation 2:
The same as variation 1 but the offence out of the first or second touch is now allowed.

Variation 3:
The same as variation 2 but with a single block against the quick hitter and/or the setter's tip/dump and a double block against the second hitter (Fig. 166c).

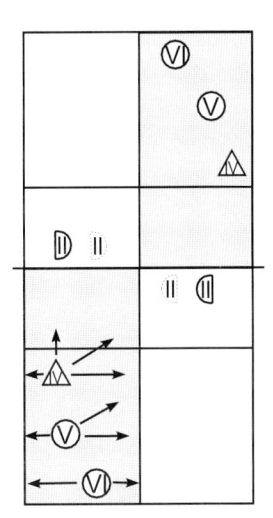

Fig. 165d

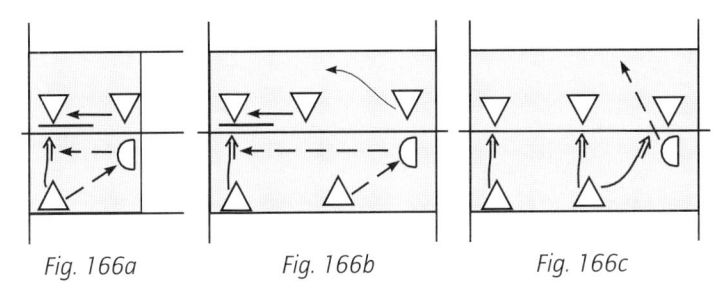

Fig. 166a   *Fig. 166b*   *Fig. 166c*

- **Game 5 vs. 5 on a Diagonal Volleyball Court Including the Entire Front-court Area (Zone)!**

There must be a high set and the formation of a double block (Fig. 167).

Variation 1:
Play using the mirror image for the defence in positions II, III, IV, VI, and I.

Variation 2:
The same as variation 1 but the setter can now tip/dump the volleyball.

LEARNING PART 3

Variation 3:
The same as variation 2 but now a quick attack is allowed.

- **Game 4 vs. 4!**
  [On a 9 x 9 meter volleyball court]

A front-court athlete, who is setting and blocking, and three defenders who are also back-court hitters (Fig. 168a). The front row athlete can tip/dump the volleyball.

Goal:
- The defender in position VI is covering outside the block shadow in the main hitting direction.

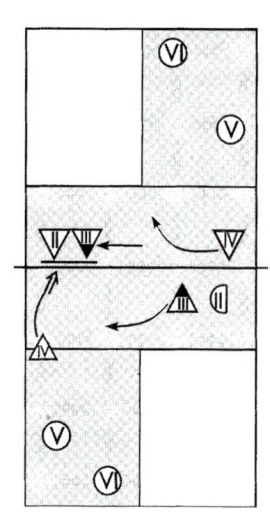

Fig. 167

Variation 1:
Game 5 vs. 5 but with two front-court athletes as blockers. The offence is still run only from the back-court (Fig. 168b).

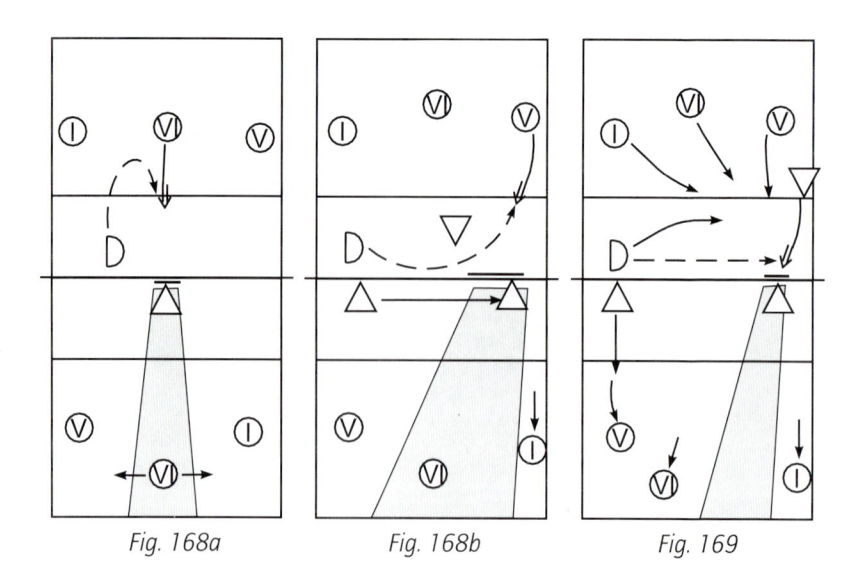

Fig. 168a *Fig. 168b* *Fig. 169*

Variation 2:
The same as variation 1 but the back-court athlete can hit from the front-court.

Variation 3:
The same as variation 1 but one front court athlete is running a quick attack and the back-court athletes are hitting back row attacks (but later switch to combination attacks).

- **Game 5 vs. 5 with Two Front-court Athletes and Three Back court** Athletes!
  [On a 9 x 9 meter volleyball court]

The offence is run from the outside positions against a single block. The setter is allowed to tip/dump the volleyball.

Goal:
- The non-blocking net athlete releases from the volleyball net and plays defence if there has been no setter's tip/dump.

- **Power Volleyball Games with an Uneven Number of Athletes on a 9 x 9 Meter Volleyball Court, and the Smaller Team Always Receives the First Volleyball!**

For example, two or three athletes vs. four, five, or six athletes! The important point here is that the defence must always be complete.

Goal:
- The correct spatial actions of the defenders according to the situation at hand.
- Training the psychological skills and abilities of the athletes.

- **Power Volleyball – 6 vs. 6!**
  [On a 9 x 9 meter volleyball court]

The volleyballs are always tossed to the same team, who runs a predetermined offensive strategy, and forces the defence to deal with different situations (i.e. the use of a front row setter). First, the volleyball is only set to the outside position, then to position II, then involving a quick and outside hitter, and finally with the use of special offensive combinations.

5.6.4 Special Training Drills to Work on the Coordinative Skills and Abilities of the Defenders

The organisation and the routines are the same as in section 4.6.4 – "Special Training Drills for the Setter and the Attacker"!

Outside Blockers:
- Outside block/defence/offence.

- Outside block/close coverage & defence/offence/block.
- Outside double block/inside double block/offence/block.
- Outside double block/defence & distant coverage/block.
- Inside double block/outside double block/self-coverage/attack.
- Outside single block/close coverage of the block/attack (1 meter behind).
- Triple block in the distant outside position/offence/block.
- Block against the setter's tip & dump/defence/combination attack at the setting position.
- Single block against an A-quick behind the setter/inside double block against a 1-meter set/offence.
- Single block against a quick attack/double block against a back row attack on the outside/self-coverage.
- Triple block in your own position/safety set/block.
- Single block/receive a free ball/combination attack (see the drills for outside/combination/diagonal hitter).

Middle Blockers:
- Single block against a quick attack/double block against a back-court hitter/B-quick attack.
- Single block against an A-quick behind the setter/double block against combination hitter in position III/block against the setter's tip & dump/fake a single block against the quick hitter/double block in the outside position II/quick attack jumping away from the setter ("flyer").
- Release from the volleyball net (free ball)/shoot without a change of direction/double block against the back-court hitter in position V/quick attack (medium-quick/3-meter shoot set).
- Double block in positions II, III, and IV.
- Single block against a quick hitter/run for a tip/A-quick behind the setter.
- Double block in positions II, III, and IV against back-court attacks.
- Triple block in position III/B-quick attack/double block in position IV against a back row attack from position I.
- Three single-block actions against "flyers" (see all drills relating to the quick hitter).

Outside Defenders (Especially the Libero) in Positions I and V:
- Defend against a setter's tip & dump/close coverage of the offence/defence.
- Save a volleyball/defend against a quick attack/cover the offence.
- Defence/safety set/cover the offence.
- Defend against a setter's tip & dump/safety set/defence.
- Back row attack/defend against a quick attack/save a volleyball/cover the offence.
- Distant coverage of the block/safety set/cover the offence.
- Defend against a setter's tip & dump/defend against a quick attack/defend against a setter's tip & dump.

- Defend against a quick attack/save the volleyball/defend against an offensive tip & dump.
- Defend a touched volleyball/distant coverage of the block/safety set/cover the offence.

Defenders (Especially the Libero) in Position VI:
- Defend against three spikes that quickly follow each other through an open double block.
- Four defensive actions with a single block (attacks should be alternating passed the block from the left side and from the right side).
- Save a touched volleyball (hit off of the block)/diagonal (cross-court) defence/safety set/cover the offence.
- Free ball situation/cover the offence/defence.
- Defend against three quick attacks in a row (without a block in his/her defensive area).
- Defend against a setter's tip & dump (played deep into a corner)/defence/cover the offence/safety set.
- Save a volleyball/cover the offence/defend against a volleyball hit off of the block.
- Back-court attack/defence/back-court attack.
- Free ball situation/back row attack/save a volleyball.
- Defend against a combination hit (without a block)/defend against a volleyball hit off of the top of the block.

Photo 65 (Schäfer)

6 Match Systems

The following basic **principles** are important for the design and choice of a match system, regardless if a team uses a libero or not:

1. One, if the not the major condition, is an exact assessment of the individual tactical abilities of each athlete, especially where his/her role as a specialist is concerned. Therefore, not only are the technical, tactical, athletic, and psychological strengths relevant but also the weaknesses in each of these fields.

Each **match system** has two different goals: On the one hand it must bring out the "best" in each athlete and the team and, on the other hand, it must cover up the weaknesses of each athlete and the team. In other words, it must make it difficult for the opposition to discover your team's weaknesses. In the end, a match system can only be further developed by maximising the team's strengths and minimising the team's weaknesses. This also includes a permanent control and comparison of the practice situation and the match situation.

2. The knowledge of the individual tactical abilities of each athlete does not help if these abilities cannot be used within the group/team tactical field. In other words, a match system based on the individual tactical strengths of the athletes will fail if they are not able to or only partly use these strengths within the entire structure of the team and within the team's tactical strategy. For example, let us say that we recognise that one athlete is by far the most effective service reception athlete. This knowledge is useless if this athlete does not acquire a larger service reception area and is given more responsibility within the contexts of the service reception.

3. Most attention is focused on the service reception and setting situations (Complex 1 – C1) and on the blocking and defensive situations (Complex 2 – C2). In the C1 field every thought is fixed on a method of improving the service reception situation – firstly by taking care of the strengths and weaknesses of the service reception athletes, secondly by developing the setting situation, and finally by organising the offensive situation. Since the attacker has three times as much time to prepare for the offence than a hitting service reception athlete every possibility to make the transition from service reception to offence easier should be taken advantage of. After the service reception, the main focus should be given to the setter and finally to the attacker.

An offensive tactic can only be successful if it is keeping in mind the sequence of the game/match. This means that the offence is not determining the setting and the service reception strategy, but rather the setting and offensive strategies are dependent upon the service reception strategy.

The principles of C2 are based according to this. First and most important are the middle blocker and defender in position VI, then the outside blockers and outside defenders, and finally the offence from a transition out of the defensive situation.

Generally, there are many possibilities for line-ups of athletes in the C1 and C2 situations and it is the job of the coach to find the appropriate one for each situation. If there are two or more possibilities for the first chain of action (service reception/defence) then the formation of the next phase (setting out of the service reception/defence) should determine the selection of which service reception formation to use.

The thoughts that are mentioned above are absolutely true for the high levels of volleyball where there are only two or three service reception athletes. At the middle and low levels of volleyball the second phase (setting situation) and the third phase (offensive situation) should be given more importance in the thoughts regarding the choice of a match system. This is because the front-court service reception athletes do not have to cover large distances in their offence because there are usually more than three service reception athletes involved in the service reception formation.

1. It is a feature of a perfect match system that all six line-ups and formations and offensive rows are equally strong. The same is true for the back rows. A result of this principle is that equal and the same types of athletes are put diagonally to each other in the line-up. If a team has only two middle blockers and/or two middle hitters they should be lined up diagonally to each other. This is a major principle for the design of a starting line-up and, respectively, the match system.

   With every principle there are thoughts and ideas that might lead to different decisions. An exception to this principle is the example in the following situation: If a team has one strong hitter and strong blocker but also at the same time two weak blockers. In this situation, it would make sense to position the two weaker blockers in a row either in front of the strong blocker or behind the strong blocker instead of positioning one of them in front of the strong blocker and the other one behind the strong blocker. By doing this we get one or two line-ups with very weak blocking rows but we also get one or two line-ups with very strong blocking rows. This starting line-up will make two strong, two mediocre, and two weak blocking/defensive rows possible instead of six mediocre blocking rows.

The strategy of this line-up is based on the thought that in situations with weak blocking rows one still wants to score "mini-breaks", but one does not want to give away any "mini-breaks". To solve this problem one strategy that can be used is that the main hitter/blocker is always able to be successful against a double-block. This is the main idea behind this concept and the change in the line-up. This intention is supported by the fact that both (or at least one of the weak blockers) are strong servers because this will bring "mini-breaks" when they go back to serve and the strongest blocking row is at the volleyball net. On the other hand, the weakness in blocking can be reduced by a strong server who makes it difficult for the opposition to run an organised offence with his/her serves.

2. It is important to put a team together that is big and strong enough to compensate for and replace athletes who suffer from injuries or athletes that are not in the proper form and conditioning. For example, this means that in a 5-1 match system the team needs a second setter and with three middle blockers the team needs a fourth middle blocker. In a match system with two service reception athletes the team needs a third service reception athlete in case it needs a replacement. Altogether, including the libero, this brings us up to ten athletes on this exemplary team with their level of play not differing too much. The other spots on the team should be given to young and not very experienced athletes that still need to learn a lot (i.e. junior athletes). These decisions should have been already made during the off-season.

3. If a team is using a libero then it will be important for this team to develop two match systems – one with and one without the use of a libero and both systems must be able to be played automatically.

4. Each match system must have modifications that are trained in practice and that can be called for by the coach during the match. In this manner, when weaknesses occur, the coach can deal with them either by substituting an

athlete or by changing the match strategy in regards to the service reception/setting/offence or blocking and defensive formations (see Chapter 7, "Defensive and Offensive Strategies").

5. All explanations and reports in the literature regarding match systems only refer to the differences in the athlete's offensive abilities (i.e. a 4-2 match system is defined as a match system which utilises two setters and four hitters (usually two main hitters and two supporting hitters). If we take a look at the structure of the sport of volleyball, it reveals the fact that an offensive action is always started with a defensive action (except for the serving situation). The marking of the different types of athletes and of the match system is not up to the complex demands that are asked from the different athletes and, therefore, not appropriate for the game/match situation.

At the low levels of volleyball it makes sense to choose the match system after the proportion of setters to all-around athletes. This is reasonable because in this situation the specialisation of the athletes is not as strong and it would not make sense for the development of the athletes to do anything different. This is why the role of the athletes in the offence and defence does not have to be ultimately differentiated here (see Chapter 6.2). At the middle and especially the high levels of volleyball, where there are specialised athletes, the roles and obligations of the different types of athletes in regards to being a front-court or a back-court athlete should be realised and taken into consideration.

Differentiation of the athletes can be as follows:

1. **Setter** – Should play in the outside blocking position and in position I when in defence.
2. **Middle Blocker** – Should play the role of quick hitter or main hitter with or without any serve receiving actions, and in the defence s/he is mainly playing in positions V and VI, but also position I if s/he is hitting back row.
3. **Main Service Reception Athlete** – Should play as an outside or middle blocker or as an outside and/or combination hitter and s/he mainly play defence in position V or VI.
4. **Supporting Service Reception Athlete** – Should play as a quick hitter, outside or combination hitter, or as a middle or outside blocker and play defence mainly in position V or VI.
5. **Diagonal Athlete** – Should play as the main hitter and outside blocker and should defend mainly in position I as a back row attacker (see Chapter 6.3).

> 6. **Libero** – Should play as the main service reception athlete and main defensive athlete. He is mainly playing in position VI with the men and she is mainly playing in position V with the women and in both circumstances is responsible for the close coverage of the offence and for the safety set if the setter is defending the volleyball.

With the explanations mentioned above, it is evident that the athletes should be identified according to their role in the offence and defence. The more different types of roles and functions an athlete is able to play, the more s/he must be recognised as a universal/all-around athlete.

6.1 Basic Starting Line-up

Based on the general thoughts mentioned above, the following ranking of importance is reasonable concerning the starting line-up in a 5-1 match system with or without the use of a libero:

1. If a team consists of one setter, two middle blockers, and three service reception athletes without any blocking roles, then the relationship between the middle blockers/hitters and setter must be solved first.
2. If there are more middle blockers/quick hitters than service reception athletes on the team, then the relationship between the service reception athletes and/or the libero must be dealt with first.
3. If the middle blockers/quick hitters have any service reception abilities or the service reception athletes have any middle blocking/quick hitting abilities, then this should be taken into consideration from the very beginning from the points mentioned previously.
4. A comparison of the offensive and defensive actions of the service reception specialists in regards to their blocking, hitting, and defensive skills.
5. A comparison of the transition game of the service reception specialists focusing on how quickly they can switch from service reception to offence. If there are any problems or weaknesses shown, then they can be solved with the correct use of the libero.
6. A comparison of the defensive and offensive skills of the middle blockers/quick hitters, especially in regards to their abilities to perform a back row attack. This will reveal if they should be replaced by the libero when they rotate into the back row.

BASIC STARTING LINE-UP

7. Compare the teamwork between the service reception specialists and how well the quick hitters work together with the setter.
8. The front row and back row should be balanced in all six line-up formations and rotations as far as block/offence and service reception/defence are concerned.
9. If the main/diagonal hitter can also take over the role of the middle blocker/quick hitter, then this must also be taken into consideration from the very beginning in regards to putting together a starting line-up.
10. If a quick hitter/middle blocker has the qualities of a back-court attacker or the main hitter has the qualities of a service reception athlete, then these factors will influence the thoughts regarding the use of the libero.
11. If there is no main/diagonal hitter on the team, it is reasonable to consider using a 4-2 match system with a second supporting setter.

The basic starting line-up will be good, possibly perfect, if the service reception specialists, the libero, and the middle blockers are optimally included in the match system. But if the coach must make a decision to support, by a calculated and well-directed measure, either the service reception athletes more or the blocking and defensive strategy more, then the decision will always favor the service reception strategy. The reason for this is that the weaknesses, respectively the errors, in the service reception strategy not only mean a score for the opposition but also a "mini-break" whereas any errors by the blocking and/or defensive strategy, especially when your own team is serving, only means a point for the opposition. There is also a situation where the opposite view (to weaken your own team's service reception) can be considered correct. This is when your team has an excellent 3-4 wave main hitter. In this case, the coach can favor the C2 over the C1 strategy.

At the low and middle levels of volleyball, a division of the athletes in the positions of setter, main hitter, supporting hitter, and libero are extremely simplified. A more reasonable and better differentiation is between the setter, middle blocker, outside blocker, and libero. At the high levels of volleyball, a differentiation between the main and supporting setters, middle and outside blockers, main and supporting service reception athletes, main and supporting defensive specialists, main/diagonal/back-court, quick, and outside hitters is necessary.

According to this, the libero may be called a main service reception athlete and/or a main defensive specialist, or a supporting service reception athlete and/or a supporting defensive specialist.

Furthermore, there is the differentiation between the serving, defensive, and coverage specialist.

Normally, there are the following types of athletes with the following combinations of specialisations:

1. A middle blocker, who is always working against quick hitters, is most of the time a quick hitter him/herself. As well, s/he will most likely have the qualities of a back-court hitter rather than the qualities of a service reception athlete.
2. A service reception specialist, who is normally an outside/combination hitter and outside blocker, rarely has the role of a middle blocker/quick hitter and rarely has the qualities of a back row attacker.
3. A main/diagonal/back-court hitter usually has offensive qualities a second, third, and fourth wave hitter, but not as much the qualities of a first wave hitter. As well, s/he usually blocks on the outside and rarely in the middle position.
4. The libero is always the main service reception athlete, at main defensive specialist, and the main coverage athlete on the team.

For these reasons, the definition of a 5-1 match system in volleyball literature is quite superficial and does not truly describe the complex profiles that are required from the athletes. Therefore, the additional qualities of the athletes at the high levels of volleyball are discussed now.

6.2 Match Systems with Two Setters

This definition only gives the information that a team is playing with two setters and four all-around/universal athletes. If a team has an all-around/universal athlete who has more qualities and/or if a team is using a libero we are not told this in the information from the definition. Since it is important to know if the libero is playing or not, it should be a part of the match system. Therefore, the definition 4-2+L match system might more clearly indicate the use of a libero.

> The 2-2-2 match system shows that there are possibly two athletes with the qualities of a main hitter, but it does not say if they have the qualities of a quick hitter or a middle blocker.

The same is true regarding the 4-2 match system, with or without a libero, and any of its variations such as the *3-2-1 or the 3-1-2 match systems.* For these reasons, a closer examination at the different types of athletes will be presented

MATCH SYSTEMS WITH TWO SETTERS

before a match system and its variations are developed. The figures are of some selected examples of the service reception formations and their different variations. At the high levels of volleyball, there are further "universal" abilities that are asked from the setter besides extraordinary setting qualities to enable him/her to play a match system with two setters, but even more so to play a match system with only one setter. For example, in a **5-1 match system** the ability to block is important. This explains the efforts at the international level of volleyball to develop and train tall setters or setters with great jumping abilities. In a match system with two setters, both setters must be offensively trained especially in executing second, third, and fourth wave attacks. This also applies to the men's middle levels of volleyball and to the women's high levels of volleyball. Therefore, a decision for a match system with two setters is dependent upon the all-around/universal abilities of the setters. For example, if one of the setters is offensively weak then the 5-1 match system should be preferred/chosen, especially if one of the athletes is able to hit from the back row and is more effective in that position than the second setter would be as a front-court hitter. If there is even a further good attacker on the bench, then s/he should be put in the line-up over the second setter. A further reason for a change to a one-setter match system is the use of an extraordinary hitter. This hitter should be positioned next to the setter in the line-up. If both setters are strong service reception athletes then this could be a reason to stay with a 4-2 or a 2-2-2 match system despite the offensive weaknesses of one of them. If both setters are offensively weak and cannot be compensated by a back row attacker or another athlete, then the team should stay with two setters, but the setting should be simplified. In other words, the front row setter should run the offence. This is especially true at the low levels of volleyball.

> If both setters are offensively weak and are also weak service reception athletes, then the back row setter should be replaced by the libero. The front row setter then runs the offence.

If a team only has one setter with offensive and service reception skills and a weaker setter in these same fields, then a "mixed" system of running the offence would be appropriate. For example, one setter is running the offence in four of the rotations and the other setter is running the offence in the other two formations. This is a "flowing" change to a 5-1 match system. In other words, it is easy to change from the "mixed" system with two setters into a system with only one setter.

In the following paragraphs, the main hitter will be defined as a quick hitter and as a main blocker. The all-around/universal athlete will be characterised as the main service reception athlete and an outside blocker. If there are no main blockers, all-around/universal athletes with similar abilities will take over this role.

> The libero will be defined as the main or supporting service reception athlete and as the main or supporting defensive specialist.

6.2.1 The 4-2/4-2+L Match System with Four All-around/Universal Athletes

The starting line-up in this situation is not very difficult or problematic (Fig. 170). This line-up also applies if all four of the all-around/universal athletes are main hitters (4-2 match system). There are no difficulties in the transition to the offence from either the four-person service reception formation or the five-person service reception formation. Whether or not the offence is run by a front row setter or by a back row setter is dependent upon the offensive skills of the setter.

> If there is a player on the bench who is stronger in the service reception and/or defence than one or two of the starting athletes, then it is reasonable to consider this athlete for the libero position and to change to a 2-2-2+L match system. Another consideration is that the coach may decide to slowly and carefully specialise his/her athletes and to train the libero.

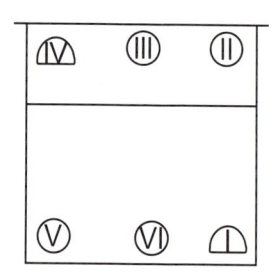

Fig. 170

6.2.2 The 2-1-3/2-1-3+L Match System with Three All-around/Universal Athletes

If the only main attacker is also a service reception athlete, then the same line-up as shown in Fig. 170 applies. The main hitter will be positioned with the setter that shows the more offensive and blocking weaknesses.

The offence out of a three-person service reception formation that is run by a front row and/or back row setter will cause no problems concerning the penetration of the setters and the approaches of the hitters if the main hitter has no service reception function. If both setters have service reception roles/skills then the use of a three-person and/or a four-person service reception formation is made much easier.

In this situation, the use of a libero makes the most sense.

6.2.3 The 2-2-2/2-1-3+L Match System with Two All-around/Universal Athletes

A further differentiation should be made regarding the block but not affecting/concerning the offence. This means that the middle blockers must be positioned diagonally to each other in the line-up. The setters can be lined up opposite to each other but not if one of them has more responsibilities in the setting duties.

If only one middle blocker is able to serve receive then the service reception skills of a substitute athlete (coming in as a libero) and of the setters must be checked and included in the thoughts and decision-making process when selecting a line-up. Fig. 171a shows a basic starting line-up with the weak service receiving middle blocker/libero in position VI, the setters in positions I and IV (main setter in position I), the serve receiving middle blocker in position III, and the two universal/service reception athletes diagonal to each other in positions II and V.

The match system would be called a 2-2-2+L. In addition, the libero can replace one or two of the other athletes when they are in the back row to help strengthen the service reception formation and/or the defence.

Another very good possibility for a line-up would be to put the middle blockers in positions II and V (Fig. 171b).

If the supporting setter has good service reception skills and the team has no libero, then the line-up in Fig. 171c will be very effective.

Fig. 171a 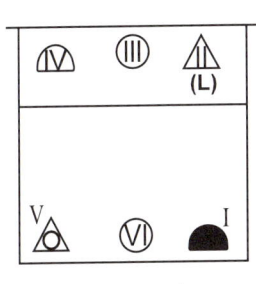   *Fig. 171b* 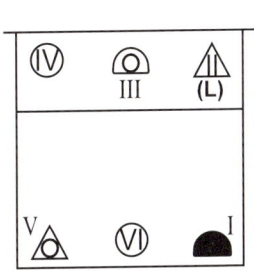   *Fig. 171c*

MATCH SYSTEMS

It can be deduced from the starting line-ups that different service reception formations can be used, especially with consideration to the possibilities of substitutions that are available with the use of the libero.

6.2.4 The 2-3-1/2-3-1+L Match System with One All-around/Universal Athlete

This particular match system can be used if at least two of the middle blockers and at least one of the setters has good service reception skills. The thoughts of section 6.2.3 apply here and offer two possible line-ups (Figs. 172a and 172b). The second option (Fig. 172b) is not reasonable for the low and high levels of volleyball, but it makes sense to use it at the middle levels of volleyball.

Accordingly, the 2-3-1+L match system will be used if at least one of the middle blockers and one of the setters is able to serve receive.

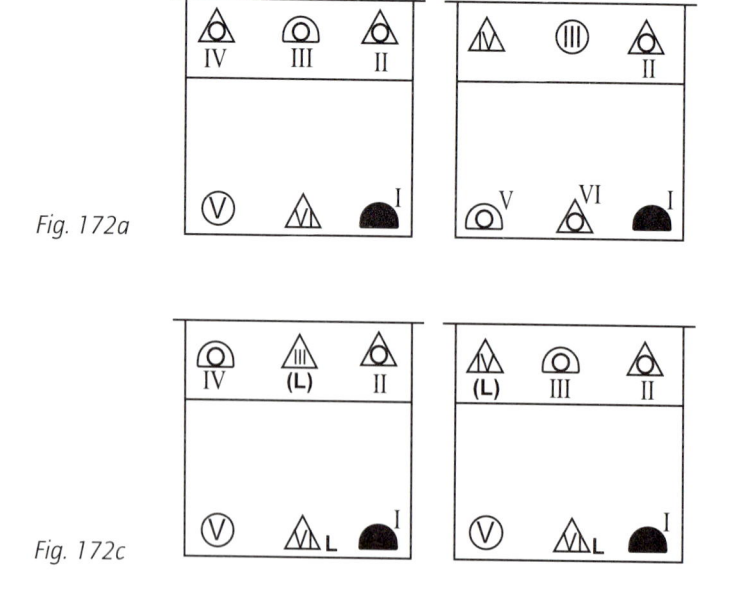

Fig. 172a

Fig. 172b

Fig. 172c

Fig. 172d

6.3 Match Systems with One Setter

According to the explanations mentioned above regarding the match systems with two setters, the transition to a one-setter match system flows better for the following possible reasons:
1. One of the setters is a very good service reception athlete.
2. One of the setters is offensively very strong and/or a weak blocker.
3. One of the setters is very effective as a back row attacker and a much better blocker than the other setter.
4. One of the setters is a weak service reception athlete and has no skills of a quick attacker.
5. One of the setters is very effective with a tip/dump or an attack out of the first pass.
6. If the service reception formation can be set up in such a way that there are no comfortable penetrating paths for the setter.
7. One of the setters is an effective hitter.
8. One of the setters is a much better setter.
9. One of the setters is psychologically much stronger.
10. One of the setters has the stronger leadership abilities.

The more true the points mentioned above are for a team, the more important is the introduction and transition of the one-setter match system.
A major advantage of this type of match system is the fact that only one setter is working more closely and intensely with the hitters and, therefore, gets to know them much better and vice-versa (the hitters get to know their setter much better). Consequently, this means that the main setter must work much more closely with all of the hitters during practice than the supporting setter.

6.3.1 Thoughts and Helpful Hints for the Development of a Basic Starting Line-up

The following basic principles will be explained, justified, and used in examples to explain them clearer. Further thoughts regarding the strengths and weaknesses of the athletes in the defence will be discussed in chapter 6.4. The aspects mentioned here are mainly concerning the abilities and skills of the main service reception, blocking, and offensive athletes. The following principles will complement and overlap each other to also show different methods of solving a problem in a particular situation. To make the points and thoughts clearer and simpler, only the main role and function of the athlete and why they are assigned to a certain position in the line-up will be stressed. Therefore, there is no order to the ranking of the principles. The less specialists that there are for a particular function/element, the more importance and priority is placed in the assignment of athletes to a particular position. This means that the first decision concerning the development of a basic starting line-up must be made here.

1. If there are only two middle blockers, then they will be placed diagonally to each other in the line-up so that one of them is always in the front row.
2. If there are only two quick hitters on a team, then they should be positioned diagonally to each other because this will increase the effectiveness of the offence. This is so because one hitter is always tying up the opposition's middle blocker.
3. If the suggestions mentioned in points 1 and 2 do not apply to the same athletes, then the following thoughts should be considered: If a team has an extraordinary hitter, then the middle blockers should be positioned diagonally to each other to have equally good blocking rows in all situations, therefore, more good chances to score "mini-breaks". If a team does not have an extraordinary hitter, then the quick hitters must be positioned diagonally to each other because the main focus is now on performing a C1 to gain the serve back without giving up any points to the opposition. This will be achieved because of the higher efficiency and effectiveness of the offence with a quick hitter always in the front row.
4. If one middle blocker is stronger than the other middle blocker, then s/he should be positioned next to the setter to make up for any possible blocking deficiencies of the setter.
5. If one quick hitter is stronger than the other quick hitter, then s/he will be lined up next to the setter to increase the effectiveness of the offence in the situations when the setter is playing in the front row and a third front row hitter is missing.
6. If the suggestions mentioned in points 4 and 5 are not combined into one athlete, then the suggestions mentioned in point 3 apply.
7. If a team has a main hitter without any back-court hitting skills, then s/he should be positioned next to the setter for the same reasons mentioned in point 5, and s/he must be replaced in the back row by the libero to save energy for his/her front-court offence.
8. If a team has a main hitter, who is also able to execute back row attacks, then s/he should be lined up diagonally from the setter to have the option of having a third hitter, even when the setter is in the front row.
9. If a team has one weak hitting and blocking athlete, then the main blocker

and/or the main hitter should be positioned next to him/her for the same reasons as mentioned above.
10. If a team has a very weak defender, then either a strong defender must be positioned next to him/her and/or s/he must always be replaced by the libero when s/he rotates into the back row.
11. If a team plays with two, three, or four service reception athletes then the stronger blocking and/or hitting service reception athlete should be positioned next to the setter. This means that when the setter penetrates from position I the athlete should be lined up in position II to strengthen the offence and the block in two of the rotations when the setter is in the front row.
12. If the service reception athlete is also a back row attacker, then s/he should not be positioned next to the setter. If a team has more than two service reception athletes then s/he can play the role of the diagonal hitter.
13. The better quick hitter should play next to the weakest hitter to create more single-block situations. As well, the weakest quick hitter should play next to the best outside hitter, who is able to attack successfully against a double block.
14. A back row attacker should either be positioned diagonally to the weakest hitter or at least two positions over to make up for his/her front-court offensive weaknesses with his/her back-court attacks.
15. If there are no back row hitters on the team, then a supporting setter/universal athlete should be positioned diagonally to the setter to be able to run the offence, especially when the main setter must play defence.
16. If a team has an exceptional front row hitter, who is also very successful against a group block (double block or triple block) in the back row, then the basic starting line-up should intentionally allow the two weakest blocking and defensive rotations follow each other. This will allow the next four rotations to be effective. The basic idea behind this concept, is that the main hitter will sideout and return the serve to the team when the two weakest rotations are playing in the front row.
17. If a team has one or two strong servers, then they should be serving when the weakest blocking rotation is at the net, and/or the weakest middle blocker is at the net to allow him/her the time to form a double-block.
18. If a team has two extraordinary front-court athletes that simply cannot play defence then they should be positioned diagonally to one another and not next to each other because this would allow the coach to replace either one of them when they rotate into the back row by the libero.

The service reception athletes and the libero have been neglected in the thoughts mentioned above because they will be separately stressed and discussed in the following paragraphs.

6.3.2 Setter with Five All-around/Universal Athletes

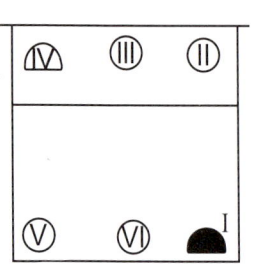

If all of the athletes are equally skilled and good in all areas of the game, then their assignment to a position in the line-up is simple. The team can either play using a five-person service reception formation or a four-person service reception formation. If a quick hitter is used, then it will be necessary to use a four-person service reception formation so as to allow him/her and the setter to be relieved of any passing duties in the service reception formation. Also it makes sense to position athletes with similar skills and abilities diagonally to each other. A change from a five-person service reception formation to a four-person service reception formation is reasonable if one of the all-around/universal athletes is clearly weaker in the service reception formation. This athlete should be positioned diagonally to the setter and play the role of a supporting setter (Fig. 173a). If the supporting

Fig. 173a

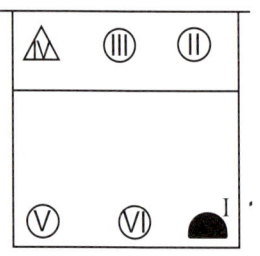

Fig. 173b

setter has the qualities of a quick hitter, then s/he can take on the role of a quick hitter when s/he is in the front row since s/he is not serve receiving. This will make up for his/her service reception deficiencies and weaknesses.

If there is a good back-court hitter, then s/he should be removed from the service reception formation when s/he is in the back row to give him/her the opportunity to execute a back row attack. In this situation s/he, should be positioned diagonally to the setter (Fig. 173b).

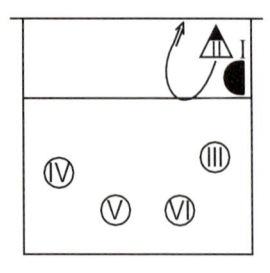

Fig. 174a 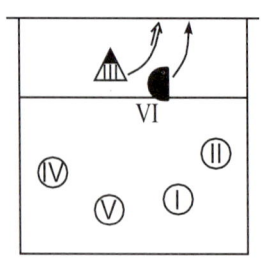   *Fig. 174b* 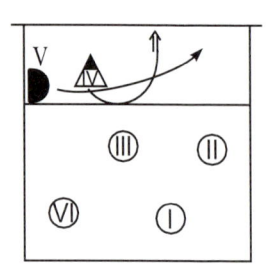   *Fig. 174c*

MATCH SYSTEMS WITH ONE SETTER 251

> If a team has a very strong defensive specialist playing in the libero position, then the libero will replace the weakest defensive athlete(s) when they rotate into the back row.

The four-person service reception formation can also be used to make the penetrating path of the setter easier (Figs. 174a-174c). The front row athletes that have been removed from the service reception formation along with the penetrating setter, will be used as quick hitters.

6.3.3 Setter with Four Service Reception Athletes in a Three-person or Four-person Service Reception Formation and One Back-court Hitter (1-1-4/1-1-4+L Match Systems)

> Basically, everything that was discussed in point 6.3.1 applies in this instance. If a team is playing with a libero as a service reception athlete, all that has been said regarding the 5-1 match system in section 6.3.2 is also relevant here.

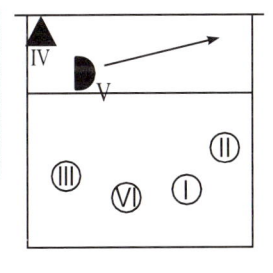

Fig. 175

With five athletes, the athletes with the quick hitting and middle blocking skills must be positioned diagonally to each other. If the main hitter is also effective as a back-court hitter, then s/he will be positioned diagonally to the setter and does not receive the serve. If the main hitter is not able to perform a back row attack, then s/he should start in position VI when the setter is penetrating from position I. This will make penetrating from position V easier for the setter (Fig. 175). In the back row, this hitter can be replaced by the libero at any time to strengthen the defence or the service reception formation.

When assigning and positioning the four-service reception athletes the following points should be taken into consideration:
1. The service reception formation is more important than the setting and the offence.
2. Choose a service reception formation that allows the setter easy penetrating paths and then worry about the approach paths of the quick hitter.
3. The more athletes that can serve receive and are in the service reception formation, the less priority needs to be given to the service reception skills and

MATCH SYSTEMS

abilities of the athletes when their positions and roles are defined in the line-up. More importantly become the other skills and abilities of the athletes (i.e. blocking and quick hitting skills before defensive skills).

The change from a four-person service reception formation to a three-person service reception formation is reasonable for match tactical reasons if there is an advantage for the offensive strategy without weakening the service reception and the involvement of the libero.

If the main hitter has the qualities of a quick hitter and a back-court hitter then there is the possibility to move two athletes out of the service reception formation (the back-court hitter and the front-court quick hitter) as long as the setter is in the front row. This means and allows for different three-person and four-person service reception formations (Figs. 176a-176f).

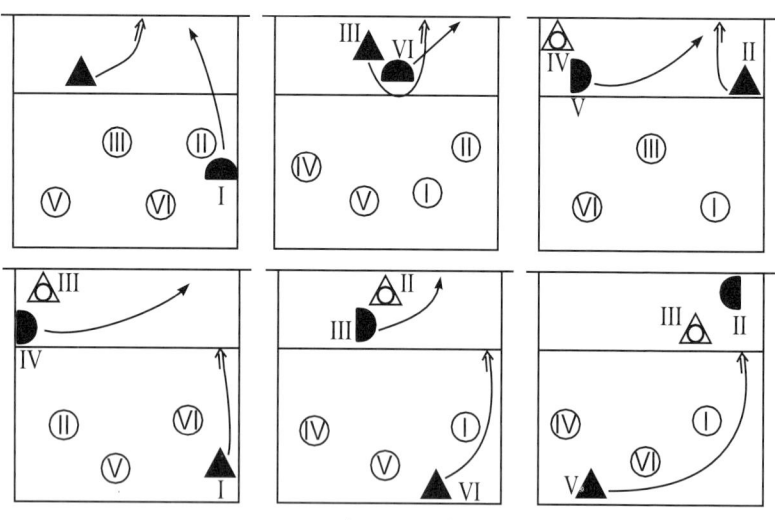

Figs. 176a-f

There is the possibility of moving two front-court hitters out of the service reception formation regardless of where the setter is positioned to give them the opportunity to exclusively focus on their offence. This is only possible if the team uses a libero and/or the main hitter has the skills and ability to be a part of the service reception formation and cannot execute any back row attacks. By not allowing the hitters to take on any serve receiving duties, the offensive strategy

MATCH SYSTEMS WITH ONE SETTER 253

will be more flexible and, therefore, more effective. This will make a three-person service reception formation necessary in all six service reception rotations (Figs. 177a-177f). The opposition can also enforce the use of a three-person service reception formation if their strategy is putting too much pressure on your team's front row service reception athletes so that they can only be used as part of the offence with high sets, then this will be the result.

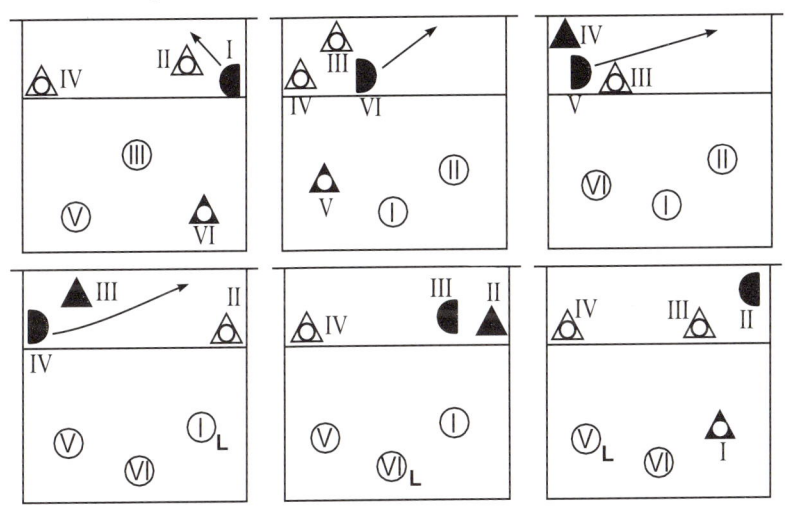

Figs. 177a-f

6.3.4 Setter with Three Service Reception Athletes in a Two-person or a Three-person Service Reception Formation and Two Quick Hitters/Middle Blockers (1-2-3/1-2-3+L Match Systems)

If a team is using a libero, then all of the points mentioned regarding the 1-1-4 match system in section 6.3.3 apply here.

If a team has two middle blockers then they must be positioned diagonally to each other to get six equally good blocking rows. Fig. 178a shows a basic starting line-up with the setter penetrating from position I and the main blocking athletes playing in positions VI and III.

If a team has to use a three-person service reception formation in all situations because otherwise the service reception will lose its effectiveness then this will cause the setter to have a longer penetrating run from position VI to get into his/her setting position. By using a zigzag formation this problem can almost be solved (Fig. 178b). This type of three-person service reception formation will allow the setter to have a shorter penetrating run to get into position.

If the team is substituting/using a libero for both middle blockers in the back row (Fig. 178a) then this will allow the team to use a three-person service reception formation in all six serve receiving rotations and, in addition, the setter will have shorter penetrating paths (see Figs. 178b-178c).

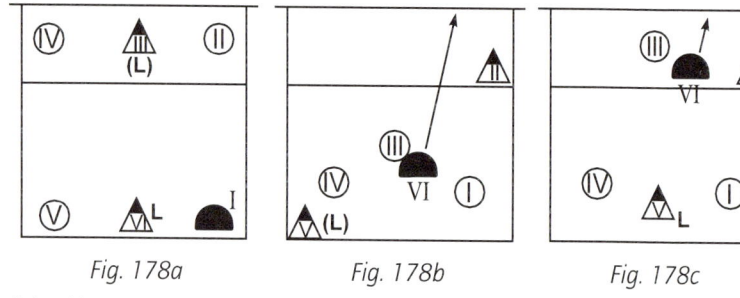

Fig. 178a   *Fig. 178b*   *Fig. 178c*

If, in this starting line-up, one of the quick hitters/middle blockers also has the skills of a back-court hitter then s/he should be assigned to the middle blocking position that is furthest away from the setter. By doing this, it allows the team to have at least two rotations when the setter is in the front row to use this hitter as a third offensive option (as a back row hitter). Therefore, this hitter should be in the line-up in position III in Fig. 178a or in position V in Fig. 178d. This second possibility of a starting line-up may cause some difficulties for the offence when the setter has to penetrate from position VI (Fig. 178e), but especially when the setter is penetrating from position V (Fig. 178f) because in this rotation the penetrating path is quite long.

> If a team is replacing a middle blocker who has no back row attacking skills (Fig. 178a) with a serve receiving libero in position VI, then there will be no long penetrating run for the setter and, therefore, no difficult service reception formations.

A very good quick hitter/middle blocker, who is able to execute an effective back row attack, can also play the position diagonally to the setter. A result of this line-up will be that there is one blocking row without a middle blocker. In this situation, the other middle blocker should start in position II instead of position VI and s/he should be replaced in the back row by the libero (Fig. 178g). An

MATCH SYSTEMS WITH ONE SETTER 255

advantage of this starting line-up is that the setter has a very short penetrating path in all six rotations (see Figs. 179a-179f). According to the basic principles outlined in section 6.3.1, the better middle blocker and/or quick hitter and the better service reception athlete in the offence and/or blocking formations should be positioned next to the setter, especially if the setter reveals any weaknesses in his/her offensive and blocking skills and abilities (see Figs. 178a, 178d, and 178g).

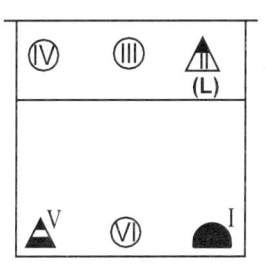

Fig. 178d

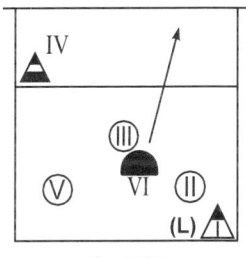

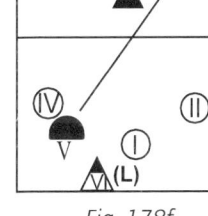

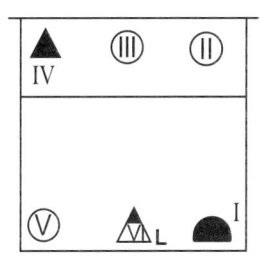

Fig. 178e

Fig. 178f

Fig. 178g

If there is a possibility of using a two-person service reception formation without weakening the quality of the service reception in general (i.e. with the use of a libero), then this should be used in certain "appropriate" situations. A possible result of this will be the use of both a two-person and a three-person service reception formation.

If there is a service reception athlete with the skills and abilities of a middle blocker. Then s/he will start according to Fig. 178f in position II because this will give the team a middle blocker in each blocking row.

If a team has a service reception athlete with the skills and abilities of a quick hitter, then s/he should be positioned in the starting line-up diagonally to the setter in position IV (the same as in Figs. 178a and 178d) and/or in position III (the same as in Fig. 178f). Based on Fig. 178a there will be used exemplary two-person and three-person service reception formations without a libero (Figs. 179a-179f) or with a libero (Figs. 179g-179l).

256 MATCH SYSTEMS

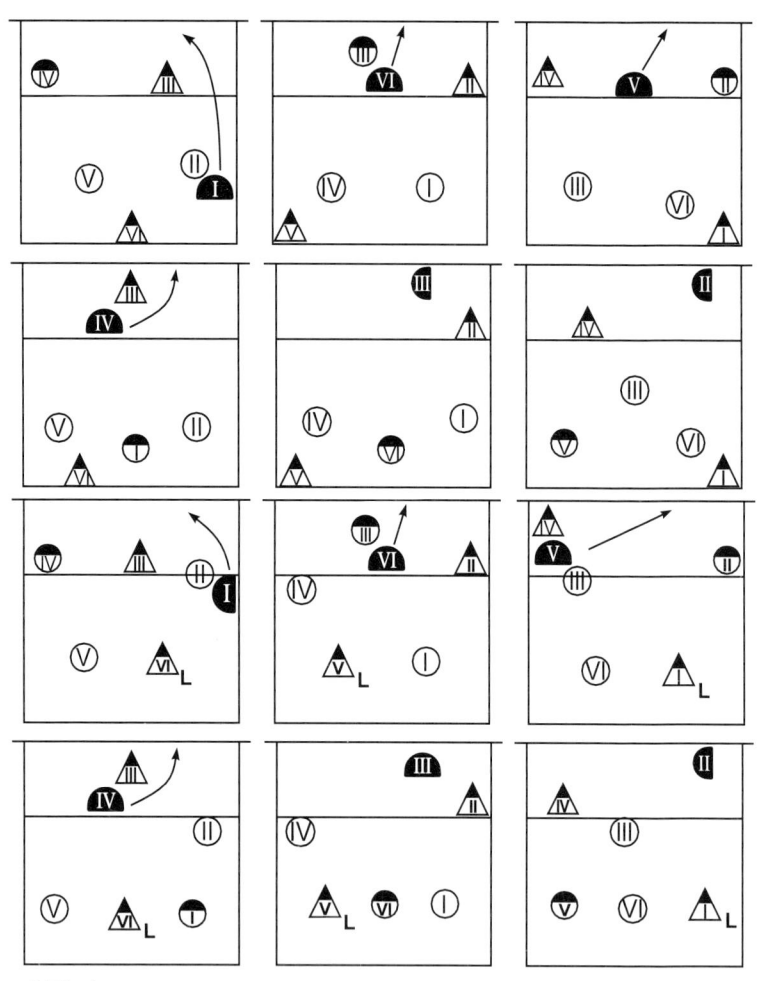

Figs. 179a-l

A comparison of match systems 1-2-3 (Figs. 179a-179f) and 1-2-3+L (Figs. 179g-179l) clearly shows the advantage of the system with the libero because with the use of the libero all of the front-court athletes can be removed from the service reception formation and can concentrate only on their offensive duties. The match systems according to Figs. 179a-179l can be described as match systems that use one setter, two middle blockers/quick hitters, two main service reception athletes, and one supporting service reception athlete with and/or without the use of a libero.

6.3.5 Setter with Two Main Service Reception Athletes in a Two-person Service Reception Formation and Three Middle Blockers/Quick Hitters (1-3-2 Match System)

In the development of the starting line-up of a 1-3-2 match system, the main priority should be directed towards the assignment of the two main service reception athletes. Based upon a starting line-up with the setter penetrating from position I the main service reception athletes should not be placed in positions IV and VI. The result would mean long penetrating runs by the setter from positions VI and V and this problem cannot be solved through any variations of this formation.

This leaves only three possible positions for the main service reception athletes (positions II, III, and V). The service reception athletes can be placed in positions III and V (Fig. 180a), positions II and V (Fig. 180b), or positions II and III (Fig. 180c). The decision in choosing which one of these three possibilities to use is dependent on the skills and abilities of the middle blockers/quick hitters. In this situation the points in section 6.3.1 should be taken into consideration.

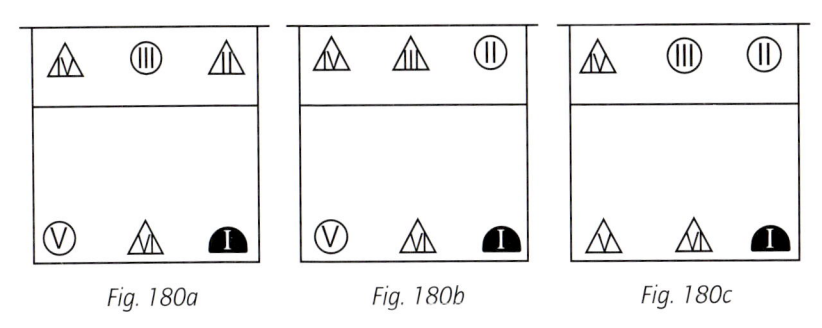

Fig. 180a   *Fig. 180b*   *Fig. 180c*

If we compare the line-ups, the one shown in Fig. 180c is the least reasonable of the three. There are two reasons for this. On the one hand, there is the situation of the setter being in position II, which would leave one blocking row without a middle blocker, even though there are three of them in the starting line-up. As well, in this same rotation there would also be no quick hitter.

Two conditions that must be met to make the use of this starting line-up reasonable are:

1. The team has an extraordinary back-court hitter and a very good server.
2. The opposition has two or three offensive rows that are clearly weaker than the others.

MATCH SYSTEMS

The starting line-ups shown in Figs. 180a-180b are both internationally and nationally played and it is difficult to distinguish which one is used more often.
1. Based on the fact that the middle blocker/quick hitter, who is positioned diagonally to the setter, is also the main and back-court hitter, both line-ups are equally effective.
2. If two of the three middle blockers are clearly better than the third middle blocker then a diagonal positioning between the two better ones in the starting line-up is recommended (Fig. 180b).
3. If there is a second main blocker with the skills of a back-court hitter, then s/he should be placed in positions VI or II (see Fig. 180a) or in position VI (see Fig. 180b) depending upon which formation is used.
4. If one of the three quick hitters is more of a main hitter and less of a middle blocker and if one of the main service reception athletes is a very good middle blocker then the line-up in Fig. 180b should be used with the main blocking service reception athlete in position III. If the line-up shown in Fig. 180a is used, then the main blocking service reception athlete should be in position II. The main hitter should be lined up diagonally to the setter in both line-ups.
5. If, besides the main hitter, there is a middle blocker with the skills of a back-court hitter, then s/he should be lined up next to the setter. In Fig. 180a this would be in either position VI or II and in Fig. 180b it would be in position VI. This ensures that the offensive rows with the setter in the front-court are almost as strong as the offensive rows with the setter penetrating from the back row. For the same reason, the middle blocker with the better quick hitting and/or middle blocking skills and abilities should also be positioned next to the setter.

The following diagrams show possible service reception formations and their variations according to the starting line-ups in Figs. 181a and 182a. Based on these diagrams a comparison of the offensive possibilities will be discussed. To do this, athletes with the same skills and abilities must be used and similar offensive combinations must be performed:
1. Main hitter/diagonal athlete with the skills and abilities of a middle blocker, a quick hitter, and a back-court hitter.
2. Middle blocker with quick hitting and back-court hitting skills.
3. Middle blocker with quick hitting skills.
4. Two service reception specialists with skills of an outside blocker and a second hitter.

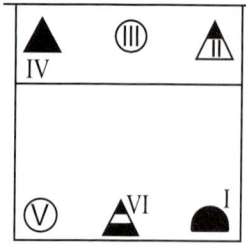

Fig. 181a

MATCH SYSTEMS WITH ONE SETTER

A comparison of the offensive possibilities of the two starting line-ups when the setter is penetrating from position I (Figs. 181 and 182) shows that the starting line-up with the two service reception specialists diagonally to each other means a longer penetrating run for the setter and reveals one service reception variation less than the other line-up for the service reception athletes. Both line-ups have two quick hitters and two middle blockers at the volleyball net.

A comparison of the course of action with the setter penetrating from position VI (Figs. 183 and 184) reveals that the diagonal assignment of the service reception athletes allows for an additional formation, although the penetrating path for the setter and the approach path for the middle hitter are not very easy with this second option. The advantage is that there are still two quick hitters/middle blockers at the volleyball net.

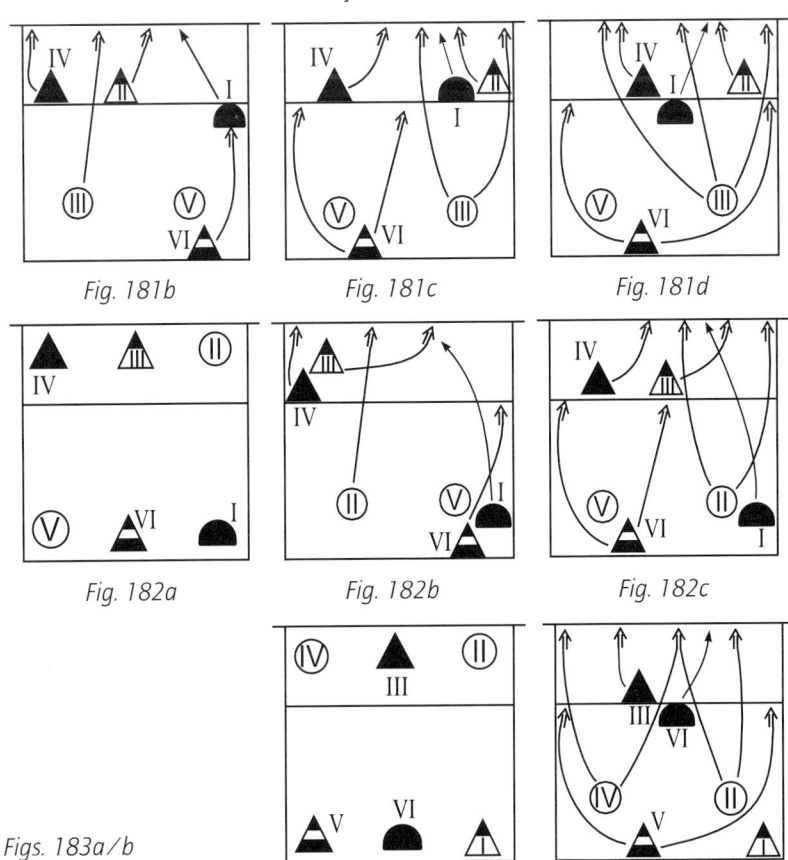

Fig. 181b *Fig. 181c* *Fig. 181d*

Fig. 182a *Fig. 182b* *Fig. 182c*

Figs. 183a/b

MATCH SYSTEMS

Fig. 184a *Fig. 184b* *Fig. 184c*

This might be a weakness for the other starting line-up because both service reception athletes are in the front row and there is only one quick hitter/middle blocker. The course of action with the setter penetrating from position V (Figs. 185 and 186) in both starting line-ups is pretty much identical. One disadvantage for the diagonal positioning of the service reception specialists is that there is the danger of illegal line-ups between position III and position VI (service reception athletes). The lack of an additional variation to this service reception formation might also make a slight difference.

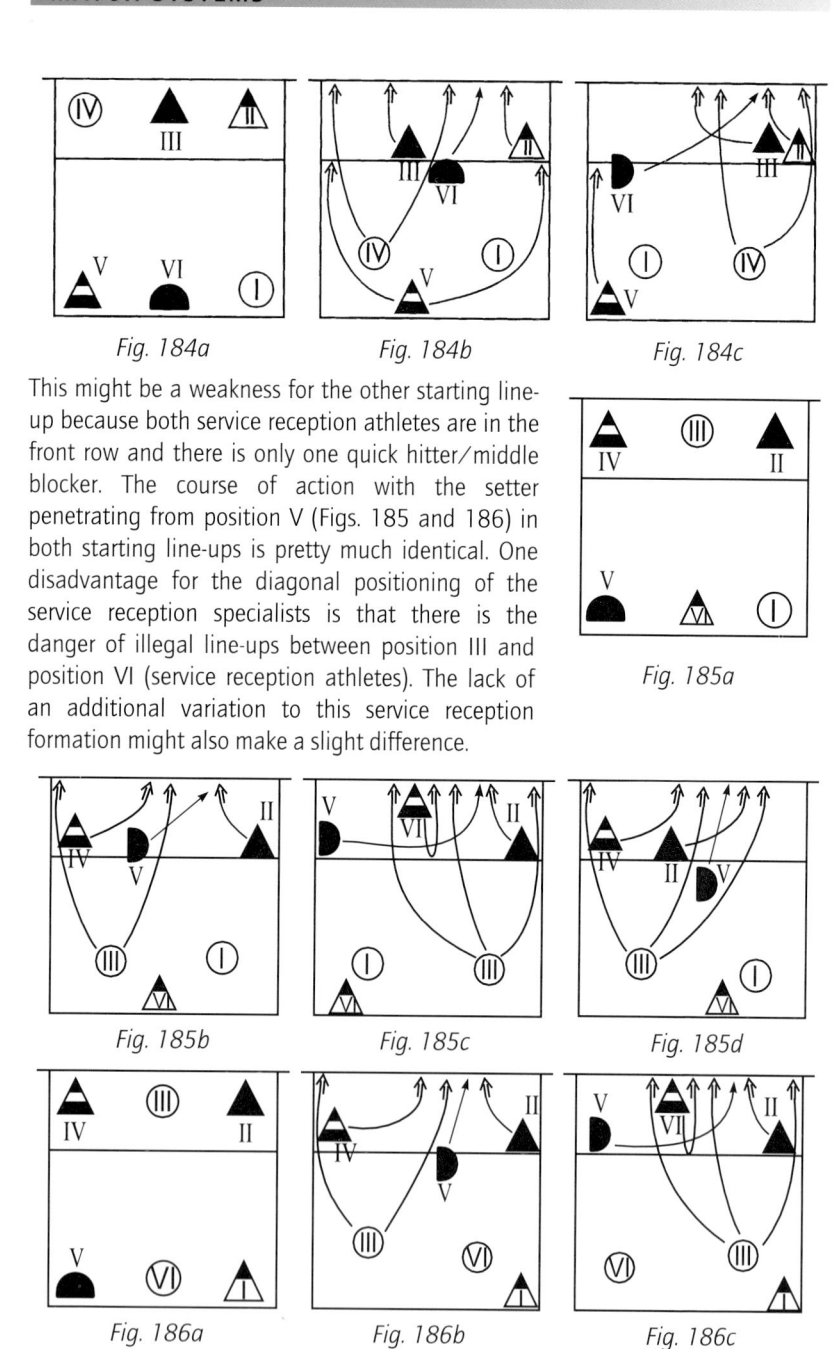

Fig. 185a

Fig. 185b *Fig. 185c* *Fig. 185d*

Fig. 186a *Fig. 186b* *Fig. 186c*

MATCH SYSTEMS WITH ONE SETTER 261

The course of action with the setter in position IV (Figs. 187 and 188) is almost the same for both starting line-ups. With the setter in position III (Figs. 189 and 190), the starting line-up with the diagonal positioning of the service reception specialists has one more variation, but an advantage of the other starting line-up is that the two service reception athletes are both back-court and, therefore, there is a middle blocker more often at the volleyball net.

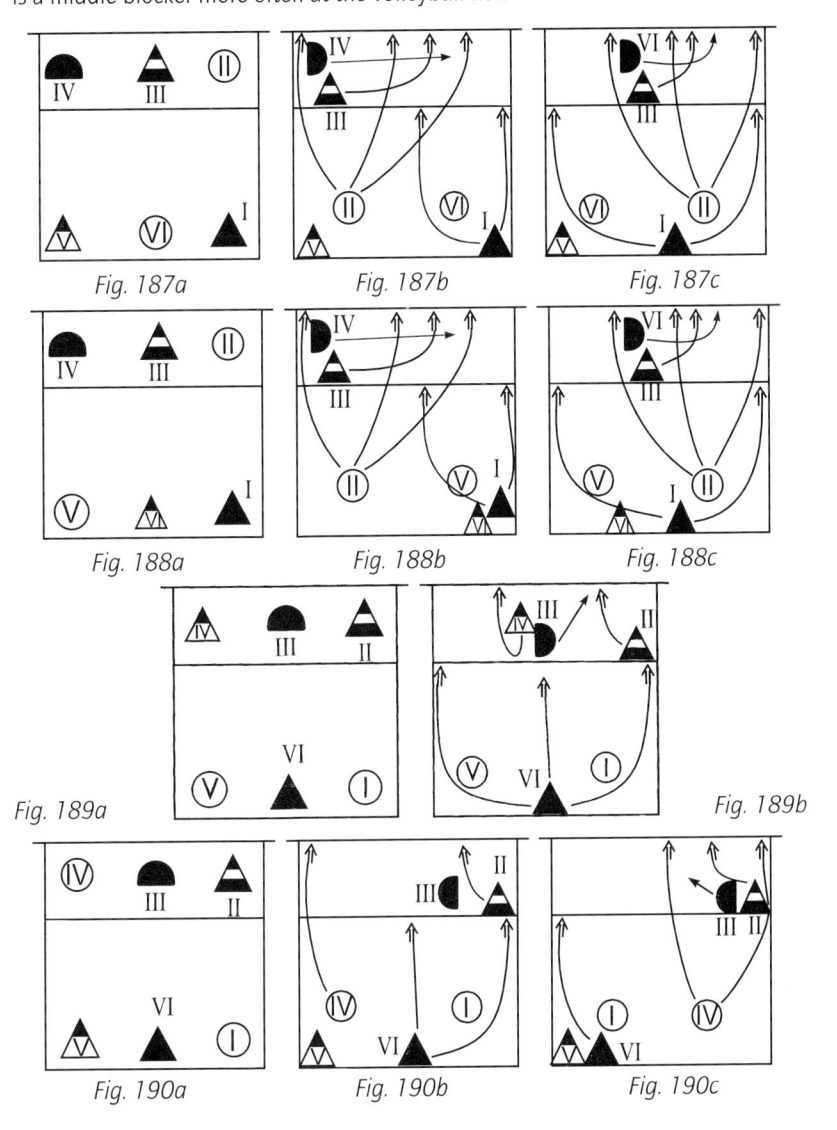

Fig. 187a *Fig. 187b* *Fig. 187c*

Fig. 188a *Fig. 188b* *Fig. 188c*

Fig. 189a *Fig. 189b*

Fig. 190a *Fig. 190b* *Fig. 190c*

MATCH SYSTEMS

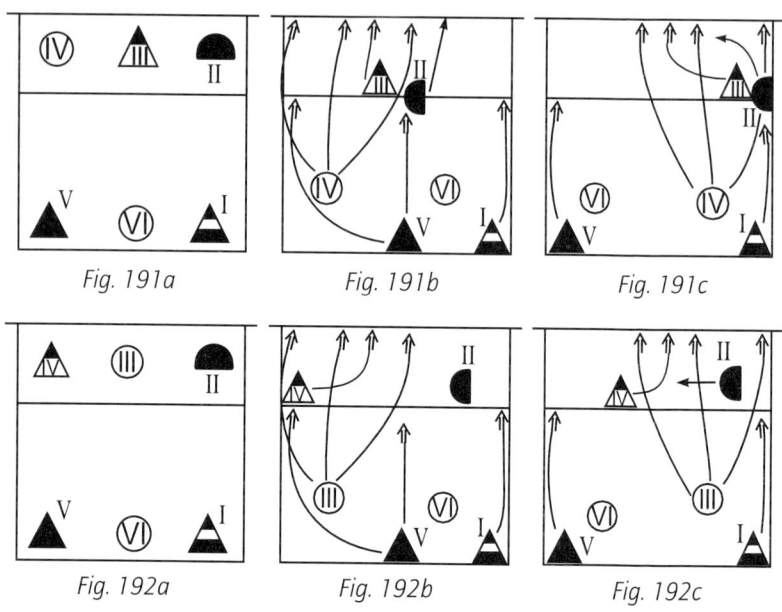

Fig. 191a *Fig. 191b* *Fig. 191c*

Fig. 192a *Fig. 192b* *Fig. 192c*

The course of action of action with the setter in position II in both starting line-ups (Figs. 191 and 192) is almost identical, but again the diagonal positioning of the service reception specialists (Figs. 192b and 192c) shows the danger of an illegal line-up if the two service reception athletes are not paying close attention to their positioning.

To summarise the comparison of the two line-ups the following can be stated:
1. The diagonal positioning of the two service reception athletes gives the opposition the opportunity to always use the same serving strategy, which always makes it difficult for the front row service reception athlete to get into a good offensive position.
2. The starting line-up with the service reception specialists positioned diagonally to each other makes it possible in all six rotations to have the setter either penetrate or to have the setter fake that s/he is penetrating from certain positions. The credible use of this fake penetrating setter is possible, which can assist in some tactical strategies for the team.
3. Both line-ups have the same number of service reception formation variations and the same number of rotations possible with quick hitters/middle blockers at the volleyball net.

MATCH SYSTEMS WITH ONE SETTER

4. A slight advantage for the line-up with the service reception athletes diagonal to each other is easily seen in the photos. In all six service reception rotations the service reception athletes are able to pass from the same side of the volleyball court. In the other line-up this is only possible in five of the service reception rotations.

Assuming that the team is able to play both match systems and that it makes no difference in the quality of play for the team which system is played, the choice of the match system will be determined by the strategy that needs to be used against the upcoming opposition, but it is important to keep in mind what consequences the choice of a particular match system has on your own team's blocking and defensive strategies, including the changes in positioning.

6.3.6 Setter with Two Main Service Reception Athletes in a Two-person Service Reception Formation, Three Middle Blockers/Quick Hitters, and a Libero (1-3-2+L Match System)

The 1-3-2+L match system is almost the same as the 1-2-3 match system in section 6.3.4 because both match systems can be played with three service reception athletes in a three-person or two-person service reception formation. With the development of the starting line-up in a 1-3-2+L match system all information from section 6.3.5 should be taken into consideration if the two-person service reception formation is used. The decisive factor in choosing a starting line-up is that with the consistent use of a libero, a match system can be developed that involves three service reception athletes, three middle blockers/quick hitters, and a setter. In this situation, the main criterion is the service reception quality and especially the skills of the service reception athletes in the starting line-up to be successful against a double block after the service reception.

1. If both service reception athletes have difficulties in attacking out of the service reception formation then they should both be positioned diagonally to each other. The same thing applies to the middle blockers/quick hitters who do not have any back row attacking skills. They also must be positioned diagonally to each other in the line-up because in this manner the libero can replace them both in all three positions (Figs. 193a-193b) when they are in the back row.

MATCH SYSTEMS

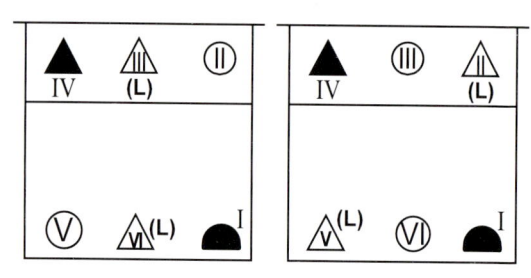

Fig. 193a

Fig. 193b

2. The diagonal positioning makes it possible in a two-person service reception formation for the libero to always be with the serve receiving back-court athlete. At the same time this allows the front-court service reception athlete without any role in the service reception formation to focus on his/her offence, especially combination plays. Additionally, the front-court service reception athlete can easily be moved back into a three-person service reception formation if the opposition is jump serving. Both starting line-ups are equally effective as far as service reception formations, penetrating paths for the setter, and approach paths for the hitters are concerned. This means that the individual skills and abilities of all of the athletes in the offensive, blocking, service reception, and defensive formations helps in deciding the choice of which starting line-up to use.

3. If one of the service reception athletes is slightly better in the offence than the other one and if we want two middle blockers/quick hitters to play next to the setter then the starting line-up shown in Fig. 193c is the correct one to use.

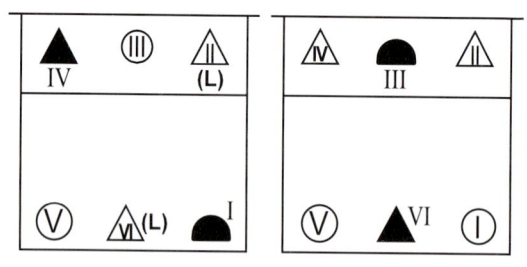

Fig. 193c

Fig. 193d

4. If the service reception athletes are not positioned diagonally to each other then the better one should serve receive in situations when they are both in the front row or both in the back row. This means that s/he is in four rotations where s/he is a part of a two-person service reception formation – once when s/he is in the front row and three times when s/he is in the back row. It does not matter for the starting line-up if s/he is starting in position III or in

position V, but it is important for all of the other offensive and defensive considerations. In the service reception situation (setter in position III and main hitter in position IV) shown in Fig. 193d, the following points regarding the libero take place:

5. If the opponent is jump serving then the libero replaces the main hitter in position VI and becomes part of the three-person service reception formation, thus neutralising the back row attack.
6. The libero will not be used to take advantage of the main hitter in position VI and his/her back row attacks.
7. The libero will replace the service reception athlete who is weakest at that particular moment.

6.3.7 Setter with One Main Service Reception Athlete in a Two-person Service Reception Formation, Four Middle Blockers/Quick Hitters, and a Libero (1-4-1+L Match System)

The 1-4-1+L match system must be seen in close relation to the 1-3-2 match system and all of the points mentioned in section 6.3.5 since both match systems use a two-person service reception formation as their main service reception formation.

In the future, this match system will be the one used at the men's high levels of volleyball as soon as the systematic training and development of the libero will have started. In this situation, the libero will have a crucial role because his/her service reception skills must be as good if not better than the service reception skills of the main service reception athlete. Furthermore, this match system requires that at least one or possibly two of the middle blockers/quick hitters will be clearly stronger outside hitters than quick hitters. It is for this reason that in the characterisation and description of the middle blocker it must be clearly differentiated between middle blockers with mainly quick hitting skills and middle blockers with very good outside hitting skills.

The positioning of the main service reception athlete is the most important decision within the development of this starting line-up because s/he is principally the only athlete who must successfully execute their following action. Also, just as important is the positioning of the middle blockers with very good outside hitting skills.

MATCH SYSTEMS

1. Generally, the main service reception athlete should not be positioned either next to the setter or diagonally to the setter. This leaves the setter, who is penetrating from position I, only the choice between position III and position V (Figs. 194a-194b).
2. Only in the situation where the main service reception athlete also has great offensive and blocking skills as a front row athlete can s/he be positioned next to the setter in position II in the line-up mentioned above (Fig. 194c).
3. If the middle blocker has extraordinary outside hitting abilities then s/he will be positioned in position II next to the setter and diagonally to the main service reception athlete/outside hitter (Fig. 194a) in position VI (Fig. 194b), or in a triangle formation with the diagonal athlete (position V) and the main service reception athlete/outside hitter (position II) in position V (Fig. 194c). In this manner it is assured that at least one front row athlete will be successful against a double block.
4. The middle blocker/quick hitter with the best back-court attacking skills will be positioned as the diagonal athlete to the setter (Figs. 194a-194b).
5. If there is an additional middle blocker/quick hitter with back-court hitting skills then s/he should not be positioned next to the setter or to the main service reception athlete if possible (position III – Fig. 194a or position V – Figs. 194b-194c).
6. The one or two better middle blockers/quick hitters should start with the setter in position II (Figs. 194a-194b) or in position VI (Figs. 194a-194c).
7. The middle blocker/quick hitter without any skills as a back-court attacker and with major defensive shortages should be replaced by the libero in all three back-court positions (L/3x – Figs. 194a-194c).
8. If the second weakest middle blocking/quick hitting defensive athlete is positioned diagonally to the weakest middle blocking/quick hitting defensive

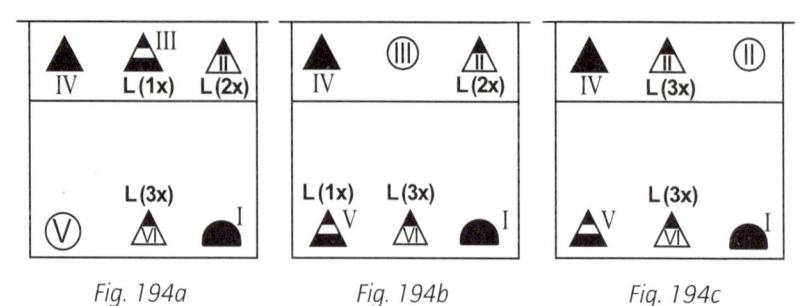

Fig. 194a   *Fig. 194b*   *Fig. 194c*

athlete then s/he should also be replaced in all three back-court positions by the libero (L/3x – Fig. 194c). If s/he is not positioned diagonally to the weakest defender then s/he will only need to be replaced in two of the back-court positions by the libero (L/2x – Figs. 194a-194b).
9. The second strongest back row attacker will only be replaced once by the libero (L/1x – Figs. 194a-194b).
10. The diagonal athlete will not be replaced by the libero when s/he is in the back row so as to be in a position to be used as a third attacker from the back row.

6.3.8 Setter with Five Middle Blockers/Quick Hitters and a Libero (5-1+L Match System)

It is possible to use this match system if the middle blockers/quick hitters have great all-around/universal skills and abilities. This is especially true regarding the service reception in the back row and the outside hitting in the front row.

The starting line-up with this match system almost exclusively takes care of one major point – to position the athletes with similar or equal abilities diagonally to each other.

This match system needs more all-around/universal athletes rather than specialists but it still can be compared to the 5-1+L match system in section 6.3.2 (setter with five all-around/universal athletes).

6.4 Switching/Changing Positions by the Athletes

The development of a starting line-up should also take into consideration some possible but necessary switches/changes in position of the athletes. The match systems and possibly the match strategies are based on the ideas regarding any switches/changes in the positions of any front row athletes or any back row athletes. The main goal is to stress the strengths of the athletes, both defensively and offensively, and to cover up and eliminate any weaknesses.

The match system must take into consideration the technical-tactical and the physical-psychological skills and abilities of the athletes. By doing this a framework of action for the individual, group, and team tactics is developed.

The match system asks for a group of decisions to be made by the coach. Since the chosen match system will be more effective the more precisely that it is adjusted and matched to the skills and abilities of the team, then the determining factors will be the level of volleyball that you are playing at and all of the other factors that are associated with it and influence the game. Therefore, the match system determines the position, role description, and the functions and actions of each individual athlete, the group of athletes, and the whole team in C1 and C2 of the match. This clearly stresses the important role that a switch/change in position has on the match/game, but this fact is not mentioned or stressed enough in the literature.

The introduction of the specialisation of an athlete is also an introduction to switches/changes in position. Generally, the match system only tells you what specialists are on a team. It does not say anything regarding the specific manner that a team is playing their service reception, what offensive and defensive strategies are used, or in the manner that the athletes switch their positions. A crucial factor in the development and use of positional switches/changes is an analysis of your own team. The specific usage of switches is dependent on the level that your team is playing at and that of your opposition.

The following points will be further developed and justified in chapter 7, "Defensive and Offensive Strategies" (also see Chapter 5, "Blocking and Defensive Formations").

There is a difference between switching positions after your own team's and/or the opposition's serve. The reason for the first one is to strengthen the block and the defence (C1), whereas the last one supports the offence (C2).

Any switches after your own team's serve are clearly done to firstly improve the defensive situation and only secondly to support a potential counter-attack. If you have two equally effective positional switches/changes, then the one that makes the transition to offence easier should be preferred. The principal switch of the setter in position II must be doubted if this switch is motivated purely for offensive reasons and not based on any blocking defensive reasons, especially if the setter is the weakest blocker in the row at the volleyball net. This switch is definitely wrong if the setter must block the opposition's main hitter in position IV (position II on your side of the volleyball court).

It must be considered switching the setter in the back row in position I (with position VI back) if s/he is a very good defensive athlete. The dominance of the offence out of the service reception formation forces the defence to use the best possible blocking and defensive formations to increase their chances of a counter-attack. Based on these thoughts, it might be reasonable during defence to switch the setter to position V or to position VI back.

SWITCHING/CHANGING POSITIONS BY THE ATHLETES

The extension of the serving zone to 9 meters has brought the result that many athletes/coaches choose the athlete's serving spot depending on the athlete's defensive area. This strategy must be rejected since the serving action always has priority over any following actions.

There is a similar problem with any switches in positions after the opposition's serve, when the switches are used to create a better transition to defence instead of to offence. At the low levels of volleyball, it can especially be seen that offensive combinations are used even though they are not effective in making the switch to the block and defensive positions easier.

Again, the second step is stressed more than the first. For example, if there is an offensive combination with the setter attacking from position IV, it must be questioned if the setter does not possess any skills of a combination hitter. This combination play would be absolutely wrong if the main reason that it is designed and used is to make the penetrating run of the setter to his/her blocking assignment (position IV) shorter and, therefore, making the next action easier.

As far as the timing and the running paths for switching are concerned, it can be stated that normally any switches after your own serve do not cause any difficulties. This is especially true for the front row athletes. Generally, all athletes who are switching their positions should have short running paths.

A reason for longer approaches and/or running paths can be the role of the athlete. For example, if an athlete is switching from position IV to position II, a middle blocker is switching from position II to position III and the final athlete is switching from position III to position IV, then the athlete with the longest run should change from the distance farthest away from the volleyball net. S/he should do this so that s/he does not force any of the other blocking athletes to move away from the volleyball net, thus, disturbing their readiness to perform their blocking duties. S/he should even accept a longer switching path if it allows the middle blocker to get to their position faster, especially if this makes it easier for the middle blocker to get into his/her starting position against a quick attack (Fig. 195a).

Another reason for deviations in the switching actions and longer running paths can be to support certain blocking strategies. A blocking strategy assigns blockers changed duties and by doing this creates different starting positions for the blockers. Fig. 195b shows the positional switch against a team that performs mainly B-quick and medium-quick attacks to the outside in their offence. By

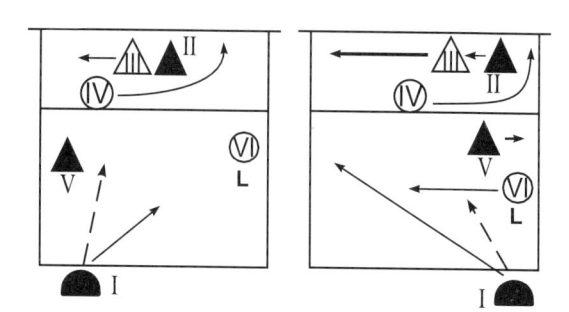

MATCH SYSTEMS

Fig. 195a *Fig. 195b*

taking into consideration the principles mentioned above, the back-court athletes are switching immediately after your team serves the volleyball – the same as the front-court athletes (Fig. 195a). The following is a deviation in the switching action to make it easier for the most important defender to get into his/her defensive position on time. Fig. 195b illustrates a shorter running path for the defender in position V to switch to his/her defensive role in position I.

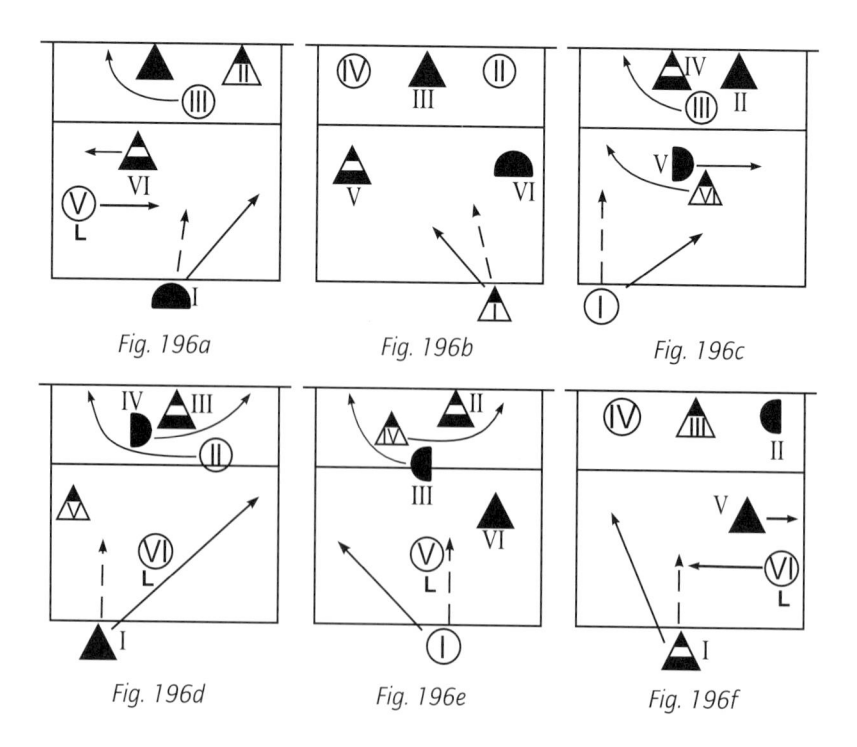

Fig. 196a *Fig. 196b* *Fig. 196c*

Fig. 196d *Fig. 196e* *Fig. 196f*

SWITCHING/CHANGING POSITIONS BY THE ATHLETES

The server as a defender has a special position if s/he is serving from the middle or long distance. Due to his/her long running approach s/he cannot play in defensive positions I and V because s/he will not get there in time to defend against a quick attack and, therefore, s/he must play in position VI back (Fig. 195a). Match strategy regarding the effectiveness of the first action, which in this case is the offensive effect of the serve, has priority over a match strategy of positioning in the defence an easy switching procedure for the back-court athletes (Fig. 195).

Figs. 196a-196f show standard switches in positions of the match system shown in Figs. 181a, 183a, 185a, 187a, 189a, and 191a after your own team serves the volleyball.

Switches by the front-court athletes and the non-service reception back-court hitter(s) after the opposition's serve aims at increasing the effectiveness of the offence. The service reception and non-attacking back-court athletes carry out their duties in the offensive coverage. The non-hitting front-court/back-court hitters provide offensive coverage after the set. Only after the volleyball has crossed the volleyball net can the switch between the blocking and defensive athletes into their original match tactical defensive positions take place.

If the volleyball is rebounding off of the block and coming back into your own side of the volleyball court and possession of the volleyball is regained, then there will be no changes to the defensive positions, but an organised offence out of the coverage will be performed. There are also no positional switches if the opposition's defence makes an offensive action from the first pass or a quick attack possible. There will simply not be enough time to change to the original assigned defensive positions and to prepare for the opposition's attack.

An interim solution for any switches over two positions can be a so-called "stage change". A "stage change" is, due to the lack of time, that there is only a change over one position (stage). To complete the "second stage", the final positional switch will be completed when the next opportunity is offered. The latest that this will occur is with the next possession of the volleyball by the opposition.

In section 4.3 and in Figs. 197a-197d, the course of action for positional switches after the offensive coverage is shown. These Figs. make the switching actions clear with an example of an offensive combination. Fig. 197a shows the planned

MATCH SYSTEMS

offensive combination out of the service reception and Fig. 197b the running paths of the hitters and coverage athletes until the moment of the attack by the combination hitter, and Fig. 197c shows the running paths to the blocking and defensive positions according to Fig. 197d.

To summarise the switching actions, the following points can be stressed:

1. Immediately after your own team's serve, the switches to optimise the block and the defence will be carried out, and immediately following the opposition's serve the switches to optimise the offence will be carried out.
2. During the play, switches occur to, on the one hand, support your own team's block and defence when the opposition has the volleyball and, on the other hand, when your team has possession of the volleyball to make your own offence more effective.
3. Before the serve is performed, certain changes regarding the defenders in positions I, VI, and V are possible (Figs. 195a, 196b, and 196e).

Considering the course of action of positional switches, it is evident to think about the possible problems that might occur with the execution of positional switches when one is developing the starting line-up of a match system. Furthermore, it must be taken into consideration that perhaps a switch to strengthen the offence might cause disadvantages for the defence and vice-versa. It is for this reason that it is very important for every coach to keep an eye on the effectiveness of the switches and to be prepared for any changes to them if necessary.

At the middle levels of volleyball, and especially at the low levels of volleyball, where not a lot of

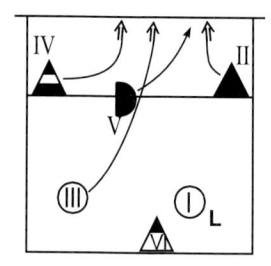

Fig. 197a

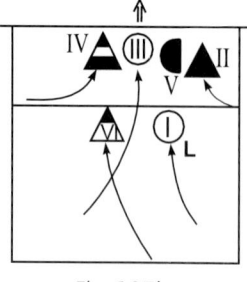

Fig. 197b

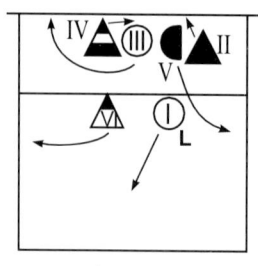

Fig. 197c

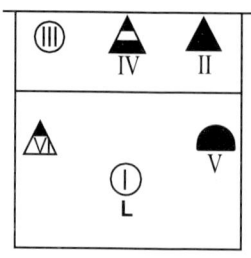

Fig. 197d

SWITCHING/CHANGING POSITIONS BY THE ATHLETES 273

specialisation has occurred, switches should not be carried out "for the sake of performing switches". On the contrary, at these levels of volleyball it is important to minimise any switching of positions as much as possible so as to omit any confusion, misunderstanding, and line-up errors.

Photo 66 (Steffen Marquardt)

7 Defensive and Offensive Strategies

In this chapter, there will be no developments of match observations and scouting techniques and systems because there are already numerous publications available on the subject. Instead, the chapter will focus on opinions regarding defensive and offensive strategies using concrete examples. The acquisition and discussion of the following determining factors is also sufficiently documented in the literature, therefore, only certain aspects and characteristics will be closely focused upon and dealt with.

Successful management of the matches and of the training sessions can only be achieved if it is combined with an analysis and discussion of all observations made. An optimisation of the practice and match can only occur with a planned and systematic observation to examine the individual, group, and team tactics. Filtering the strengths and weaknesses of each attains a better understanding of one's own team and the opposition. An unsystematic or carefree approach to athlete and match observations is unacceptable at the high levels of volleyball because the results cannot be examined and may only be obtained by pure chance. At middle levels of volleyball, taking into account the financial and logistical restrictions and limitations, it is recommended to observe and analyse only the team's closest oppositions and competitors. Besides scouting the opposition it is important to observe and analyse one's own team in practices and mainly competitions. At the low levels of volleyball, if observation of matches is at all possible, mainly one's own team should be the one observed and analysed.

The sport of volleyball is perfect for athlete and match observations and analysis because it is almost exclusively based upon standard situations and the volleyball court is easy to look over. The key for the successful use of athlete and match observations is the seizing and the isolation of the determining factors and key elements at the different levels of volleyball. Therefore, it does not make any sense at the low levels of volleyball, for example, to try to discover the serving strategy of the opposition because chances are that they do not have any and it does not make any sense to have any knowledge of their serving strategy if no counterstrategy by your team has yet been developed in practice. Observation of the opposition requires that a team have alternative defensive and offensive strategies to be able to take advantage of any possible weaknesses of their opposition. Also, observations are useless if a team's athletes have not yet learned in practice to effectively execute any successful counter-strategies.

The preceding information allows us to deduce the following general principles:
- The correct choice of **determining factors.**
- The use of the correct **observation methods.**
- The **number and type of observation criteria** in relation to the importance of the distinctive features and criteria looked-for at the level that will be observed.
- **Development, Training, and Use of Counter-strategies** in practice and in match situations.
- Each **strategy** has the goal of emphasising a team's own strengths by taking advantage of the opposition's weaknesses. This also works the other way around where a team must not let their opposition's use their strengths against your own team's weaknesses. It is important for a team to try and hide their weaknesses thus effectively neutralising their opposition's strategy.
- *The successful use of each strategy requires* an exact assessment of the individual, group, and team's tactical abilities, especially their technical-tactical skills and their psychological composition. Therefore, it is reasonable to use the second-best strategy first if it is easier to carry it out than the first strategy.
- At high levels of volleyball, each team should have a "scout/analyser", who is not only respected by the coach but also by the athletes. If there is no scout/analyser, this role will be the main responsibility of the assistant coach.
- A systematic and long-term structured training and development of the athletes to teach them the ability to execute instructions, coaching strategies, and counter-strategies.
- Ask and support an involvement by the athletes in helping make observations, analysis, and in the development of counter-strategies against opponents because the opinions that are recommended will only be successful if the athletes inwardly identify themselves with the decision made.
- *A systematic training and teaching of the athletes* to read and interpret the results from observations and analysis by themselves. Correspondingly, the goal is to have the athletes analyse the videotape themselves.
- *Counter-strategies* can only be successful if they are theoretically understood, accepted, and most importantly intensively practiced.
- The *training and development of the athletes is a continuous process*. Therefore, against weaker opponents certain strategies should be attempted and experienced which would allow a team to possibly use these strategies against their next and/or stronger opponent.

- The higher the level of volleyball that is being played, the greater the importance in the observation of athletes and matches.
- The more "specialists" that play on a team, the greater the priority towards athlete observation. The more "all-around" athletes that play on a team, the greater the priority towards match observation.

The match/athlete observation is an essential and important requirement by the coach:
- To improve the effectiveness of his/her team's practice.
- To optimise the management of matches.
- To be able to control and compare practices and competitions.
- To be able to make impartial and objective judgments of an athlete(s). The same is true for the athlete to be able to make the same impartial and objective judgments.
- To test the effectiveness of his/her own team's strategies.

The significance of each observation is dependent on the following factors:
- The more of an opposition's matches that are analysed, the more accurate and reliable that the results will be.
- The longer, more important, and contested that a match is and observed, the more significant are the facts and observations gathered.
- Videotape analysis of many of the opposition's matches is important to be able to recognise and identify the opposition's strategies in all types of match situations. The result of this will be that during the match against this opposition the coach and team are better prepared to see what the opposition's strategy is and to counter-attack with their own strategy.

In addition to the systematic athlete and match observations the collection of any additional information concerning the oppositions is of major importance. Examples of this can be the relationship between the athletes (friendships, aversions, inner-team competitions (especially if it concerns the setter), the relationship between the coach and the starting athletes, the relationship between the coach and the substitutes, and even the relationship between the starting athletes and the substitutes. This information may lead to simple yet effective strategies against the opposition, especially if it has been confirmed by the videotape analysis. For example, if a hitter has a bad relationship with the setter, it should be studied to see if the hitter only receives sets after a poor first pass, whereas a hitter who is a friend of the setter may receive the sets after a good first pass. The setter does this to make their friend look good and the other hitter look bad. This does not have to be done purposely by the setter. In this scenario, the blocking strategy can be as simple as: *If the first pass is poor as a group block the disliked hitter and with a good first pass as a group block the liked hitter.* As well, if a coach has a troubled relationship with one of his/her best starting athletes, then a simple yet effective strategy can be to put as much pressure on that athlete as early in the match as possible so they can start making errors. This strategy is based on the idea that the coach might substitute this athlete sooner than another athlete and may not even return this athlete into the match again.

Information regarding such team dynamics can be found through the media, from people associated with the team, and from conversations between the coaches and the athletes with each other. It is important if a coach has athletes who know athletes from other teams very well, that his/her athletes do not divulge any information regarding their own team to them, but conversely they should try to gather as much information about those athletes, their team, and even their coach as possible. It is just as important to know the behavior and strategies of the opposition's coach to purposely tempt him/her should the situation arise during a match to make certain decisions.

Athletes that have lengthy experience in the league, have played for different teams, and have played for several different coaches should be involved in the development of strategies. Knowledge regarding the game, behavior, and strategies of former teammates and coaches can be valuable information when developing strategies and making certain decisions.

Seemingly unimportant, but very true information, can have a large impact on the effectiveness of the strategy developed.

In the following chapters, very practical strategies and counter-strategies will be explained that are always based on systematic match and athlete observations. *Choosing a strategy, from the numerous strategies available after scouting, observations, and analysis have been performed, that has the greatest effectiveness and that can be easily executed by a coach's own team is the* **art of coaching**.

7.1 Strategies for the Starting Line-up

With the new rule changes, especially with the rally-point scoring system, it is much more difficult to make a comeback once you have fallen behind (see Chapter 1.1 "The New Rules and their Effects on Practice and Matches"). Therefore, the focus should generally be with a basic starting line-up and formation whose main concentration is on the team's own strengths. On the one hand, this will respectively bring an advantage at the beginning of a match to the team and, on the other hand, it will prevent the team from falling behind at the beginning of a match.

Further thoughts and opinions regarding the starting line-up and formation at the beginning of a match are based on the following observations:

Observation 1
The opposition always starts with the same starting line-up and rotation or it is only different depending on either their own or their opposition's serving situation. For example, a team always begins with their setter in position I if they are serving, or in position II if their opposition is serving.
Strategy:
If a coach knows the opposition's starting line-up then s/he can arrange his/her starting line-up in such a way as to take the most advantage of his/her team's defensive and offensive strengths. For example:
- Line up the team's best blocker against the opposition's main hitter.
- Set the team's weakest hitter against the opposition's weakest blocker.
- Have the team's strongest and most effective server(s) serve against the opposition's weakest service reception formations.
- If one of the opposition's starting athletes has a lot of respect for or is afraid of one of your team's athletes, then line up your athlete in such a way that they will play against each other at the net.

Observation 2
The opposition starts each game/match with a different rotation and/or line-up depending on who is serving (them or their opposition) and what starting line-up that their opposition is using.
Strategy:
- Consider and analyse what strategy the opposition's coach might use and try and use a counterstrategy against it. You may have found a solution right from the beginning of the game/match! If not, then you will have to analyse the situation during the game/match and adjust your strategies accordingly.

- The specialists on a team must be theoretically and practically prepared to play against the opposition's specialists. For example, a team's middle blockers must know the idiosyncratic characteristics of the opposing team's quick hitters, or each server on a team must be aware of the strengths and weaknesses of all six of the opposition's service reception formations.

Observation 3
If you, as a coach, know that the opposition's coach is doing a very detailed analysis and scouting report on your team and then vigorously prepares them for the match against you, the following are some strategies that you could use to prepare your team:
- Make changes to the beginning position of the starting line-up by, for example, starting the setter for the first time in position IV.
- Change the starting line-up by *switching the service reception athletes*. This might put an end to the serving, blocking, and even offensive strategy of the opposition. This strategy will be more effective if the opposition specifically trained their athletes to play against their opposing athlete – in other words, if the opposition did an athlete vs. athlete preparation.
- *Change the position of the middle blockers/hitters* to aggravate the opposition's quick hitters/middle blockers.
- Start *the team's main hitter in another position* in the starting line-up. For example, if the hitter was positioned next to the setter, move them to play the opposite diagonal position to the setter.
- *Change the alignment of the athletes in the service reception formation.* For example, instead of having the service reception athletes in positions II/V and the setter penetrating from position I, change the service receptions, athletes' position to III/V but the setter still penetrating from position I. This also means changing the team's match system.
- *Change the team's match system* with the use of fake formations, a fake penetrating setter, and/or fake hitters/blockers.

Once again, it must be pointed out that only *counter-strategies that have been practiced and that have become second nature to the athletes will be successful.*
It is also important to know that very experienced coaches know of several methods of finding out the opposition's starting line-up ahead of time, which will give them the opportunity of selecting and matching their line-up against their oppositions. For example:

- Send a person to inconspicuously observe the opposition's coach while s/he is preparing his/her starting line-up for the official and try to see the starting rotation, what position the setter will start in, what athletes will be in the starting line-up, etc.

Strategy:
Always pay attention and be cautious (this includes making sure the assistant coaches and statisticians are also doing the same) that nobody looks at your team's line-up card while or just after you have filled it out. As well, the coach can fill out a fake line-up card to give any observers false information regarding the starting line-up, thus maintaining an upper hand in strategy. Other methods of getting information can include:
- Arrangements can be made between the home team coach and the person that officially fills in the starting line-up in the match scoresheet to find out the opposition's starting line-up ahead of time.

Keep in mind to hand in the line-up card after the opponents have finished their serving warm-up. When your team is serving remind the official to keep the line-up card until s/he also has the opposition's line-up card, thus handing them to the official scorer at the same time not allowing for any further changes to the line-ups. This makes the official and scorer feel observed, not allowing for any giving of information to the opposition. Unfortunately, there is nothing that can be done regarding secret signals between the home team's coach and the scorer once both line-up cards have been handed in. This might give the home team coach the opportunity to prepare his/her athletes just before the match/game starts for a possible new line-up by the opposition or a fake line-up strategy (i.e. fake setter penetrating from position I when the setter is actually in position II).

7.2 Serving Strategies

To develop a serving strategy the following ***observable characteristics*** are important:
- *The number of available service reception specialists and their abilities.* The fewer main service reception athletes a team possesses, the more intensively their main strengths and weaknesses must be captured, trained, and improved upon. This is especially true for the libero. This large but decisive analysis of the service reception athletes must focus upon the following main targets:

- *The quality of the pass by the service reception athletes from movement* (i.e. to the front, to the back right, to the back left, to the left side, and to the right side). Most often, service reception athletes tend to favor and have a stronger service reception passing side (called their "preferred side"). For example, left-handed service reception athletes usually have difficulties passing from their right side, especially with serves that must be passed from their front right side (Fig. 198). The service reception will be observed and recorded as a three or four level quality scale in each service reception zone.

Photo 67 (Martin)

The quality of the pass by the service reception athlete in relation to their role as either a front-court or back-court athlete. It can be observed very often that the quality of passing by the service reception athlete is different and related to their role and position on the volleyball court. For example:

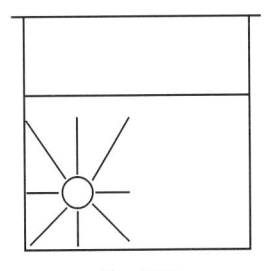

Fig. 198

- A front-court service reception athlete brings a better quality of service reception because they have to better prepare themselves for the entire play (service reception and offence), therefore, they are more focused at the task at hand. This athlete is often a weaker service reception athlete when they are in the back-court.
- If a front-court service reception athlete is passing ineffectively because s/he is already preparing for his/her offensive role rather than focusing on his/her service reception duties, s/he will be a much better and more effective service reception athlete when s/he rotates into the back-court because s/he will now only focus on his/her service reception role.
- A service reception athlete is stronger when s/he can use the overhand pass to play tactical serves by the opposition and use the forearm pass to play the other types of serves by the opposition.
- Discovering the physical skills and abilities of the service reception specialist, especially their speed and coordination skills.

- Most front-court service reception specialists have problems executing a combination attack if they must pass long deep hit serves. They are only able to execute a 3-4-tempo attack.
- Some service reception specialists have problems passing short serves because they cannot release quick enough from their position at the net to be ready in time for an offensive attack.
- Other service reception specialists have problems passing volleyballs served to a particular location.
- *Discovering the strengths and weaknesses of the service reception specialist's psychological state of mind.*
  During critical game/match situations many service reception specialist's service reception and offence skills worsen. A comparison of the service reception using the 10-point system will give some information regarding the psychological ability of the service reception athlete.
- There is often a *connection between the service reception and the offence,* therefore, it should be specifically examined and analysed to see if individual athlete mistakes in the offence are followed by mistakes in the service reception. The comparison of the possible correlation between the service reception and the offence and vice-versa should be accomplished by developing a system that follows a specific sequence or series of actions.
- *Discovering the teamwork and communication abilities of the service reception athletes,* especially when volleyballs are served to areas with overlapping coverage by the service reception athletes.
- *The assessment of certain idiosyncratic characteristics by the setter in his/her teamwork and communication skills with the service reception specialists.* Specifically, it should be examined to see if the service reception athlete receives sets after s/he passes the volleyball or only after one of their teammates passes the volleyball.
- *The assessment of possible idiosyncratic characteristics of the offence after the volleyball is served to a specific target on the volleyball court.* It should be examined to see if after a service reception from a specific area on the volleyball court (i.e. position V) if the setter will set more to a certain hitting position (i.e. left-side hitter or right-side hitter).

To discover the strengths and weaknesses of the service reception athletes is relatively simple because they have to perform many service reception actions during a game/match. To discover the main characteristics of the two or three

main service reception athletes is much more important than discovering information on the five main hitters. The reason for this is that not only is it easier and more accurate information to gather and analyse, but it is also much easier to implement a service strategy. This is also an easy strategy to implement and execute because the server, after every break and interruption in the match, can receive, without any problems, additional information from the coach before s/he actually serves the volleyball.
- *Discover the exact six service reception formations, including the offence that their opposition uses.*

The following points should be discovered for all six rotations to find out any correlations between the serve, block, and defensive strategy:
- Find out if most attacks are executed by a certain hitter or from a certain attacking position.
- Examine the service reception formations in respects to weak service reception areas and weak areas in the execution of the offence (i.e. penetrating path of the setter, quick hitter, back-court hitter, etc.).

The goal of the following serving strategies is to allow the formation of a double block, thus increasing the chances for the defence to play the volleyball. In international volleyball, there are already signs that the serving strategy is now based upon the team's blocking and defensive strategy. If this is the case, the middle blocker not only organises the block strategy but s/he is also directing the serving strategy.

7.2.1 Serving Strategies vs. a Two-person Service Reception Formation, which Utilises Two Service Reception Specialists but without a Libero

Generally, jump serves and tactical serves are very effective offensive strategies against a two-person service reception formation.
*The **jump serve** is recommended especially:*
- If the opposition is lacking or has a poor third service reception athlete.
- If the third athlete in the three-person service reception formation is the back-court attacker, this serve will essentially neutralise him/her.
- If the opposition has no jump servers chances are their service reception athletes will have difficulties passing jump serves because they cannot practice against them during training.

- To force a front-court athlete, who has moved out of the service reception formation because of the assistance of the libero, back into the service reception formation.
- To push a front-court service reception athlete deep into the back-court. This forces them to make a longer approach to get back to their attacking position. This extra time only allows the hitter to be available for a third or fourth tempo attack. For example, to neutralise service reception athletes in position V serve from service zone I into their service reception area, and to neutralise service reception athletes in position I serve from service zone V into their service reception area.

The *tactical serve* is recommended:
- To take advantage of the weaknesses of the service reception specialists, by making them move to pass the volleyball using their weaker side, etc.
- To use long and deep serves to push the front-court service reception athlete deep and to the side of the volleyball court to make their transition to offence much more difficult, thus neutralising him/her as an attacker.
- To put pressure on a technically and/or psychologically weaker service reception athlete by continually serving him/her. This is especially true when the substitute service reception athlete is even weaker in those or other areas than the athlete that s/he just replaced. It is even better yet if the server can maintain an intentionally prolonged eye contact with the psychologically weaker athlete to put even more pressure and nervous tension on them.
- To make the transition to offence more difficult. For example, use a tactical serve to a) the setter's spot, b) in the running path of the setter, or c) in the area of the quick hitter, especially if s/he has trouble passing using the overhand pass technique.
- To potential influence where the set will or will not be made. For example, serve the volleyball short and diagonally to the main hitting spot or serve to position II to make it more difficult to set to the hitter in position IV.
- To cause miscommunication by the service reception athletes by serving the volleyball to the overlapping areas that are being covered by the opposition. This strategy is absolutely recommended if both of the service reception athletes are in the front-court because it will interrupt their transition to offence, at least for a short period of time.
- To neutralise the libero. By doing this it may force the opposition to change their service reception formations, possible even removing the use of the libero.

- To provoke line-up errors by serving the volleyball to the opposition when they are in an overlapping diagonal assignment in two of their service reception formations (i.e. positions III & VI). Therefore, according to Fig. 199, the athlete in position VI is standing behind the athlete in position III, thus pushing him/her back even farther. It is for this reason that volleyballs served short from serving spot V/VI in the marked area are hard to pass for the athlete in position VI.

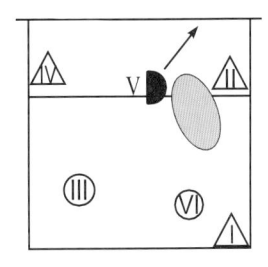

Fig. 199

- To make the use of the quick hitter playing in front of the setter more difficult. In other words, serve the volleyball to position II so the quick hitter can only be utilised with the use of a backset.
- To stop or to make the use of an expected offensive combination much more difficult by serving the volleyball to the zone where the offensive play is supposed to occur.
- To serve the volleyball in the service reception area of a front-court service reception athlete who is either frequently or rarely used as a hitter.
- To omit serving a service reception athlete or libero with strong leadership abilities on the team and is important to that team's psyche. The intention by not serving them is to take them out of the game/match and disturb their rhythm.
- To make the penetrating/running path of the setter longer, especially from the serving spot opposite to the starting position of the moving setter.
- To make it much more difficult for the service reception athlete to anticipate if the volleyball is going to stay in or go out of the volleyball court with the use of diagonal serves.
- To force inaccurate service reception passes with the use of diagonal serves from serving zone V, because the service reception athletes are still not used to the different "angle of incidence and angle of reflection" of the serves from that side of the volleyball court, therefore, the flow of movement from the service reception athletes and the quality of the pass may not yet be sufficiently established.
- To shorten the anticipation time of the service reception athletes by choosing the serving spot opposite to the serving target. This is especially true for volleyballs served from serving zones V and VI because the reasons given in point 15 are also true in this instance.
- To serve the volleyball with a lower and shorter high risk serve because the volleyball is now allowed to make contact with the volleyball net during the serve.

If the tactical serves from a short distance, with the goals and intentions mentioned above, are not effective it should be tested to see if the outcome and results intended can be better achieved with tactical serves *from the middle distance and from different serving spots.*

It has been established that if a team is without a service reception specialist who can pass *serves from the long distance,* that the tactic against them should be to serve the volleyball from serving zone VI and from the long distance. The reasons for this are a) that no athlete on the service reception team is using this type of tactical serve and/or b) the team has no opportunities to practice this type of serve because the size of their gym or training facility does not allow for this to be possible.

7.2.2 Serving Strategies vs. a Two-person Service Reception Formation, which Utilises only One Service Reception Specialist or Libero

This denotes that the one service reception specialist is passing the volleyball in all six rotations and formations and is supported by two other service reception athletes. The supporting service reception athlete who is in the back row will always form the two-person service reception formation with the main service reception specialist.

All of the strategies discussed in section 7.2.1 against the two-person service reception formation also apply in these situations. Further strategies that also apply are:

- If a team does not have a second main service reception athlete that can come into the match as a substitute, it might be reasonable to serve to the main service reception specialist all of the time even though s/he is the better passer. This strategy is meant to put continuous psychological and physical pressure on the main service reception specialist so that possible weaknesses and mistakes caused by the service reception will also cause problems for the service reception team's offence and blocking.

Photo 68 (Marquardt)

- If the service reception specialist is not a particularly good blocker, the opposition will always use their offence to hit overtop of him/her. This offensive strategy is interrelated with the serving strategy and vice-versa.
- Remove the main service reception specialist, most likely the libero, completely out of the team's serving strategy, thus eliminating that athlete's contacts with the volleyball, which is what is his/her main role in the match.
- If the main service reception athlete has only a small role in the offence then do not take him/her into account in the serving strategy.
- The supporting service reception athletes should be put under continuous pressure with serves in their serving areas because any difficulties in their service reception will also weaken their offensive play at the volleyball net.
- If a service reception specialist is also a good back-court hitter then s/he should be served short volleyballs in front of him/her to make his/her use as a back-court attacker less effective and even more difficult for his/her team's offence to utilise him/her.

7.2.3 Serving Strategies vs. a Three/Four-person Service Reception Formation, which Utilises Three/Four Service Reception Athletes

Generally, it can be stated, "The more athletes that are receiving the serve, the more that tactical match related serves lose their effectiveness and legitimacy." This is especially true for volleyballs that are served at certain service reception athletes because the service receiving areas are much smaller and the use of the overhand pass makes the service reception situation much easier. Another effect is that the movement areas are shorter, therefore enabling a service reception athlete to hide his/her weaker passing side. **Tactical serves** used to disrupt and cause problems for the opposition's offence are still an important tactical strategy. All of the previous strategies mentioned can still be used according to the scouting report and analysis of the opposition.

The following strategies are particularly recommended:
- If all of the service reception athletes are equally good passers, high risk serves from the middle/long distance and/or jump serves should be used. The target/location of these serves should be an area deep and in position I because it will make it much more difficult for the setter to watch the opposition's blockers in relation to his/her own hitters.
- The same strategy is recommended if the setter is in the front-court and has

only two front-court hitters and no back-row attacker available. In this situation a short serve behind the setter will cause him/her the most difficulty.
- If a three/four-person service reception formation is used, the volleyball should be served deep and to the side of the service reception athlete's serve receiving area (head or shoulder height next to the front-court athlete) to make their transition to the offence more difficult.
- If the service reception front-court athletes are pushed up because they can effectively use the overhand pass, the best strategy to use is to vary the serves between hard and deep regular and float serves from the short distance to the baseline-serving zone.

7.2.4 Serving Strategies During a Tiebreak

- Essentially, the serving strategy should not change or be any different from the strategy already being used, especially if there have not been any errors caused directly related to the serving strategy.
- If there have been a lot of errors made which are directly related to the serving strategy, and the effectiveness of the serve related directly to any points scored by the opposition is very low, the serving strategy must be changed by slightly reducing the risk factor of the serves to help omit direct service errors. This might result in the situation that every athlete is still using his/her specialty serve with the same amount of risk as before, but without following the serving strategy.
- Safety serves must not be performed because they only help make the opposition psychologically stronger. Safety serves only make sense if the team's front-court blocking and defence is strong in the situation being encountered and/or the opposition's front-court offence in this situation is particularly weak.
- If one or two of the substitutes are stronger or more effective with their serve than any or all of the starters or if a team has service specialists, then they should definitely be used. It is advisable to use these athletes/substitutes during the first part of the game to help gain the scoring lead.
- The starting line-up in the final game should be adjusted in such a way that the server who has scored the most points in the match so far should begin the rotation by being the first to serve. One point to keep in mind is that this change should not considerably weaken the team's other offensive and defensive strategies.

7.2.5 General Principles for a Serving Strategy

In addition to the explanations mentioned above the following are some principles and strategies that generally apply as well as some individual tactical characteristics:

- There are certain factors that can change the serving strategy: the score, the psychological state of mind of either team, the circumstances of introducing into the match an opposition's service reception athlete, an athlete that is upset about a poor call that the official made, and many other similar situations. Some possible serving strategy changes could be to serve to the excited athlete or to the athlete that was just recently substituted into the game/match, etc.
- If a team has weaknesses in their blocking and/or defence, they should perform higher risk serves.
- If a team is extremely dominant in their offensive transition from service reception (C1), but shows clear deficiencies in their blocking and defence (C2), they should carry out extremely high-risk serves.
- If in certain rotations the opposition has a great deal of effectiveness in executing their offence, then they should be served high risk serves during these rotations.
- If in certain rotations the opposition has a weak offensive execution, then the risk of the serves carried out should be reduced during those rotations.
- If a team has a good front-court blocking rotation, then the risk of the serves that they carry out should be reduced during that rotation.
- If a strong blocker is substituted into the game/match for a weaker blocker (i.e. the setter) in certain situations, then the risk of the serve must also be low so that the blocking strategy is not ruined.
- If the opposition successfully attacks from the outside using high sets against a team's double block, then the blocking strategy should be changed (i.e. change to a triple block) not the degree of risk of the serve.
- The risk of the serve must be low: a) after timeouts, b) after a long and difficult rally, c) after service errors by teammates, d) after an athlete missed their previous serve, e) after a team's spectacular attack, f) in specific situations in which the serving strategy is based upon the blocking and defensive strategy, and g) after several consecutive points.
- The server should always try to obtain eye contact with the service reception athlete that they are going to serve the volleyball to, consequently disturbing that athlete's concentration and putting more psychological pressure on them.

Serving strategies that do not show any immediate results or effectiveness should not be abandoned as long as they are based on systematic observations and scouting of the opposition. The serving strategy does not begin at the start of the match, but rather at the beginning and end of the warm-up time. The purpose of the hitting and the serving during the warm-up time is to get the athletes adjusted to the environmental conditions (i.e. lighting, space outside of the volleyball court, height of the ceiling, etc.) of the gymnasium that they will be competing in.

This time also allows the athletes to test the distance of their serve from their serving position to the opposition's baseline from the middle and long distances and, if necessary, to mark these positions on the court. During the warm-up the athletes should intentionally:
- Serve harder than they would during the match to impress and intimidate the opposition's service reception athletes, but this must not lead to an athlete's psychological insecurity and instability because of too many serving errors committed.
- Serve together as a team at the same time at the opposition's service reception athletes because by doing so the service reception athletes cannot properly prepare themselves for the serves.
- Serve in a manner that disturbs the opposition.
- The libero, who is not allowed to serve, should pass the opposition's serves to prepare him/herself for his/her main role during the match.

Finally, it must be stressed that there is no single serving strategy in a match that can be executed by all of the athletes in the team. *Instead there will be a serving strategy developed for each athlete according to the individual skills and abilities of the server and to the specific service reception situation.* All of the information regarding the serving strategies needs to be examined in a close correlation with the Learning Part I (Chapter 3.4, "Selected Drills to Train the Individual Tactics of the Server and the Service Reception Players, and the Training of the Service Reception Formation"). The main focus of the individual tactical training of the server is discussed in this section.

7.3 Service Reception Strategies

Just as the serving strategies are allocated to the offensive strategies, so are t*he service reception strategies allocated to the defensive strategies.* Service reception strategies can also be termed counter-strategies because they are strategies put into place to counter the serving strategies enacted upon them.

SERVICE RECEPTION STRATEGIES

For the development of a service reception counter-strategy the following observational characteristics are important:
- *Type of Serve*
- It should be found out and noted which athletes jump spike/float serve and which athletes do not, as well as which athletes specialise in tactical serves. Furthermore, it must be noted with tactical serves from which area of the serving zone that they are served from.
- *Serving Spot/Target*
- It should be noted from which serving zone each athlete is serving and to what distance that s/he is serving the volleyball to. It must be noted if the athlete is changing their serving zone and varying the distance of their serves.
- *Identifying the Opposition's Serving Strategy*
- Do all of the athletes serve the same way regardless of whom their opponent is or do they change their method of serving according to whom the opponent is that they are competing against?
- Do the athletes have serving alternatives?
- Is the opposition using high-risk serves with or without a tactical reasoning/ strategy behind their serves?
- Does the team have an individual or a team assigned serving strategy?
- Does the opposition alter/change their serving strategy during the match?
- Do the servers use safety serves after a break in the game or after an error and/or does the opposition even make any serving errors?
- Does the serving strategy change during critical situations in the game/ match?

A successful service reception strategy requires that a team's own service reception athletes have been closely observed and analysed. *Especially within a team's own service reception formations, the coach has the opportunity to stress the strengths of each athlete and to hide each of their weaknesses. This is even more so now that the libero athlete has been introduced into the game.*

A systematic analysis of the service reception athletes, which is also accomplished by the opposition, has the goal of optimising the service reception training and to eliminate its weaknesses (see Chapter 7.2). The same is true regarding the identifying of the effectiveness of all six service reception formations. Particularly at this time a close eye must be kept on the teamwork and communication between the setter and the service reception athlete, especially if there are certain systems or idiosyncratic characteristics to be recognised. If these are identified by the opposition, this will be a large disadvantage to your team. For example, it is often observed that a front-court service reception athlete is only used as a hitter after they execute a good pass or after a good pass by one of his/her teammates. It can also be stated that a service reception athlete is either being used only as an outside hitter and/or only as a combination hitter.

7.3.1 Service Reception Strategies for a Two-person Service Reception Formation, which Utilises Two Service Reception Specialists with or without a Libero

If the opposition uses jump serves, the service reception for these types of serves must be intensified during practice. Also, they must be received using a three-person service reception formation. An absolutely necessary strategy is to train at least two additional athletes as service reception specialists for jump serves. These two athletes should possibly be positioned diagonally to each other in the rotation to be able to turn the two-person service reception formation into a three-person service reception formation, with one of the two athletes being a back-court athlete. The direction of the server must be taken into account by the newly created three-person service reception formation, ensuring that at least one of the service reception specialists is covering the zone that the server is facing. The higher the risk of the opposition's jump serve and the harder that it is served, the more focused the service reception athlete must be to avoid any individual mistakes by trying to pass a good, but not perfect, volleyball up to the setter target (safety first!).

Photo 69 (Martin)

Depending on the type and arrangement of the service reception formation, the effectiveness and strategy of the offence should depend and be based upon the quality of the service reception pass. If there is no jump server on the team who serves as hard as the opposition, the distance of the jump serves in practice

SERVICE RECEPTION STRATEGIES

should be made shorter (i.e. use the 6 meter line as the baseline) to allow the training of the service reception during practice that corresponds as closely as possible to the opposition's jump serving style during the match.

Observation 1
The opposition uses tactical serves from the short or middle distances and from different serving positions to:
- *Make the service reception specialist use their weaker passing side.*
  Strategies for your own team:
  Change the service reception formation in such a way that this athlete is using his/her stronger passing side to cover more area or position this athlete in such a manner, separate from the service reception formation that only allows the athlete movements to his/her stronger passing side or that only forward and/or backward movements are allowed to be in a situation where only the overhand passing technique needs to be used or to change from a two-person service reception formation to a three-person service reception formation by taking into account the use of the libero.
- *Make the transition to offence much more difficult for the service reception front-court athlete:* Divide the service reception areas of the volleyball court in such a way that the back-court service reception athlete must cover more space (ie. 2/3 to 1/3 or 3/5 to 2/5) or change to a two-person service reception formation with three service reception athletes or change from a two-person service reception formation to a three-person service reception formation by especially involving the libero.
- *Place psychological pressure on one of the service reception specialists or the libero.*
  Strategies for your own team:
  Prepare the athletes ahead of time to be ready for such tactics by the opposition's serving strategy with the use of mental/psychological and special training methods and drills. As well, train and prepare the athletes in the use of a group tactical strategy involving the service reception athletes with the main goal and purpose being to deceive the opposition's server (Fig. 200).

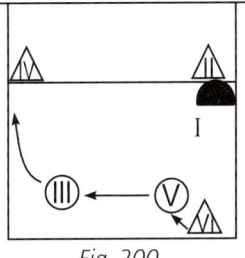

Fig. 200

At the very moment that the server tosses the volleyball into the air to serve, the athlete who is being put under pressure will leave his/her service reception area and as a front-court athlete move forward or as a back-court athlete move backward or to the side. At the same time, the other service reception athlete is taking over the uncovered area. A third, normally a non-service reception athlete, is also prepared to cover the now empty service reception area that has just been left vacant by the service reception athlete who just moved over to cover the area left vacant by the original service reception athlete that was under pressure or change the service reception areas to be covered by changing the service reception formation or do a transition to a two-person service reception formation with three service reception athletes including the libero replacing the athlete that is under pressure (note – if the athlete is in the front-court, then s/he should not receive) or do a transition to a three-person service reception formation to make the service reception areas smaller especially with the use of a libero or use another service reception formation without the libero.

- *Make the transition to the offence more difficult for the quick hitter.*
  Strategies for your own team:
  Make sure that the quick hitter is aware that s/he must serve receive the volleyball in his/her area by using the overhand passing technique. To accomplish this the quick hitter must take the following points into account: His/her service reception pass needs to be good – not perfect. This pass should be played high enough to the setter that s/he, as a quick hitter, is still credible and able to execute his/her offensive role. Also, if the service reception is to be performed by three athletes, the libero should be included.

- *Put pressure on the setter and his/her setting* (i.e. serve to the setting spot, in the running path of the setter, in the area of an offensive combination, etc.).
  Strategies for your own team:
  Make sure that the combination hitter, if s/he receives the serve, will use the overhand passing technique to play the volleyball. Furthermore, the service reception specialists should pass the volleyball higher to give the setter and the hitters more time for their transition to offence or change the starting positions of the specialists to provoke a deep serve to the back area of the volleyball court or change from a two-person service reception formation to a three-person service reception formation by including the libero.

- *Disturb the setter and his/her setting with serves in behind them.*
  Strategies for your own team:
  The shorter the serve is, the higher the pass must be to give the setter enough time to turn to the hitters (III/IV) or as a tactic with his/her service reception athletes the setter penetrates to his/her position by going to the sideline, thus enabling him/her to watch his/her hitters and the opposition's blockers.

- *Cause difficulty for the setter by serving the volleyball to the overlapping areas of the service reception athletes.*

Strategies for your own team:
The stronger service reception athlete should generally do the bulk of the passing or, with equally strong service reception athletes, always the athlete in the back-court or the libero should pass the volleyball or the service reception athlete with the better movement and passing to the setter target should play the volleyball or the service reception athlete who is in a position to use his/her stronger passing side should play the volleyball or the service reception athlete that allows a better execution of the offence with his/her pass should be the one to play the volleyball.

Observation 2
The opposition is using serves from the long distance zone (the area 7 meters or greater from behind the baseline).
Strategies for your own team:
It is an absolute necessity to train the team's service reception against serves of this type as soon as possible, even if the training must occur in another gymnasium.
It is a major task for each team to develop and train at least one service reception specialist, usually the libero, to be able to pass serves from the long distance zone. This athlete will endure more, if not the entire, responsibility of the service reception under these types of serves. This allows a change to a **one-person service reception formation** strategically possible and, based upon the long traveling distance of the volleyball, relatively easy to perform.

7.3.2 Service Reception Strategies for a Two-person Service Reception Formation, which Utilises One Service Reception Specialist and Libero

In this instance, it means that a team is always using a two-person service reception formation, where only one of the three service reception athletes is the main passer with the libero, who is one of the two passers in all six of the service reception formations.

All strategies mentioned in section 7.3.1 are also true for this service reception formation. The difference is that in this service reception formation the main passer is the libero, thus s/he is always covering a larger area of the volleyball court and has the most responsibility during the service reception. The two supporting service reception athletes must be prepared, in case the situation arises that one of the two passers is showing weaknesses or vulnerability, to be ready to back him/her up.

In case the situation arises that this service reception strategy will be performed without a libero, it is important to have trained and developed a second main service reception athlete that can be used as a substitute. This would also help in omitting any possible major changes to the match strategy and system that needs to be used.

If the opposition purposely does not serve the main service reception athlete/ libero, then this athlete should cover even more court space or change the service reception formation so s/he can cover the "endangered" area that the opposition is serving or change from a two-person service reception formation to a three-person service formation.

7.3.3 Service Reception Strategies for a Three/Four-person Service Reception Formation, which Utilises Three or Four Service Reception Athletes

If *tactical serves from the short distance* are highly effective against the three-person service reception formation, it should then be changed to a four-person service reception formation. This also applies in the case of jump serves. *With tactical serves from the middle distance* one of the athletes, who was preselected through an analysis and study of all of the service reception athletes, will receive more responsibility. With *tactical serves from the long distance* a two-person service reception formation should be used if one or two of the service reception athletes are qualified to receive this type of serves. To be in a position to outsmart and foil the opposition's serving strategies a team must have already practiced and worked on alternative service reception strategies for the ones that they currently employ.

This is especially true if a team has service reception formations that fully utilise the libero.

With these changes in place the "endangered" service reception zones and the serving areas that the opposition can serve to are constantly changing. This includes the areas and positions that athletes have to cover and play.

7.3.4 Service Reception Strategies During a Tiebreak

- If there have not been any major errors in the service reception, then the service reception strategy should not be changed during the tiebreak.

- If there have been many direct service reception errors in the game, then the service reception strategy should be changed. A perfect first pass should no longer be the goal but rather a good, decent first pass. If the main hitter is in the front-court and is very effective, it might be wiser to play all service reception passes safely.
- The starting line-up for the final game should be the service reception formation and rotation that had the most success in bringing the serve back without losing any or the least amount of points. Of course, the blocking and defensive strategy must also be taken into account with any decisions made.

7.3.5 General Principles for the Service Reception Strategy

The following explanations are general principles that complement and complete the strategies mentioned thus far and, to a certain extent, also deal with individual tactical characteristics:

- The psychological situation of the service reception athlete, his/her teammates, and of the opposition, the particular situation that a service reception specialist is brought into the game/match, the score, and situations where there is a high potential of hostility or aggressiveness of the individual athletes on the volleyball court must all be taken into account for the determination of the individual tactic and strategy of the service reception athlete.
- A perfect pass off of the service reception should try to be achieved if a team has difficulties with a 3/4-tempo attack. This also applies if the opposition has a very good block and defensive arrangement.
- If a team is clearly superior in C1 and clearly inferior C2 a good pass off of the service reception is preferred over a perfect pass. This also applies if the server is very effective or if the opposition has a very weak block and defensive formation.
- If your team's main offensive strategy is to use outside attacks after medium-high/high sets, then a good pass off of the service reception is adequate. If your team's main offensive strategy is to use quick and combination attacks, then a perfect pass off of the service reception must be performed.
- The willingness to take risks in the service reception should be minimal, especially:
  - After you commit an unforced error.
  - After your teammates commit an unforced error.
  - After a timeout.
  - When the opposition is going to jump serve or use a very effective tactical serve.
  - When offensive errors occur following the change in the service reception.

- If the setter is in the front row, a higher risk service reception formation and/or tactic can be used, especially if the setter is a strong hitter/blocker. A lower risk service reception formation should be used if the setter is penetrating from the back row.
- A service reception pass that is purposely played higher is recommended if:
  - The setter and/or hitters have longer distances to cover to get to their positions.
  - The combination hitters use a change in direction in their approach.
  - The service reception front-court athlete has to dive to play the volleyball.
- Individual tactical actions that only concern the server or the service reception athlete are very effective if:
  - A service reception athlete feels strongly that s/he can present the server some space in the service reception area either by eye contact or by signaling to him/her to make or entice the server to change his/her original serving strategy. This may make the server feel unsure of him/herself and cause him/her to make a service error.
  - After a good service reception the service reception athlete should continue to show the opposition his/her strengths by "exhibitionism" (i.e. emotions, eye contact, gestures, etc.) and, if the service reception athlete made an error, s/he should continue to act as if nothing had happened (i.e. act cool and not bothered by the error).
- In critical situations the service reception athlete must be prepared for service deceptions. For example, s/he must be aware of long or short serves that are executed by using the same hitting motion but the volleyball trajectory is changed because of a different use of the wrist, or s/he must expect float serves even though the opposition is going through the jump serve action, or s/he should not be surprised if the opposition is serving the volleyball in a diagonal direction yet they are facing forward.
- If the athlete is a strong service reception athlete, they should be prepared for a change in the opposition's serving strategy at the end of a game/match, after a timeout, or during a critical moment or situation in the game/match, especially if they have only received a few serves up to that point in the game/match.
- The service reception strategy should not begin with the start of the match, but should have already begun with the warm-up. The athletes should test the serve/service reception situation and conditions so that they can get familiar and used to the gymnasium and the environment that they are going to compete in.

SETTING STRATEGIES 299

- During the warm-up, the service reception athletes should prepare themselves for their service reception duties by performing special specific passing drills behind the volleyball court.
- At the end of the warm-up, the service reception athletes should pass the volleyballs served by their opposition, but they must pay close attention to the following points:
  - If the opposition is only serving to one service reception athlete, then a second or third service reception athlete should replace or rotate with them so they can each alternate and pass some volleyballs.
  - If the opposition is trying to disturb your own team's serving actions, especially the jump servers, by serving diagonally across the volleyball court, then the service reception athlete(s), the assistant coach(s), and any injured athlete(s) should stop these tactical maneuvers by the opposition by covering these diagonal serves and/or any other areas of the volleyball court that they may be serving to.

Finally, it must be stressed that there are not many service reception strategies and that the existing ones have a group, and especially, an individual tactical focus. In addition, the service reception strategy is very much related to the offensive strategy.

All of the information that is discussed above is directly related to the service reception strategy and the explanations of the Learning Part I (Chapter 3 – "Service Reception Formations"). The main focus in chapter 3 is the individual tactical training of the service reception athlete.

7.4 Setting Strategies

The setting strategies are closely related to the offensive strategies. The two form an integrated whole. A setting strategy will only be successful if the hitters execute it and see it through to its end. Despite this fact, the setting strategies will be discussed separately because they are the first step of any offensive strategy and they are the decisive and crucial requirement to perform a successful following action.

The setting strategy is generally designed and developed by the coach in cooperation with the setter, based on an analysis of their own team and their opposition.

The *analysis of their own team* should focus on the following main observable points:
- Individual tactical abilities of the setter.
- Individual tactical abilities of the hitter.
- The group tactical abilities of each offensive hitter and/or rotation of hitters in all six rotations.

The *analysis of the opposition* should focus on the following points:
- The individual tactics of the athletes in their blocking and defensive roles.
- The setup and formation of the block and back-court defence, including any planned positional changes and any fake blocker schemes.
- The block and defensive formations, including the possible variations.
- An analysis of the opposition's offence to gather observations and conclusions to help your team prepare for the type of block training to do in practice (i.e. if the opposition, but not your team, is using 61s (quick sets behind the setter) or if they are using any special offensive combinations behind the setter, it might be assumed that your team will have extra difficulties in blocking and defending against these type of offensive tactics, therefore, extra training focusing on the skills needed to defend against these types of offensive tactics will be needed).
- A detailed analysis of the opposition's middle blocker concerning:
  - *His/her strategy* (i.e. is s/he jumping before, with, or after the set?).
  - *His/her technical skills* (i.e. does s/he penetrate immediately and is his/her starting position with his/her arms extended in the air before s/he jumps, or does s/he have any strengths/weaknesses with his/her footwork to one blocking direction, or does s/he have a tendency to close the block or to leave it open in favor of a good penetrating but open block?).
  - *His/her athletic abilities*, especially speed, coordination, and his/her physical characteristics (i.e. size).
  - *His/her psychological abilities*, especially after a successful and/or not successful action or after any of the following actions: Does the middle blocker change his/her actions after the opposing quick hitter successfully hits over his/her position once or twice (with and/or without a block) or after s/he has successfully blocked the quick hitter?

From this, it follows that the setter must take into account most of the factors within his/her control. Therefore, the individual tactics of the setter are a crucial

factor in the match. The setter must have the following abilities to execute the setting strategy:
- *The ability to quickly analyse and interpret tactical offensive actions.* For example, to recognise if the offensive action was successful because s/he faked the middle blocker or was it successful because of an error made by the opposition at the net.
- *The ability to memorise and assign the results of certain actions to specific setting situations and plays.* For example, to remember the situation where s/he penetrated from position I, performed a combination attack behind him/herself, and to recall if the execution was successful or not. This is very similar to performing the skills in point 1.
- *The ability to recognise and take advantage of the strengths and weaknesses of the athletes in the respective situation.*
- *The ability to change the tempo and rhythm of the match/game.*
- *Extraordinary teamwork with the coach.*

The following are simplified strategies with only the most important aspects being discussed; it is for this reason that they only apply to one particular situation during the game/match.
It is the art of the coach and the setter to pick from several offensive strategies the one that will bring the greatest possible success from the situation at hand whilst taking into consideration all of the factors that can influence the play. For the transition from defence to offence, a separate setting/offensive strategy must be developed.

7.4.1 Setting Strategies that Take into Consideration the Opposition's Offensive Combinations

The opposition's offensive tactics will mostly provide you with the information regarding their **block training**. From this information, the following important conclusions regarding what offensive tactics that your team can implement can be presumed:
- If the opposition is not using a quick attack **behind** their setter, it can be assumed that they will have difficulties in blocking against the same play performed against them.
- If the opposition is not using a back-court attack, then your team's offence should carry out a back-court attack against the opposition.

- If the opposition's quick hitters are not able to hit a particular type of set, then it is assumed that they will have trouble blocking against the same type of set used against them.
- If the opposition does not execute certain offensive combinations in the middle, then it can be assumed that they will have trouble blocking against these same types of combinations.

7.4.2 Setting Strategies that Take into Consideration the Starting Positions of the Blockers and the Defensive Athletes

- If the opposition's blockers are standing close together in the middle, then medium-quick sets to the outside will cause them difficulties in trying to form a double block.
- If the blockers are spread out across the net, then it is possible to use combination attacks in the middle, depending on the actions and skills of the middle blocker.
- If the outside blocker in position IV is looking to block an A-quick set behind the setter, then second tempo or combination attacks behind the setter are good strategies.
- If the middle blocker chooses his/her starting position as the attacking location of the quick hitter, then shoot sets should be used more often.
- If one of the opposition's athletes is blocking in a switched position perform:
  - Quick & medium-quick sets to the outside.
  - A change of direction attacks.
  - Shoots.
  - Offensive combinations with a double-quick attack (two hitters attacking at the same time).
- If the starting position of your team's blockers reveals that the opposition is expecting your team to execute an offensive combination, it is recommended to allow your quick hitter to run in the direction of the blockers and to change the position and attacking spot of the second hitter or to use another type of combination attack.
- If it can be assumed by the starting positions of your team's blockers that the opposition is using a one-one blocking strategy, then the setter should use the second hitter more often.

- If the opposition is serving from the long-distance zone and s/he is not able to get to his/her defensive starting position on the volleyball court, then it only makes sense to:
  - Have the setter tip/"dump" the volleyball to the open defensive area;
  - Have the setter use the quick hitter.
- If the setter is not blocked when s/he is in the front row and tipping/dumping the volleyball, then s/he should use this play early in the game/match to freeze one of the opposition's blockers for the rest of the game/match.
- If the outside blocker in position IV is positioned to block the setter's tips/dumps, then it will help to allow the quick hitter to perform quick attacks behind the setter or to use the back-court hitter in position I to perform second tempo attacks or to let the second hitter execute an attack behind the setter.

7.4.3 Setting Strategies that Take into Consideration the Actions of the Middle Blocker

- If the middle blocker *jumps after the set is made,* then it is important to use the quick hitter \as much as possible with A & B quick attacks, in addition to the setter jump setting all of the time to speed up the tempo of the game/match. This will continue to be carried out until the middle blocker changes his/her strategy.
- If the middle blocker *jumps after the set is made* because his/her own hitters are not able to execute a quick attack and, therefore, does not know any better, the attacking spot of the quick hitter should be clearly moved to one side of the volleyball court to make the middle blocker also follow to this side of the volleyball court.
  If the middle blocker moves to this side of the volleyball court, then the hitter that is the farthest away from the middle blocker should be the one to receive the set to possibly create an attack against a single block.
  If the middle blocker does not move with the quick hitter, then the quick hitter should be the one who receives the set.
- *If the middle blocker is not fully jumping,* it must be checked to see:
  - If the height of the reach of your own team's hitter is clearly better than the opposition's middle blocker. If this is the case, then the quick hitter should be used more often.

- If the middle blocker is effective or not with a passive block. With an effective block, the attacking spot of the quick hitter should be clearly moved to one side of the volleyball court to make the middle blocker move over as well.
- If the middle blocker is clearly shutting down the main hitting direction of the quick hitter, then the setting should be performed in such a manner as to allow a quick attack against the direction of the approach. The same applies if the middle blocker is standing near the setter.
- If the middle blocker is jumping **with the quick hitter**, the offence should mainly execute outside/combination attacks or shoot attacks. If the middle blocker is not effective even though s/he is jumping with the quick hitter, then the quick hitter should also be used.
- If the middle blocker shows **weaknesses in his/her movement** to the side (i.e. moving to form the double block in position IV), then the combination attack should be started on the middle blocker's stronger side but the attack should be executed on the middle blocker's weaker side. For example, start the first hitter in a combination of a B-quick in position III/IV and the second hitter finishing the attack in position I/II. If the middle blocker is weaker on his/her left side (position II on your side) an A-quick behind the setter should be combined with a half-quick set to position IV.
- If the opposition has small blockers that must jump fully, combinations should be run at their blocking positions.
- If the opposition has tall blockers, the setter should make the second hitter attack from different positions and with changes of direction to make the blockers have to move. These movements and changes of direction will not allow the blockers to get easy blocks.
- If the opposition has a very high reach on their block and a very aggressive blocking style, then the setter should not set the volleyball too tight to the volleyball net.

Photo 70 (Schäfer)

The setting strategy against the skills and tactics of the opposition's middle blockers requires very good communication and teamwork between the setter, each quick hitter, and the coach because the others support the setter with observations and analysis of the opposition's blocking strategy. The quick hitter should provide specific information regarding the opposition's blocker (i.e. does the opposition's blocker perform fake movements?). The coach must provide information to the setter regarding changes in the opposition's blocking strategy.

7.4.4 Setting Strategies that Take into Consideration the Weaknesses of a Blocker

The weaknesses of a blocker can be of an athletic, technical or tactical nature:
- If the blocker is small and not very athletic, a very good hitter should play opposite him/her and hit tight set volleyballs over top of him/her.
- If the opposition's blockers have technical deficiencies (i.e. late hand/arm penetration, hand and arm movements during their jump, their landing position is far away from the take-off spot, etc.), then the attack should be executed over/against these athletes. In addition, the attack should be carried out with the assistance of a quick hitter, whose main duty is to move the middle blocker away from the weaker blocker, thus separating the two of them and allowing the opportunity for a one-one attack match-up.
- If the outside blocker is poorly anticipating and late in getting to the attacking spot, as well as obstructing his/her middle blocker teammate, the attack should be performed in the blocking zone outside of the blocker.
- If a weak blocker is late in switching to his/her blocking position combined with a fake blocking line-up, a teammate (i.e. the second hitter) that will attack against him/her or a back-court athlete should call out to the setter and tell him/her what blocking zone that athlete is taking.

7.4.5 Setting Strategies that Take into Consideration Your Own Team's Attackers

The following points and the previous items mentioned are directly related to each other and are overlapping, completing, and/or complementing each other. Offensive strategies are always effective if a team's own strengths can be practiced against the known and analysed weaknesses of their own block and defence. This is easier achieved if the **team's attacking side can act,** whereas the **team's defensive side must react.**

DEFENSIVE AND OFFENSIVE STRATEGIES

- If a team has an extraordinary hitter, s/he will be particularly used out of the service reception formation and almost exclusively out of the defensive transition.
- In combination plays the attackers will be used out of their favorite attacking positions and with receive their favorite sets.
- If an athlete on a team has a lot of functions, the setter should not set him/her too many volleyballs so s/he does not get overexerted.
- Successful offensive combinations that the opposition cannot adjust to or stop should continue to be used. Combination plays that are unsuccessful must be changed by moving the position of the attacking spot and/or changing the type of quick attack that is being performed.
- If an attacker in a certain position has not been successful in several attempts, then s/he should be used in a different attacking spot and against another one of the opposition's blockers.
- To be in a position to surprise or to confuse the opposition in critical situations the setter must use an offensive combination that has not been used in the game/match until that point.

The setter must always be aware of the psychological state of his/her hitters to be in a position to use the psychologically most stable athlete in critical situations and to build the confidence of the weaker athletes in less critical situations.

- If, after an error, an athlete on your own team has been put under a lot of pressure by the opposition, the setter should take any opportunities in favorable game/match situations to build this athlete's confidence up again.
- If an athlete is not receiving any volleyballs from the opposition in either blocking and/or service reception situations, then the setter should use this athlete more offensively in order to keep him/her in the flow of the game/match.
- If an athlete is in a critical situation and at a critical moment in the game/match, then the setter should try to successfully set him/her up against a single blocker by having the quick hitter run a play far away from the attacking spot.
- If the main hitter is matched up against an opposition's great blocker then the setter should try to take advantage of the hitter by having him/her hit from a different attacking spot with the use of a combination play.
- If the first volleyball in play is passed more to position II and the opposition's middle blocker is focused on the volleyball and on the quick hitter (at the

setter), the attack should be carried out in position IV because the middle blocker must change the direction of his/her running/steps and must cover a larger distance to get into position.
- The setter must omit any idiosyncratic characteristics, tendencies, and schemes when s/he is setting.

The explanations regarding the setting strategies are closely related to the Learning Part II (Chapter 4 – "Offence"). The crucial section here is the individual tactical training of the setter and, directly related are the strategies of the server, the service reception athletes, and the hitters.

7.5   Offensive Strategies

These strategies are directly related to the offensive actions and, therefore, the third touch of the volleyball. It is more reasonable to discuss the individual tactical actions than of strategies. It is for this reason that this section is referred to the explanations in Learning Part II – Chapter 4, especially section 4.5 "Individual Tactics of the Hitter".

In the following paragraph only practical hints for the hitter are given:
- The **quick hitter** needs to know, after an **analysis of the opposition's middle blockers:**
  - If the opposition's middle blockers are following a blocking strategy and if they change throughout the game/match.
  - If and what type of technical deficits the opposition's middle blockers have, especially regarding the arm/hand posture and position.
  - Which hitting direction are they mainly covering and blocking.

The quick hitter especially should be assisting the setter carry out the offensive strategies (see Chapter 4.5.1 "The Quick Hitter").

For **the main/diagonal hitter** details can be located in section 4.5.2, for the **back-court hitter** details can be located in section 4.5.3, for the **outside hitter** details can be located in section 4.5.4, and for the **combination hitter** the details can be located in section 4.5.5.
- If the **middle blocker** is waiting to perform his/her blocking duties, the quick hitter must be even quicker in the offence.

DEFENSIVE AND OFFENSIVE STRATEGIES

Photo 71 (Martin)

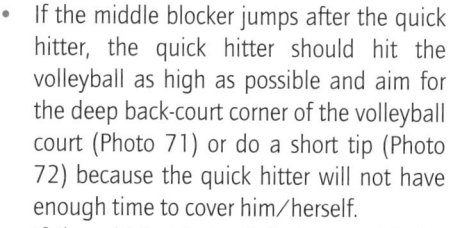

Photo 72 (Marquardt)

- If the middle blocker jumps after the quick hitter, the quick hitter should hit the volleyball as high as possible and aim for the deep back-court corner of the volleyball court (Photo 71) or do a short tip (Photo 72) because the quick hitter will not have enough time to cover him/herself.
- If the middle blocker fully jumps with the attacker, then the quick hitter should hit the volleyball hard past one side of the block (Photo 73) and/or hit shoot sets.
- If the outside blocker covers the quick hitter, then s/he could try tipping/dumping the volleyball.

For the *second hitters* an *analysis of the opposition's double-block formations* regarding their athleticism, technique, and tactics is very important.

Photo 73 (Marquardt)

OFFENSIVE STRATEGIES

- If the opposing athlete blocking at the volleyball net is with the non-blocking front-court athlete, a successful strategy is to hit volleyballs at an extreme diagonal angle. If the setter is covering closely behind the block, a tip in the area of the setter can cause difficulties for a counter-attack by the opposition.
- Find and use uncovered areas in the opposition's defence.
- If the block is positioned normally, then your team should try and hit past it or to use the top and/or the side of the block (Photo 74). If the block is flying or moving in the air, the volleyball should be hit at the side of the block with a delayed hit. The last strategy also applies to volleyballs that are set too tight to the volleyball net.

Photo 74 (Marquardt)

- If the opposition's middle blocker is late in closing their double block, then the "blocking seam" should be seen and used as a weakness and the volleyball should be hit through it (Photo 75).
- If the middle blocker is fully jumping with the quick hitter, then the combination hitter should hit the volleyball over the middle blocker during his/her landing phase of his/her block attempt.
- If the block is positioned very precisely, then the block should be used in such a manner that the volleyball can go off of the block for a sideout or the volleyball should be hit in such a manner that it can be blocked back into the hitter's own side of the court and be played up by his/her teammates and start a new attack. Alternatively, a strategic hit at a weaker defender can be used or an attack in the defensive area of the setter to remove him/her from the rest of the play.

Photo 75

- Similar to the setter, each hitter should have a high percentage "safety hit" in their offensive attack that can be used in critical situations of the game/match.
- If the setter is penetrating too early to the net from the back row, strategic attacks to his/her defensive area should be used.

It is very important for the *attackers* to know precisely what defensive formations the opposition is using.

Therefore, it is important to find out and analyse:
- If and what type of block coverage the opposition uses (i.e. is the coverage at a close distance or further away from the block?).
- If the defence varies throughout a game/match.
- If the athletes have fixed and specialised defensive roles and positions.
- If and where does the setter change to and cover in the defensive formation.
- How the defender in position VI reacts to a single- or double-block formation by his/her team (see Learning Part III "Blocking and Defensive Formations").

The points discussed above are closely related to the following block and defensive strategies and depend and rely on each other.

7.6 Defensive Strategies

Defensive strategies (i.e. block and defensive actions) will only be successful if the opposition views them as tactical strategies. The knowledge regarding the skills and actions of the middle blocker and the outside blockers are decisive factors that influence a successful defence. Therefore, continuous communication between the blocking athletes and the rest of the defensive athletes is a crucial condition for a successful team defence.

A team that will not or is not capable of changing and adjusting their block and/or defensive formations during the season or even against a particular opposition's offensive strategy in a certain game/match situation will not be successful in the long run. Each block and defensive strategy is based on a team's own strengths and by taking into consideration the strengths and weaknesses of their opposition.

By *analysing your own team* the following main observations must be taken into account:

DEFENSIVE STRATEGIES

- The technical/tactical and physical/psychological skills and abilities of the blocking and defensive athletes.
- The starting line-up of the team and the resulting six rotations and position changes of the athletes.
- An analysis of your own team's offence to gather information and draw conclusions for your own blocking and defensive training.
- Even if your own team does not use an A-quick behind the setter or a B-quick in the offensive scheme, you should still practice these and other offensive skills in order to better prepare your team's block and defence against opponents who do use these offensive actions.
- A detailed analysis of the middle blockers and the defensive athletes in position VI and also of the libero in his/her role as a defensive specialist and the director of the defence.

These explanations are related to the main observational points in chapter 7.4 in regards to the development of setting strategies and Learning Part III (Chapter 5 "Block and Defensive Formations and the Individual Tactics of the Blocking and Defensive Athletes").

The *analysis of the opposition* should follow the following main points/observations:
- Strengths and weaknesses of the service reception athletes including the libero and of each service reception formation as far as the transition from passing the volleyball to the execution of the offence is concerned (see Chapter 7.2 "Serving Strategies").
- Analysis of the setting in relation to the following points:
- Does the setter tip/dump the volleyball only during critical moments in the game/match?
  - Does the positioning of the setter change when s/he performs backsets?
  - Is the quick hitter only used when the setter jump sets or only after a perfect pass?
  - Is the second hitter only and always used after high passes?
  - Does the setter have a particular and favorite hitter that s/he prefers to set the volleyball to in critical situations?
  - Is there a particular hitter who only receives sets after a perfect first pass and only when it is not a critical situation?
  - Does the hitter immediately receive a second set after s/he just made a hitting error?

- Does the quick hitter also get used in critical situations?
- Does a team only use combination attacks in non-critical situations (i.e. at the start of a game or the match)?
- Does the setter execute different types of sets or attacks when s/he jump sets than when s/he just stands and sets?
- A detailed study of the frequency and the efficiency of the hitters including their hitting direction from all six rotations. In this scenario, the following items must be observed:
  - In each of the six rotations is there either a main attacking position or a main hitter that is used?
  - In each of the six rotations is there only one or several combination plays used?
  - Are there any rotations where a fake penetrating setter and/or a fake hitter used?
  - Is there only one combination hitter?
  - Are there different combination plays used when the setter is in the front row than when the setter is in the back row?
- Teamwork between the setter and the quick hitter(s).

The following observations serve as a basis for the actions of the middle blocker and for the actions of the defender:

- Are real or only fake quick attacks used?
- With regards to the time-spatial orientation of the quick hitter, are there any differences in the teamwork between the athlete and the setter?
- What is the main hitting direction of the quick hitters:
- Do the quick hitters ever tip/dump the volleyball?
- Do the quick hitters ever execute and hit any shoot sets in the offence?
- A detailed analysis of the actions of the outside hitter including the following:
  - Is the hitter successful as a combination hitter when s/he must also pass the volleyball as part of the service reception formation?
  - Is the hitter able to execute quicker sets if s/he is not a part of the service reception formation?
  - Does the hitter have difficulties in carrying out a combination attack if they are a part of the service reception formation?
  - Does the hitter have difficulties in executing a successful attack against a double block if they are a part of the service reception formation?
  - Do the outside hitters each have a favorite hitting direction?
  - Does the hitter aggressively hit the volleyball down or place the volleyball deep into the back-court?

DEFENSIVE STRATEGIES 313

- Does the hitter disguise his/her hits and/or does s/he hit using her wrist?
- Does the hitter approach the volleyball straight on or with a change of direction?
- Does the hitter hit high set volleyballs straight ahead and medium set volleyballs at an angle?
- Does the hitter hit the volleyball hard and straight down against a single block and/or does s/he hit the volleyball hard off of the top of a double block?

These observations require methods that especially show action sequences and their differences in critical (i.e. from 10 points and beyond) and in not critical situations, as well as the frequency and effectiveness of the actions.

To summarise the previous paragraph, it can be stated that the observations of the teamwork between the setter and the quick hitter is directly related to the actions of the opposition's middle blocker and the defenders in positions V and I. Also, the teamwork between the setter and the second hitter is related to the actions of the opposition's entire team, but especially the middle and outside blocker and the defender in position VI.

7.6.1 Defensive Strategies in Association with Serving Strategies

On the one hand, a combined action between the block and defence and/or on the other hand on the server may be aimed at accomplishing the following goals:
- To try to **neutralise the service reception front-court athlete** from second tempo attacks by serving him/her with long serves to the side of the volleyball court. This allows the block of the quick hitter after a very good first pass with the use of one and possibly even two blockers.
- **To force a change of the service reception formation** from a two-person to a three-person service reception formation or from a three-person to a four-person service reception formation by using jump serves. This binds the non-service reception front-court athlete and/or the back-court hitter in the service reception formation.
- **To neutralise the service reception back-court hitter** (i.e. with jump serves) will make it easier for the blockers because it means that there will be one less attacker for them to have to pay attention to (see Chapter 7.2 "Serving Strategies").
- **To neutralise the quick hitter** (by serving in his/her area or running path) will allow the middle blocker to focus on the second hitter(s).

7.6.2 Defensive Strategies that Take into Consideration the Actions of the Quick Hitter

If the quick hitter jumps with or after the set (fake A-quick), the middle blocker must also take action after the set in all situations.

If the quick hitter jumps before the set, then the following factors will determine the strategy of the middle blocker:

- The middle blocker jumps with the quick hitter and is covering his/her main hitting direction because the quick hitter is receiving many sets (man-man coverage).
- The middle blocker is fully jumping with the quick hitter because s/he cannot make it to the outside to close out the double block because of a quick set to the outside.
- The middle blocker is jumping before the quick hitter (fake jump) to trick the setter into setting the second hitter.
- At the beginning of a game the middle blocker is jumping with the set, but later in the game the middle blocker jumps after the set to be able to have time to form a double block.
- The middle blocker jumps after the set but also tries to slow down the attack with the use of a passive hand/arm posture.
- The middle blocker is jumping after the set because the quick hitter is not very effective or is using a lot of tips.
- The middle blocker is switch-blocking, which means that another blocker is taking the quick hitter while s/he is trying to form a double block.
- The middle blocker should jump after the set if the height of the reach of the quick hitter is not very high.
- If the quick hitter is mainly hitting shoot sets, then the middle blocker should watch the volleyball and jump after the set. The middle blocker's starting position in this situation should be between the setter and the quick hitter.

In the development of strategies for the middle blockers all idiosyncratic characteristics and schemes of the opposition's setter and his/her teamwork with his/her quick hitters should be taken into account.

7.6.3 Defensive Strategies According to the Actions of the Offence

If the *setter is in the front row* and often tips and/or fakes (often to the main hitter in position IV), the following blocking strategy may be used:

The blocker in position IV has two tasks to perform. Firstly, s/he will block the setter's tip/fake and secondly s/he will block the back row attack. It is the job of the middle blocker, together with the outside blocker, to cover the quick hitter and the main hitter in position IV (Fig. 201a).

If, in the same situation, the main attack is coming from position I, then the middle blocker can block the quick hitter in position III and the outside hitter in position IV by him/herself. This will leave the blocker in position II free to cover the back row attack from position I. This would also mean that the blockers in positions II and IV could form a double block against the back row attacker while the middle blocker covers the rest of the attacks (Fig. 201b).

If the outside hitter in position IV is receiving most of the sets as mentioned above, and the quick hitter is carrying out an A-quick in front of the setter, then the middle blocker will cover three attackers by him/herself (the setter, quick hitter, and the back row hitter) while the other two blocker will cover the main attacker (Fig. 201c).

If all of the hitters are used equally, then every blocker will be responsible for a hitter to which s/he is assigned.

If the outside hitters are used with quick and low sets, then every front-court athlete will block his/her direct opponent.

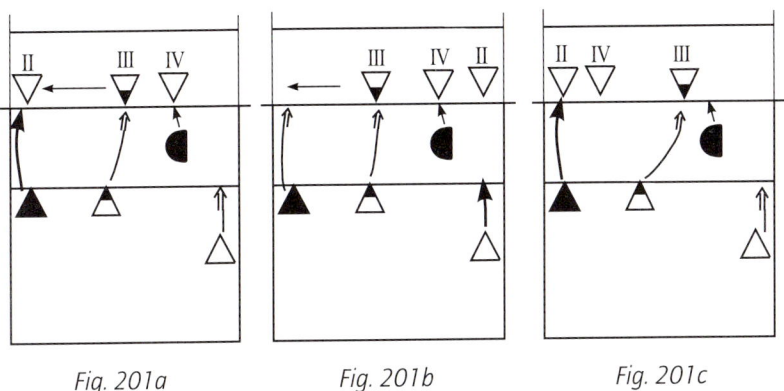

Fig. 201a   *Fig. 201b*   *Fig. 201c*

DEFENSIVE AND OFFENSIVE STRATEGIES

If the quick hitter is moving towards the setter, then the middle blocker is also responsible for covering the setter; if the quick hitter is moving away from the setter, then the outside blocker in position IV will be responsible for covering this situation. If the quick hitter is receiving many sets in this situation, then it is possible to cover him/her by using two blockers: In this situation the middle blocker will cover the second most used hitter in either position IV or I alone (Figs. 201d and 201e).

If the opposition is using two back row hitters (positions VI and I), the block can be organised in this manner: It is the duty of the middle blocker to cover the quick hitter and to form a double block against the second hitters. The blocker in position IV is responsible for watching the setter for fakes/tips and the back-court hitters. The blocker in position II is responsible for covering the hitter in position IV and the back-court hitter in position VI (Fig. 201f).

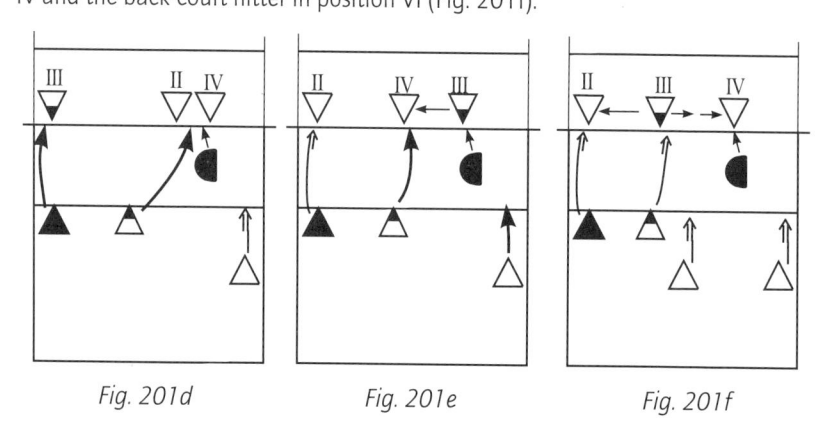

Fig. 201d *Fig. 201e* *Fig. 201f*

If, in this situation, combination plays in the middle are used, then the middle blocker must stay in the middle to cover the quick hitters and the combination hitters, whilst the outside blockers will move closer to the middle to be in a better starting position to cover the combination attackers.

If the setter is penetrating and there are three front-court hitters, all of the strategies mentioned above according to Figures 201a-201f can be used.

If there are just as many combinations being performed behind the setter in position II as there are to the outside hitter in position IV with three hitters in the front row, then the main blocker may take the outside hitter in position IV alone and the other two blockers can cover the combination hitters or the other way around (Figs. 202a-202b).

The same blocking strategy should be used with a combination attack in position IV and the main hitter in position II.

DEFENSIVE STRATEGIES 317

If there is a combination attack expected in the middle, then the main blocker will be the middle blocker. If there are two combination plays used in two positions at a distance from each, and they are used equally, then the main blocker should take one of the combinations and the other two blockers should cover the other combination (Figs. 203a-203b).

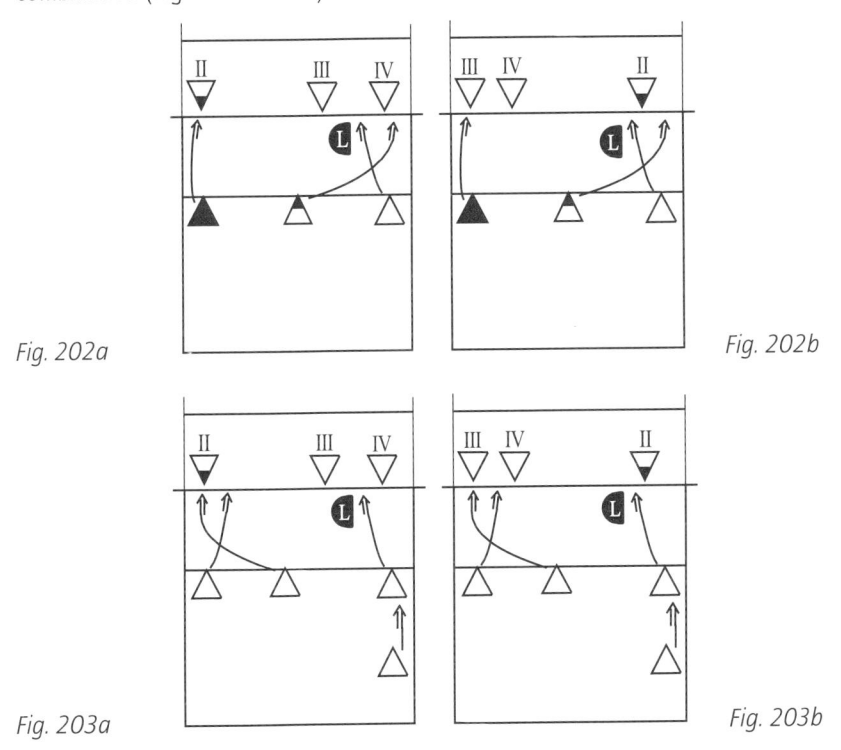

Fig. 202a *Fig. 202b*

Fig. 203a *Fig. 203b*

Combination plays with two quick hitters by the setter and a second hitter at a distance from them, and all hitters are an offensive threat, then the following situation must occur: the main blocker will cover the quick hitter behind the setter and the second hitter in position I, the second blocker will cover the second quick hitter in front of the setter, and the third blocker will cover the second hitter in position IV (Fig. 204a).

If, in this situation, the outside hitter in position IV is getting by far the most sets, then the main blocker will be responsible for both quick hitters and the second hitter in position I, while the other two blockers will make sure that the main hitter is always being double-blocked (Fig. 204b).

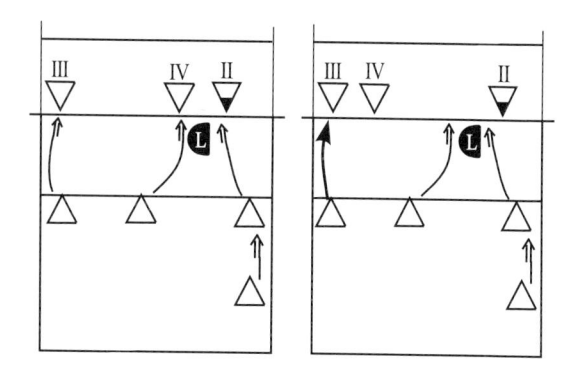

DEFENSIVE AND OFFENSIVE STRATEGIES

Fig. 204a *Fig. 204b*

Combination plays in the middle or the use of two back-court hitters (positions I and VI) requires the main blocker to take on the role of a middle blocker.

In the aforementioned example, the row of blockers always reacts to the actions of the opposition's offence (hitters), but it also makes sense (this can be accomplished as part of the defensive strategy) that the row of blockers also react early enough so that the opposition's offence, especially the setter, will react or will have to react against it! For example, an early jump by the middle blocker – before the quick hitter – tempts the setter to use the hitter in the outside position. Similarly, the starting position of the blockers at the net may also force the volleyball to be set to a certain position.

To summarise the above points the following ***principles*** and ***blocking strategies*** can be stated:

- The main blocker must do the most work in the strategy.
- The second best blocker has the task with the second most responsibility.
- The weakest blocker has only to deal with problems that are easy to solve.
- The more athletes on a team that can take on more than one task, then the more blocking strategies that become possible for the team to perform in the same game/match situation.
- If having to deal with several tasks is too great of a responsibility for the blockers, then simple and clear strategies should be chosen.

If several tasks mean that the blockers will show their technical deficiencies when they are blocking, then strategies that are less difficult and technically easier to execute should be used.

7.6.4 Defensive Strategies for Block and Defence

All explanations regarding defence can only be successfully executed with the involvement of defensive strategies. *Only attacking positions, not hitting direction, and how often the offence has been carrying out attacks from these positions has been the main basis of the blocking strategies discussed.* All strategies discussed above regarding the actions of the middle blocker relate to the quick hitter, and the group tactical actions of the blockers relate to combination plays all with one goal – the formation of a double block.

Generally, teams can be divided into three categories according to the offence that they run:

- Teams that use hard and powerful spikes/hits.
  Against these types of teams, the blockers must cover the main hitting direction of the attacker, the defensive athletes must be in a very low defensive ready position, and the athlete in position VI should be in a middle defensive ready position far enough back in the "block's shadow" and, if necessary, outside of the volleyball court.
- Teams that use more tactical spikes/hits.
  In this situation, the athlete playing in position VI should always stay inside of the volleyball court and defend at the edge or just outside of the "block's shadow".
- Teams that use both of the above types of offensive hits.
  In this situation, a counter-strategy would be a mixture of the strategies mentioned above or a change of the strategy depending on the offence.

The following strategies are focusing their attention to the frequency of the attacking spots used in relation to the hitting direction of the volleyball. These strategies will be shown based on the following selected practical examples:
- The opposition is attacking over the weakest blocker.
  - The weakest blocker must change, as late as possible, his/her blocking position.
  - The change must be combined with a fake blocking line-up.
  - Fake a change to a blocking position and then play the role of a covering athlete behind the block at the latest possible moment. This should definitely be done when the opposition is using high sets.
  - The weakest blocker is blocking line at the antennae in position II. This means that the main blocker in position III is preparing him/herself early

enough to support this blocker at the outside position. The defenders in position IV and V will cover the diagonal direction and the athlete in position VI is at or behind the baseline, ready to run for any volleyballs that are hit off of the block. The strongest defender in the defensive back-court, usually the libero, is changing to position I and defends deep in the back-court volleyballs that are hit over the block (Fig. 205a). In this manner, the attacker only has a small zone along the line available to hit the volleyball against the weakest blocker; therefore possibly causing some troubles resulting in some hitting errors.

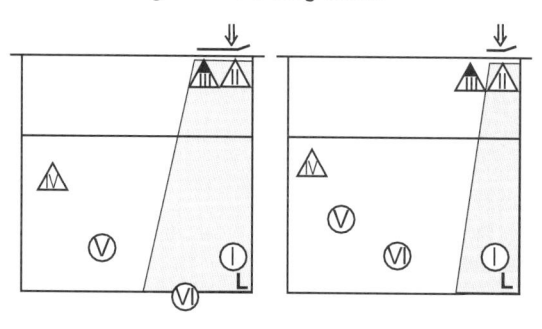

Fig. 205a   *Fig. 205b*

- Just the same as in 1, but the main blocker in position III reaches over the weaker blocker and blocks still penetrating over his/her blocking zone and the area of the weaker blocker. The athlete in position VI, in this situation, is changing his/her position to also defend the diagonal direction (Fig. 205b).
- The weakest blocker is changing to the middle blocking position and jumps with the quick hitter.
- The weakest blocker is changing to the outside position IV and only blocks the zone against the back-court hitter in position I.
- The weakest blocker is always blocking the weakest hitter or the hitter with the least reach height.
- The opposition is using their main hitter in position II or IV.
- The main hitter receives medium sets most of the time and mainly hits the volleyball in the diagonal direction: according to Fig. 206a the double block will cover the diagonal direction. The athlete in position VI (usually the libero) covers half of the diagonal direction.
- The main hitter is mainly attacking deep line: Fig. 206b shows the changed defensive formation.

DEFENSIVE STRATEGIES   321

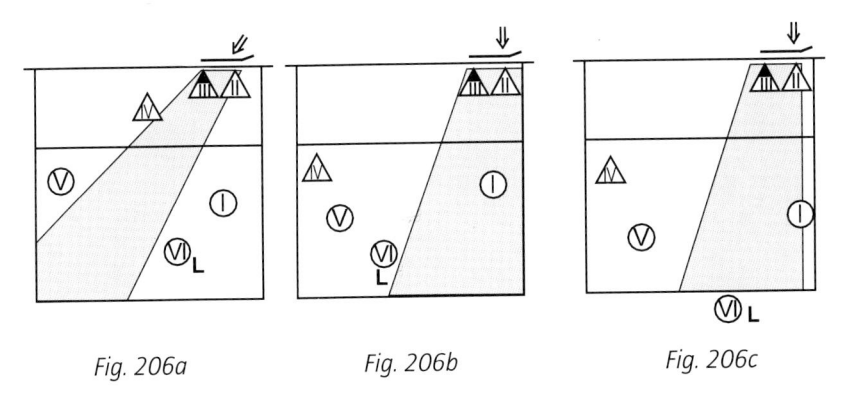

Fig. 206a *Fig. 206b* *Fig. 206c*

- The main hitter is purposely hitting off of the top of the block: Position VI/libero is defending outside of the volleyball court behind the baseline in the "block's shadow" (Fig. 206c).
- The main hitter varies his/her approach but always hits down his/her power line: The outside blocker organises the block by blocking the volleyball with his/her inner hand. Depending on the direction of the hitter's approach, the defensive formations of Figs. 206a-206c apply.
- The main hitter is hitting hard past the double block after a high set: Formation of a triple block with coverage in the diagonal direction (Fig. 207).
- The main hitter is often using tips against a triple-block: Defence such as in Fig. 207, but the athlete in position I must move up and cover behind the block.
- The opposition is using medium quick sets to attack over the outside hitters in positions II and/or IV.

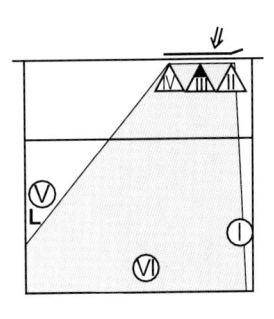

Fig. 207

Generally, attackers who hit medium quick sets should be blocked in their power line because this could be seen as their main hitting direction, and also the athlete in position VI/libero will cover the main hitting direction.

- If the middle blocker is signaling that s/he will wait for the set before s/he jumps against the quick hitter, then the athlete in position VI/libero must take a new starting defensive position in the main hitting direction of the quick hitter. Fig. 208a shows the double block and the defence.

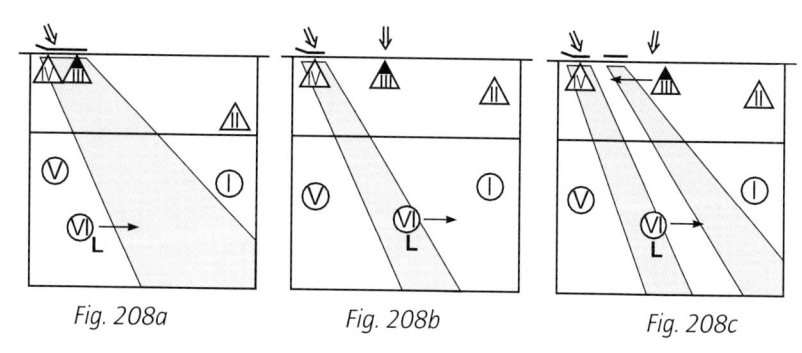

DEFENSIVE AND OFFENSIVE STRATEGIES

Fig. 208a *Fig. 208b* *Fig. 208c*

- If the middle blocker is signaling that s/he will jump with the quick hitter and if the setter is penetrating, then the defenders in positions I and V must move back and position VI/libero must move to the area of the main hitting direction of the second hitter (Fig. 208b).
- If the middle blocker is signalling that s/he will wait for the set before s/he jumps with the quick hitter and that s/he expects a B-quick set, then the defence has to be prepared for the formation of an open double block. This means that the athlete in position VI/libero must start their position in the main hitting direction of the quick hitter (Fig. 208c).

The opposition is using their combination hitter.

- The formation of a double block against the combination hitter on the outside position, forces the actions of the blockers to depend upon the direction of the approach of the power line of the hitter. The defensive athlete in position VI/libero must try to either take the position at the "seam" of the double block in the block shadow or in the area of the main hitting direction at the edge of the block-shadow or s/he must make his/her starting position deep back at the baseline.
- If the middle blocker is signaling that s/he will jump with the quick hitter and the setter is penetrating, then both defenders in positions I and V must move their defensive areas further back and position VI/libero must take his/her area in the main hitting direction of the combination hitter (Fig. 209b).
- If the combination hitter attacks in the middle and the middle blocker is waiting for the set before s/he blocks, then the athlete in position VI/libero must start in the main hitting direction of the quick hitter. If the quick hitter is not getting the set, the athlete in position VI/libero must either move to the "seam" of the double block in the block shadow or s/he must push back deep or at the edge of the block shadow (Fig. 209c).

DEFENSIVE STRATEGIES   323

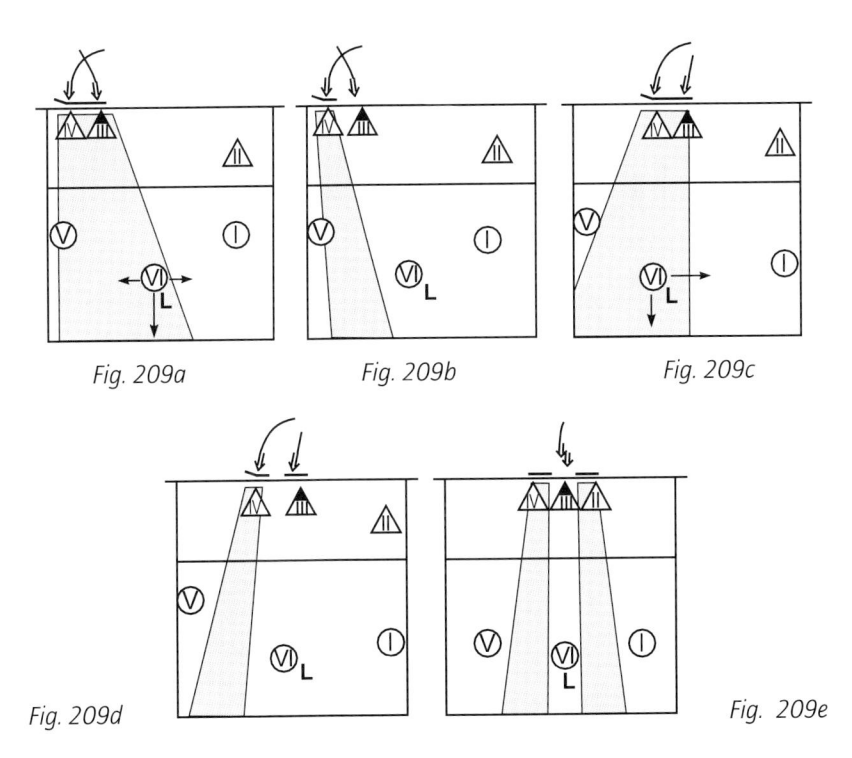

Fig. 209a   *Fig. 209b*   *Fig. 209c*

Fig. 209d   *Fig. 209e*

- If the middle blocker is jumping with the quick hitter and single-block situations are occurring, then the defender in position VI/libero must cover the main hitting direction of the combination hitter, but outside or at the edge of the block shadow (Fig. 209d).
- If the middle blocker is jumping with the quick hitter and an echelon combination attack is taking place behind the quick hitter, then both outside blockers must form an open double block right next to him/her (Fig. 209e).
- The opposition is using a back-court hitter.

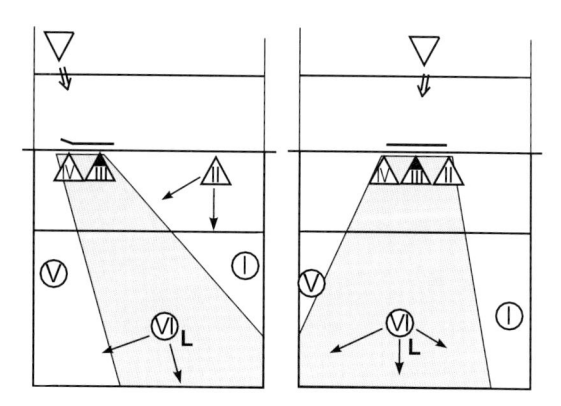

DEFENSIVE AND OFFENSIVE STRATEGIES

Fig. 210   *Fig. 211*

- A back-court hitter in position I is attacking a medium-high set. According to the following principle: "the line will be left open and, if necessary, covered by two defenders" (Fig. 210).
- If the attacker in position I is receiving medium-quick sets then the team must carry out the defensive strategies according to Figs. 209c, 209e, and/or 211.

Regarding positional changes in the back-court and further possibilities to take action in the defence, it must be referred to the Learning Part III (Chapter 5).

The following *generally applicable characteristics* that are based on individual and group tactics will be discussed. To be in a position to use them and to carry them out requires a very good understanding and communication between the blockers and the defenders.

- The blockers must acquire and analyse both the setting rhythm and the idiosyncratic characteristics of the hitters. Only this ability allows for new and/or changed strategies possible.
- The same applies for the observation and analysis of the psychological-physical abilities of the setter and the hitters.
- The blocking position against left-handed hitters must follow the principle of "cover the volleyball and the hitting arm" and, therefore, changes in comparison to right-handed hitters in the same position.
- If the quick hitter is often and very effectively used, then the middle blocker might jump fully at the beginning of a game to force the opposition to change their offensive strategy.
- If a blocker is very effective against the opposition's star athlete, then s/he should possible play against him/her.
- The outside blocker should move to the middle and stay there if his/her direct opposition is neutralised from the offence because of a service reception or a defensive action.

DEFENSIVE STRATEGIES   325

- The blocker should be able to quickly switch from a blocking action to an offensive action. This is especially true with a bad first pass by the opposition in the area of the net where the blocker is positioned. The blocker should also know if the setter is a front row or a back row athlete and know the setter's blocking abilities.
- Sticking to a particular defensive strategy makes the opposition's setting strategy easier. It is for this reason why variations of the defensive strategy are necessary and tactically reasonable.
- A long self-confident eye contact with the opposition's hitter might put him into a state of uncertainty. The same is true for signals with the hands and arms before the block or the serve.
- If a hitter is varying his/her hits and always hits past the block, then the blocker can use, in a single block, an open blocking posture with spread arms (called an "eagle" (spread wings) block) (Photo 76).
- After long rallies or in critical game/match situations, it has been found that hitters use their most successful spike.
- After a successful blocking action, it might be expected that the same rejected hitter will use a different hitting direction or a different offensive action the next time s/he receives the set.
- With inaccurate sets, the blocking strategy must be changed. With sets that are too tight to the net the volleyball must be blocked and with sets that are far away from the net the diagonal area must be blocked.
- Instead of trying to form a double block with only one arm to attempt to try and close it, an open double-block formation with penetration is preferred. A one-armed block only makes sense if the blocker miscalculates the set, but the volleyball is set too tight to the net and the defenders will not have any chance to defend against the attack (Photo 77).

Photo 76 (Sabarz)

Photo 77 (Kuzian)

- If an attacker is not hitting very hard, but s/he uses the outside of the block very often, then it would be reasonable to use a zone block to cover the diagonal hitting direction and to leave the line open. Two defenders, like it is shown in Fig. 206a, must still cover the deep line.
- If the middle blocker is not able to close the double block or even to form an open double block, then s/he should signal this to the outside blocker by calling out to him/her. The same applies to the outside blocker when it comes time to form a triple block.
- If a hitter has been blocked twice in a row, the blockers should neglect this hitter the next time, and they should tell this to the back-court defenders so they can adjust their defensive formation to this new strategy.
- If a hitter misses the volleyball court twice in a row, the blockers should cover a more diagonal direction.
- Small, but very athletic blocking athletes should not be used to block offensive combinations.
- If the blockers know the expected offensive combination, then this fact should be hidden by the starting position of the blockers at the net as long as possible.
- If the attackers are hitting volleyballs out of a change of direction approach, then the blockers should communicate this by calling it out and helping each other as much as possible.
- At the end of a game or in critical situations, it might be an advantage if the blockers all of a sudden matched up against different hitters than before because this will introduce a new and not prepared attacking situation for the hitters.
- If a hitter is always successful against his/her blocker, a change of the blocking formation by suitable positional changes will surely be positive.
- After a timeout, a new offensive tactic is to be expected.
- Athletes with the same reach height should block together rather than athletes with very different reach heights.
- The defenders in positions I and V should move further back if a bad service reception pass is played and no quick attack is to be expected. The same applies for the athlete in position VI, who must also cover the main hitting direction.
- In anticipation of a tactical and/or long serve to the back-court, the athlete in position I should move his/her defensive starting position further back.
- With frequent attacks off of the service reception by the setter, the defender in position VI/libero should cover the setter's main hitting direction from the very beginning of the game and not the hitting direction of the quick hitter.
- The higher the reach height of the blockers, then the further the starting position of the defenders can be pushed back.

- The more passively the double block, then the further back the player in position VI should be defending.
- If two defenders are defending the same side of the volleyball court, then they should be positioned next to each, but at a distance from each other and with staggered positions to the volleyball net. In this manner, volleyballs in an overlapping area can be better defended and without any miscommunication.
- If the opposition is attacking against a weak blocker or even against no block, then the defenders should move to the middle of the volleyball court because that is the most endangered and likely to be hit at area.
- Against very good tactical hitters that very often use the block to their advantage, it might be successful to move the hands away just before the hit, but the defenders need to know this so they can be ready just in case this strategy does not work out.
- If the attacking spot is outside of the volleyball court or even outside of the antennae, then all the defenders should defend outside of the block shadow in the diagonal direction because there is no other direction possible for the volleyball to travel in this situation (Fig. 212).
- Tall athletes can move up further in the defence because tactical hits cannot as easily be played over them due to their size.
- If the setter is defending in position V or VI, then every volleyball should be played very high to give the setter more time to run to set the volleyball.
- The service reception athletes should generally take all free balls.

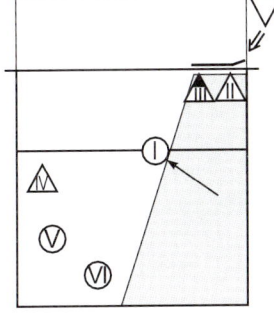

Fig. 212

7.6.5 Determining Factors in the Men's and Women's Game

In this section, important influences will be assigned to their respective level.

Low Level
At this level, the decisive element of the game is the serve. *It is for this reason that the service reception formation must be an element of each practice.*
The practicing of the offence out of the service reception/defence must include, to a large extent, the **safety set**. This play is often needed at the low levels of

volleyball, therefore, every athlete must be able to set a high diagonal volleyball, but not too tight to the volleyball net so it is hittable by a teammate.

In block and defence, especially with women, a single block with close coverage by the athlete next to the blocker and with the athlete in position VI pushed back is preferred over a double block with the athlete in position VI moved up. With men, the goal must be the formation of a double block, especially in position II. If the block is well-positioned, the athlete in position VI should be moved up, but with a bad block the athlete in position VI should be moved back.

It must be an important goal of each practice to reduce the number of unforced errors that occur. The following measures can help to achieve this goal:

- Serves from serving zone VI should mostly be hit in the frontal direction, and serves from serving zones I and V should be hit in a diagonal direction to help omit serves that go out of play.
- The serve from serving zone I should be hit diagonally to position I or between position I and VI to make the opposition's attack from position IV more difficult because it forces the setter to backset the volleyball if they want to put it into that position.
- The serve from serving zone V should be hit diagonally to position V or between position V and VI to force the service reception athlete in this new and still unusual service reception situation to pass the volleyball and to possibly cause trouble for the opposition's offence in position II.
- The service reception athlete should use the overhand pass to play any volleyball that is served high, but not very fast.
- The first pass, especially out of a defensive formation, should be played high and not too tight to the volleyball net.
- The setter should only perform a backset after a perfect pass. If a pass is of a medium quality, the setter should prefer to use a safer set. The set should be higher and use the whole width of the net. The same applies for the use of a "safety set".
- The attackers should use tactical hits (i.e. roll shots or tips, etc.) after a bad or medium quality set. Only after a perfect set should an attack be hit deep and into the back area of the volleyball court.
- The outside blockers should be able to reach the blocking spot with one step and always block the diagonal direction. A double block in position III should only be formed after a medium-high set so that the blocker will have time to get to the correct blocking spot and to jump out of a standing position and not from a moving position.

- The middle blocker should never jump with a real or fake quick attack but only with medium or higher sets from position III. The blocker should generally go for a double block in position II and try and form that block from a standing position. If the blocker has to block from a moving position then s/he should choose to allow the outside blocker to execute a good single block rather than to form a bad double block.
- The defenders should start from a position far enough back so that they only have to move forward and/or to the side to get to a defensive position. They defend at a line approximately 7 meters back from the volleyball net so that they will not have to defend attacks that come at them above their chests because those volleyballs will be out of play.
- A front-court athlete rather than a setter penetrating from the back row should run the offence. This also applies to free ball situations.
- The use of the libero should not be used as an introduction of this new specialised athlete and position but rather to improve upon weaknesses of certain athletes in service reception and defensive formations and situations.

Finally, it can be said that a 4-2 or 3-3 match system with a front-court setter running the offence will be the best and correct match system for this level.

Middle Level

At this level, especially with women, many of the above points also apply.

Determining factors at this level are:

- A serve from the middle distance zone and at least two different serving spots are possible.
- A service reception formation and skill that allows at least two different sets to be performed. With women, a safety set from the back-court is still very important.
- Setting and attacking from both outside positions is important, whereas position IV still remains the main attacking position for women.
- The actions of the middle blocker and the formation of a double block at both outside positions is the decisive factor in the men's game. The formation of a double block in position II is important for the women's game.
- The men should work equally as well with the athlete in position VI playing up and/or back in block and defence situations. The women should play with the athlete in position VI back and a close coverage of the block through the other directly positioned back row athletes.

DEFENSIVE AND OFFENSIVE STRATEGIES

Thanks, largely in part to the rally-point scoring system, it is still an important and major factor to omit unforced errors if success is to be achieved in a match.

The following points should be taken into account and used as part of the match tactics because they will make the transition to the higher level much easier:

- Tactical serves from serving zones I, V, and VI to remove the service receiving front-court hitter from the offence or behind the setter to make the setting much more difficult should be used.
- In the service reception formation, stronger passing athletes and/or the libero should cover a much larger area.
- If the setter is penetrating, the service reception formation should not be played too tight to the volleyball net. If the setter is in the front row, the service reception athletes can take a greater risk.
- The setter should only jump-set with a perfect pass and the jump-set should be used only when the setter is in the front row rather than when the setter is penetrating from the back row.
- The set must not be worse than the pass from the service reception.
- The quick hitter must be used with short balls or fake A-quicks to bind the opposition's middle blocker without too many unforced errors.
- A simple and effective offence should be chosen over a complicated combination offence.
- The offence out of the defence should still be run by a front row setter rather than by a setter penetrating from the back row.
- The middle blocker should only jump to block the quick hitter after the set is made so that s/he is prepared to form a double block.
- The women's defence should be strengthened by positioning the libero in the diagonal hitting direction. Whereas with the men the long line hitting direction, along with the diagonal, should also be covered.
- The strongest defensive athlete/libero should be put in position V and the weakest defensive athlete should be placed in position VI.

Finally, the following match systems are recommended for the men, assuming that there is one back-court hitter being used: 5-1 or 4-2. For the women, where there is no planned back row attack the 4-2 match system is recommended.

Also, for both the men and the women, a planned use of the libero should be started. The new rules, especially the rally-point scoring system and the introduction of the libero, had the following effects in their first season of use:

DEFENSIVE STRATEGIES   331

- The effectiveness of the service reception and the directly related service reception errors hardly changed.
- The setter's actions, especially the distribution of the sets, changed slightly in favor of the outside hitting position (by approximately 3%). The setters still set to the outside hitting position in critical match situations.
- The effectiveness of the offence slightly worsened (by approximately 1%), but the attackers made more errors in critical game/match situations (by approximately 9%).
- The effectiveness of the serve dropped by approximately 3%, but at critical moments in the game/match it was higher than the previous average. Direct service winners dropped by approximately 5%.

All of the above statistics become clearer if one takes into account the fact that only about 15% of the teams at this level have been using a libero.

Even at the highest national amateur level, in this case the third division (the German "Regionalliga"), less than 40% of the teams used the libero.

It is expected that with a better use and understanding of the libero rule, the effectiveness in the C1 situation will increase.

High Level
The following points apply to the top national level:
- Jump serves as well as tactical serves are much more important in the men's game than in the women's game. In the women's game, serves from the middle distance dominate.
- It is expected that because of the rule change that allows the serve to touch the volleyball net legal, serves from the middle and long distance zones will lose their effectiveness and importance. Their role will be replaced by tactical serves from the baseline and by jump serves.
- With the use of the libero, it is expected, especially by the men, that jump serves and jump float serves will increase to force the front-court and/or a back-court hitter to pass in the service reception formation.
- Where in a women's team up to five athletes are in the service reception formation the men are only using two or three service reception specialists.
- With women, position IV is still the main attacking spot (photo 78), while with the men the back-court hitter in position I has to be added and, therefore, position II must be added as a second main attacking spot (photo 79).
- The jump-set is an absolute must for a successful offence by the men, whereas jump-sets are not necessary for an effective offence in the women's game.

DEFENSIVE AND OFFENSIVE STRATEGIES

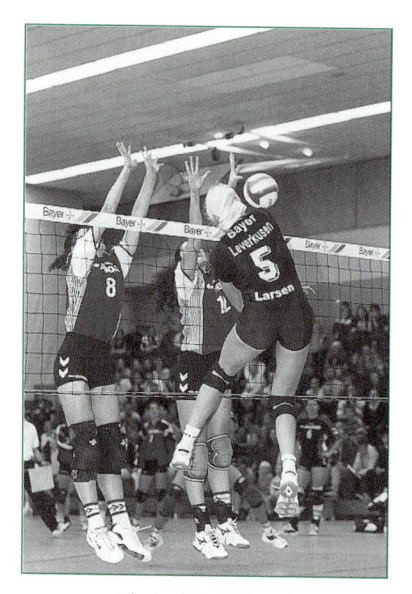

Photo 78 (Zeimer)   *Photo 79 (Martin)*

- Quick attacks by the men are rather "real" while quick attacks by the women are rather "unreal".
- The men overwhelmingly use A-quick and B-quick attacks while the women almost exclusively use A-quicks.
- The women often use one-legged quick attacks (slides) behind the setter, the men prefer two-legged shoot sets.
- Out of the service reception formation, women use up to three hitters while the men use many combination plays with up to four and even five hitters.
- Especially with the men, it might be expected that with the use of the libero and the services of an additional front-court athlete because of the changes that are possible in the service reception formations, that more and quicker sets to the outside will be used and that more special offensive combination plays will be introduced.
- Women mostly execute a counter-attack in position IV. The men execute a counter-attack in position IV as well as in position I/II.
- The actions of the middle blocker are much more decisive in the men's game than in the women's game. On the other hand, defence is much less important in the men's game than it is in the women's game where there it is the deciding factor.

- The men always try and block aggressively (photo 80) while the women block much more passively (photo 81).
- Triple-block formations are more often seen in the men's game than in the women's game.
- There are less blocking and defensive strategies to be found in the women's game than in the men's game.
- It is to be expected that the libero will be permanently used to strengthen the service reception and the defence.
- It is also predicted that all front-court athletes will have very good middle blocking skills. The differentiation of the front-court athletes will be done by comparing their hitting skills such as executing a quick attack, outside hit, or their role in a combination play.

In the women's international level there are tendencies to be seen in the world's best teams that they are adjusting their game technically-tactically and psychologically-physically to mirror the men's game and style.

Photo 80 (Martin)   *Photo 81 (Zeimer)*

8 Specific Principles for the Training of the Sport of Volleyball

The following principles are mainly based upon observations and analysis of the training sessions at the different levels of volleyball. These principles are supposed to assist the coach in designing his/her training sessions as close as possible to the sport of volleyball and furthermore to correspond as precisely as possible to the exact match situations that may be encountered.

This volume purposely excludeds match skills and drills for the introduction and development of technical and tactical variants. The methodical practice sessions regarding the basic techniques and tactics can be easily transferred from the first volume Volleyball – A Handbook for Coaches and Players; *these skills are also sufficiently covered by many periodicals and other publications. Therefore, more training will be discussed rather than educational and systematic principles (chapter 1.1 – "The New Rules and their Effects on the Practice and Matches").*

These ideas have to be looked upon in context with the practice sessions of the different learning components and they support the coach in his/her efforts to develop and achieve a systematic practice session.

Generally, this implies that the **training session** has to be specifically designed for the sport that it is going to be utilised in. Analysis of the structure of the sport of volleyball displays the following parameters for high levels of national volleyball:
- Short to very short highly intensive exertions on the athletes alternating with phases of regeneration.
- The duration of the exertion that is put upon the athletes averages 7.9 seconds.
- The time between rallies averages 12.5 seconds.
- From a physiological standpoint, these short exertions of the muscles are almost exclusively of an anaerobic alactacid nature.
- The amount of running averages 3.2 meters per sprint.
- The time of the sprints averages 17.4 seconds.
- The amount of sprints performed in an hour match averages 190 dashes.
- The average time that passes in-between the jumping actions of an athlete at the volleyball net is approximately 26 seconds.

- The amount of jumping performed in an hour match averages 71 jumps per athlete.

It can be clearly deducted from the explanations mentioned above that for the volleyball related training (except when training endurance and psychological skills), the repetition method must be used. In other words, short (approximately 6 seconds) maximum intensity exertions followed by an active and complete break for regeneration (1-3 minutes).

*The following **principles** are absolutely necessary for training and only partly necessary for the teaching of new techniques and tactics. Here, it is not about the learning of techniques or tactics, but about the learning of specific match related situations and/or the training of a technical-tactical action under competitive circumstances.*

8.1 Principles for a Volleyball-related Warm-up

1. *The athlete should perform their warm-up game perpendicular to the volleyball net*, because all service reception and/or defensive actions are carried out in the direction facing the volleyball net. By doing this, only the net athletes are allowed to perform accurate or inaccurate offensive actions, while the back-court athletes should try to always execute a perfect first pass to the volleyball net. The only exception is the setter's warm-up game, and that should be done as close to and parallel to the volleyball net as possible to simulate their match actions.
2. *The net athletes should, as often as possible, perform jumping actions.* This means to move quickly from executing hits and/or tips from a standing position to offensive actions where the athlete is jumping at the volleyball net.
3. *The athlete closest to the end line must not play any volleyballs that are out of play.* This is a principle that should be followed in training sessions as well, because it creates the habit of recognising what is in play and what is out of play during match situations. The execution of this simple concept will improve the athlete's spatial orientation and actions from an early stage of learning.
4. *Three-person warm-up games should be used over two-person warm-up games*, because to play in a triangle is the basic concept of the sport of volleyball. In this situation, two of the athletes can be either at the volleyball net or at the end line of the volleyball court.

SPECIFIC PRINCIPLES

5. *During the warm-up, drills should be chosen that make the athletes focus on some skill to train their ability to anticipate.* For example, if an athlete at the net is hitting a volleyball towards the end line but at different points of the end line, then the athlete at the end line will have to move as early as possible to the anticipated defensive spot to pass the volleyball.
6. The principles mentioned above require a change in the function of the athletes every two minutes to ensure that each athlete is getting a turn at practicing both positions.
7. *Warming-up with small-court games that include the volleyball net and volleyball specific movements and actions ensures a preparation that reflects certain volleyball match situations.* Appropriate games include one-on-one, two-on-two, and three-on-three with or without a setter that sets for both groups.
8. *Warm-up hitting should always be carried out indirectly.* This means that prior to the offensive action (the hit) there is a service reception and/or defensive action (a pass and/or set). This trains the setter and the hitter to set and hit after a perfect first pass.
9. *Warm-up hitting should be carried out from the very beginning against a single and/or double block.* In this situation, the second hitter in line will play the volleyball to the setter (third athlete passing). The setter and hitter then do the same thing as stated in 8. The setter and third athlete passing then play defence and cover the hitter so as to be able to execute another attack if the volleyball is blocked.
10. *Attackers must not cross underneath the volleyball net to the other side of the volleyball court after their hit.* They must go around the volleyball net at the side of the volleyball court. It is best if the athletes hit from only one side of the volleyball net and block and defend on the same side as well.
11. *The rules of the sport of volleyball must always be adhered to during warm*-up (i.e. a back-court hitter must not touch and/or step beyond the ten-foot line when hitting a volleyball or touching the volleyball net and/or stepping over the center line as a front-court hitter).
12. *Warm-up hitting of quick attackers should only be executed with a third athlete passing the volleyball (simulating different passes to the setter) and against a block.*
13. *If the setter is jump-setting during matches then s/he should be jump-setting during the warm-up and, if possible, s/he should begin with a small penetrating run.* If the setter is not expected to jump-set during matches then s/he should perform a jumping action (i.e. block) after each third set.

PRINCIPLES FOR A VOLLEYBALL RELATED WARM-UP   337

14. A warm-up involving a volleyball should prepare the team for the main goals of the training session. For example, if the main focus of the coach is to train the team in counter-attacking after a defensive dig then a "safety" set should be a part of the volleyball portion of the warm-up.
15. A volleyball-related warm-up is extremely important if training sessions are not often and/or they are in short duration.
16. The running portion at the beginning of each warm-up should always take place in the volleyball court (no running in circles). An arm and shoulder stretch and warm-up should also be included right from the beginning.
17. Taking into account that the matches are being played using the rally-point scoring system, the warm-up should include moments where the athletes must mentally, psychologically, and physically reach their match level and be ready to play. Therefore, drills after the initial part of the warm-up should be of a competitive nature and put psychological pressure on the athletes.
18. **Warm-ups before matches** should take into account the preceding principles and the following points:
    - Generally the portion of the warm-up that does not include the use of a volleyball should mirror the same warm-up that is used at the start of each practice and should also be done in the same time frame. This portrays the team in a state of unity and may put them in a more positive psychological state of mind amongst themselves and may put their opponents into a more negative psychological state of mind. A similar result can also be achieved if a team is talking positively and encouraging each other throughout the warm-up. Athletes that are easily susceptible to injuries or are extremely over-motivated should follow their own programme or routine.
    - During the warm-up but before any hitting occurs, at the very least the service reception athletes and the libero should pass volleyballs that are served (or hit like serves) using the forearm and overhand passing techniques. This service reception drill can be conducted outside of the volleyball court simultaneously as the defensive drills are being carried out inside of the volleyball court.
    - During the warm-up, athletes should be assigned their warm-up partners based upon observations made in training that have proven to show that the two athletes complement each other. For example, setters should warm-up together or the setter and the hitter opposite diagonally to them should partner together. During this time, the starting athletes will warm-up inside of the volleyball court while the substitute athletes will warm-up outside of the volleyball court.

- The libero should be warming-up with a substitute athlete or the assistant coach on his/her service reception skills while the other athletes are hitting, and/or s/he should play defence in positions V and/or I against the opposition's hits.
- During the warm-up serving, the libero should be passing the opposition's serves.
- *It may be an advantage to ask for a separate hitting warm-up* (i.e. each team takes its own turn hitting at the net by themselves) if a team is ready but the opposition is not.

8.2 Principles for the Organisation and Use of Practice Drills in Volleyball

Specific hints as to the principles for the training and taking action of specialists are to be found in the chapters related to individual tactics and also in the following practice drills.

1. *If complex game drills or small-court games are used the athletes should be put and play in their specialised positions.* This is especially important during the volleyball season. Athletes performing specific roles should also take on other roles to eliminate longer break periods. *This will also give specialists help in their anticipation skills if they play other roles from time to time.* Therefore, a second hitter should also practice the role of a quick hitter, because in a match situation s/he may often have to block against a quick hitter. Also, the athletes/specialists can better understand the "stress" that their teammates experience. This will help them develop more completely as volleyball athletes and can assist the coach in preparing more all-around and advanced practices. It is also recommended to use other service reception athletes in the role of the libero.
2. *Drills that continually change the roles of the athletes should be omitted.* Drills must be chosen where the athlete can develop and train his/her skills and role using as many repetitions as possible. This allows the coach to observe each athlete closely, correct, and control any changes that need to be carried out properly.
3. *During a training session, it is preferred to work on only a few but complex drills.* All types of match situations should be practised but only focusing on one or two main points at a time.

4. *The intensity and frequency of volleyball related actions can be measured and controlled quite easily with the use of several volleyballs.* The use of a second volleyball gives the possibility to force the desired action by the athlete(s) or to finish the outcome sought after.
5. *The use of several volleyballs can also show in a team tactical training session the incorrect choice and action of an athlete and how to correct it.* For example, if the non-blocking athlete at the net is not stepping away from the net in time, the coach can then use a second volleyball to make the athlete perform the correct action and be in the correct position.
6. *At high levels of volleyball, technical corrections of athletes should only be made during the pre-season phase if possible.* During the season phase, mainly tactical errors should be corrected and not technical ones – with the exception of serving, blocking, and defence. It is very important that the setter and the service reception athletes are not made hesitant and/or indecisive by too many corrections. The exception is **rookies** who are supposed to become starters. *In other words, the effectiveness and not the accuracy of a technical skill is much more important, therefore this is what should be stressed during this phase.*
7. *During the competition period training should focus more on individual and team tactics against a team's opponents.* In other words, it does not make sense to train the serve and offence if service reception and defence are not practiced at the same time.
8. *Drills should be designed in such a way that the training of the preliminary phase, the action phase, and the finishing phase are all included during the execution of the skill.* For example, when training the service reception athlete, the skill should be followed by either an offensive action and/or offensive coverage of the hit.
9. *As part of every drill, no matter what main skill is trained, every play must be completed and a "rally" performed.*
10. *Independent of the main focus of the drill, it is not allowed to receive or defend any volleyballs that are out of play* – not even to keep the drill running. Instead, a second or third volleyball should be tossed in to keep the drill running.
11. *Traditional drills, such as hitting volleyballs to targets (i.e. mats or pylons) should be omitted.* Closer to match situations is the use of an athlete as a target – which means the drill must be practiced in such a way as to imitate a match situation as closely possible (including the score).

13. *During technical training it is important to pay close attention to the fact that the skill is used correctly according to the match situation encountered.* This means that speed and accuracy of the movement or action must be practised simultaneously. In this situation, drills that follow a triangular pattern are of the highest priority.
14. *In training, there must not be a single deviation as to the rules of the sport of volleyball. For example, crossing the centerline or touching the volleyball net is not permitted at all.* This also means that antennas must always be used in practices.
15. *Serves in training must always be performed and hit exactly as they would in a match situation as far as serving location, type of serve, and standing position of the server are concerned.* The only exception is when an athlete is asked to imitate the serving strategy of their opponents.
16. When a match element is introduced and developed at a specialised high training level, the athlete must not be allowed to immediately repeat an incorrect action. This rule will increase an athlete's **attention and awareness** during the practice.
17. *Training of the defence should always be carried out with a complete defensive back-court of athletes;* otherwise there will not be match or space-related defensive actions possible. As well, the counter-attack must be kept in mind. If the initial pass is flawed, this can also be done by tossing in a second volleyball and/or by changing the rules of the drill.
18. *To ensure the individual tactical training of the service reception athlete and/or the defensive athlete,* any volleyball that is played directly across the volleyball net to the opposition will be called an error.
19. The training of offensive combinations should be executed at the same time as the training of the setter. At this time, immediate **feedback** will help improve teamwork between teammates.
20. *To imitate certain match conditions during training,* the setter must not only set in practice but also serve, play defence, and block.
21. The second or **substitute setter,** whose timing during sets is different than the starting setter's, *should mainly set to the substitute athletes in practice,* otherwise the timing and any rhythm between the starting setter and starting hitters may suffer. It is for this reason that after a sudden substitution of the starting setter (i.e. the setter gets injured) less quick sets should be attempted to omit a team's own unforced errors. Although, there is an opportunity to eliminate and/or reduce the risk of this from occurring through the use of additional training and enforcement.

22. *Small-court games are used as preparatory drills during the warm-up and the main segment of the practice process.* They are used to teach and improve the accuracy of the athlete's movements and actions.
23. *The teams in the small-court-games should always be selected according to the athletes that compromise the starting line-up.* Athletes that play side-by-side in a match should also form a small-court team to help improve their teamwork and understanding of each other.
24. *It must be taken into account that the effort in practice for the athletes participating in small-court games is higher than the effort produced playing the small-court games before matches.*
25. *During the development and practicing of strategies and counter-strategies, substitute athletes play important supporting roles such as simulating the actions and strategies of a team's oppositions.*
26. *When training individual tactics, the strengths of the athlete should be developed first and then the focus should turn to improving upon their weaknesses.*
27. *When performing any types of drills in practice, the starting athletes should always participate first and then followed by the substitute athletes.* This allows the substitute athletes an opportunity to learn from observing the starting athletes.
28. *When training the individual tactics of an athlete, his/her counterpart should also be trained.* The training of the defending athlete should also come before training the offensive athlete. For example, if the goal of the training is to improve upon the attack of the outside hitter, then it will begin by first dealing with some aspect of training the outside blocker.
29. *Actions that are not practiced during training will never be successfully used in a volleyball match.*
30. *Offensive coverage must always be stressed in all practice drills, especially in men's volleyball.*
31. *The actions of the athletes without the volleyball must always be observed and corrected if they are wrong during all practice drills.* This is especially true for movements that occur in any defensive position, the offensive coverage position, athletes who must support teammates that have difficulties in completing their actions with the volleyball, the preparatory phase of getting ready to switch to offence, etc.
32. Shorter volleyball set and match times, the substitution of the non-service reception athletes by the libero, and the timeouts require shorter training phases that must be at a high qualitative level.

> - The ten-minute breaks should reasonably involve a practice. For example, a short discussion should take place regarding the last and next volleyball set to be played and then the athletes should perform a small warm-up with a volleyball to get ready for the volleyball match again.

8.3 Principles for Training under Psychological Pressure in Volleyball

A practice that is based upon and carries out all of the principles stated earlier will still not be effective during a volleyball match situation, unless the practice is able to create similarly intensive psychological pressure situations as they would occur during a volleyball match. Especially in the sport of volleyball, the following **factors** cause immense difficulty in the development of the athlete's psychological state of mind:

- The length of a volleyball match is not predictable.
- Direct contact with the opposition is missing.
- Every play in the match is short and has an impact on the score.
- Every volleyball contact is short and requires very quick reaction time by the athlete, especially in more difficult situations.
- Volleyball techniques and skills are very complex and complicated and require accuracy in their execution.
- With the new scoring system in effect, the intensity and attention of the athletes is very high.
- The main characterisation of the volleyball athlete is his/her **"actions and movements during a volleyball match without the volleyball"**. In other words, is the athlete ready and prepared for a possible action or reaction to a situation that may occur? The portion of a volleyball match that takes place with the athletes without the volleyball has a much greater influence in a volleyball match than the portion of the volleyball match with the actions of the athletes with the volleyball.

In summary, the **structure of the sport of volleyball** shows that it is a very emotional sport.
It is a sport that creates psychologically difficult and huge problems for an athlete's self-control. Therefore, training should motivate athletes, mobilise their activity and attention, and create stressful situations.

This can be achieved by the following measures:
1. Play small games, with the main focus on a particular match element, competitively or as part of a mini-tournament;
2. Serve the volleyball to a certain zone or athlete.
3. Perform several repetitions of a skill or a drill until it is executed without any mistakes and/or effectively mastered.
4. Summarise the positive and negative actions of the athletes during a practice or drill.
5. Use complex practices or drills that always control the accuracy of the athlete's actions. For example, the server should make the service reception athlete move with the serve, the penetrating setter should create one-on-one blocking situations for his/her hitters, or the hitter should hit the volleyball past the block. How the athletes solve or are expected to solve each situation imposed upon them will be the focus of their actions and the drill.
6. A drill will be performed until one, three, or five errors are made or until a specified number and/or consecutive number of successful actions are achieved.
7. The athlete, group, or team selects how many successful actions must be reached in a drill (i.e. 10 repetitions).
8. The A-team (six starting volleyball athletes) will play against the B-team (substitutes) but will begin with a handicap against them. For example, the B-team will begin with a score of 5-0 or 10-0 in their favor.
9. Play tournaments of small-court games where teams start off with different scores according to their strengths and weaknesses. For example, each match is started with the strongest team having 0 points, the second strongest team having 3 points, the third strongest team having 5 points, etc. Every small- court match would begin with the score assigned to each team.
10. Play "short games" where the game ends when one team leads by a certain number of points (i.e. 3 points, 4 points, etc.). For example, a set might end with the score 3-0, 7-0, etc. depending on the rules imposed.
11. Play games with a particular goal in mind, such as one team trailing and trying to equalize the score. For example, one team begins with a 3-0 lead over their opposition and can finish the game if they reach five points.
12. Play games that are based on the principle of a progressive scoring system. For example, the serving team scores one point for their first successful action, two points for their second consecutive successful action, three points for their third consecutive successful action, etc.

13. Play small-court games where the winner always remains on the court. Here, games with short goals or point totals are recommended.
14. Play a tournament with only three teams competing. The winner is the team that wins five games first or that wins five games in a row. The winner of a game always stays on the court.
15. Play games where you must score two or three points to win one "big point". The winner is the team that has the accumulated or reached the number of "big points" needed to win the game.

The following measures create complex, match-related situations, which can increase the psychological pressure on the athletes by introducing "punishment":

16. Play very short tiebreak games.
17. Create "critical" situations. For example, start the game with the score 20-20 or let one team begin with a point advantage.
18. Give certain athletes more responsibility.
19. Double the score after certain actions are executed and/or after a certain score is reached points will be doubled for correct actions performed and/or points will be taken away for incorrect actions performed.
20. Create unbalanced conditions. For example, have the hitters vs. the service reception athletes, older athletes vs. the younger athletes, etc.
21. Play practice matches against better teams with the goal being to win a game or attain a certain score.
22. Practice under challenging conditions (i.e. noise, light, temperature, etc.).
23. Simulate the absence of top athletes from the starting line-up and pass on their responsibilities to other athletes on the team.
24. Create overtaxing situations for the athletes. For example, a single block against two hitters, an attack against a triple block, etc.
25. Request additional actions to be performed. For example, a defensive action must be performed after an offensive action.
26. Add extra tension on the athletes by covering their ears, changing the size of the volleyball court, changing the height of the volleyball net, use different volleyballs, use two volleyballs at the same time, etc.
27. Make sure that the athletes have a higher and more intensive physical pressure in the practice than in their matches.
28. Purposely provoke the athletes by being strict and unfair with them.
29. Athletes that are in competition for a position or role on the team with each other should play against each other.

30. Create extreme situations in technical and tactical skills that must be used. For example, the practice will end only after ten perfect service receptions are made or five successful jump serves are executed or five successful blocks are formed, etc.
31. Play games in which the coach arbitrarily and without preliminary warning to the athletes will:
    a) Stop the set or match and start it all over again;
    b) Change the score of the set/match;
    c) Order the next point or the next "big" point to be the final and deciding point.

Reward and punishment are very effective methods of obtaining competitive levels in the practice process:

32. Try to get the athletes to do what is required of them by giving them positive verbal feedback.
33. Offer material rewards (i.e. a good dinner, a single room, the best seat on the bus, a bonus, etc.).
34. Remind the athletes of the accolades that victory carries (i.e. honour, glory, championships, titles, medals, etc.).
35. Punish the individual athlete after an error/failure by making them perform additional actions such as block jumps, sprints, push-ups, etc.
36. A group/team punishment after an error by one of their teammates. This punishment will be even more infuriating if the athlete who committed the error is excluded from the punishment.
37. Play games in which the winner gets to punish the loser or the loser will receive a punishment that was determined before the game was played.
38. Perform fitness and skill checks, but it must be possible to measure them fairly and objectively. If the athlete fails them, then s/he will have to deal with the discipline.
39. If the athletes do not practice and perform as they are expected, their rewards will be revoked (i.e. bench a starting athlete, cut any bonuses offered, do not renew an athlete's contract, etc.).
40. Suspend an athlete for a short or long period of time depending on the error made in training.

Finally, many of the rewards and punishments mentioned above can be used at all levels of the sport of volleyball, but some are obviously only used at the professional level, and even a very few of them can only be used at the international level.

8.4 Principles Related to Coaching/Managing a Volleyball Practice

In the sport of volleyball there are generally two kinds of coaching functions that occur in practice:
- The coach and/or assistant coach perform all of the supporting roles and responsibilities to make a drill work.
- The coaches leave the supporting roles and responsibilities up to the athletes to perform.

Unfortunately, the second point rarely occurs and is almost exclusive to the men's game. If we examine the first point above, it will often reveal that the coach has 5-10 times more contacts with the volleyball than do the athletes.

This is incorrect because *it is not the role of the coach to physically manage the drills but rather to guide and correct the athletes.*

Therefore, the first act that every coach must do is to convert his athletes into assistant coaches. In other words, the athletes will be trained and developed to be in a position to perform every supporting role that would be needed to make a practice run. The coach will control the intensity and quality of the practice and make sure that the drills performed will be as close as possible to match situations. The coach is both the director and instructor rolled into one person.

A coach who carries out the supporting functions by him/herself can only be seen as an "assistant coach". S/he can see the proper combination between high-energy training and recovery time, but s/he cannot enforce any specific measures of correction of the athlete's errors.

Correcting must be viewed as the process that begins with the awareness and analysis of an error. Specific measures must be then taken to correct the error. Finally, the effect of these measures must be controlled and the observation starts from the beginning again. A small correction without control of the result must also be seen as a "mediocre and poor correction". It is for this reason that the second type of coaching function is preferred, especially since individual tactics and techniques are very important to the sport of volleyball. Only this type of coaching method allows the coach to get to know his/her team. By taking advantage of this method the coach can observe the technical/tactical and the psychological aspects of his/her athletes and detect weaknesses very early.

Finally, the coach can observe the humanistic behavior of the athletes, which in turn can give the coach an idea of the "person" behind the athlete.
If, despite all of these lines of reasoning, the situation is as such that the coach must carry out the supporting functions on his/her own, then it is very important that s/he warms up properly.

The following principles are important to the proper management of a practice:
1. When implementing new drills it is important to tell the athletes the purpose and goal behind the drill!
2. Since motor learning works mainly by observation and performance, long explanations are to be omitted. Follow the saying, "I hear – I forget, I see – I remember, I do – I understand and memorise"!
3. Provide concrete and positive corrections and do not discuss probabilities.
4. Take athlete's comments seriously and allow the athletes, depending on the importance of the comment, to quickly argue their point. Sort out the problem immediately if possible. This is especially true for negative comment.
5. Athletes that never cause any troubles for the coach during practice will also never cause any troubles for their opponents in matches.
6. If an athlete is not allowed to practice as hard as the other athletes or if s/he is allowed to come late to practice because of an injury the team must be told before the practice begins!
7. The coach's role, such as correcting, providing positive feedback, etc., must be intensified towards the end of practice for two reasons – 1) the athletes are asked to intensify their performance by the end of practice, therefore the coach must lead by example, and 2) the athletes must also "feel" watched.
8. The coach must differentiate between the athlete and his/her skills and the personality of the individual.
9. The coach must always remember that volleyball is a sport of errors; therefore, it is important for him/her to differentiate precisely what mistakes are acceptable and unacceptable in practice. These rules must be athlete- and team-related and not changed from practice to practice.
10. The coach must analyse the intensity of each practice by assigning each drill to one of the following three categories of intensity:
    a. "Above match level" – higher intensity than in a match;
    b. "At match level" – the same intensity as a match;
    c. "Below match level" – lower intensity than in a match.

11. The coach must always pay attention to the fact that the athletes that are substituted in or out of a match for the libero must receive the same interruptions in their rhythm in practice as they would receive in a match. This must be done in such a way that there is no drop in their mental, psychological, and physical play.
12. *It is the main responsibility of the coach to design the practice that the technical/tactical and psychological/physical components reflect the match conditions to be encountered as much as possible!* This means that the following components must be taken into account in each drill:
a) General willpower that is closely related to motivation.
b) Situation-related willpower that requires maximum management of the control abilities (i.e. determination, courage, etc.) in specific match situations.
13. The coach should thoroughly prepare each practice beforehand and then evaluate it afterwards. Everything should always be written down so as to always be able to control his/her planning and structure of the practice! To do this, drill checks make sense and are reasonable.
14. Talking to the athletes after practice may provide the coach with valuable information regarding the physical intensity and/or psychological demands of the practice!
15. The coach should ask more from his/her athletes in practice than their opponents would in a match!
16. Observation and correction of blocking and offensive skills requires the positioning of the coach at the net. Observation and correction of blocking and defence and of the service reception formations, including the attack approaches of the hitters need the coach to be positioned behind the baseline!

8.5 Principles Related to Coaching/Managing a Volleyball Match

The following explanations are directly related to the explanations in chapter 7 regarding defensive and offensive strategies. For this reason, only general statements concerning coaching during matches are discussed here:
1. *If the athletes are training for a competition, then the practice will also be training for the coach and his/her actions/behavior during a competition.* In

other words, each observation made by the coach in practice concerning an athlete, group, or team must be watched to see how it can and will be used in a match. Therefore, each post-practice evaluation by the coach is preparation for him/her during a match.

Photo 82 (R. Ischerland)

2. *The coach must systematically plan and prepare him/herself for each match.* In other words, the coach must sort out the most important and key elements of information that s/he has in combination with what his/her match strategy is. The coach must then write this information down so as to take advantage of it during critical match situations. Since the information is written down it allows the coach to compare his/her strategy with his/her observations during a match and then make any necessary corrections and adjustments.
3. *Exhibition matches, practice matches, and tournaments are the best opportunities for a coach to learn, practice and refine his/her coaching skills.* For this reason, the coach should prepare for these situations just as s/he would for a regular season match.
4. The coach should, not only in matches but also in practices, provide the libero and the athletes that s/he will replace in a match the same individual and team tactical information and strategies. During the practice, the coach should convey this information to his/her athletes from the new "coaching zone" so as to have an opportunity to practice communicating via this method.
5. *The coach must be honest, open, and always ready to speak with his/her athletes.* S/he should spend a lot of time with the athletes and should make an effort to discover all of their problems in life. The coach may even be able to help the athletes with these problems.
6. *The coach should develop and maintain a positive attitude and rapport towards all of his/her athletes.* Do not favor any athlete over another or put any of them in an awkward position because success can only be achieved with the team as a whole.

SPECIFIC PRINCIPLES

7. *Mutual trust and respect between the coach and athletes are major components and requirements for successful teamwork to occur.*
8. *Problems arising must be brought forth immediately and discussed. Under no circumstances should problems be suppressed or covered up.*
9. *The coach must also allow for his/her actions to be observed and analysed in the same manner that s/he observes and analyses his/her team.* This is the only method in which s/he can have his/her actions during a match analysed and then receive feedback as to how the athletes perceive his/her behavior and coaching style. From these results any necessary changes can be made.
10. *Every so often the coach should allow for his/her actions to be controlled by the athletes.* If this is to be done it is very important to discuss it with the athletes.
11. *The coach must display the same behavior in practice as in competitions.* S/he must not "act" or "react" because s/he expects the same behavior from his/her athletes from either practices or matches.
12. *The coach, just like his/her athletes, must learn some relaxation techniques to be able to deal with stressful situations.*
13. *The coach must always be prepared for interviews with the media and think about the consequences of any statements that s/he may give before they are made.* The coach should also be aware of the influence of reports and commentaries by the media on the team, especially certain athletes, to be able to intervene and correct the situation or to at least counteract the statements in the future.
14. *The coach, just like his/her athletes, should consider what appearance s/he should portray for the spectators/fans,* thus enabling him/her to win the spectators'/fans' support for his/her team.
15. *Just as the athletes must be able to anticipate the actions of their opponents, the coach must always try to predict and anticipate the strategy and counter-strategy of the opposition.*
16. Just as the athletes must react and change according to the actions of their opposition, the coach must *be willing to change his/her strategy and tactics according to each situation encountered.* This requires from a coach, not only the instinct to change, but the strength of character and willingness to make and/or change a decision.
17. *The coach must always be willing to take the responsibility for the match strategy and the coaching decisions.* This applies for decisions in critical situations and for the lack of success that was expected from a team.

18. The athletes need to know and understand the strategy to be able to successfully execute it during a match, because the more that they are influenced and persuaded to adhere to it the more they are willing to make it successful. *It is the responsibility of the coach to convince the athletes to follow the strategy.*
19. *Scouting and analysis of the opposition is an important requirement for a successful coach.* If only one match is analysed the observations and conclusions made can only be seen as ideas, but if two or more matches (especially important matches) are analysed then the observations and conclusions made can be seen as reliable and concrete information.
20. *The coach's actions must be the same in matches as they are in practices and must be directed mostly to individual athletes.* Only if a coach knows each athlete in every discipline can s/he coach a team in a competition. This could be coaching one athlete in a tactical strategy, another athlete in psychological preparation, and nothing at all for another athlete. It could also be to get one athlete motivated for a certain match situation while another athlete must be calmed down for the same match situation.

It is for this reason that one athlete can be given more responsibility based upon their personality and ability to respond in critical match situations over another athlete.

In conclusion, it can be stated that *a coach should be a good teacher, a good psychologist, and a good strategist.*

21. *Concerning the preparation of a team for their next opposition, the defensive strategy should always be developed first followed by the offensive strategy.* This will begin by discussing the opposition's offensive strengths followed by discussing a team's own offensive strengths. By doing this a team will be psychologically stronger and better prepared to play the match.
22. *It is one of the coach's main duties to prepare a team's schedule for the day of a competition, especially when the team is traveling.* This not only includes scheduling the morning practice (approximately 7 hours before the match), but also to choose the right food to be eaten at the right time. Therefore, it is very important to work closely with the manager.
23. On the day of the match the coach should provide a final explanation of the offensive and defensive strategies to be employed in the match in conjunction

with the morning practice. This should not only include the team tactical strategies but also any instructions for individual athletes. Also, information regarding the officials, the spectators, the gymnasium layout, etc. should be discussed.

24. *Just before the start of the warm-up, the main points of the strategy to be used should be stressed once again. This should be accomplished in a stimulating and motivating manner.* Part of this is to again emphasise a team's own strengths and their opposition's weaknesses.
25. *The coach should have a short, relaxed, and positive conversation with the officials before the match.*
26. *The coach should take full advantage of the rule that allows him/her to provide his/her athletes with information from the "coaching zone".* The communication should be verbal and/or with the use of signs, and it should be directed more to individual athletes than to a group and/or to the team (Photo 83).
27. *From the coaching zone, the coach should provide team-related instructions to one athlete who then transmits the message across to the rest of the team.*
28. *If the coach calls out information so the opposition can hear it,* especially when it is regarding the blocking assignments of his/her athletes regarding the opposition's setting and offensive strategy, it can very often be irritating to the opposition.

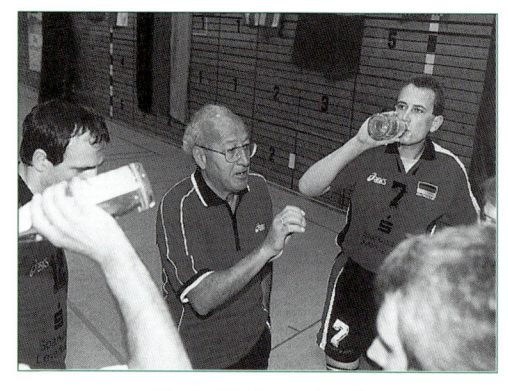

Photo 83 (Ischerland)

29. *The coach should not wait a long time before calling a timeout.* The latest that the coach should wait before taking a timeout is three points in a row by the opposition.
30. *The coach should try to have a positive impact on his/her athletes.* S/he should not make any disrespectful remarks and/or gestures from the bench. It is also important that the coach provides helpful instructions during a

PRINCIPLES RELATED TO COACHING

timeout. The coach should not repeat all of the mistakes that have been made because the opposite results are expected from the athletes. In other words, move forward after unforced errors occur and focus on the upcoming events in the match.

31. *The coach should manage the athletes with the help of the assistant coach during a timeout.* Only two important instructions and/or pieces of information should be provided to the athletes. If the coach is providing instructions on team strategy, then it is important and noticed that all of the athletes are listening.
32. *One of the substitute athletes must be included in every timeout* so they can convey the information provided, especially when it is regarding changes to team strategy, to the other substitute athletes.
33. *It is important that the coach is observing his/her own team and that the assistant coach is observing the opposition* or the coach is responsible for his/her team's serving and offensive strategy and the assistant coach is responsible for the team's defensive strategy.
34. *A coach should not change his/her coaching style whether or not it is s/he or the opposition who calls a timeout.* The stimulation and motivation of the athletes in both situations is equally important.
35. *The coach must prepare and train the substitute athletes and the libero in a manner that is consistent to the manner that they will be used in a match.* The individual tactical strategy of a substitute athlete should be the following: s/he should stay warmed-up during the entire match in case a substitution occurs and s/he should signal to the coach that s/he is ready and willing to play. Trying to make eye contact with the coach as much as possible accomplishes this. Substitute athletes must develop a feeling of readiness for the moment that their skills and services are required and learn to ask to play or that they are ready to play in critical situations.
36. *Substitutions are only effective if they are prepared.* In other words, they must have been practiced before. It makes sense to provide the substitute athlete with specific instructions at the moment right before they enter the match.
37. *Serving and defensive specialists and substitutes that are strong blockers should try and be used in every match.*
38. *If the coach has no more timeouts remaining,* but would like a stoppage to break the momentum and rhythm of the opposition then it might be the only acceptable occasion to use an unplanned and possibly not even practised substitution.

SPECIFIC PRINCIPLES

39. A *substitution* can also be reasonable in the following situations:
    - To provide a psychologically and physically strained athlete an opportunity to relax.
    - To prepare one of the top athletes on the team for the next match, especially if the match taking place at the moment can be concluded as either being won or lost.
    - To provide a substitute athlete and/or especially a rookie some match exposure. There should never be any substitutions for social reasons.
40. A *double substitution* (i.e. substituting the setter in position IV and their diagonal counter-part athlete in position I for a setter in position I and their diagonal counter-part athlete in position IV) only makes sense if the two athletes that are substituted in work perfectly well together in setting and offence. The shorter sets (i.e. 2.5 rotations) are more in favor of a positive well-prepared double substitution.
41. *The individual care of the athletes, especially in-between sets, is important for the next set.* To be in a position to completely utilise the time available during the break, the coach should already have prepared the starting line-up and rotation for the next set. Any possible changes can be handled by the assistant coach and they must be shown to the coach as early as possible so that the coach can examine the changes and either agree or disagree to them.
42. *An analysis of the match is another important role of the coach and assistant coach.* The analysis will be the basis for the structure of the following practice, to examine if the team followed the match strategies that were outlined, and if the athletes executed their individual roles properly. The analysis of the match is the basis for the evaluation, critical discussion, and for any disputes that occur afterwards between the coach and the athletes.
43. *For rational reasons, a subjective analysis and discussion of the match should not be allowed immediately following a competition because the arguments and discussions that take place will be purely emotional.* Each athlete should have access to the results of the match analysis and the videotapes, so they can watch the match by themselves and make up their own minds and judgments.
44. **The coaching style and technique for the shorter and more decisive fifth set cannot be practised often enough.** The peculiarities of the fifth set should not be underrated because with only 15 points needed to win the set is reduced by 60% of total points needed to finish as compared to the previous four sets where 25 points were needed to finish. Therefore, the set will be determined much earlier than the previous sets. This leads us to the following principles:

- Take any timeouts needed earlier than in the previous four sets.
- Use all six substitutions by taking into account the use of the serve and defensive specialists and the strong blockers.
- Give more responsibility to the psychologically stronger hitter(s).
- Give more responsibility to the psychologically stronger service reception athlete(s).
- Match the blockers to the opposition's psychologically stronger hitter(s)

Finally, it must be stressed again that special coaching strategies and principles (i.e. serving strategies, techniques of the middle blockers, coaching in tie-break situations, etc.) are discussed in more detail in chapter 7 – „Defensive and Offensive Strategies".

Photo & Illustration Credits:

Cover Photos: Steffen Marquardt
Illustrations: Rainer Christ
Inside Photos: see credits underneath each photo.
Cover Design: Birgit Engelen, Stolberg

Literature:

The authors used an extensive list of literature for this book. But since all of the material used is in German, we decided not to include it in this English version. It is available on request.

MEYER & MEYER SPORT

Please order our catalogue!
Please order our catalogue!

„Competitive Volleyball" is just one example of our varied sports programme.

Meyer & Meyer publishes many other English titles under the following categories:

▼

Aerobic ■ Bodywork ■ Endurance
Fitness & Recreation ■ Fun
Games & Sports ■ Golf ■ Gymnastics
Health ■ Martial Arts ■ Rowing
Running ■ Soccer ■ Surfing ■ Tennis
Triathlon & Duathlon
Volleyball ■ Winter Sports

Meyer & Meyer also publishes various international journals and a series of scientific sports titles.

---

service

If you are interested in Meyer & Meyer Sport and our large programme, please visit us **online** or call our Hotline ▼

online:
▶ www.m-m-sports.com

Hotline:
▶ +49 (0)1 80 / 5 10 11 15

We are looking forward to your call!

MEYER & MEYER Verlag | Von-Coels-Straße 390 | D-52080 Aachen, Germany | Fax +49 (0)2 41- 9 58 10-10

Basic Training

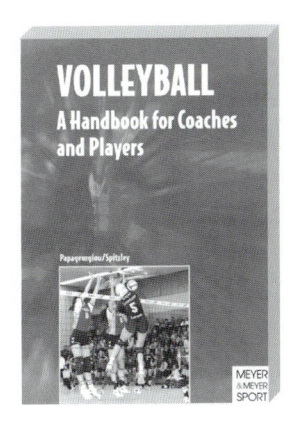

Athanasios Papageorgiou/
Willy Spitzley/
Volleyball
A Handbook for Coaches
and Players

This handbook, divided into 16 „learning objectives", offers a structured approach to basic training for volleyball. The manual aims at providing volleyball players with a wide range of individual-, group- and team tactical action patterns, and it wants to make the player able to exercise them as the game and the situation require. This book provides a fundamental basis for the training of specialists to top-players.

360 pages
380 figures, 10 photos
Hardcover, two-colour print,
14.8 x 21 cm
ISBN 1-84126-005-3
£ 14.95 UK / $ 19.95 US/
$ 29.95 CDN / € 22.90

MEYER & MEYER Verlag | Von-Coels-Straße 390 | D-52080 Aachen, Germany | Fax +49 (0)2 41-9 58 10-10

MEYER & MEYER SPORT

Beach Volleyball

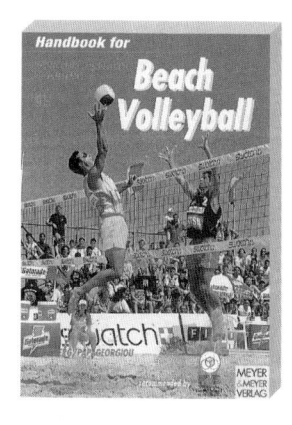

Stefan Hömberg/
Athanasios Papageorgiou
**Handbook for
Beach Volleyball**

Internationally, this is the first instructional handbook on Beach Volleyball. It deals with the special techniques and tactics as well as with attack and defence strategies. Additionally, drills, exercises and game forms for the learning and further training of technical and tactical movement and action sequences are given. Likewise, principles for training of the player are offered.

296 pages
Hardcover, 14.8 x 21 cm
ISBN 3-89124-322-7
£ 17.95 UK / $ 29.00 US/
$ 39.95 CDN / € 22.90

MEYER & MEYER SPORT

MEYER & MEYER Verlag | Von-Coels-Straße 390 | D-52080 Aachen, Germany | Fax +49 (0)2 41-9 58 10-10

Fit for Success

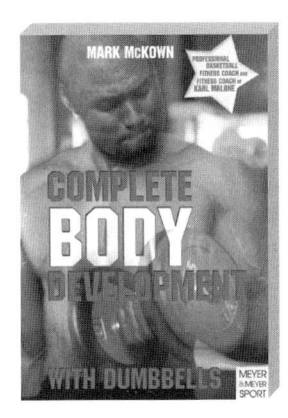

Mark McKown
Complete Body Development with Dumbbells

- Maximise your physical potential
- An excellent route to a better physique
- Get a healthier and fitter body

Mark McKown
- Player Development Coach for the Utah Jazz of the NBA
- Strength coach of NBA-star Karl Malone

About 128 pages,
Two-colour print, 100 photos,
50 drawings and tables,
Paperback, 14,8 x 21 cm
ISBN: 1-84126-087-8
£ 12.95 UK / $ 17.95 US/
$ 25.95 CDN / € 16.90

Fitness

MEYER & MEYER SPORT

MEYER & MEYER Verlag | Von-Coels-Straße 390 | D-52080 Aachen, Germany | Fax +49 (0)2 41-9 58 10-10